History of World Architecture

Architecture of the Nineteenth Century

R. Middleton / D. Watkin

Electaarchitecture

Photographs: Electa (Bruno Balestrini)
Drawings: Studio Lodolo-Süss

1003653144

Distributed by Phaidon Press
ISBN 1-9043-1309-4

www.phaidon.com

© 1980 by Electa, Milano
All Rights Reserved

www.electaweb.it

First English translation of PART I published in 1980
by Academy Editions, London
First English translation of PART II published in 1980
by Harry N. Abrams, Inc., New York

© 2003 by Electa Architecture
Mondadori Electa spa, Milano
All Rights Reserved

Printed in China

TABLE OF CONTENTS

The architecture of the eighteenth and nineteenth centuries was conditioned largely by two traditions of thought, the French rationalist tradition emerging from a Cartesian delight in clarity and mathematical certainty, and the English or rather British Empirical tradition that was to suggest another system of ordering, ultimately to be popularized as the Picturesque. The two phenomena were quite distinct and were independently developed, though by the late eighteenth century their particular qualities were clear enough for them to be taken up and adapted to new situations. The impact of Marc-Antoine Laugier's somewhat simplistic rationale of architecture, the primitive hut, was felt throughout Europe, in England no less than in Italy and Germany, while that particular expression of the Picturesque, the *jardin anglais,* was to taken up not only in Italy and Germany and the outer states of Europe but in the home of rational enlightenment itself—not that the French ever understood the subtleties of Picturesque composition or grappled long with the problems. Likewise, the geometrical ordering principles evolved by Jean-Nicolas-Louis Durand at the turn of the century were to be adopted by architects throughout Europe, but in England with noticeably less enthusiasm and effect than anywhere else. But the rational interpretation of Gothic that the French had evolved from the sixteenth century onward was to be introduced into England in the early nineteenth century by A. W. N. Pugin with the most profound and dramatic results. Even John Ruskin, that man of sensitivity and feeling who cared little enough for the way in which a building was organized or the techniques of its construction, was conditioned to the deepest respect for the rigidly deterministic analyses of Gothic made by the Frenchman Eugène-Emmanuel Viollet-le-Duc.

There was thus much exchange of thought and opinion and no little interaction of opposed ideas, but the main development of the two traditions of thought remained separate and distinct, and they are best dealt with independently.

The French rationalist ideal demands the first attention, for it provided the framework of thought for the whole of the Enlightenment. The beginnings, for our purposes, lie in the works of Claude Perrault (1613-1688), a doctor, anatomist, and experimenter in all kinds of devices, mostly mechanical, who turned unaccountably to architecture when he was already over fifty. His chief architectural works were the Observatoire in the Faubourg Saint-Jacques, Paris, a decidedly gaunt and singular building, dating from 1667 to 1672; the east facade of the Louvre, begun in the same year and more or less completed by 1674; and a triumphal arch for the Porte Saint-Antoine, also in Paris, designed in 1668 (started at once, mocked up in lath and plaster, which deteriorated, it was torn down in 1716). The key work is the Louvre facade, which may or may not be Perrault's own composition. It was the outcome of a combined effort by a committee composed of Louis Le Vau, *Premier Architecte du Roi;* Charles Le Brun, *Premier Peintre du Roi;* Perrault himself; and his brother, Charles, who acted as secretary and

stand-in for his master, Jean Baptiste Colbert, the king's chief adviser. Claude Perrault's contribution has often been called in question, first by Nicolas Boileau soon after his death, but those who saw the relevant documents and drawings before they were destroyed in the fire at the Hôtel de Ville in 1870 found no evidence to dispute his claim to authorship.

The whole enterprise was an occasion, almost, of national importance. Le Vau had done the first project, but this was little admired by Colbert, who submitted it to the judgment of an array of Italian architects, among them the great Bernini, who was induced to journey to Paris to undertake the design himself. The pope's release of his favorite architect was a triumph for French diplomacy. But having gotten Bernini to Paris, they feared that national prestige might suffer should an Italian complete the royal palace. Bernini's robust, grandiose designs were not, in any case, to French taste. He was sent home, richly rewarded with gold but enraged. Instead, the committee set up by Colbert built the majestic, calm, and rhythmical facade that stands today and that has been regarded always as a model of excellence by architects and connoisseurs of French architecture. Le Corbusier himself found it in him to admire it. Its particular qualities may seem to us negative rather than positive, but they have nonetheless been potent influences. There is very little emphasis in the facade. The traditional French composition of a central feature with outlying pavilions is still in evidence, but there is scarcely a break in the plan, scarcely a break in the outline. The composition is neat and rectangular. The pediment in the center is low and unobtrusive. The essence of the architecture seems to reside in the rows of coupled freestanding columns that link the main elements, a curious paradox but one that evidently embodied Perrault's intentions. He aimed that the column should resume its antique role as a supporting element, thus constituting the architecture and no longer appearing as an applied decorative device. This clear and honest expression of the role and the form of the main elements in the architecture was a quality he thought to discern not only in ancient Greek temples but also, it may be surprising to learn, in Gothic cathedrals. He defended his arrangement of columns on the Louvre facade with reference to the clustered shafts of Notre-Dame in Paris.

In consciously renewing the French tradition by a return to sources, he referred thus to both classical and national prototypes. But he pleaded for no simpleminded return to the past. He was trained as a doctor and a scientist and took it for granted that the contemporary endeavor would be in advance of that of the past. He looked to the past only as a point of departure in the establishment of principles. His most earnest achievement in this respect was the translation of the ten books of architecture ascribed to Vitruvius, the only architectural treatise to survive from antiquity. This was another venture abetted by Colbert. Jean Martin and Jean Goujon had published a French translation in 1547, but the text was unsatisfactory and the plates were culled for the most part from earlier Italian editions. Perrault's professional grounding in Latin and Greek stood him in good

1. *Claude Perrault, Observatoire, Paris, 1667-72*

stead. In 1673 he issued the first edition of his scholarly and altogether competent text. It was not an antiquarian exercise but rather a polemical work. It was illustrated with magnificent plates—the finest by Sébastien Le Clerc, who was later to attempt an architectural treatise on his own account—featuring all of Perrault's own works and an array of suggested reconstructions of antique buildings intended to set a new standard for contemporary architecture. The forms are precisely defined and rectangular; freestanding columns are in evidence everywhere. A revised edition appeared in 1684 with a great many footnotes that make more clear Perrault's theoretical standpoint, though this had been expressed clearly enough the year before in his *Ordonnance des cinq espèces de colonnes selon la méthode des anciens.* This was, as the name implies, largely concerned with the orders. But in it Perrault was to introduce his theory of beauty that served to shatter the Renaissance and post-Renaissance belief in the transcendental role of the orders. There were, Perrault declared, two types of beauty in architecture, positive and arbitrary. Positive beauty was based quite simply on the quality of materials, on precision and neatness of execution, on size, on sheer magnificence, and on symmetry—values that must have seemed obvious enough in the reign of Louis XIV. Arbitrary beauty resided in such qualities as proportional relationships, form, and shape. It was in his ability to manipulate these and compose his designs that the real talent of the architect rested. For there were no sure guides, no fixed rules, only custom. Perrault rejected quite rudely the idea that there was an absolute criterion for architectural proportions. The architectural proportions derived from the orders, he said, were not related to the scale of musical harmonies as was commonly thought; they were in no sense a feature of a divine or universal order; they were simply a matter of custom. The cultivated eye had grown used to certain proportions and was thus shocked by any departure from the norm. Perrault himself respected the norm—like Descartes and even Pascal he upheld an ideal of "médiocrité." He thus determined to investigate the welter of proportional systems that had been proposed by theorists from the Renaissance onward and to find a workable mean. Antoine Desgodets's carefully measured drawings of forty-nine buildings in Rome, to be published in 1682 as *Les édifices antiques de Rome,* confirmed his belief that there was no consistency in antique proportions. His own system was based on a single module, readily applicable to all parts of each of the five orders.

Perrault does not appear to have been a member of the Académie Royale d'Architecture that Colbert established in 1671—one year after Le Vau's death—but he nonetheless attended some of its meetings and proposed that the Académie take up his system of proportioning and adopt it as its own. The members were shocked by his rude disregard for the Renaissance system of belief and were confused, moreover, by his suggestion that a new set of rules be substituted for the old. They did not grasp clearly his determination, like that of Colbert in all his undertakings, to establish a

2. Claude Perrault and others, east facade of the Louvre, Paris, 1667-74
3. Frontispiece of Claude Perrault's translation of Vitruvius, 1673. Represented are three of Perrault's works; in the background, the Observatoire; in the middleground, the east facade of the Louvre, to the left, the triumphal arch for the Porte Sainte-Antoine (now the Place de la Nation)

common and sensible working standard. To what extent Perrault's system was adopted is impossible to judge until the buildings of the period have been measured. We can be sure, though, that his published works were widely read. He was staunchly upheld during the eighteenth century by that most respected, and indeed academic, of teachers, Jacques-François Blondel (1705-1774). In England his architectural works had been translated and issued by the end of the first decade of the century, and, perhaps more significant, they were embodied in Isaac Ware's *Complete Body of Architecture* in 1756.

Though he offered a more reticent and rational architecture as a model and radically reinterpreted and reassessed accepted assumptions, it is clear that Perrault did not provide a coherent body of theory. His commonsensical approach, however, was to be followed up and rendered more useful in two small books published early in the eighteenth century, Michel de Frémin's *Mémoires critiques d'architecture,* of 1702, and Jean-Louis de Cordemoy's *Nouveau traité de toute l'architecture; ou, l'art de bastir: utile aux entrepreneurs et aux ouvriers,* of 1706. Neither if these men was an architect. Frémin appears to have been a tax collector; Cordemoy (1631-1713) was settled in the church, a cousin, or brother even, of Gerauld de Cordemoy, upholder of Descartes, author of that pioneering study of language the *Discours physique de la parole,* of 1668. Frémin's book is a plea for a reasoned approach to design, expressing a concern for the restrictions imposed by the site, the qualities of materials, the cost, and the needs of the client. The orders and the classical measures were of no real importance in architecture, he said, and in demonstrating his convictions he compared St.-Eustache and Le Vau's church of St.-Sulpice with Notre-Dame and the Ste.-Chapelle and concluded forcefully that the Gothic buildings were more rationally designed and thus preferable as architecture. This sympathy for Gothic arrangements and, in particular, structural manipulations is a feature also of Cordemoy's treatise, though the latter was intent to show that the qualities he admired in Gothic architecture could be interpreted in classical terms. Cordemoy required an architecture that was made up of rectangular forms, largely unadorned, with plain masonry walls or series of columns supporting lintels. He disliked arches and all acute angles, including those of the classical pediment. The ancien, he said, would have preferred the mansard roof to the pitched roof, had they known it, because it more nearly approximated to the rectangle. He proposed a model church with freestanding columns between the nave and aisles, supporting horizontal entablatures (absolutely not arches, he insisted) and, above, a barrel vault. For the west front he suggested a portico of columns with a balustrade over them, not unlike that built many years before by Inigo Jones at St. Paul's in London. He was consciously emulating both Gothic and, he fancied, Early Christian and Greek models. The structural supports, indeed, the whole structural system, were to be expressed and made evident so as to constitute the architecture, as in pre-Renaissance times. He wanted a trabeated architecture. Michelangelo's

4. *Claude Perrault and others, east facade of the Louvre, Paris, detail of the colonnade, 1667-74*

5. *Philibert de l'Orme, structural frame of a Gothic vault illustrated in his* Architecture, *1567*

6. *Interior perspective of a basilica, illustrated in Claude Perrault's translation of Vitruvius, 1673. Engraved by Sébastian Le Clerc.*

La hauteur des Colonnes des Basiliques sera égale à la largeur, des Portiques, & cette largeur sera de la troisième partie de l'espace du milieu. Les colonnes d'enhaut doivent être

portion des Basiliques de la ville de Chalcis : mais la construction du texte ne peut souffrir cette interpretation.

Comme je ne trouve aucune de toutes ces interpretations differentes qui me satisfasse, j'en forme une nouvelle, que je fonde sur les autoritez des plus anciens Interpretes de ce mot : & estant assuré par le témoignage d'Ausone, que *chalcidica* estoit un lieu élevé que nous appellons un premier étage, & par le témoignage d'Arnobe, que *chalcidica* estoit un lieu ample & magnifique, j'estime que ces Chalcidiques estoient de grandes & magnifiques salles où on rendoit la justice, situées aux bouts des Basiliques de plain-pié avec les galleries par lesquelles on alloit d'une salle à l'autre, & où les Plaideurs se promenoient, car ces Galleries hautes sans ces Salles semblent estre inutiles. Suivant cette interprétation, lorsque Vitruve dit que s'il y a assez de place pour faire une Basilique fort longue, on fera des Chalcidiques aux deux bouts, il faut entendre que si elle est courte, on ne fera qu'une Salle à un des bouts, ou que si l'on en fait à chaque bout, elles seront trop petites pour pouvoir estre appellées Chalcidiques, dont le nom signifie une grandeur & une magnificence extraordinaire. Palladio semble l'avoir entendu autrement, parce que dans la figure qu'il a faite de la Basilique, il luy a donné beaucoup moins de longueur que le double de sa largeur, peut-estre parce que n'ayant pû se determiner à ce qu'il devoit entendre par Chalcidique, & par cette raison n'en voulant point faire aux bouts de sa Basilique, il l'a faite plus courte, pour faire entendre qu'il croyoit que les Basiliques qui estoient sans Chalcidiques n'avoient pas la proportion que Vitruve leur donne en general.

7 DES PORTIQUES. Il faut entendre par Portiques les ailes qui sont aux costez de la grande voute du milieu, & que l'on appelle bas costez dans les Eglises.

plus petites que celles d'embas, comme il a esté dit.* La cloison qui est entre les colonnes d'enhaut ne doit avoir de hauteur que les trois quarts de ces mesmes colonnes, afin que ceux qui se promenent sur cette

8. LA CLOISON. Vitruve met icy *Pluteum* pour *Pluteus*, ainsi qu'il fait en plusieurs autres endroits. Philander & Barbaro ont pris ce *Pluteum* ou *Pluteus* pour l'espace qui est entre les colonnes d'embas & celles d'enhaut, & ils ont crû que Vitruve ayant dit *Spatium quod est inter superiores columnas*, il falloit suppléer & *inferiores*, mais il n'est parlé dans le texte que de la *cloison* qui est entre les colonnes d'enhaut, ce qui peut avoir un fort bon sens, pourveu qu'on entende que Vitruve a conçû que cette cloison qui estoit comme un piedestail continu sous toutes les colonnes d'enhaut, ne devoit passer pour cloison qu'à l'endroit qui répondoit entre les colonnes : parce que l'endroit de ce piedestail continu qui estoit immediatement sous les colonnes, devoit estre pris pour leur piedestail. Il est amplement prouvé sur le 7. chapitre de ce Livre, que *Pluteus* ne sçauroit signifier icy que Cloison, Balustrade ou Appuy.

EXPLICATION
DE LA PLANCHE
XXXVIII.

Cette Planche contient l'élevation perspective de la Basilique. Il faut entendre que de mesme que l'on a fait servir un seul Plan pour les deux étages de la Basilique ; on n'a aussi mis icy qu'une partie de son élevation, supposant que l'on comprendra aisément que ce qui est icy ne represente qu'environ un quart de tout l'Edifice, representé dans le plan par ce qui est renfermé dans des lignes ponctuées.

7. *Claude and Charles Perrault,*
project for Ste.-Geneviève, Paris,
c. 1680

work at St. Peter's, Rome, was to be dismissed in the second edition of the *Nouveau traité,* published in 1714, though Bernini's colonnade on the piazza was to be admired. The real source of inspiration for Cordemoy's model church, however, was a design made about 1680 by Claude and Charles Perrault for the new church of Ste.-Geneviève in Paris. Freestanding columns line the long nave, carrying a horizontal entablature with a curved vault above. There was at that time no church like this, though the genesis of the arrangement can be traced back to the plan of an entranceway in Fra Giocondo's edition of Vitruvius, of 1511, and then to the work of Raphael and his pupils on the entrance of the Palazzo Farnese and its imitation in France by Le Vau, on the south side of the Louvre. An antique precedent was concocted also at this time by the engraver Jean Marot, who inaccurately illustrated the interior of the Temple of Bacchus at Baalbek in this form, perhaps at the behest of the Perraults. It was Charles Perrault who, as

Colbert's secretary, was responsible for issuing instructions and payments to travelers to the east who went in search, for the most part, of manuscripts for Colbert's collections. Claude Perrault himself acknowledged the use of some drawings done by one such traveler, M. de Monceaux, who was to visit Baalbek in 1668; however, it is possible that the reconstruction was based on the observations of Balthasar de Monconys, who was there in 1647.

But even as Cordemoy was writing, a church was being put up in France that embodied some of the qualities he demanded—the royal chapel at Versailles. Once again, Claude Perrault appears to have been involved in the early design, though the building begun in 1698 is generally attributed to Jules Hardouin Mansart, with Robert de Cotte responsible for its completion. The lower level of the chapel has heavy piers and arcades between the nave and aisles, but at the upper level, from which the king was to follow the service, there are majestic, widely spaced Corinthian columns with a horizontal entablature and vault above. The details are all classical, but the effect is of the spacious Gothic kind, with flying buttresses outside to confirm the hybrid basis of the inspiration.

The play of Gothic that is so curious a part of the architectural theory of Perrault, Frémin, and Cordemoy requires, perhaps, further explanation. It was not an isolated and idiosyncratic excursion into thought, but part of a long-standing French tradition, upheld, as a rule, by adventurous thinkers. Gilles Corrozet, a humanist scholar, translator of the works of Leon Battista Alberti and Trissino (Palladio's patron), and author of one of the first guidebooks to Paris, issued first in 1532, chose, surprisingly, to study Gothic buildings and to praise their manner of construction. His lead was taken up, in the years that followed, by other such authors, many of them associated with the Benedictine congregation of St.-Maur, the founders of French historical study. Terms such as "hardiesse," "légèreté," and "délicatesse" are invariably encountered in descriptions of Gothic buildings in these popular guidebooks or histories—of which there were many. In the more restricted field of architectural theory there was a similar emphasis on the structural finesse of Gothic architecture. Philibert de l'Orme, who thought of himself as the first architect to introduce classical refinements into France, nevertheless described and illustrated the construction of a Gothic vault in his *Architecture,* of 1567. And it is evident that he thought of the columns and ribs as an independent and clearly expressed structural scaffold supporting the webs of the vault above. This separation of the structural features from the enclosing elements was to assume great importance in the years to come. François Derand, the Jesuit mathematician and architect, author of *L'architecture des voûtes; ou, l'art des traits et coupe des voûtes,* a standard work on building construction published first in 1643, but issued again in 1743 and yet again in 1755, emphasized not only the structural elegance of the Gothic columns and ribs but also the role of the flying buttress and the outer buttress. He saw Gothic architecture as the solution to a problem in equilibrium.

A great deal more evidence could be adduced to show the vitality of this tradition of thought in France, in particular, the works of Amédée-François Frézier (1682-1773), who, in a lively exchange of letters in the *Mémoires de Trévoux* early in the eighteenth century, was to disparage Cordemoy's conception of a trabeated architecture, noting correctly that with the small stones available in France it was sounder to put arches rather than lintels over columns. Frézier attacked Cordemoy on many other points, but he proved himself equally sympathetic as an interpreter of Gothic, and far more knowledgeable than his predecessors. In his *Théorie et pratique de la coupe des pierres et des bois pour la construction des voûtes...; ou, traité de stéréotomie à l'usage de l'architecture,* published first between 1738 and 1739, he described Gothic architecture as a precisely calculated affair, dependent on a carefully worked out system of vaulting. And he extended the usual structural analysis to show that the webs of the vaults were particularly light and strong because they were slightly concave. His analysis was more subtle and penetrating than any yet made. He was not, however, an admirer of Gothic architecture. Like most interested Frenchmen he intended to analyze Gothic architecture and to infuse its principles of organization and construction, not its forms, into contemporary building. The detailed study of Gothic in France was thus in no way a preliminary to a revival of the style, though it is noteworthy that the Benedictines of the congregation of St.-Maur did uphold the Gothic style as such: St.-Wandrille, for example, was constructed in the Gothic manner between 1636 and 1656, and at their center, St.-Germain-des-Prés, in Paris, the Benedictines introduced Gothic vaults of stone over the nave and transepts, in 1644. When they came to build the west front of St.-Pierre at Corbie, in the first decade of the eighteenth century, they substituted a design in the Gothic mode for the proposed classical facade that was submitted earlier, a decision parallel to that made at the same time for the west front of Orléans cathedral, where the king, possibly under the influence of the Maurist scholar Bernard de Montfaucon, demanded that "l'ordre gothique" be adhered to. These, though, may all be interpreted as examples of Gothic survival.

More problematical and far more challenging was the design prepared in 1718 by the master mason of Orléans cathedral, Guillaume Hénault, for a Maurist chapel in the same town. For the interior he adapted the chapel at Versailles, for the exterior he provided a Gothic pastiche, complete with pointed windows, finials, and flying buttresses. This was not built. And nothing like it was to be designed in France until the end of the century, when the introduction of a playful Gothic mode in garden architecture resulted in something of a Gothic revival. But this was an English intrusion.

Cordemoy's ideas were not to be taken up immediately in France; the columnar screen around the forecourt of Pierre-Alexis Delamair's Hôtel de Soubise, of 1705-9, may owe something to his suggestions, as may the columnar episodes that appear so frequently in Germain Boffrand's early works, but only the chapel that Boffrand designed for the château at

11. St.-Pierre, Corbie, west facade, begun, c. 1706

12. Guillaume Hénault, design for Notre-Dame-de-Bonne-Nouvelle, Orléans, 1718, a chapel for a Benedictine Congregation of St.-Maur, 1718

Lunéville in 1709—to be completed several years later—demonstrably fulfilled Cordemoy's program. The first architect to develop Cordemoy's ideas with any real consistency was the Parisian Pierre Contant d'Ivry (1698-1777), who designed the church of St.-Vasnon at Condé-sur-l'Escaut, in 1751, and that of St.-Vaast at Arras a year or two later, both with freestanding columns supporting horizontal lintels of stone and, above, barrel vaults. But by then another propagandist and interpreter of the ideas of both Perrault and Cordemoy had emerged, the Abbé Marc-Antoine Laugier (1713-1769). His starting manifesto, the *Essai sur l'architecture,* was first issued anonymously in 1753.

Laugier dutifully paid his respects to Perrault, praising highly the Louvre facade—though he noted that it would have been improved if the central pediment had not broken the line of the balustrade—and was careful to acknowledge his debt to Cordemoy, but he was more radical than either of his predecessors. In his determination to purge and invigorate the tradition of architecture by a return to sources, he was led to entertain the idea that the basis of all architecture should be envisaged as the rustic hut, a hut stark and almost natural in its forms. It consisted of four tree trunks, still growing, as supports, with logs as lintels, and smaller branches above making up a pitched roof. This was to be illustrated as the frontispiece in the second edition of the *Essai,* in 1755. The concept was not new. Commentators of Vitruvius, including Perrault, had illustrated the origins of architecture in the guise of the rustic hut, but none had proposed that it be taken as the model of excellence in architecture. The essential elements in architecture, in Laugier's analogy, were, thus, the freestanding column, acting as a support, the attendant lintel, as a beam, and the pediment, as an expression of the pitched roof. Everything else was to be regarded as secondary. The rich heritage of Renaissance forms and ornamentation was to be disregarded. Inevitably, for practical design purposes, walls were to be provided, doors and windows accepted. But there was to be nothing superfluous to necessity.

Laugier's ideal, as may be imagined, was best adapted to the design of churches, and, like Cordemoy, he proposed one made up with single or coupled freestanding columns in one or two tiers along the aisles, all supporting horizontal entablatures without cornices, and a barrel vault above. As before, the arrangement was related to both the temples of ancient Greece and the cathedrals of Gothic France. But Laugier's moving descriptions of the interior of Notre-Dame show that new emotions, new feelings, had come into play. He admired the lightness and the structural strength of Gothic architecture and hoped to incorporate these qualities into contemporary design in the most rational way possible. But he was susceptible also to those more intangible qualities of mystery and sublime grandeur of the Gothic. That he was influenced by these tastes beyond the bounds of restraint usually accepted in France was particularly evident in 1765, when he published his *Observations sur l'architecture.* Therein he

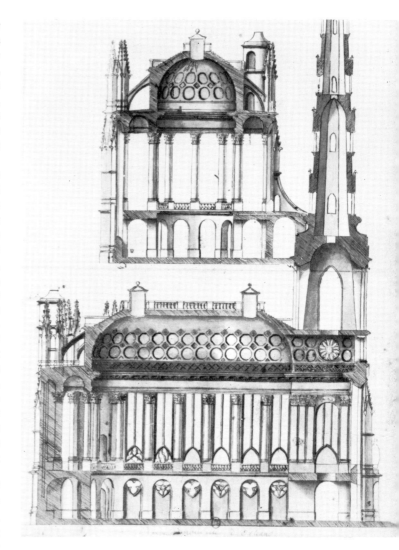

proposed churches no longer based on Latin- or Greek-cross plans, but of a variety of shapes, ordered internally with soaring columns bursting at their tops into formalized palm fronds and an array of richly decorated vaults. Gone were the lintels and entablatures, gone were the classical measures, though for the exterior, he insisted, classical forms were to be retained. But for domestic architecture, he suggested, Gothic effects might be conjured up externally by introducing turrets and broken roof lines. In compensation, perhaps, the ideal system of proportioning that he proposed in the *Observations* was more limited and restrictive than ever before. The ideal ratio was 1:1; the best figure the square; the best volume the cube. Not surprisingly, his second book was regarded as quirky and highly idiosyncratic. His first book, however, was acclaimed and eagerly read throughout Europe; it was considered a revolutionary tract.

The first major building that might be seen as an illustration of Laugier's ideal, and one that Laugier himself was to praise as "le premier modèle de la perfaite architecture, le véritable chef-d'oeuvre de l'architecture française" ("Discours sur le rétablissement de l'architecture antique," Lyons, Académie des Sciences, MS 194), was the church of Ste.-Geneviève, now known as the Panthéon. The architect was Jacques-Germain Soufflot (1713-1780). Soufflot had been to Rome as a young man and had spent seven years there, from 1731 to 1738, during which time he measured St. Peter's and other Italian churches, including the Milan cathedral. He then returned to his native Burgundy, settling in Lyons, where he was to build the great Hôtel-Dieu, a grand if unlovely building, stretching over two hundred fifty meters (eight hundred twenty feet) along the banks of the Rhône. The prestige it brought him prompted Mme. de Pompadour to select him as companion to her brother, soon to become the Marquis de Vandières (later the Marquis de Marigny), on his grand tour of Italy, in preparation for the young man's assumption of the position of *Directeur Général des Bâtiments.* Their journey was begun in December 1749; by February 1751 Soufflot was back in Lyons. But in the following year he was installed in an apartment in the Louvre and in January 1755 was made *Contrôleur des Bâtiments du Roi au Département de Paris* and commissioned to design the church of Ste.-Geneviève. This was intended to initiate a new departure in architecture. The plan was a Greek cross, to which Soufflot was forced by the clergy to add two bays and flanking towers at the east end, making the geometry less pure. Inside, the nave and aisles were divided by rows of giant Corinthian columns, supporting a continuous entablature from which sprang an array of lightly constructed and cut-away vaults and domes. The spatial elegance of the whole was extraordinary. But even more extraordinary was the structural finesse of the whole undertaking. "Le principal objet de M. Soufflot en bâtissant son église," his pupil Maximilien Brebion wrote later, "a été de réunir, sous une des plus belles formes, la légèreté de la construction des églises gothiques avec la pureté et la magnificence de l'architecture grecque" (Brebion to Ch. Cl. de Flahaut de

14. *Pierre Contant d'Ivry,
St.-Vasnon, Condé-sur-l'Escaut,
interior, 1751*

15. *Jacques-Germain Soufflot, Hôtel-
Dieu, Lyons, facade and central
feature, 1741–48*

la Billarderie, Comte d'Angiviller, October 20, 1780, Paris, Archives Nationales, 0¹ 1694-[43]).

During the long period of construction, Soufflot and his friends the engineer Jean-Rodolphe Perronet (1708-1794), *Inspecteur Général des Ponts et Chaussées,* and founder in 1747 of the École des Ponts et Chaussées, and his pupil Émiliand-Marie Gauthey (1732-1808), scoured France for stones, building machines to test their compressive strengths in a laboratory set up in the Louvre, coordinating and interpreting their results, and arriving at formulas and equations that they applied to the design of Ste.-Geneviève. They continued to refine the structure and whittle away the masonry mass but were forced to justify their procedures to the members of the Académie, particularly when the main piers were found to be cracking. They might be said to have mounted a campaign, presenting drawings of a whole range of lightly constructed churches for inspection: S. Agostino in Piacenza, the Cappella della SS. Sindone in Turin, S. Maria della Salute in Venice, and a number of French Gothic churches. The Gothic parallel remained of paramount importance in the justification of Ste.-Geneviève. Soufflot's pupil Jallier sent painstaking measured drawings of Notre-Dame in Dijon, in 1762, the first such drawings of a Gothic church to be made. Soufflot himself read a paper on Gothic architecture, chiefly on the proportional system involved, that he had delivered first to the Académie des Sciences in Lyons in 1741, when it was probably heard—or heard of—by Laugier, then at the Jesuit college there.

The discussion occasioned by the building of Ste.-Geneviève was of the highest importance in furthering theories of construction in France. Soufflot and his associates stressed the development of abstract theories based on experiment and mathematical calculation; their adversaries, chief among them the architect Pierre Patte (1723-1814), relied rather on empirical knowledge alone. But even Patte was to extend greatly the common understanding of structure, especially Gothic structure. He planned a treatise on this subject that he was never to finish, but when that great pedagogue Jacques-François Blondel died in 1774, Patte took over and completed the last two volumes of Blondel's *Cours d'architecture,* devoted to building materials and construction. These were issued in 1777. Blondel's *Cours d'architecture,* the issue of a lifetime's teaching—first at an independent school that he started in 1743, then from 1762 onward as an authorized professor of the Académie—served to consolidate and disseminate French doctrine at its most sound and most sensible. His judgements were always cautious and carefully explained. He could scarcely be thought intolerant, though he was not too adventurous. Tradition and reason conditioned all his attitudes. He did, however, take up the idea of designing churches with freestanding columns along their naves—but with arches above, as Frézier had shown that they were more sensible in France—and was fully aware of the Gothic sympathies thus involved, defending them in terms that were to be taken up by A. W. N. Pugin and the Ecclesiologists in nineteenth-

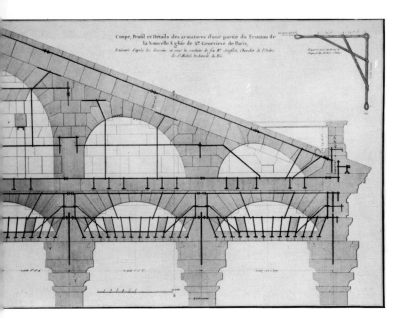

Coupe, Profil et Détails des armatures d'une partie du Fronton de la Nouvelle Eglise de S.ᵗᵉ Geneviève de Paris.

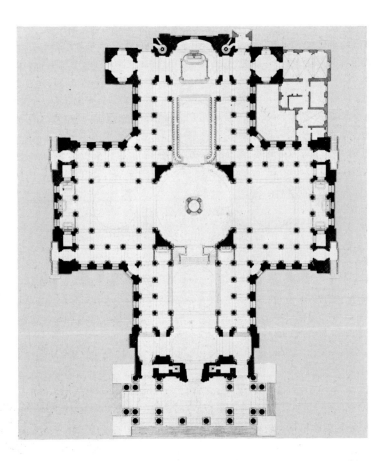

century England, on the grounds of religious tradition.

Blondel was in no sense a connoisseur of construction. "La magie de l'art," he wrote, "veut des bornes; trop de hardiesse étonne plus qu'elle ne satisfait" (*Cour,* vol. 4, p. 315). He lagged in completing the last two volumes of the *Cours* through lack of vital interest. But Patte had a long-sustained and inquisitive concern with the techniques of building. He had already written several memoirs on the subject, and he returned in the *Cours* to his attack on Soufflot's great church and to the intricacies of Gothic engineering.

To illustrate his text, Patte chose drawings of Notre-Dame in Dijon that Jallier had prepared for Soufflot, and, in analyzing the section, he showed that not only were the ribs of the vaults, the flying buttresses, and the outer buttresses essential structural features—nothing more—but so also were the finials, which acted as counterthrusts to the forces directed through the flying buttresses. He thought that even the timber trusses over the aisles were designed as buttresses. His ingenuity in isolating what he recognized as the Gothic principle never deserted him. He discerned it even in the Augustinian church at Lille, where iron tie-rods rather than buttresses were used to restrain the thrust of the vaults. Whatever their basic disagreements, like Soufflot he sought an architecture that was altogether economical and honest in its expression.

Something of this spirit, it should be noted, was developed independently in Venice, during the first half of the eighteenth century, by Carlo Lodoli (1690-1761). Lodoli was not an architect; he was a brilliant, radical polymath, a Franciscan friar, who started a small academy about 1720 for the sons of Venetian noblemen, teaching them languages, mathematics, law, and statesmanship for a few hours each day. He also taught them something of architecture, his favorite subject. He evolved no fully worked-out theory of architecture but some highly original notions, based in part on the experiments and mathematical theories of a succession of Scottish engineers active in Padua, among them James Gregory and James Stirling. Lodoli's ideas were to be recorded by two of his disciples, the fashionable gadabout Francesco Algarotti (1712-1764), whose ironical commentary, the *Saggio sopra l'architettura,* was to be published in 1757, and the more staid but dreadfully muddled Andrea Memmo (1729-1793), who did not start to write his account until 1784. It was published in two parts: the first, *Elementi dell'architettura Lodoliana; ossia, l'arte del fabbricare con solidità scientifica e con eleganza non capricciosa,* in 1786, reprinted together with the second in 1833 and 1834. It was once thought that Laugier—who published the *Histoire de la République de Venise* between 1759 and 1768, and is known to have been in Venice in 1757, and perhaps in 1752, to collect material for this work—was directly influenced by Lodoli when he came to write the *Essai sur l'architecture.* But this has been disproved. To judge by the references made to French architects and ideas in both Algarotti's and Memmo's accounts, the Venetian was strongly influenced rather by the works of

Perrault, Cordemoy, Frézier, and others. But Lodoli was more extreme in his views; he held that architecture should derive entirely from the nature of materials and the laws of statics. Ornament or decoration might be applied, provided that it did not disrupt the basic forms and shapes. But he rejected outright the whole range of forms, moldings, and details belonging to the classical language of architecture, for they had been evolved originally, he said, in timber. The temples of ancient Greece were made first of timber. They were therefore unsuitable as models for buildings in stone. All the architecture of the Romans and by the men of the Renaissance was thus lacking in honesty; it was to be dismissed. The only true architecture of stone, Algarotti noted, was that of Egypt and Stonehenge.

Neither the niceties of argument offered by Lodoli nor the refinements of structure proposed by Soufflot and his friends were to be greatly favored in late eighteenth-century France. Architects were no longer interested in structural elegance and lightness of form: they had learned by then to appreciate the strong sculptural qualities of the architecture of antiquity, Greek no less than Roman, and had begun to cherish in their own work large and simplified mass. Those uncomplicated proportional relationships that Laugier had so much admired had come into their own. The square and the cube had passed into favor, and with them the sphere. But whatever the mathematical certainties relied upon to produce this purified geometry, there was a delight in large-scale elementary forms for their visual effects alone. Explanations offered were often, as we shall see, of a sophisticated kind. Étienne-Louis Boullée (1728-1799), the greatest of the visionary architects, who had intended at first to pursue a career as a painter, saw embodied in the sphere all manner of marvelous qualities.

The irrational, emotive streak that appears in architectural theory in the late eighteenth century was no doubt conditioned by the complete break in building activity during the French Revolution, so that the practicalities of architecture could be set aside for a time in favor of the production of grand and ever more vast imaginative projects. But this tendency was evident even before 1789, when the less restrictive, sensational English attitudes toward beauty—and, in particular, Edmund Burke's concept of the Sublime—were introduced into France in the form of Picturesque gardening theory. The first significant book on the subject to appear in France was the translation and extension of Thomas Whately's *Observations on Modern Gardening,* itself the first coherent attempt to systematize Picturesque theory. This was issued in 1771, only a year after its publication in England. The translator was François de Paule Latapie, a protégé of Montesquieu, who is often credited with having laid out the earliest *jardin anglais* in France, at his estate at La Brède, soon after his return from England in 1750. No record or trace of this survives. A better-known and certainly more influential exemplar of the natural garden in something of an English manner was that begun soon after 1754 at Moulin-Joli near Bézons, by

20. *Jacques-Germain Soufflot,*
Ste.-Geneviève, Paris, detail of the
vaults, 1756–90

21. *Jacques-Germain Soufflot,*
Ste.-Geneviève, Paris, interior,
1756–90

Claude-Henri Watelet, who was to record his experiences and all his intentions in his *Essai sur les jardins,* of 1774. This was intended as only a part of a general treatise on taste and beauty. Its influence was considerable. The fashion for Picturesque gardens in France dates from its publication. More important, it introduced a whole new range of ideas and notions into artistic theory. *Le génie de l'architecture; ou, l'analogie de cet art avec nos sensations,* issued in 1780 by Nicolas Le Camus de Mézières (1721-1789)—the architect of the great circular Halle aux Blés in Paris, who was to dedicate his work to Watelet—marks a new departure in French architectural thought. For the first time, a major part of an architectural treatise was devoted to the idea that architecture should be pleasing to the senses and that it should, in addition, induce elevating impressions on the spirit and soul. This heady, speculative venture was to be balanced in the second part of the book by a detailed discussion of the matter-of-fact problems of planning. In the following year Le Camus was to publish an even more practical manual on building construction, *Le guide de ceux qui veulent bâtir.* But it was his more rarefied notions that were to appeal to such architects as Boullée. Boullée virtually gave up building at this time and turned instead to that sublime abstract architecture of monuments without practical function, for which he is famous, and to the composition of his *Essai sur l'art.* A measure of how far he had moved from any acceptance of the standard French criteria for architectural excellence is evident in his opening lines: "Qu'est-ce que l'architecture? La définirai-je avec Vitruve l'art de bâtir? Non. Il y a dans cette définition une erreur grossière. Vitruve prend l'effet pour la cause. Il faut concevoir pour effectuer. Nos premiers pères n'ont bâti leurs cabanes qu'après en avoir conçu l'image. C'est cette production de l'esprit, c'est cette création qui constitue l'architecture, que nous pouvons, en conséquence, définir l'art de produire et de porter à la perfection tout édifice quelconque. L'art de bâtir n'est donc qu'un art secondaire, qu'il nous paraît convenable de nominer la partie scientifique de l'architecture" (J. M. Pérouse de Montclos, ed., *E. L. Boullée: Architecture, essai sur l'art,* 1968, p. 49).

There is nothing in his essay on that scientific aspect of architecture, nothing on those practical, rational notions that had occupied architectural theorists in France from Perrault onward, though there was a great deal on Perrault's proposition that beauty be regarded as both positive and arbitrary, with interest directed in particular to the arbitrary, fantastical forms. Not that Boullée's architecture was ever wayward or disorderly. Though he and most of his contemporaries were sympathetic to the theories that sustained the Picturesque movement, they were intent to interpret them always in compositions of a rigid symmetry and pure geometrical form. Clear-cut geometry for the French (Jean-Jacques Lequeu apart) remained all. The legacy of eighteenth-century architectural thought in France was to be contained and summed up in two books, the *Traité théorique et pratique de l'art de bâtir,* issued between 1802 and 1803, and the *Précis des leçons*

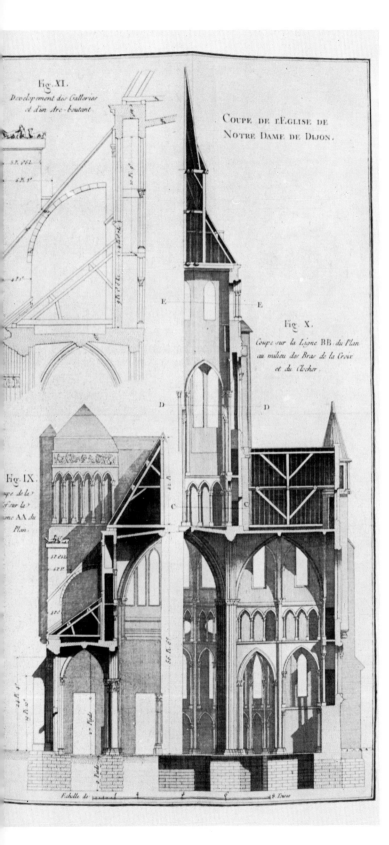

22. Drawings by Jallier of Notre-Dame, Dijon, 1762, illustrated in Jacques-François Blondel's and Pierre Patte's Cours d'architecture, *1777*

d'architecture données à l'École royale polytechnique, published between 1802 and 1805. They were to remain standard texts for fifty years and more. The first was written by Jean-Baptiste Rondelet (1734-1829), a pupil of Soufflot, who had been responsible for the completion of Ste.-Geneviève and had later reinforced the main piers with inestimable tact and skill when they were found, for the second time, to be collapsing. Rondelet's knowledge of building construction was unsurpassed. The second book was the work of Boullée's favorite pupil, Jean-Nicolas-Louis Durand (1760-1834), who was made professor of architecture at the École Polytechnique in 1795 and was to teach there for the rest of his life, mainly instructing surveyors and engineers. The only architects of note who passed through the school were Hubert Rohault de Fleury and his son Charles and Émile-Jacques Gilbert. But Durand exerted his enormous influence on architects through the medium of books. In addition to the *Précis,* he wrote the *Recueil et parallèle des édifices de tout genre anciens et modernes,* of 1800, and an appendix to the *Précis,* the *Partie graphique des cours d'architecture faits à l'École royale polytechnique,* of 1821. His works propounded the strictest standards of formal geometry and design.

Rondelet's book is probably unique among architectural treatises in that it contains almost no general discussion of architecture, apart from a few pages at the beginning (published twice, separately) that make it clear nonetheless that his treatise was to be regarded as a comprehensive foundation for the study and practice of architecture. Architecture was constituted entirely in "l'art de bâtir." "La théorie," he wrote, "est une science qui dirige toutes les opérations de la pratique. Cette science est le résultat de l'expérience et du raisonnement fondé sur les principes de mathématique et de physique appliquées aux différentes operations de l'art. C'est par le moyen de la théorie qu'un habile constructeur parvient à déterminer les formes et les justes dimensions qu'il faut donner à chaque partie d'un édifice en raison de sa situation et des efforts qu'elle peut avoirà soutenir, pour qu'il résulte perfection, solidité et économie" (vol. 1, p. v.).

Architecture, Rondelet insisted, was not an imaginative art but a science, controlled by need and necessity. The five volumes of his treatise were therefore devoted to lengthy accounts of building materials, their properties and their strengths, the techniques of all manners of building, and the most efficient means of estimating and calculating costs. There was much challenging reinterpretation of Gothic construction, as one might expect from a pupil of Soufflot, and much more up-to-date information on the latest experiments in building in iron, once again reflecting an interest of Soufflot. Most of the new bridges in iron in both England and France were illustrated, with suggestions as to how their design might have been improved. French theorists, whether they looked to the architecture of the past or the present, sought always to refashion it in terms of their own ideals.

Durand took as part of the frontispiece of his *Recueil et parallèle* that view of the Propylaea in Athens that had first appeared in Julien-David Le Roy's

23. *Plate from Jean-Baptiste Rondelet's* Traité théorique et pratique de l'art de bâtir, *1802-3*

24. *Julien-David Le Roy, reconstruction of the Propylaea, Athens, from his* Ruines des plus beaux monuments de la Grèce, *1758*

Ruines des plus beaux monuments de la Grèce (1758) in which all the elements are rearranged in axial symmetry around a monumental flight of stairs. Throughout, Durand redrew the buildings in the illustrations so that they might appear more neat and orderly, for though he selected his examples from all periods of history—from Egyptian, Greek, Roman, Gothic, or Renaissance times—he was intent to disregard their oddities and stylistic characteristics and to present them all drawn to the same scale and arranged for comparison, as particular building types. Temples are grouped together on one page, churches on another, theaters on yet another, and so on. Once again the initial idea can be traced back to Le Roy, who illustrated a set of plans thus in the second edition of his book on Greek architecture, though the idea was initiated by Soufflot's pupil Gabriel-Pierre-Martin Dumont (1720-1791), who issued two such plates illustrating theaters in 1764 or 1765.

Durand's theoretical approach to architecture is contained in the *Précis* and the *Partie graphique*. He refused to consider Laugier's rustic cabin as the model for all architecture; it was no more, he said, than a rude beginning. Architecture was a reasoned affair, a considered and evolving solution to practical problems. "Soit que l'on consulte la raison," he wrote, "soit que l'on examine les monuments, il est évident que plaire n'a jamais pu être son objet. L'utilité publique et particulière, le bonheur et la conservation des individus et de la société, tel est le but de l'architecture" (*Précis,* vol. 1, p. 18).

Such high-minded sentiments, however, cannot be taken as grounds for considering Durand as a strict utilitarian; his language is only an aspect of post-Revolutionary cant. Though he proposed that architecture be conditioned by social demands, convenience, and economy, his criteria in designing were symmetry—at best, true symmetry—and a simplified geometry, which happened to be his aesthetic preferences. He developed his themes with logic, but it is a logic not free from naivety. He argued that symmetry and regularity resulted in economy of means and were thus ideals. The circle and the sphere were the finest figures because they enclosed the maximum area—or volume, in the case of the sphere—for the minimum circumference or surface area. He accepted, though, that these figures might be impractical in building design and chose, therefore, as the next best, the square and the cube. To learn to be an architect, he said, one had only to learn to divide a square into a regular grid. Architecture, he claimed, was a graphic formula. His method of composition was to start with the plan (almost invariably a square), to transform this into a grid, to draw on the main and subsidiary axes required to link the rooms, and then to impose upon this grid what he recognized to be the elements of architecture: the walls and columnar supports, together with such "negative" elements as doors and window openings. To arrive at the section and form of the building, the established grid was projected vertically. Durand had no feeling for form and volume. Even his plans were altogether unsatisfactory from the point of view of human requirements, though as geometrical

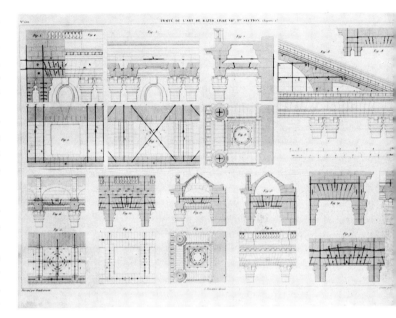

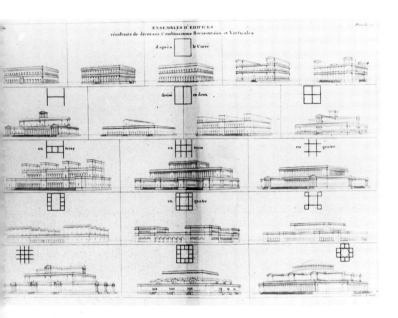

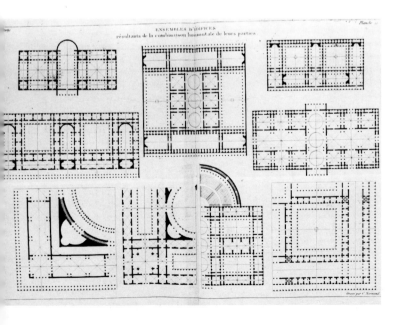

patterns they are undeniably impressive. Certainly they were to impress architects throughout Europe, and in Germany in particular. It is of some significance, perhaps, that the one building he was to approve without restraint, the vast circular Hôpital Ste.-Anne in Paris, begun in 1788 by Bernard Poyet (1742-1824), was stopped soon after on grounds of inefficient planning and inordinate cost. But there was more to Durand's theory than grid planning; he wished to do away with all unnecessary extravagance and decoration in architecture (the normally accepted forms of expression), and he proposed therefore that the style of a building be the visible expression of its functioning parts. The walls were to appear as plain masonry surfaces. The independent supports were to be in the form of piers or columns, equally spaced and made of materials that were demonstrably stronger than those used for the rest of the structure. There was to be a minimum of adornment and molding, and what there was had to present a palpable argument to the spectator of the role of the form to which it was applied. For richness or variety architects were to turn to plants, and many of Durand's stark and barren buildings were relieved with vines and creepers.

Rondelet and Durand together reduced architecture to two of its component parts, structure and formal geometry, and though Rondelet cared little for formal planning and Durand knew next to nothing of the art of construction (he had relegated it to a few notes at the back of the *Précis,* he was to explain in a later edition, lest it disrupt the thread of his argument), their books were by no means opposed in spirit; indeed, most architects regard them as complementary studies summarizing and reformulating the chief interests of the architects of the eighteenth century. Architecture entered a period of doctrinaire orthodoxy in the early years of the nineteenth century, and these books were to provide suitable formulas for building countless *mairies, palais de justice,* hospitals, prisons, and barracks throughout France. Émile-Jacques Gilbert, Durand's most enlightened pupil, was to make a sustained and serious attempt to reinvigorate architecture by introducing into it those humanitarian and social concerns of the early penal and health reformers, and later the ideas of Claude-Henri, Comte de Saint-Simon himself. Gilbert devoted his life to building no more than a prison, an asylum, a hospital, and a police barracks—and also, one might note, a morgue—yet he reflected faithfully in all his work and in all his teachings the ideals of Durand and Rondelet. The only other attempt to disrupt the torpor of architecture in France in the early decades of the century was the desperate bid by Jacques-Ignace Hittorff (1792-1867)—born in Cologne, but trained in France under François-Joseph Bélanger—to justify the application of riotous surface coloring to architecture. He fought bitterly to prove that the ancient temples of Greece had been richly colored. He recorded and publicized the murals and decorations of Pompeii and Herculaneum and even Raphael's grotesques. He sought to decorate his own buildings with enameled plaques, but such was not the means to renew

27. Eugène-Emmanuel Viollet-le-Duc,
house built between 1860 and 1863
in the valley below the Château de
Pierrefonds (now École Secondaire
d'Agriculture du Prieuré)

architecture. Yet there can be no doubt that Gilbert and Hittorff prepared the way for those riformers of the middle years of the century Guillaume-Abel Blouet, Félix-Jacques Duban, Pierre-François-Henri Labrouste, Louis-Joseph Duc, and Léon Vaudoyer. Only the eldest of these, Blouet, was to attempt a full-scale exposition of his theory, and it is scarcely surprising to find that as his architectural activity was close in its range to that of Gilbert (he designed prisons and built a penal colony), his ideas were no more than an extension of those expounded many years before by Rondelet. Indeed, Blouet's treatise took the form of a *Supplément à la traité théorique et pratique de l'art de bâtir de Jean Rondelet,* issued in two volumes in 1847 and 1848.

This is essentially a catalogue of nineteenth-century engineering achievements, though there is a clear enough exposition of the theoretical underpinnings of such structures. Blouet's arguments are based on two tenets, which are worth quoting at length, for they served to reaffirm and reestablish the rationalist position worked out half a century before.

1°—à concevoir ce qu'il faut, rien de plus, et à le réaliser le plus simplement possible, ce qui ne peût être obtenu qu'en subordonnant d'abord ses conceptions, qui doivent devenir des réalités, aux moyens d'exécution et aux propriétés des materiaux dont on dispose.

2°—à n'employer la décoration que pour compléter l'expression en ébauché dans la disposition et la construction, accentuer les parties en raison de leurs fonctions relatives et déterminer par suite, avec plus de précision, le caractère de l'édifice à l'aide des moyens qui favorisent les matériaux auxquels ils sont appliqués, de moyens, en un mot, rendant sensible à la fois le but de l'édifice et sa construction, tant sous le rapport du mode de l'exécution que sous celui de la nature des matières employées (vol. 2, pp. ix, 227).

There is scarcely any need to comment on this program, though it is worth noting that it served from 1846 until 1853, when Blouet was *Professeur de Théorie* at the École des Beaux-Arts, as the official doctrine. At the École Polytechnique itself, oddly enough, a rationalist doctrine of considerably less intellectual rigor and restrictiveness was being propounded from 1837 onward by François-Léonce Reynaud (1803-1880), the engineer, who was to publish his *Traité d'architecture* in two volumes in 1850 and 1858. This is devoted largely to building materials, methods of construction, and various building types, but the seventeen pages of theoretical text and the introduction make the guiding principles disarmingly clear. The aim of architecture, Reynaud declared, was beauty, not utility, though practical requirements must always be carefully fulfilled. Taste was to be the ultimate arbiter of architectural harmony and expression. Ornament and decorative forms, though certainly not to be regarded as essential, were vital to such expression and might give value to architecture. But in other respects Reynaud was far less lax and tolerant than Blouet; whereas Blouet extolled the economy of Gothic construction and was even prepared to set up programs for his students for churches in the Gothic style, Reynaud disliked

all aspects of the Gothic and dreaded lest there be a Gothic revival. "L'art du moyen âge est mort," he wrote, "aussi bien que son esprit et ses institutions, et leur résurrection est impossible. On peut galvaniser un cadavre, mais non le rappeler à la vie" (vol. 2, p. 270).

It was precisely those men of Gothic inclination who were to take up the rationalist doctrine of Blouet and his circle—in particular, that transmitted by Henri Labrouste—and who were to demonstrate that, by a renewed and more thorough analysis of Gothic architecture, more stringent principles yet might be adduced that could even lead to an architecture with style, but one that owed nothing to any styles of the past. Eugène-Emmanuel Viollett-le-Duc (1814-1879) was the chief exponent of this brand of rationalism. He was the bugbear of the École des Beaux-Arts. And it is not without irony that Jean-Louis-Charles Garnier, architect of the Paris Opéra—who was to destroy, almost, the intellectual tradition of architecture in France, and to show that by conjuring up a whole medley of styles, forms, and motifs a vigorous architecture could be produced—should have been asked, as a student, to swear "Haine à Viollet-le-Duc" on the "Grand Durand," the *Recueil et parallèle des édifices de tout genre anciens et modernes.*

The Gothic movement in nineteenth-century France sprang from romantic beginnings, from Alexandre Lenoir's atmospheric museum in the Couvent des Petits Augustins, later to become part of the École des Beaux-Arts, where fragments from the past were reassembled after the Revolution and imbued with an aura of poetry and mystery. Chateaubriand's

28. *Eugène-Emmanuel Viollet-le-Duc, project for a* hôtel de ville *with cast-iron struts, from his twelfth* Entretien sur l'architecture, *c. 1866*

Gothic leanings were first nurtured there; so also were those of the historian Jules Michelet. But though Michelet's brilliant *Introduction à l'histoire universelle,* of 1831, and the six volumes on French medieval history that followed were to arouse a popular passion for the Gothic past—particularly in Catholic circles—he was to find that his ideal image had little relation to reality and he was to become the leader of an anticlerical coterie of historians who despised the Middle Ages. The Catholic national credo and the manifesto for the restoration, if not the revival, of Gothic architecture was, in fact, a novel, Victor Hugo's *Notre-Dame de Paris,* issued first in February 1831, but republished in the following year with three additional chapters that made quite explicit Hugo's aims: "Inspirons," he wrote, "s'il est possible à la nation l'amour de l'architecture nationale. C'est là, l'auteur le déclare, un des buts principaux de ce livre; c'est là un des buts principaux de sa vie" (1832 ed., preface).

Viollet-le-Duc was inspired by such works, and he was to retain always a romantic, emotional sympathy for the Gothic, but it was rather those self-sure Protestant historians of the Middle Ages grouped around François-Pierre-Guillaume Guizot—and, in particular, Guizot himself—who were to supply his knowledge of the national past and to give him the opportunity to devolop his inclinations. When Guizot assumed political power, he at once established the Commission des Monuments Historiques and began to provide money for the restoration of historical buildings. Viollet-le-Duc was drawn early into this orbit by Prosper Mérimée, *Inspecteur Général des Monuments Historiques.* In 1840, at the age of twenty-six, he was appointed to restore Ste.-Madeleine at Vézelay; later in the same year he joined Labrouste's pupil Jean-Baptiste-Antoine Lassus (1807-1857) on the restoration of the Ste.-Chapelle; and in another four years they began the restoration of Notre-Dame. His career was to be largely concerned with restoration. This was the source of his immense knowledge and understanding of Gothic architecture and the basis of those two great works for which he is famous, the *Dictionnaire raisonné de l'architecture française du XIe au XVIe siècle,* published between 1854 and 1868, and the *Dictionnaire raisonné du mobilier français de l'époque carlovingienne à la renaissance,* issued from 1858 to 1875.

In his early years Viollet-le-Duc's energies were directed not only to the restoration of Gothic architecture but also to a revival of the style itself. Lassus, together with a group of Gothic enthusiasts and archaeologists, chief among them Adolphe-Napoléon Didron, was then busy restoring the church of St.-Germain-l'Auxerrois, and was showing both there and at the Ste.-Chapelle that an image of the Middle Ages could conjured up that was quite as colorful and rich as that proposed at the same time by Hittorff for Greek architecture. They all propagated their ideas in Didron's *Annales archéologiques,* begun in 1844. But from Lassus Viollet-le-Duc also learned something of that rationalist doctrine of the Gothic that was contained in the works of Rondelet and that had been transmitted by Lassus's master,

29. Eugène-Emmanuel Viollet-le-Duc
and Félix Narjoux, gallery in the
Château de Pregny, near Geneva,
1875

Labrouste. Already, in his first major series of articles, "De la construction des édifices religieux en France depuis le commencement du Christianisme jusqu'au XVIᵉ siècle," published in the *Annales* between 1844 and 1847, Viollet-le-Duc indicated that he had absorbed all that his predecessors could teach him on the structure and the rational nature of the Gothic. Soon after, he was to reject the idea of a revival of the style and to turn his attention instead to the most rigorous analysis of every form, every detail, of Gothic, to arrive at a set of principles for design that he hoped might be applicable to the nineteenth century. The architecture of the nineteenth century was thus to be analogous to, though distinct from, that of the thirteenth century; it was to be the visible expression in contemporary terms, using contemporary materials such as iron, of a system evolved in the thirteenth century. In the *Dictionnaire raisonné de l'architecture française* he illustrated a section through the aisle and nave of a church showing how timber props might be substituted for the stone of the flying buttresses, and cast-iron columns used in place of the piers of the nave; this, in its most elementary form, was the way in which he thought Gothic structural principles might begin to be reinterpreted. His analyses were to become far more complex and subtle than this, for he was led to believe that every feature, every molding, of a Gothic building could be interpreted as a functional device, whether as part of a supporting system or to throw off rainwater. He was convinced that architecture was a clear expression of function, a function that embodied political and social aspirations, material limitations and needs. His analyses

of medieval social organizations were marvelously distorted so that they might accord with his architectural theories.

Later, he assaulted the citadel of classical rationalism, the École des Beaux-Arts itself, first, in 1857, by opening an independent *atelier* of his own in the Rue Bonaparte, taking over some of Labrouste's students, and then, in 1863, by intriguing with Prosper Mérimée, a long-standing friend of the Empress Eugénie, to have himself appointed *Professeur d'Histoire de l'Art et Esthétique* at that venerable institution. He retired soon after, rudely rebuffed by the students. He had attempted to show that the rational theories he had evolved in relation to the Gothic style were applicable also to all great architecture—among which he ranked Greek and Byzantine architecture, with some reservations as to the quality of Roman buildings. Roman structure was sound enough, he thought, but the decorative overlay adopted had been evolved in relation to Greek architectural forms and was altogether inappropriate. His exposition of these ideas took the form of the *Entretiens sur l'architecture,* appearing in chapters from 1858 onward; the first volume was completed in 1863, the second in 1872. The second volume reveals Viollet-le-Duc at his most adventurous. He was a dogged theoretician who argued his way through even the knottiest problems with determination and an air of success, but he was never able to give convincing form to his ideas. His restorations apart, he designed almost one hundred buildings on his own account (often credited to his students and associates), but he never once built anything that accords successfully with his theories. His buildings, individual houses for the most part, are lackluster and commonplace, conceived in a range of styles from Gothic to late Renaissance. The ultimate disappointment was his gallery, of 1875 in the Château de Pregny, on the outskirts of Geneva—built in 1860-64 for the Baron de Rothschild by none other than Sir Joseph Paxton, designer of the Crystal Palace of 1851. The gallery is a fussily decorated period pastiche.

Yet in a handful of plates in the twelfth *Entretien,* issued about 1867, he showed that with dogged determination he could produce a visual embodiment of his theories that was to be almost as memorable to twentieth-century architects as the Crystal Palace itself. Viollet-le-Duc's designs are awkward and ungainly, but the system of angled iron struts that he indicated first for a town hall, then in increasing complexity for a series of large covered spaces, and finally for a concert hall for three thousand people, provided just that liberating stimulus required by architects trained in a rational functionalist ideal but encumbered always by a range of historical styles. Viollet-le-Duc suggested how they might abandon these and evolve a new style for the future. This not only was to be an expression of a solution to a problem in structure but was to embody also an absolute geometrical ideal based on the form of the equilateral triangle. Viollet-le-Duc's giant concert hall is an illustration of his belief that everything in nature, indeed the whole universe, was built up of polyhedra based on the equilateral triangle. This was, to him, the essence of style.

Perhaps the most striking architectural impact of the Picturesque was the new emphasis it placed on architecture as part of an environment. We may interpret the word *environment,* so fashionable today, in a rather broad way so as to refer not merely to the physical setting, whether rural or urban, but also to the historical setting. Architecture, in other words, came to be regarded as possessing evocative narrative or literary powers. This emphasis on architecture as part of something else, as an incident in history or in a landscape, encouraged the concept of growth, of flexibility, in architecture; thus, buildings were thought to have a special merit if one could read in them the process of their alteration during the years or even centuries of their existence.

One of the clearest ways in which this new approach to architecture was expressed in the eighteenth century was, perhaps ironically, in the obsession with the ruin. Admiration for ruins is an obvious indication of a belief that there are more important aspects to a building than the functional and visual roles its designer intended it to fulfill. Thus some architects, at once frustrated and excited by this implied shift in their role, began to imagine what their own buildings would look like when change and decay had reduced them to ruin. Perhaps the first English design that is clearly part of the international neoclassicism developed in Franco-Italian circles in the 1740s is the one for a mausoleum for the Prince of Wales, of 1751-52, by Sir William Chambers. Yet its monumental neoclassicism, doubtless derived from designs by such architects as Louis-Joseph Le Lorrain for the Festa della Chinea in Rome, is dissolved by Chambers's unexpectedly Romantic decision to show the mausoleum not merely in a landscaped setting but also as it would appear when ruined. Few went so far as Racine de Monville, who, with help from the architect François Barbier, in 1780 built a house for himself in the form of a ruined column, at the Désert de Retz, not far from Paris. The essentially pictorial character of this enterprise is emphasized by the fact that the *jardin anglais* that surrounded this bizarre dwelling was designed with assistance from the painter Hubert Robert. The continual dissolution of neoclassicism by the Picturesque is a particularly English phenomenon, and it reached a climax with Sir John Soane (1753-1837), who commissioned Joseph Michael Gandy (1771-1843) to depict his vast rotunda at the Bank of England, London, at a point when it could be said to possess the status of a Piranesian ruin.

Sir John Vanbrugh's memorandum of June 11,1709, arguing for the preservation of the ruins of Woodstock Manor in the park at Blenheim is a key document in the history of eighteenth-century ruin mania. Vanbrugh (1664-1726) urged the upkeep of buildings of distant times because "they move [inspire] more lively and pleasing Reflections (than History without their aid can do) on the Persons who have inhabited them; on the remarkable things which have been transacted in them, or the extraordinary occasions of erecting them." Vanbrugh went on to argue that because the park at Blenheim "has little variety of objects" it "stands in need of all the helps

30. *Sir William Chambers, project for the mausoleum of Frederick, Prince of Wales, 1751–52.*

that can be given... Buildings and Plantations." These, in his opinion, "rightly dispos'd will indeed supply all the wants of Nature in that place. And the most agreeable disposition is to mix them in which this old Manour gives so happy an occasion for; that were the enclosure filled with Trees (principally fine Yews and Hollys) promiscuously set not grow up in a wild thicket, so that all the buildings left might appear in two risings amongst'em, it would make one of the most agreeable objects that the best of Landskip painters can invent" (*The Complete Works of Sir John Vanbrugh,* ed. B. Dobrée and G. Webb, 4 vols., 1928, vol. 4, pp. 29-30). This quotation encapsulates the Picturesque tendency to dethrone architecture, to replace the traditional Renaissance architect with historians, Romantics, painters—people who see a building as an incident in an environment, whether natural or historical. We can usefully tabulate the three principal points of Vanbrugh's thesis as follows: "1. Buildings can bring the past to life more vividly than written history; 2. Buildings can be composed as an integral part of a landscape; 3. In mingling buildings and trees in a designed landscape we should take seventeenth-century landscape paintings as a model if we want the result to be authentically 'Picturesque.' "

From Vanbrugh in the early eighteenth century to Edwin Lutyens in the early twentieth we can trace the development of the ideas contained in these three points. An intense emphasis on architecture as part of a landscape or of a natural setting, which was so much to characterize the work of John Nash, led in time to an emphasis on local materials and local techniques, which marks the work of Philip Webb and Lutyens.

Vanbrugh lost his battle with the forceful duchess of Marlborough over the preservation of Woodstock Manor, but the victory was ultimately his since his ideas were adopted later in the eighteenth and nineteenth centuries. Thus the ruins of medieval houses or castles were preserved as Picturesque objects in the landscaped parks of many new houses: in the 1760s, at Tabley house, Cheshire, by John Carr (1723-1807); in the 1770s, at Wardour Castle, Wiltshire, by James Paine; in 1807, at Belsay Castle, Northumberland, by Sir Charles Monck; and, most strikingly of all, in 1835, at Scotney Castle, Kent, by Edward Hussey, Anthony Salvin (1799-1881), and William Sawrey Gilpin. At Scotney, Salvin's new house is, in a sense, a mere window placed to catch a view of the Picturesque ruins of the moated castle in the valley below. Hussey and Salvin made these ruins even more "Picturesque" by eliminating most of the additions made to them in the seventeenth century. With further help from the landscape gardener Gilpin, son of the celebrated Picturesque theorist, the castle was linked visually to the house by a landscaped garden of dreamlike quality and intense beauty. At Peckforton Castle, Cheshire, Salvin provided a different interpretation to a similar theme. Here, from 1844 to 1850, he created a vast new castle on a hill adjacent to the thirteenth-century Beeston Castle. As at Scotney, the principal rooms commanded views of the nearby ruins, but the parallel ends there since Beeston Castle plays only a very minor role in the whole composition. It is the expansive new castle of Peckforton and not the landscape or the ruins that is the center of attention.

The story of the Picturesque begins not with architecture but with gardens. The Romantic "natural" garden, or park, developed in England in the eighteenth century, had undoubtedly been anticipated in Renaissance Italy. So far, research into either the Italian gardens themselves or English knowledge of them has been insufficient to enable us to assess the measure of their influence. The groves, grottoes, nymphaea, and irregular areas of Italian gardens were as rich with antique literary and mythological symbolism as Stourhead was to be in the eighteenth century. In the Vatican gardens, the early sixteenth-century Fontana dello Scoglio was a cross between a grotto and a ruin that would have delighted the poet Alexander Pope, while the largest of the four sections of the grounds of the Villa Borghese was laid out as a park at the beginning of the seventeenth century in a way that might similarly have pleased the designer William Kent (1685-1748). A description of the Villa Borghese written in 1700 claims that the inspiration for this part of the garden was antique and that it "seems irregular but art and industry have so well regulated it that it alternates from hill to plain and from wild to domesticated valleys" (see G. Masson, *Italian Gardens,* 1961, p. 154).

Among the first English landscaped parks and gardens were Pope's own at Twickenham, Middlesex (begun 1719), with its little wilderness, shell temple, and grotto. The new movement had strong literary and philosophical overtones, not only in the writings of Pope but in those of the first earl of Shaftesbury and Joseph Addison as well. The gardens of Stephen Switzer and the writings of Batty Langley (*New Principles of Gardening,* 1728) lent support to a movement that reached a climax in William Kent's garden at Rousham, Oxfordshire, in the 1730s. The second phase in the history of the Picturesque is represented by Lancelot "Capability" Brown (1716-1783), whose work from about 1750 to about 1780 is an extension and popularization not so much of what Kent had achieved at Rousham—which is still essentially a *garden*—but of the bigger, barer *parks* he had projected at Euston and Holkham Hall. Reaction quickly set in to Brown's rather bland landscapes, thus producing the third phase of the Picturesque, associated with the writings of Sir Uvedale Price (1747-1829) and Richard Payne Knight (1750-1824) in the 1790s. For our purposes at the moment this third phase is the most significant, since it had more impact on architectural design than the other two phases. Nonetheless, we should look at some of the great landscaped parks of the mid-eighteenth century with their pictorial treatment of nature and architecture.

A contemporary described the Elysian Fields at Stowe, Buckinghamshire, as "the painting part" of the gardens. In this "sacred landscape," with its complex mythological and political iconography, Kent designed the circular Temple of Ancient Virtue (1734), based on Palladio's drawing of the Temple of Vesta at Tivoli. The antique source makes both the building and

I. Jules Hardouin Mansart and
Robert de Cotte, Versailles, Royal
Chapel, interior, 1698-1710

II. Jacques-Germain Soufflot,
Ste.-Geneviève, Paris, interior,
1756-90

31. Joseph Michael Gandy,
The Bank of England, *c. 1830*

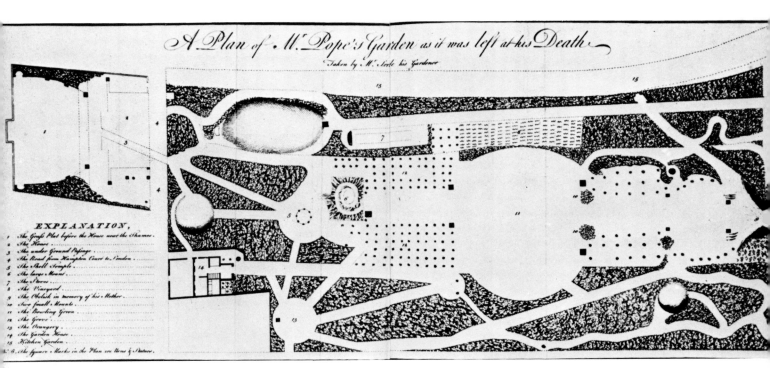

the pastoral scene of which it is part important in the history of neoclassicism since the temple and gorge at Tivoli are the only Roman "sacred landscape" to survive. However, Kent was equally susceptible to Italian Renaissance sources, as is shown in the remarkable Temple of British Worthies on the other side of the Elysian Fields. This may have been inspired by the exedra, or circus, on the grounds of the Villa Mattei in Rome. Thus it is probably not quite accurate to say that Kent was attempting to re-create paintings by Claude Lorrain or Poussin, though such an attempt may be seen in the Grecian Valley, which extends from the upper end of the Elysian Fields. Laid out in the 1740s—probably from designs by Lord Cobham, after Kent had left Stowe—and dominated by the imposing Temple of Concord and Victory, designed by Cobham's nephew, Lord Grenville, about 1748, it is a landmark in the history of British neoclassicism. On another part of the grounds, Kent had designed a temple perhaps as early as 1731 that is also unique for its time in Europe. This is the Temple of Venus, in which a Palladian quadrant theme is handled with a neoclassical austerity. The open screen of columns before a coffered apse was to recur more than thirty years later in the work of Robert Adam and Claude-Nicolas Ledoux. At Rousham, Oxfordshire, in the 1730s, Kent laid out a garden that had much in common with the Elysian Fields at Stowe but that was at once more varied and more unified. It is approached from a remarkable balustraded terrace called the Praeneste, which may have been based on the pedimented arcades of the Roman Baths as illustrated by Palladio in the *Fabbriche antiche disegnate da Andrea Palladio Vicentino,* published by Lord Burlington in 1730. The source of the Praeneste itself is the Roman Temple of Virtue; with its ramped terraces commanding distant views, it is itself the prototype of continental garden design from the Villa d'Este to Versailles. From the Praeneste a path leads to the small valley originally laid out by Charles Bridgeman as a wilderness with tortuous paths. This was opened out by Kent so as to become Venus's vale, with "the opening and retiring shades" admired by Horace Walpole. Kent remodeled Bridgeman's uncompromisingly square pool into an octagon, which, though perhaps softer on the eye than the square, was still a long way from the dreamy undulations of Capability Brown. The pool is flanked by an Upper and Lower Cascade in the form of grottoes, perhaps based on the Fontana Rustica at the Villa Aldobrandini, Frascati.

The type of garden represented by the development from Twickenham to Rousham was popularized much later in France as the *jardin anglais.* Characteristic examples, crowded with naive architectural incident, are the gardens at Ermenonville (1766-76) and Louis Carrogis de Carmontelle's Jardin de Monceau, Paris (1773-78).

Stowe and Rousham are essential preliminaries to an appreciation of the work carried out at Stourhead, Wiltshire, in the 1740s and 1750s. At Stourhead, more than anywhere else in Europe, one can admire the way in which poetry, painting, gardening, architecture, travel, the study of antiquity, and topography blend to form the single art of Picturesque

landscape. Both the house and its contents—pictures, books, and furniture—and the grounds and their contents—trees, water, and temples—merge to form an idyllic, narrative, cultural picture dominated by a profound sense of place. That sense of place, that *genius loci,* was perhaps the particular legacy to Europe of the English Picturesque movement. What Alexander Pope had written in his "Epistle to Lord Burlington on the Use of Riches," in the 1730s, sums up the spirit that created Stourhead:

> "Consult the Genius of the Place in all
> That tells the Waters or to rise or fall
> Or helps th'ambitious Hill the heav'n to scale,
> Or Scoops in circling theatres the vale,
> Calls in the Country, catches opening glades,
> Joins willing woods, and carries shades from shades,
> Now breaks or now directs th'intending Lines,
> Paints as you plant, and, as you work, designs."

Stourhead lies at the center of a historic and beautiful part of English geography and history, at the point between Salisbury Plain and Glastonbury where myth and history have been intertwined for centuries. There, at the remote meeting point of three counties—Somerset, Dorset, and Wiltshire—Henry Hoare, a rich city banker, built a large, bleak Palladian villa, designed by Colen Campbell (1676–1729), in 1718. Situated on a height, the house faces east across the bare plain. But just three hundred yards to the west, the ground drops sharply into a lush, almost tropical, hidden valley, long known as "Paradise," which contains the tiny village of Stourton. In 1743 Hoare's son, also Henry, began to plan a Picturesque circuit tour around the sides of the valley, in the manner of Stowe and Rousham. In August 1744, in a letter to Henry Hoare, Henry Flitcroft (1697–1769), who was completing the interiors of the house, referred to his designs for a "Circular Open Temple of the Ionic order, Antique." He also sent "a sketch of how I conceive the head of the lake should be formed. Twill make a most

36. Charles Bridgeman plan of the
gardens at Rousham, Oxfordshire,
before William Kent's alterations,
1715-20

37. William Kent, plan of the
gardens at Rousham, Oxfordshire,
1730 and later

38. William Kent, Venus's Vale,
Rousham, Oxfordshire, after 1730

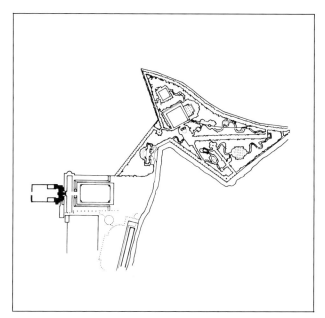

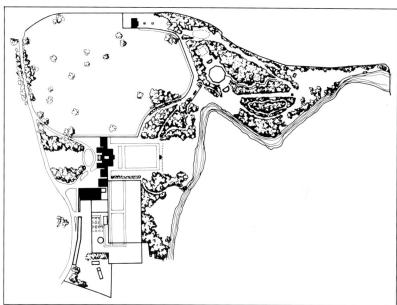

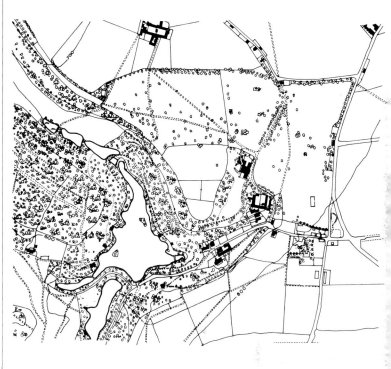

agreeable scene with the solemn shade about it and the variety of other agreeable circumstances." The letter establishes that as early as 1744 Hoare envisaged uniting his garden buildings within the valley by means of a lake. In fact, the dam that made the lake possible was not formed until ten years later. Flitcroft's Temple of Ceres (or Flora) contains altars designed by Flitcroft as well as an inscription over the door from the sixth book of Virgil's *Aeneid:* "Procul, o procul este profani" ("Begone all you who are uninitiated"). The lakeside Virgilian overtones were thus established from the first, though it is possible that in creating his lake landscape—which is what distinguishes Stourhead from Stowe and Rousham—Hoare may also have had in mind Pliny's description of the Source of the Clitumnus (*Letters,* book 8, chapter 8).

On the other side of the lake from the Temple of Flora an elaborate grotto was created, in 1748, containing a statue of the Nymph of the Grot carved in white lead by John Cheere, after the antique. The grotto is very much in the style of Italian Mannerist gardens and would have appealed to Pope. Indeed, a suitable quotation from Pope is carved in the marble bath within

*41. Henry Flitcroft, Temple of the
Sun, Stourhead, Wiltshire, 1765*

the grotto. Hoare wrote in 1765: "I have made the passage up from the souterrain serpentine & will make it easier of access *facilis descensus Averno,*" thus confirming the notion that the path around the lake is an allegory of Aeneas's journey through the underworld.

From the grotto we reach the Claudian and Virgilian Pantheon, a remarkable neoclassical building completed in 1756 from designs by Flitcroft. Its impressively austere interior contains statues of Hercules and Flora by John Rysbrack, and an antique marble figure of Livia Augusta as Ceres, brought from Herculaneum. Here the analogy with landscape painting, adumbrated by Vanbrugh, becomes more relevant than ever, for the form, position, and iconographical significance of the Pantheon seem to have been inspired by Claude's *Coast View of Delos with Aeneas.* We know that Hoare owned a version by Andrea Locatelli of Claude's *View of Delphi with a Procession,* which contains just such a pantheon temple. Higher up on the other side of the lake is a companion piece to Flitcroft's Pantheon, another "antique" temple, which was completed in 1765. Flitcroft took its

design from the late Roman Temple of Venus at Baalbek, which had been included in Robert Wood's *The Ruins of Balbec,* published in 1757. This wholesale incorporation of antique monuments into a landscaped scene is significant enough, but the deliberate inclusion of views of the village of Stourton into the composition is equally worthy of comment. Whereas at Stowe the medieval parish church was deliberately planted out, at Stourhead one of the great composed vistas is of the medieval church tower rising above cottage roofs and a village cross. This incorporation of the quintessence of the English rural scene into the Picturesque elegiac idyll is, of course, a make-believe in every possible way. The village cross is not the village cross but a sophisticated urban market cross of 1373 brought to Stourton from Bristol High Street in 1768. Moreover, it is not even in the village at all—though it appears to be, from the Pantheon—and the triangle of grass behind it, which looks like the village green, is also within the park boundary. The Picturesque make-believe is exposed in a letter written by Hoare to his daughter, in 1762, about the bridge that he constructed in front of the cross: "I took it from Palladio's Bridge at Vicenza, 5 arches, & when you stand at the Pantheon the Water will be seen thro the arches & it will look as if the River came down thro the Village & that this was the Village Bridge for the Public use; the view of the Bridge, Village and Church altogether will be a charming Gaspard view at the end of that Water". Hoare's words remind one forcibly of Vanbrugh's claim half a century earlier that if architecture and trees were combined at Woodstock Manor "so that all the buildings left might appear in two risings amongst'em, it would make one of the most agreeable objects that the best of Landskip painters can invent."

Robert Adam's Culzean Castle, Ayrshire (1777 onward), towering dramatically above the rocky coastline, is a realization in stone of the imaginary landscape architecture Adam (1728–1792) spent so much of his spare time painting. A celebrated example of an architect's deliberately designing a building that appears to have strayed from a painting by Claude is Nash's Cronkhill, Shropshire (c. 1802). The undoubted source for this round-towered villa is the buildings that appear in the backgrounds of such paintings as Claude's *Landscape with the Ponte Molle.* Moreover, the Ponte Molle is very close in form to the bridge at Stourhead. A curious example of the pictorial approach to architecture and landscape is afforded by an aquatint of the front door of Sezincote House, Gloucestershire, of 1810, by John Martin, showing the Picturesque park reflected in the glass. As soon as this remarkable Indian-style country house was completed, its owner commissioned the aquatints from Martin—which suggests that a house that came into being as a realization in architecture of Picturesque drawings and views of India could only be fully appreciated once it had been translated back into pictorial imagery.

Even an architect so imbued with classical archaeology as Charles Robert Cockerell (1788–1863) found it impossible to look at William Wilkins's

Grange Park, Hampshire (1809), without immediately recalling landscape paintings by Claude and Poussin. It is not clear whether Wilkins (1778–1839) had such analogies in mind when designing the great temple-like house, but to Cockerell, in a now-celebrated passage in his diary for 1823, "nothing [could] be finer, more classical or like the finest Poussin. It realises the most fanciful representations of the painters pencil or the poets description . . . there is nothing like it on this side of Arcadia." More surprisingly, it occurred to Cockerell only *after* he had designed the Hanover Chapel in Regent Street, in 1821, that its source lay in a painting by Claude. Looking at some of Claude's seaport scenes in the collection of J. J. Angerstein, in 1823, Cockerell noted in his diary: "much flattered at Claude's pictures & finding in 2 of the 5 pictures in this collection the idea of the two turrets at the entrance of a building as in my chapel. I have little doubt that the idea of this adoption arose in my mind from having seen these pictures and engravings. In these wonderful pictures one feels the balmy rosy atmosphere of the Mediterranean, that agreeable air . . . which I so well remember in those parts." Rather unexpectedly, Cockerell also found that his twin-towered chapel reminded him of Vanbrugh's Morpeth Town Hall, Northumberland (1716). After passing through Morpeth, in July 1822, he noted in his diary that the town hall was "picturesque *like my chapel.*"

There can be no doubt that the heroic romance of Vanbrugh's buildings, of his "Castle style" in particular, was a source of inspiration to his successors from Adam to Cockerell, even though they worked in a style different from his. Adam's eulogy of Vanbrugh in the preface to his *Works in Architecture of Robert and James Adam, Esquires* (1773) is well known, but as a central and beautiful text in eighteenth-century aesthetics it must be quoted here. He begins by describing the revolution his own architecture had achieved in defeating neo-Palladianism: "The massive entablature, the ponderous compartment ceiling, the heavy frames . . . are now universally exploded." In their place he had established what he called "movement," a quality he defined as follows: "*Movement* is meant to express, the rise and fall, the advance and recess, with other diversity of form, in the different parts of a building, so as to add greatly to the picturesque of the composition. For the rising and falling, advancing and receding, with the convexity and concavity, and other forms of the great parts, have the same effect in architecture, that hill and dale, fore-ground and distance, swelling and sinking have in landscape: That is, they serve to produce an agreeable and diversified contour, that groups and contrasts like a picture, and creates a variety of light and shade, which gives great spirit, beauty and effect to the composition . . .

We cannot however allow ourselves to close this note without doing justice to the memory of a great man, whose reputation as an architect has been long carried down the stream by a torrent of undistinguishing prejudice and abuse.

45

43. *Robert Adam, Culzean Castle,*
Ayrshire, aerial view, 1777–90

Sir John Vanbrugh's genius was of the first class; and, in point of movement, novelty and ingenuity, his works have not been exceeded by anything in modern times (*The Works in Architecture of Robert and James Adam, Esquires,* vol. 1, 1773, p. [4]).

How far Adam achieved this movement in his own architecture is a matter for debate. One distinctly Vanbrughian building by him is his last work, Seton Castle, East Lothian (1789–91), which seems to have been inspired by Vanbrugh's own house at Greenwich, Vanbrugh Castle (1718, with later additions). The combination at Vanbrugh Castle of symmetrical with consciously asymmetrical forms in the disposition of both the house and its linked outbuildings was fraught with consequences for the future. However, it was not this aspect of Vanbrugh's work that, on the whole, was to influence Adam. It was in the subtle variety of the volumes of his rooms and in his internal planning that Adam sought to recapture the "movement" that had marked Vanbrugh's handling of exterior forms. A characteristically beautiful example of this is Adam's Syon House, Middlesex (1762–69), of which he claimed, in 1773, that "the inequality of the levels has been managed in such a manner as to increase the scenery and add to the movement so that an apparent defect has been converted into a real beauty" (ibid., p. 9). Here, another central tenet of Picturesque theory is stated: that the architect should make use of, note ignore or conceal, natural accidents.

A quintessentially Picturesque environment was created at Strawberry Hill, Middlesex, from 1749 onward, by Horace Walpole (1717–1797). The slow growth of his villa was emphasized, not concealed, so that one could follow its development northward from the simple cottage he found on the site. Strawberry Hill was consciously asymmetrical, and the architect's choice of the Gothic style consciously associational. Its principles were further elaborated upon in a brilliant, asymmetrical house created by the greatest theorist of the Picturesque movement, Richard Payne Knight. Knight's own house, Downton Castle, Herefordshire (1772–78), superbly sited above the deep valley of the Teme River, with views to the Welsh hills beyond, is the first and most influential of those houses that rely for their effect on painterly and asymmetrical massing and grouping. Fortunately, Knight gave a clear account of his intentions at Downton in his distinguished and stimulating book, *An Analytical Inquiry into the Principles of Taste* (1805): "It is now more than thirty years since the author of this inquiry ventured to build a house, ornamented with what are called Gothic towers and battlements without, and with Grecian ceilings, columns, and entablatures within . . . It has, however, the advantage of being capable of receiving alterations and additions in almost any direction, without any injury to its genuine and original character.

The best style of architecture for irregular and picturesque houses, which can not be adopted, is that mixed style, which characterizes the buildings of Claude and the Poussins: for as it is taken from models, which were built piece-meal, during many successive ages, and by several different nations;

46

44. Robert Adam, Seton Castle, East Lothian, 1789–91

45. John Nash, Cronkhill, Shropshire, c. 1802

it is distinguished by no particular manner of execution, or class of ornaments; but admits of all promiscuously, from a plain wall or buttress, of the roughest masonry, to the most highly wrought Corinthian capital . . .

In choosing a situation for a house of this kind, which is to be a principal feature of a place, more consideration ought to be had of the views towards it, than of those fromwards it: for, consistently with comfort, which ought to be the first object in every dwelling, it very rarely happens that a perfect composition of landscape scenery can be obtained from a door or window; nor does it appear to me particularly desirable that it should be: for few persons ever look for such compositions, or pay much attention to them, while within doors. It is in walks or rides through parks, gardens or pleasure grounds that they are attended to and examined, and become subjects of conversation . . .

Sir John Vanbrugh is the only architect, I know of, who has either planned or placed his houses according to the principle here recommended; and, in his two chief works, Blenheim and Castle Howard . . . The views from the principal fronts of both are bad . . . but the situations of both, as objects to the surrounding scenery, are the best that could have been chosen" (4th ed., 1808, pp. 225–27).

This passage makes clear the revolutionary way in which the Picturesque dissolved the compositional techniques that were traditional in Palladian and Baroque architecture in favor of an architecture of growth and change, designed pictorially so as to be absorbed into its landscape setting. In emphasizing this point Knight found it necessary to censure the great Capability Brown, whose landscaped parks, which seem so beautiful to us today, were too smoothly artificial for Knight's tastes, and whose designs for country houses were for the most part conventionally Palladian. Less fairly, Knight associated Humphry Repton (1752–1818) with his attacks on Capability Brown. Yet it is the executed work of Repton and his partner John Nash (1752–1835) that most closely approximates the ideals laid down by Knight, Uvedale Price, and William Gilpin. It was Gilpin (1724–1804) who had first popularized the term Picturesque in a book called *Observations Relative Chiefly to Picturesque Beauty* (1789). This was quickly followed by three important publications, of 1794: his own *Three Essays on Picturesque Beauty,* Knight's *The Landscape, a Didactic Poem* (dedicated to Uvedale Price), and Price's *Essay on the Picturesque.* In 1795 Humphry Repton produced his own contribution to the corpus of Picturesque theory, *Sketches and Hints on Landscape Gardening,* which was, of course, more practical and less theoretical than the work of Price and Knight. Indeed, in the next year, 1796, Repton formed an alliance with John Nash, a practicing architect, to show how architecture and landscape could be designed according to the same principles.

Perhaps the principal achievement of the partnership between Repton and Nash was Luscombe Castle, Devon (1799–1804), built for Charles Hoare, great-nephew of Henry Hoare of Stourhead. The *Red Book* in which Repton

48

*III. Sir William Chambers, Project
for the Mausoleum of Frederick,
Prince of Wales, section, 1751–52*

February 1752 Section of the Mausoleum for the P. of Wales.

presented his proposals to Mrs. Hoare contains a view of Luscombe as developed according to Capability Brown's ideas, contrasted with a view showing Nash's and Repton's proposals for a more dramatic and Picturesque scheme in accordance with the ideas of Price and Knight. Derived from the asymmetrical composition of Downton Castle, the smaller Luscombe pivots on an octagonal tower containing a drawing room leading into a large conservatory. Varied, compact, and practical, with all the groundfloor windows coming down to floor level so as to make the most of the views across the park and valley to the sea, the plan is totally original. Such planning anticipates the "organic" sophistication of Frank Lloyd Wright's so-called Prairie Houses. Certainly no other European country could produce plans as revolutionary as this as early as 1799.

Other architects adopted Nash's daring and delectable asymmetry, notably Sir Jeffry Wyatville (1766–1840), who, at Endsleigh, Devon (1810–11), created one of the most striking houses of the nineteenth century. With a view to the erection of a large cottage orné, the duke of Bedford had selected a superb site in the wooded hills above the Tamar River already occupied by a simple cottage. Repton was called in to landscape the grounds while Wyatville provided a long, low house of astonishing freedom of plan in a mixed vernacular style, the whole anticipating the Shingle style of later nineteenth-century America. With the strange diagonal articulation of its plan, the rustic verandas and bay windows, Endsleigh, like Salvin's Scotney, is a perfect visual expression of the essential Picturesque idea so clearly stated by Uvedale Price: "If the owner of such a spot, instead of making a regular front and sides were to insist on having the windows turned towards the points where objects were most happily arranged, the architect would be forced into inventing a number of picturesque forms and combinations which otherwise might never have occurred to him; and would be obliged to do what has so seldom been done—accommodate his building to the scenery, not make that give way to the building" (*Essays on the Picturesque,* 2d ed., vol. 11, 1810, p. 268).

Another Picturesque extravaganza, with a plan as bizarre and unprecedented as that of Endsleigh, is Highcliffe Castle, Hampshire (1830–34), by W. J. Donthorn (1799–1859). The first Lord Stuart de Rothesay employed Donthorn to blend the transported fragments of an early sixteenth-century French Flamboyant Gothic mansion into a sympathetic modern re-creation. The deliberate blurring of the visual boundary between what twentieth-century man would call "original," on the one hand, and "fake," on the other, must be regarded as characteristic of neoclassical and Picturesque taste. Lord Stuart's daughter complained that Donthorn "was ambitious of his own fame and wanted to emulate Fonthill and Ashridge"—and certainly the astonishing composition of Highcliffe, with its aspiring verticality and its tangential wings thrusting forward along the cliff top, owes much to the planning revolution effected by the practitioners of the Picturesque in late eighteenth-century England. Highcliffe was also Picturesque in the literal

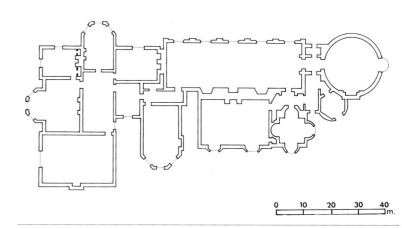

0   10   20   30   40
———————————————m.

49

48. *Richard Payne Knight, Downton Castle, Herefordshire, entrance facade, 1772–78*

sense in that, in reconstructing this Normandy château, Donthorn relied on views of it *in situ,* by J. S. Cotman, made before Lord Stuart de Rothesay brought the house to England in 1830.

A very different house built at about the same time as Endsleigh shows that an irregular building could be designed in a style other than Gothic or Tudor and still fit appropriately into a dramatic or Picturesque landscape. This is Dunglass, Haddingtonshire, executed from 1807 to 1813 for the architectural historian Sir James Hall (1761–1832), from designs by Richard Crichton (1771–1817). Pivoting on a tower perched at the head of a rocky glen, Dunglass has some stylistic affinities with the Vanbrugh/Nicholas Hawksmoor approach and recalls the enthusiasm for Vanbrugh shared by Price and Knight. Hall went so far in following Price's recommendations as to employ the services of a landscape painter, Alexander Nasmyth, to settle the site of the house, before calling in the architects.

Another rather later Picturesque house which seems to owe something to Vanbrughian composition is Beaufront Castle, Northumberland (1836–42), by John Dobson (1787–1865). A prolific north-country architect, Dobson is today best remembered for his austere, late neoclassical country houses, but the pictorial massing of Beaufront reminds us that he had been a pupil of the watercolorist John Varley, and that one of his first commissions had beed to carry out alterations at Vanbrugh's powerfully romantic Seaton Delaval, also in Northumberland.

Dodington Park, Gloucestershire (1798–1808), by James Wyatt (1746–1813), and Sezincote House, Gloucestershire (c. 1805), by Samuel Pepys Cockerell (1753–1827)—though one is neoclassical and the other neo-Mogul—are among the most successful examples of pictorially composed houses, blending nature and architecture by means of long quadrant greenhouses. Equally significant, though now demolished, was Thomas Hope's remarkable country house, The Deepdene, near Dorking, in Surrey. This was a late eighteenth-century house that Hope (1769–1831) bought in 1807 and to which he made a series of irregular Picturesque additions in 1818–19 and 1823. First of all came a new entrance front and private wing, with exteriors ranging stylistically from Gothic to Pompeian and culminating in an asymmetrically placed, loggia-topped tower of Lombard or Tuscan origin. With this striking object Hope had created, at a stroke, the language in which so many Italianate villas of the first half of the nineteenth century—by such architects as Sir Charles Barry (1795–1860) and Thomas Cubitt (1788–1855), and their many followers—were to be composed. In April 1819 Hope's friend, the novelist Maria Edgeworth, recorded in a letter that the house appeared ''grotesque and confused among trees in no one particular taste.'' Had she been more familiar with the writings of Knight she might have welcomed the blending of styles as a realization of his recommendations concerning ''that mixed style, which characterizes the buildings of Claude and the Poussins.'' The irregular skyline of The Deepdene, the tower and the detached group of kitchen

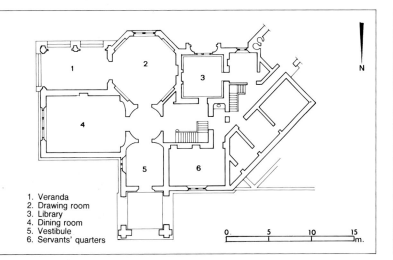

1. Veranda
2. Drawing room
3. Library
4. Dining room
5. Vestibule
6. Servants' quarters

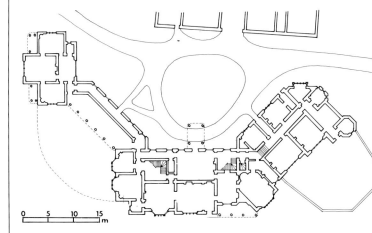

offices placed among trees on sloping ground and sporting a belvedere and spire, similarly followed advice given by Sir Uvedale Price.

Thomas Hope was, of course, himself a Picturesque theorist. In 1808 he published an article "On the Art of Gardening," which was reprinted in Mrs. Hofland's *A Descriptive Account of . . . White-Knights* (1819). Here Hope developed further the occasional expressions of regret made by Price and Knight at the way in which Capability Brown swept away all survivals of formal gardens, terraces, and balustrades, so as to bring his shaven lawns right up to the house. Thus Hope felt able to speak warmly of "the suspended gardens within Genoa, and of the splendid villas about Rome . . . those striking oppositions of the rarest marbles to the richest verdure; those mixtures of statues, and vases, and balustrades, with cypresses, and pinasters, and bays; those distant hills seen through the converging lines of lengthened colonnades . . ." (pp. 11–13).

By developing ideas outlined by Price and Knight, Hope anticipated, as with his loggia-topped tower, later nineteenth-century practice: in this case the vast, formal Italianate gardens laid out by Barry and William Eden Nesfield (1835–1888). In the same essay he wrote of the new Picturesque architecture; he wished to establish that "the cluster of highly adorned and sheltered apartments that form the mansion . . . should shoot out, as it were, into . . . ramifications of arcades, porticos, terraces, parterres, treillages, avenues. . . ." He gave a striking demonstration of this in the additions he made to The Deepdene, in 1823: a bizarre complex of conservatories,

sculpture galleries, and orangeries from the house down the hill at an angle of about forty-five degrees. This represented the height of the Picturesque ambition to break down the barriers between nature and architecture. In general, this ambition was, in these years, a particularly English one—indeed, it was England's gift to Europe and North America—but we can also find it clearly stated in the work of the German Karl Friedrich Schinkel (1781–1841).

In 1824 work began on Schloss Glienicke, a villa near Berlin, by the side of the Potsdam Bridge over the Havel River. Schinkel built it for the twenty-five-year-old Prince Karl, one of the sons of King Friedrich Wilhelm III of Prussia. The house is simple, asymmetrical, and low-spreading and pivots around a tower. It forms a courtyard of simplified Italianate architecture on the walls of which are displayed antique Roman sculpture and casts acquired by Prince Karl in Italy. The small, undulating park, prettily landscaped by P. J. Lenné (1789–1866), contains numerous garden buildings by Schinkel as well as the remarkable Klosterhaus, a small cloister in a rich Byzantine style, built shortly after Schinkel's death in order to house the collection of Byzantine sculptures that the prince brought back from Venice, Padua, and elsewhere. Near the edge of the river are two additional buildings by Schinkel, the gardener's house and the Kasino (1826). With its vine-clad loggias looking out across the water, the elegant Italianate Kasino reminds one how much Berliners must have wished to forget the forbidding Prussian climate and imagine themselves on the shores of Italian

*54. John Dobson, Beaufront Castle,
Northumberland, stable courtyard,
1836–42*

55. *James Wyatt, Dodington Park, Gloucestershire, 1798–1813*

56. *Samuel Pepys Cockerell, Sezincote House, Gloucestershire, c. 1805*

57. *Thomas Hope and William Atkinson, The Deepdene, Surrey, plan, 1818–23*

58. *Thomas Hope and William Atkinson, The Deepdene, Surrey, conservatory wing, 1818–23. British Architectural Library Drawings Collection*

lakes. Also from 1826 is the Schloss Charlottenhof at Potsdam, designed by Schinkel on his return from an important visit to England. This was a pleasure pavilion for Prince Karl's brother, the crown prince, an architect manqué to whom the general disposition of the buildings is due. The relationship of the low, Italianate house with its Greek Doric portico to the gardens, loggias, canals, and pavilions, is masterly. In 1829–36 Schinkel and Ludwig Persius (1803–1845) greatly heightened the Picturesque charms of Charlottenhof by laying out a water garden punctuated by irregularly placed buildings such as the court gardener's house, the Tea House, and Roman Bath. The subtle and delectable blending of nature and architecture, though developed from hints in the writings of J.-N.-L. Durand, J. K. Krafft, and Pierre-Nicolas Ransonnette, closely parallels both what Thomas Hope had achieved at The Deepdene from 1818 to 1823, and the remarkable village of Clisson in the Vendée, built from 1805 to 1820 in an Italianate vernacular style.

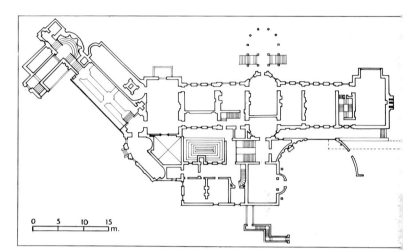

For yet another of King Friedrich Wilhelm's sons, Prince Wilhelm, Schinkel designed the extensive Schloss Babelsberg near Potsdam (1833) in Nash's castellated style; its turrets can be glimpsed through the trees from Schloss Glienicke. The crown prince certainly had a hand in selecting the style of Schloss Babelsberg, which is so closely based on such castles by Nash as Luscombe, Caerhayes, and East Cowes that it must be one of the most English buildings in Germany.

So far, we have spoken as though the Picturesque could be realized only in the country, but John Nash showed brilliantly its suitability for urban design. In 1811 his Blaise Hamlet near Bristol, curiously similar to Richard Mique's *hameau* at Versailles, of 1778–82, was a foretaste of subsequent garden suburbs from Richard Norman Shaw's Bedford Park onward, but it is Nash's redevelopment of central London, also initiated in 1811, to which we should now turn our attention.

John Fordyce, Surveyor-General of the Office of Woods and Forests, was a great believer in comprehensive town planning. Seeing that the king's largely rural Marylebone estate, which was leased to the duke of Portland, was to revert to the Crown in 1811, Fordyce argued for the creation of a new major road leading to the estate from Charing Cross. In 1806 he appointed Nash as one of the two architects in the Office of Woods and Forests, and in October 1810 the department commissioned two alternative schemes for the development of the Marylebone estate and the new road. The architects invited to submit designs were Thomas Leverton and Thomas Chawner, the department's surveyors, and Nash and James Morgan. When Nash's plans were accepted in July 1811 the Prince of Wales was so pleased with their magnificence that he exclaimed: "It will quite eclipse Napoleon."

If he had in mind such schemes as the Rue de Rivoli by Charles Percier and Pierre-François-Léonard Fontaine he was quite right in supposing that Nash's genius in town planning was of an altogether different order. Instead of covering Marylebone with a grid of streets and squares, as Leverton and

59. Karl Friedrich Schinkel, Schloss
Charlottenhof, Potsdam, 1826
60. Karl Friedrich Schinkel and
Ludwig Persius, court gardener's
house, Schloss Charlottenhof, Potsdam,
1829–36

Chawner envisaged, Nash realized that since many people living in London would prefer to live in the country, the most popular way of developing the Marylebone estate would be to turn it into a Picturesque rural park dotted with villas and flanked by broken runs of terraced houses glimpsed irregularly through trees. In fact, Nash's first plan of 1811 was rather more stilted than the final proposals. Nevertheless, in 1812 a part of the 1811 plan was begun, the southern half of the circus at the north end of Portland Place, but the builder went bankrupt so that the northern half was never built. The result is more is more in keeping with Nash's eventual proposals since it enables the greenery of the park to be seen from Portland Place. In 1812 Nash also presented his scheme for linking the new buildings in the park with the prince's dwelling at Carlton House, and from there, by implication, to the seat of government at Westminster. Nash saw immediately what no one else had thought of, that the line of his new road should follow that curious division between the sleaziness of Soho to the east and the elegance of Mayfair to the west. Thus he could buy up property fairly cheaply at Soho prices and sell it at Mayfair prices. Henry Holland's impressive colonnaded screen in front of Carlton House provided the visual climax at the southern end of Nash's scheme, but, since Portland Place and the entrance to the Marylebone estate lay to the northwest of this, the new processional route would necessarily have to follow a convoluted course. Here Nash heeded the advice of the Picturesque theorists—to make use of, rather than to conceal, natural accidents. Hence the celebrated Picturesque curve of the Regent Street quadrant, which he justified as "resembling in that respect the High Street at Oxford." Hence also the scenically placed if eccentrically planned All Souls' church, Langham Place, which subtly and seductively directed one's glance around an awkward shift in axis.

Behind the sweeping terraces surrounding Regent's Park, Nash developed a Picturesque enclave of Italianate villas and cottages ornés known as Park Village East and Park Village West. An outgrowth of his Blaise Hamlet theme, these were the prototypes of subsequent garden suburbs.

The strong emphasis that the Picturesque theory of the eighteenth century placed on domestic architecture led, in the nineteenth century, to a not unhealthy preoccupation with the house as a building type. This preoccupation survived the Gothic Revival of the first half of the century and its concern with church building and reemerged in the so-called Queen Anne movement, or Domestic Revival, of the 1870s, which had been created by Nesfield and Shaw in the 1860s. Indeed, there was an almost moral seriousness in the approach to house design after 1850. It became a kind of sacred task. We can sense something of this in the lectures on architecture that Ruskin delivered at Edinburgh in 1853. His lecture on domestic architecture proclaimed a belief in the value of vernacular buildings and the country cottage, which linked him, ironically, with the Picturesque movement and the Regency pattern-books of rural architecture. What

61. Karl Friedrich Schinkel,
Schloss Charlottenhof,
Potsdam, 1826

62. John Nash, the Regent Street
quadrant, London, 1818–20

63. John Nash, Regent Street
and Regent's Park, London, plan,
1811–30

64. John Nash, Chester Terrace,
Regent's Park, London, 1820
and later

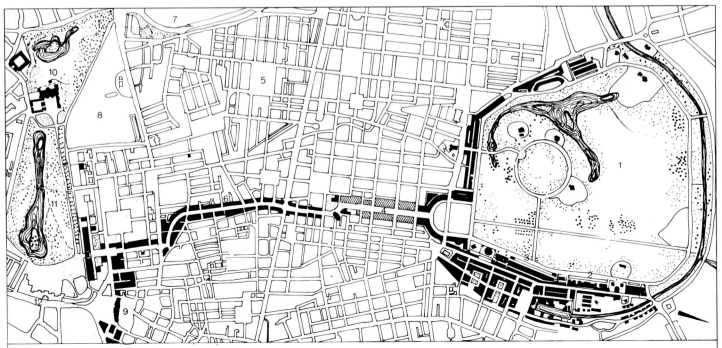

1. Regent's Park   3. Chester Terrace   5. Grosvenor Square   7. Hyde Park   9. National Gallery   11. St. James's Park
2. Cumberland Terrace   4. Portland Place   6. Regent Street   8. Green Park   10. Buckingham Palace   12. Whitehall

68. *George Devey, Betteshanger, Kent,*
1856–61
69. *George Devey, cottages, Penshurst,*
Kent, 1850

distinguished such cottages from the boxlike neoclassicism he so much despised was their roofs. These, he felt, were not merely Picturesque in themselves but deeply expressive of the human need for shelter. He argued that the cottage was "really more roof than anything else." For him, "The very soul of the cottage—the essence and meaning of it—are in its roof; it is that, mainly, wherein consists its shelter; that, wherein it differs most completely from a cleft in rocks or bower in woods. It is in its thick impenetrable coverlid of close thatch that its whole heart and hospitality are concentrated. Consider the difference, in sound, of the expression 'beneath my roof' and 'within my walls.' " Ruskin went on to ask: "Do you suppose that which is so important in a cottage can be of small importance in your own dwelling-house? . . . It is vain to say you take the roof for granted. You may as well say you take a man's kindness for granted." Second only to the roof in architectural and spiritual significance was the bay window: "You surely must all of you feel and admit the delightfulness of a bow-window; I can hardly fancy a room can be perfect without one."

In fact, there were a good many architects who shared Ruskin's fancies and, from George Devey (1820–1886) in the 1850s to Edwin Lutyens (1869–1944) in the 1890s, they put them unceasingly into practice. At Penshurst, Kent, in 1850, Devey designed cottages for Lord de l'Isle that are narrative statements about the Old English rural way of life. They are Picturesque not only for that reason but also because they remind one of both old country cottages and *pictures* of such cottages. Devey had been trained as a watercolorist under J. D. Harding, and Penshurst in the 1840s and 1850s became something of an artists's colony. Devey's patrons at two of his major country houses in Kent, Sir Walter James at Betteshanger and W. O. Hammond at St. Alban's Court, were both keen watercolorists and appreciators of Old English rural traditions. At Betteshanger, from 1856 to 1861 and in 1882, Devey created "instant history" by echoing the enthusiasm of eighteenth-century Picturesque theorists for buildings in which one could read a process of growth and change. The historical and pictorial fantasy which Devey created at Betteshanger is that of a late-medieval house, successively altered, extended, and patched with different materials in the Elizabethan period and in the seventeenth and eighteenth centuries. A lazy, spreading plan of the type pioneered by Wyatville at Endsleigh, in 1810, heightens the impression of informal growth. St. Alban's Court (1874–78) is a more unified design, but even here the lower parts of the walls are of stone, ending in a ragged, uneven line, and the upper parts are of brick, so as to suggest, falsely, the re-use of an earlier house on the site. In fact, the earlier house lay in the valley below, and its remains, suitably restored and romanticized by Devey, form a Picturesque object much as the old Scotney Castle does on the grounds of Salvin's new Scotney.

Greece was described in 1650 by Roland Fréart de Chambray as "the divine country." Claude Perrault declared that he aimed to renew architecture by reverting to the purity of the temples of ancient Greece, and in his translation of Vitruvius's works he illustrated a baseless and fluted Doric column, a concept that had been illustrated also by Renaissance commentators, though never as accurately. But though Greek architecture was long regarded as the basis of all excellence, and though there were attempts to conjure up and explore its visual forms, almost nothing was known about it. It remained, largely, a literary ideal. Not until 1750, when J.-G. Soufflot and his pupil G.-P.-M. Dumont measured the Doric temples of Paestum, were French architects to begin to make any serious inspection of the ruins of Greek antiquity. They were not quick, however, to use this information. Soufflot introduced an engaged version of the Paestum Doric column, with a base and pedestal, into the crypt of Ste.-Geneviève about 1758, but not until 1764 was Dumont to publish the results of their fieldwork in *Suite de plans . . . de trois temples . . . de Paestum,* and even then it was the first publication of its sort. One may wonder at their lack of response. The answer lies in their aesthetic preferences. Not until the late eighteenth century did architects in Europe learn to respond to the bold sculptural qualities of the Doric. They followed their Renaissance predecessors in finding their inspiration rather in the forms of Roman antiquity. When Colbert thought to ensure that his architects might have the correct antique models, he sent Antoine Desgodets to Rome, where he measured no less than forty-nine Roman monuments; engravings of these were published in 1682 in the sumptuous *Les édifices antiques de Rome.* This was to remain the standard reference for two hundred years. Colbert made no attempt to sponsor a similar publication on the monuments of Greece. Yet for twenty years and more, at considerable expense, he sent out agents to the mainland of Greece, to the islands, to Turkey, Palestine, Syria, and even to Persia and beyond to collect manuscripts, medallions, and coins for his extensive collections. And though these agents were instructed by Claude Perrault's brother, Charles, and told to take their copies of Pausanias with them and to visit all possible ancient sites, they can scarcely be said to have enhanced existing knowledge of Greek architecture. Early travelers to Greece—and there were many who went on trade and diplomatic missions—stopped at Athens and penetrated to the Parthenon, then more or less intact, and recorded their wonder. Robert de Dreux, for instance, who was there in 1668, said that it appeared so magnificent that, having seen it, there was no need to look further for architectural perfection.

That most enlightened of early ambassadors, the Marquis de Nointel, explored Athens and several of the islands in 1674 with a carefully chosen and extremely costly retinue, including the author of *Les mille et une nuits,* Antoine Galland, and two artists, Rombaut Faydherbe and Jacques Carrey, who were to record the sculptures of the Parthenon, but they did very little, indeed, to publicize the results of their investigations. Nointel did, however,

70. *Jacob Spon, engraving of the Parthenon, Athens, from his* Voyage d'Italie, de Dalmatie, de Grèce, et du Levant, *1676*

71. *Jacques Carrey (attributed),* The Expedition of the Marquis de Nointel to Athens. *Chartres, Musée des Beaux-Arts*

send back to France some notes and observations made by the Jesuit missionary J.-P. Babin, which were published at once by the scholar and doctor Jacob Spon. Spon himself was inspired to travel to Greece and—financed by Colbert—he set out; in Venice he encountered the English botanist George Wheler, whom he took with him. By 1676 he was back in his native Lyons, where he published his *Voyage d'Italie, de Dalmatie, de Grèce, et du Levant.* This was to remain for almost seventy years the most reliable and, from an architectural standpoint, most illuminating account of the buildings of Athens. It contained a miserable engraving of the Parthenon, showing that the columns were heavily proportioned, fluted, and baseless. Although the illustration was not of the sort to inspire architects, it nonetheless became famous, having been reproduced by Wheler in his plagiarized account of the journey with Spon, published in England in 1682, and in a description of Athens by Cornelio Magni, issued in Italy from 1679 to 1692. When Bernard de Montfaucon published his monumental compilation of all the known artifacts of antiquity, *L'antiquité expliquée,* issued in fifteen folio volumes, from 1719 to 1724, he was still forced to rely on Spon's record of the Doric temple. Similarly, for the temples of Baalbek, the only ones in Palestine that he was able to illustrate, Montfaucon was compelled to turn to seventeenth-century engravings, those made about 1680 by Jean Marot, probably on the basis of drawings, provided by another of Colbert's agents, M. de Monceaux, who visited the site in 1668. The Perrault brothers, as we have seen, may have had a hand in Marot's distorted reconstruction of the Temple of Bacchus at Baalbek, endowing it with a nave and aisles separated by columns, and a coffered barrel vault above. This variant, however incorrect, had its appeal, and soon after its appearance in Montfaucon's work it became the basis for the reconstruction drawings of the temples at Palmyra and Olympia by Johann Fischer von Erlach (1656-1723), author of that first extensively illustrated history of architecture *Entwurff einer historischen Architektur,* issued first in 1721, and then in 1725, 1730, 1737, and 1742. This was a book to which architects could respond; the text was limited to a few lines underneath each engraving.

The plates depicted an extraordinary and breathtaking array of buildings, real and imaginary, including the wonders of the ancient world, the mosques of Constantinople, the palaces and bridges of China, and also a sheaf of Fischer von Erlach's own designs. At the end of the eighteenth century Boullée was basing his pyramids on those reconstructions by Fischer von Erlach, while in the early years of the next century Fischer's naumachia was being adapted for an arena in Milan by Luigi Canonica. Fischer's imagery was to remain potent for almost one hundred years, although there was no great accuracy of observation in his views.

A more informed knowledge of Greek architecture became possible only in the middle years of the eighteenth century when measured drawings of the temples of Athens were included in the third volume of Richard

72. *Johann Fischer von Erlach, plates
from his* Entwurff einer
historischen Architektur, *1721,
showing Chinese buildings, artificial
rock mounds and a suspension bridge*

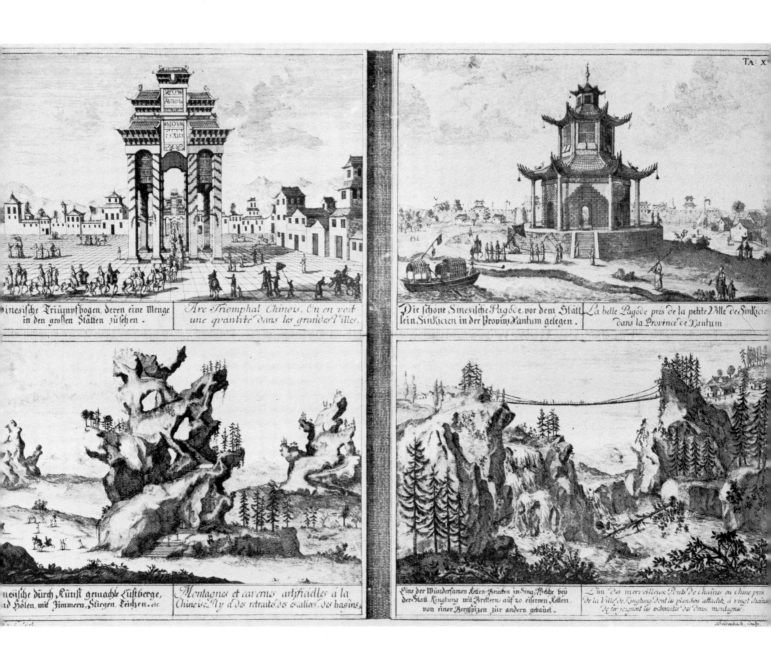

73. *Johann Fischer von Erlach, reconstruction of the Temple of Zeus at Olympia, from his* Entwurff einer historischen Architektur, *1721*

74. *Johann Fischer von Erlach, plates from his* Entwurff einer historischen Architecktur, *1721, showing the Egyptian pyramids*

Pococke's *Description of the East and Some Other Countries,* of 1745, to be followed in 1752 by the work of another Irishman, Richard Dalton's *Antiquities of Greece and Egypt.* Something of the nature of the Doric temples of Sicily was made known also at exactly the same time with the appearance of the second volume of G. M. Pancrazi's *Antichità siciliane.* However, there was nothing either reliable or captivating in these works. Among the first of that succession of scholarly studies that were to open up a real knowledge of antique architecture and provide models for emulation and even imitation were *The Ruins of Palmyra,* of 1753, and *The Ruins of Balbec,* of 1757, the results of an expedition undertaken in 1750 by James Dawkins and Robert Wood (1716–1771) together with John Bouverie and the draftsman Giovanni Battista Borra. These books marked the ascendancy of the British, and in particular the Society of Dilettanti, as patrons and explorers of antiquity. All the important archaeological publications to follow emanated from the British Isles. In France—Dumont's publication of the temples of Paestum apart (and he was to issue a revised edition in 1769)—only Julien-David Le Roy's *Ruines des plus beaux monuments de la Grèce,* of 1758, may be said to have provided hard archaeological information of the sort required by practicing architects. The information contained there, however, was soon shown to be less hard than might have been expected. In the first volume of their *Antiquities of Athens,* of 1762, Le Roy's rivals James Stuart and Nicholas Revett were to remark that his errors "have most of them been made before, tho'in fewer words by Wheler and Spon" (vol. 1, p. 35). Le Roy's work was, in fact, inspired by Stuart's and Revett's; in 1751 they published two detailed proposals for their work and began their proctracted studies in Greece. By the beginning of 1754 Le Roy was in Greece and, soon after, he published a proposal of his own, based on one of Stuart's and Revett's; by 1758 he had published his own book. This in turn was to be plagiarized when Robert Sayer issued his *Ruins of Athens and Other Valuable Antiquities in Greece,* in 1759. Le Roy's publication, for all its haste and inaccuracy, offered a most seductive array of views and measured drawings of the antiquities of Athens, Attica, and Corinth. Its impact in France, at least, was considerable. When he issued a second edition in 1770, he rearranged all his plates as a rebuke to Stuart and Revett, demonstrating that the monuments included in their first volume—the Temple on the Ilissus, the Choragic Monument of Lysicrates, the Tower of the Winds, and the Stoa at Athens—were all post-Periclean works, and thus somewhat lax in style. And he answered their gibes at his errors by pointing out that he was in no way interested in the minutiae of measurements. He did not wish to provide models for imitation. He was intent to conjure up only the effects and the qualities of architecture. And this statement might be taken as a hint as to why the French, though they continued to visit classical ruins with great eagerness—witness the studies of the French *pensionnaires* (students, usually winners of the Grand Prix, sent to study at the Académie de France in Rome) and the magnificent volumes of the Abbé Richard de Saint-Non's *Voyage*

75. Julien-David Le Roy, view of the
Parthenon, Athens, illustrated in his
Ruines des plus beaux monuments
de la Grèce, 1758

76, 77. Louis-Joseph Le Lorrain,
designs for the first Festa della
Chinea, Rome, 1746, 1747

pittoresque; ou, description des royaumes de Naples et de Sicile, issued between 1781 and 1786, Jean-Pierre Houel's *Voyage pittoresque des isles de Sicile, de Malte, et de Lipari,* of 1782 to 1787, and the Comte de Choiseul-Gouffier's *Voyage pittoresque de la Grèce,* of 1782 and 1809—did not at any time instigate a Greek or even a doctrinaire Roman revival. The French were not interested in copying Greek and Roman forms. As with their study of Gothic architecture, they were concerned only to discover principles, methods of grouping and composing, means of handling scale and proportion, and techniques of building. They sought the spirit of antiquity—and also of Gothic architecture—not the detail.

Yet there was something of a minor Greek revival in France in the 1760s known as the *goût grec,* and also a fierce polemic waged against the fiery Piranesi in Rome as to the merits of Greek architecture.

The *goût grec* was the creation of the Comte de Caylus (1692–1765). He had, in fact, set out in 1716 to search for the site of Troy and had spent almost a year wandering in Asia Minor, visiting the Temple of Diana at Ephesus, but he returned home when recalled by his mother without having explored Athens itself. He was to become a connoisseur and antiquarian, and in 1729 he began to form a mixed collection of antiquities similar to that begun by Montfaucon in 1693. This was to become the focus of his salon and to serve as the basis for the seven volumes of his *Recueil d'antiquités* that appeared between 1752 and 1767. There was not much in these on architecture, though the later volumes did include the Gallo-Roman antiquities of southern France. His influence was exerted rather through his friends, the collector and publisher Pierre-Jean Mariette, the critic Abbé Jean-Baptiste Leblanc, and the Abbé Jean-Jacques Barthélemy, and through his personal efforts.

The young painter Louis-Joseph Le Lorrain (1715-1759) was a *pensionnaire* in Rome who had made something of a name for himself with three designs for the Festa della Chinea of 1745, 1746, and 1747 that may be said to have taken up where Perrault left off. He was warmly recommended by Caylus to Ange-Laurent La Live de Jully, master of ceremonies at court, for whom, in 1756, he designed a suite of furniture, in ebony and gilt-bronze, a writing table, cabinet, and clock that were regarded as startlingly Greek in inspiration and form. Each object was decidedly heavier and clumsier than contemporary French furniture, recalling that of Louis XIV's reign, but was in no sense antique. Yet this furniture led, at once, to a wide if ineffectual fashion for things *à la grec*—fans, snuff boxes, occasional chairs or tables, and a handful of houses. Details for the more authentically antique works were taken from such early publications on the ruins of Herculaneum—where excavations had started in 1738—as that produced in 1751 by Soufflot's companion on his voyage C.-N. Cochin. Even in its revised form of 1754, this was not particularly informative. Revelation had to await the appearance of the nine large volumes of the *Antichità d'Ercolano,* which appeared from 1755 until 1792. But the

disclosures they contained were taken up by painters rather than by designers and architects. Joseph-Marie Vien, a protégé of Caylus, introduced an authentic-looking antique tripod into his insipid Grecian study *Une prêtresse qui brûle de l'encens sur un trépied,* of 1763 (later to become known as *La vertueuse athénienne).* In Rome, it should be noted, such attempts to depict antique furniture had already been made in 1761 in Gavin Hamilton's *Andromache Bewailing the Death of Hector,* and, in the same year, in Anton Raphael Meng's *Augustus and Cleopatra.* But the French, as we have seen, were not greatly interested in archaeological accuracy.

The Abbé Laugier acclaimed the Hôtel de Chavannes on the Boulevard du Temple, in Paris, built between 1756 and 1758 by Pierre-Louis Moreau-Desproux (1727-1793), as an exemplar of the new Greek mode, but the surviving drawing of the elevation shows that the only features that might connect it to Greek architecture were some bands of fretwork—and they were probably derived from Renaissance buildings—and an unusual largeness of scale conveyed by the use of giant pilasters. The fashion was soon ridiculed both by that spry entertainer Louis Carrogis, known as Carmontelle (1717-1806), in some masquerade costumes, and later, in 1771, in a similar set of costumes designed by Ennemond-Alexandre Petitot (1727–1801), who had been a student in Rome with Le Lorrain but had been sent as architect to the court of Parma in 1753 at the instigation of Caylus himself. On Caylus's recommendation Le Lorrain was employed to tidy up Le Roy's drawings for *Les ruines des plus beaux monuments de la Grèce* and was then given a post in Russia, where he died in 1759.

The *goût grec* was an ephemeral fashion, but it cannot be overlooked. Yet another of Caylus's protégés, the Belgian-born architect and engraver Jean-François de Neufforge (1714–1791), who was to engrave more than half the plates for Le Roy's publication, began to issue his *Recueil élémentaire d'architecture* in 1757. It comprised nine volumes and a total of nine hundred illustrations by 1772. Because these diffused and popularized a coarsened and heavy geometrical style thought to be antique in manner, they may be held to have prepared the ground for the more considered classicism of Louis XVI's reign. The first full-scale example of the new taste was the Hôtel de Varey, in Lyons, designed about 1758 by Toussaint-Noël Loyer (1724–1807), a pupil of Soufflot. There is no feeling for the refinements of classical architecture either in the facades on the Rue Auguste-Comte or on the Place Bellecour, or in the moldings of the salons of this *hôtel,* although they very convincingly reflect the coarsened taste inspired by Caylus and his associates.

Piranesi's quarrel over the merits of Greek architecture, instigated in 1761 with Le Roy and then with Mariette, was prompted more by nationalistic pride and a very real concern for his own livelihood than by any scholarly convictions. Giambattista Piranesi (1720–1778) arrived in Rome at the age of nineteen; he came from Venice, where he had learned etching and may have absorbed some of Carlo Lodoli's radical notions. In Rome he was stunned and then stirred by the sight of the ruins and

influenced by a whole range of artists and stage designers such as the Bibienas and the Valeriani brothrs, by the architect Filippo Juvarra, and, in particular, by the painter Gian Paolo Panini, who, in 1711, had himself come south from Piacenza to Rome, where he had established himself as the most prolific painter of scenes of ruins, both real and imaginary. Panini was to teach perspective drawing at the Académie de France and to open the eyes of a whole generation of French architects to the picturesque qualities of ruins—and thus to a more atmospheric view of architecture. He taught them to see architecture in painterly terms. Jean-Laurent Legeay (c. 1710–c. 1788), G.-P.-M. Dumont, Nicolas-Henri Jardin, Charles-Louis Clérisseau, Jérôme-Charles Bellicard (1726–1786), and Petitot, all of whom were in Rome in the 1740s, learned to present their projects in an atmospheric and painterly manner—a manner that conferred more interest on their works than they sometimes merited. Piranesi was in close contact with all these architects, an also with those French painters and sculptors studying in Rome—Jean-Baptiste Lallemand, Le Lorrain, the Challe brothers, Jacques Saly, Claude-Joseph Vernet, Vien, and, later, Hubert Robert. One of the first works to which Piranesi contributed, Fausto Amidei's *Varie vedute di Roma antica e moderna,* issued in 1745, also contained plates by Legeay, and in later editions views of Bellicard were to be added.

But Piranesi soon established himself on his own merit. Already in July 1743, he had published his first suite of etchings, the *Prima parte di architetture e prospettive,* which, though influenced by the works of Fischer von Erlach and the Bibienas, was to influence, in turn, Le Lorrain's designs for the Festa della Chinea of 1746 and 1747. Then in 1748 came the *Antichità romane de tempi della repubblica, e de primi imperatori,* which established his style and his reputation as a recorder of buildings old and new, in and around Rome. Some more idiosyncratic works followed, the four plates of the *Grotteschi,* mysterious rococo confections influenced by his contact with G. B. Tiepolo in 1744, and the fourteen plates of the *Invenzioni capric. de carceri,* the initial version of his theatrical prison designs. All these works were combined and published together in various combinations, for they were not equally successful. What the connoisseurs and cognoscenti who visited Rome wanted, above all, were renderings of the monuments of the city. For four years Piranesi worked feverishly, excavating and measuring ruins, using his imagination for what he could not inspect for himself. In 1756 he began to issue the grandest and most stunning of all his works, the *Antichità romane,* to run eventually to two hundred plates, each two feet across. He had used his wife's dowry to pay for the plates and his strongest influence to secure a tax exemption to cut the cost of the paper. His future was thus tied up in the enterprise. When Le Roy's volume of Grecian antiquities appeared in 1758, with the threat of Stuart's and Revet's to follow, Piranesi determined to shatter all rival claims to originality and magnificence in architecture. With the aid of several local scholars he concocted the long and muddled text and the thirty-eight plates of *Della magnificenza ed*

81, 82. *Ennemond-Alexandre Petitot,*
Berger et Bergère à la grecque,
costumes for a masked ball at the
court of Parma, 1771

architettura de' Romani, which appeared in 1761. Refuting both Le Roy's claim that Roman architecture was derived from that of the Greeks—whose architecture was based, in turn, on that of the Egyptians—and a similar historical analysis made in a *Dialogue on Taste,* published as far back as 1755 by the Scottish painter Allan Ramsay, he sought to prove that Roman architecture owed nothing to Greece, that it developed rather from ancient Etruscan architecture, and that if there was not much of that at hand to prove his point, there were at least stupendous engineering works such as the Cloaca Maxima, substructures, aqueducts, and roadways extant. Greek architecture had no such logic and splendor of engineering. Roman architecture, moreover, was richer and far more varied than that of the Greeks, and thus infinitely to be preferred. Reason played small part in Piranesi's propaganda. Caylus's friend Mariette responded succinctly to this outburst in November 1764, in the *Gazette littéraire de l'Europe,* adding to Le Roy's summary history the suggestion that not only was Roman architecture altogether dependent on that of the Greeks, but that it owed whatever finesse it might possess to the labors of Greek slaves. Incensed, Piranesi rushed into print in 1765 his rebuttal of Mariette's arguments, the *Osservazioni . . . sopra la lettre de M. Mariette,* and the related *Parere su l'architettura* with its handful of extraordinary compositions, in which he abandoned all archaeological verisimilitude in favor of original composition. This was followed in 1769 by his equally outrageous, altogether shocking designs for the *Diverse maniere d'adornare i camini.* "Je pense absolument comme vous," Caylus wrote to the archaeologist Paolo Maria Paciaudi, in 1765, "sur l'excès de l'encre et du foin de Piranesi, mais que voulez-vous? C'est sa manière . . ." (*Correspondance,* 1877, vol. 2, p. 95). Caylus could admire only the early works. But by then Pierre Patte was selling copies of Piranesi's etchings in Paris. Piranesi's reputation remained strong and his works continued to sell. The feud with the French was soon forgotten. Just before he died, in 1778, he produced the boldest, most somber of his works, a sheaf of etchings of the temples at Paestum, the title in French, *Différentes vues de quelques restes de trois grands édifices qui subsistent encore dans le milieu de l'ancienne ville de Pesto.* The solemn magic of these plates, more than anything else, perhaps, was to reveal to architects the solid splendor of Greek antiquity.

There were other propagandists, however, the greatest of them Johann Joachim Winckelmann (1717–1768), with whom we still associate the ideal of the "noble simplicity and quiet grandeur" of Greek art. Like Caylus, Winckelmann never visited the temples of Greece itself, though he was invited on three occasions to do so. He preferred that Greece remain a remote landscape. He wanted an ideal image, not reality. When he wrote his first invocation to Greek art, the *Gedanken über die Nachahmung der griechischen Werke in der Malerei und Bildhauerkunst,* in Dresden, in 1755, he had not even traveled to Rome. For his ideas on Greek art he relied on the writings of Pliny the Elder and Pausanias. He visualized Greek art

entirely in terms of that of Raphael—in particular, the *Sistine Madonna,* with which he was familiar in Dresden. Raphael's smooth and rounded forms established Winckelmann's ideal. This was sapless and colorless. "Color," Winckelmann wrote in the second chapter of his *Geschichte der Kunst,* "should have but little share in our consideration of beauty, because the essence of beauty consists not in color but shape, and on this point enlightened minds will at once agree." Elsewhere he wrote that great art should have no flavor, but should be like pure water.

Winckelmann's interest, as one might expect, was focused on sculpture, on the *Apollo Belvedere* and on the *Laocoön.* He did not know the works of Phidias, never saw a statue dating from before the fifth century B.C., and never really experienced the noble simplicity of the Greek art that he extolled. His concern for architecture was strictly limited. He described the temples of Agrigento, but summarily, in 1759, in *Amerkungen über die Baukunst der alten Tempel zu Girgenti in Sizilien,* relying on the observations of the Scottish architect Robert Mylne (1734–1811), and, for the rest, limiting himself to general remarks on the subject of Greek and Roman architecture. He lauded rather the works of Michelangelo, as represented at St. Peter's. None of his writings was illustrated in a way calculated to stir architects. His direct influence on architecture may thus be dismissed. Yet he did prompt a reassessment of Greek art among connoisseurs that was to affect architecture. For however shaky his premises, however personal his interpretations, his accounts of the stylistic evolution of Greek and Roman art, couched in elevated and rapturous language, riveted the attention of his contemporaries (and even his successors, as late as the end of the nineteenth century, when Walter Pater was still quoting him with the highest admiration). There can be no denying the dramatic impact of Winckelmann's writings, in particular the *Geschichte der Kunst des Altertums,* of 1764, the first systematic account of the evolving forms of antique art. He was the most important propagator of the Greek myth in the late eighteenth century. His books were translated into French almost immediately on publication, though they were less quick to appear in English. The Swiss painter Henry Fuseli translated some of Winckelmann's earlier works in the late 1760s but the *History of Ancient Art Among the Greeks* did not appear until 1849, and then in America.

Winckelmann's life, one may note, also had its dramatic side, not uninteresting to his contemporaries. Son of a Prussian cobbler, he rose rapidly from schoolmaster, to reader, to librarian; then, like Jean-Jacques Rousseau, he turned to Catholicism to further his career. In 1755, at the age of thirty-eight, he moved to Rome to become librarian to Cardinal Archinto. Archinto died, and three years later Winckelmann graduated to the library of Cardinal Albani, where he may have advised Anton Raphael Mengs on the famous ceiling fresco *Parnassus,* of 1760, and the architect Carlo Marchionni on the three *tempietti greci* just being completed outside the cardinal's villa.

In 1763 Winckelmann moved to the Vatican itself, where he became Keeper of Antiquities. He was an active and influential propagandist, regarded as a man of the highest sensibility, but on occasion his perception failed him. His friend Mengs, whom he had even known in Dresden, painted a fresco of Jupiter and Ganymede in the antique style in imitation of one from Herculaneum. Winckelmann acclaimed it as an antique original. He liked the cupbearer. "Jove's paramour," he wrote to his friend Friedrich Reinbolt von Berg, "is certainly one of the most extraordinarily beautiful figures that has come down to us from antiquity, and I could not hope to find anything to compare with his face, it breathes so great a voluptuousness that his whole soul seems to be drawn into this kiss." Goethe, too, liked this Ganymede.

There were shadows in Winckelmann's life. In 1768 he was brutally murdered by a hustler in Trieste. Such scandalous incidents served, however, to attract more than usual attention not only to the man, but also to his work and all that he upheld. The French were particularly intrigued, but they were not to be spurred to the extent of initiating a Greek Revival.

England made the most determined effort to apply the new archaeological information to the creation of a new architecture directly inspired by the antique. English architects were less troubled by theory and ideas than their French counterparts and their powers of invention were further stimulated by the growth of the Picturesque tradition.

The new wave of enthusiasm for the antique, which enables us to see the middle of the eighteenth century as a turning point in British architecture, had been anticipated by Lord Burlington (Richard Boyle; 1694–1753) and his neo-Palladian circle. Thus, although England could scarcely parallel the long French tradition of theorists proposing a new rational architecture shorn of Baroque trimmings, many of the forms that were to be characteristic of neoclassical architecture had already been exploited by the Burlingtonians—in particular, the sequences of domed and apsed spaces derived from the Roman Baths. Lord Burlington was determined to purify British architecture of Baroque extravagance by recapturing that classical harmony which, he believed, had been codified and enshrined in the architecture and theory of Palladio. This obsession with the antique, if only at second hand through the eyes and researches of Palladio, made England unique in Europe at the beginning of the eighteenth century and helps explain why English architecture was out of step with, and, in some ways, stylistically in advance of, that of the rest of Europe.

One of the most influential products of Burlington's ruthless and doctrinaire classicism was the Assembly Rooms at York, which he designed in 1730. In his search to discover how the ancients would have designed a festival hall he was directed, probably by Giacomo Leoni (1686–1746), to Palladio's reconstructions of a hall in the "manner of the Egyptians," based on a description in Vitruvius, and of the courtyard of a Greek house.

88. *Plate from Giambattista*
Piranesi's Antichità romane, *1756*
onward showing the foundations of
the Theater of Marcellus

89. *Plate from Giambattista*
Piranesi's Prima parte di
architetture e prospettive, *1742*

90. *Plate from Giambattista*
Piranesi's Antichità romane, *1756,*
showing visitors in the Tomb of
Arruntius

Leoni himself had published a similar design in his *Designs for Buildings both Publick and Private,* which appeared in 1726–29. However, the credit for realizing the idea for the first time in an actual building must go to Burlington, since not even Palladio had been able to carry his scheme into execution. Similarly, at Holkham Hall, William Kent and Lord Burlington were able to realize a plan type invented though never fully executed by Palladio. Burlington's chill hall at York, with its insistent freestanding columns carrying an unbroken horizontal entablature, set a precedent that was to be followed throughout the eighteenth century and later, from Mereworth church, Kent (1744–46; anonymous), via Adam's hall at Kedleston, Derbyshire (1760–70), to Leo von Klenze's throne room at the Munich Residenz (1832).

In the same year as his York design, 1730, Burlington printed for private circulation an edition of Palladio's original drawings for the restoration of the Roman Baths that Burlington had bought from the Bishop of Verona. Entitled *Fabbriche antiche disegnate da Andrea Palladio Vicentino,* this important contribution to archaeology gave Burlington the inspiration for the round and apsidal rooms that flank the great colonnaded hall at York and also for the remarkable entrance facade (now destroyed) with its curved portico containing windows similar to those of the Baths of Diocletian.

Burlington was an important forerunner of the architect as archaeologist, as exemplified during the next hundred years in England by Stuart and Revett, Adam, William Wilkins, C. R. Cockerell, and Henry W. Inwood. Another architect who had been interested in Palladio's reconstruction of Vitruvius' Egyptian Hall was Inigo Jones's pupil John Webb (1611–1672). We should not forget that the seventeenth century in England had enjoyed its own Palladian Revival. In the 1630s Jones added a colossal Corinthian portico to Old St. Paul's cathedral on a scale that still impressed Cockerell two centuries later, and about 1655 Webb provided The Vyne, Hampshire, with a giant Corinthian portico probably inspired by Palladio's chapel at the Villa Barbaro, Maser. Webb's was the first portico ever to adorn an English country house and is thus the father of the countless examples erected in Europe and North America during the following century.

Burlington was a learned and influential architect but he lacked flare and panache as a designer. Those qualities were possessed in abundance by his intimate friend and follower, William Kent. Burlington and Kent's collaboration on the design of Holkham Hall, Norfolk, for Lord Leicester, produced one of the most spectacular interiors of eighteenth-century Europe: the entrance hall of about 1734. To the basic theme of Palladio's Vitruvian Hall, as revived at York, has been added a great apse partly inspired by Palladio's reconstruction of the antique basilica and partly by his own Venetian churches. The rich frieze, the coffered cove, and the details of the eighteen fluted Ionic columns from the Temple of Fortuna Virilis in Rome are based on plates in that popular work of archaeology Desgodets's *Édifices antiques de Rome* (1682). The light coloring of the Derbyshire

alabaster and the prominent Greek-key and Vitruvian-scroll friezes also help
to create a thoroughly classical effect in a room whose disposition obviously
has a certain Baroque or threatrical drama.

Of the many sides to Kent's genius that cannot be fully explored here,
one of the most significant is his interest in the Etruscan or Pompeian type
of interior decoration that had been revived by Raphael and Giovanni da
Udine in Renaissance Rome and that was to be given prominent emphasis
in a number of celebrated interiors by Robert Adam. Kent painted ceilings
in this festive classical taste in the Audience and Council chambers at
Kensington Palace, London (1724), and in the parlor at Rousham,
Oxfordshire (1738–40). The Rousham ceiling, framed within a striking
Greek-key border, is especially noteworthy since it contains two Romantic
landscape paintings by Kent, which also point the way to future developments in painting.

From Kent's revolutionary interiors of the 1720s and 1730s it is but a
step to what is sometimes regarded as the first neoclassical interior in
England, James Stuart's Painted Room at Spencer House, London (1759),
and to Clérisseau's celebrated room in the Hôtel Grimod de la Reynière,
Paris (1774 or 1775). To mention the name of James Stuart is to recall the
Society of Dilettanti. Founded in 1733-34, this remarkable institution may
justly be regarded as the fountainhead of English neoclassical architecture.
A group of about forty rich young noblemen and gentlemen, mostly in their
late twenties and in the process of making their *grands tours,* got together
to form a club to promote what they called "Greek taste and Roman spirit."
Their aim was to institutionalize, as it were, the interest in the antique
expressed more indirectly by Burlington and his circle, and for the next
century successive members of the society, by acting as patrons of designers
and architects and by financing archaeologists and scholars, were able to
exercise great influence over the development of taste. In some ways the
most characteristic members were the architects Stuart and Revett in the
mid-eighteenth century, and Wilkins and Cockerell in the early nineteenth,
for all four combined the roles of archaeologist and architect. But the
patrons, following in the footsteps of Lord Burlington, were almost as
important: such men as Sir George Beaumont, elected in 1784, and Thomas
Hope, elected in 1800. Though the Society of Dilettanti was aristocratic
in impetus, its membership reflected both the social mobility of England
and the strength of the Whig oligarchy. Nothing like it could have existed
in any other European country.

James Stuart (1713-1788) was born into humble circumstances. He first
found employment with Louis Goupy, a fan painter who had accompanied
Lord Burlington on an Italian tour. Goupy's fans were decorated with views
of classical buildings. Stuart set out for Rome in 1742; there, he acquired
a reputation as a connoisseur of pictures and probably acted as *cicerone* to
Englishmen on the *grand tour.* In 1748 he accompanied Gavin Hamilton,
Matthew Brettingham, and his future partner, Nicholas Revett, on an

92. *Plate from Giambattista Piranesi's* Parere su l'architettura, *1765*

V. Robert Adam, Kedelston Hall, Derbyshire, the Marble Hall, 1760–70

VI. *William Kent, Holkham Hall,*
Norfolk, hall, c. 1734

expedition to Naples, during which the plan to visit Athens was first discussed. Revett (1720-1804), the son of a Suffolk squire, was very different in background from Stuart. In 1742 he traveled to Rome to study painting with Cavaliere Benefiale. The friendship of these four widely different men—Hamilton, Brettingham, Stuart, and Revett—led to their decision to measure the buildings of Athens, and they were encouraged by such English dilettanti in Rome as Lord Malton, Lord Charlemont, James Dawkins, and Robert Wood. Money was raised to finance the expedition, though in the end Brettingham and Hamilton were unable to take part. In 1748 Stuart and Revett issued their "Proposals for Publishing an Accurate Description of the Antiquities of Athens." Their aim was to parallel the way in which "Rome, who borrowed her Arts, and frequently her Artificers, from Greece, has by means of Serlio, Palladio, Santo Bartoli, and other ingenious men, preserved the memory of the most excellent sculptures and Magnificent Edifices which once adorned her." They also pointed out that "A work so much wanted will meet with the approbation of all those Gentlemen who are lovers of Antiquity, or have a taste for what is Excellent in these Arts, as we are assured that those Artists who aim at perfection must be infinitely more pleased and better instructed the nearer they can draw their Examples from the Fountain-head."

This clear statement of a neoclassical aesthetic in 1748 emphasizes the close connection between the study of archaeology and the practice of architecture. Stuart and Revett left Rome for Greece in 1750. They spent some time on the way in Venice, where the British Resident, Sir James Gray, procured their election to the Society of Dilettanti. They arrived in Athens in March 1751 and returned to England four years later to prepare their drawings for publication. Naturally, those members of the Society of Dilettanti who had helped finance the expedition were impatient for the results. In Germany Winckelmann himself shared their impatience as we know from the preface to his *Anmerkungen über die Baukunst der Alten* (1762), written in 1760, two years before Stuart and Revett's first volume was published.

Between 1748 and 1762 Stuart and Revett changed their ideas as to the contents of the first volume, so that it eventually contained not the major buildings of the Acropolis but the smaller, later, and minor buildings in the city of Athens. These, they modestly hoped, might furnish hints concerning "the different Grecian modes of decorating buildings." Indeed, the buildings they chose to illustrate, such as the Choragic Monument of Lysicrates, the Tower of the Winds, and the Gateway to the Agora, were Hellenistic, note Greek, and lent themselves particularly to a process of transformation into garden ornaments for English parks. This is an early instance of the way in which, in England, the tradition of the Picturesque tended to dissolve any expression of pure neoclassicism. Stuart himself had contributed to this process even before the first volume of his *Antiquities of Athens* appeared in 1762, so that the first Greek Revival building in

Europe is, characteristically, a garden ornament in an English landscaped park. This is the temple at Hagley Park, Worcestershire, designed by Stuart for Lord Lyttelton in 1758. Built of red sandstone originally covered with stucco, it is not an exact copy of any Greek building but, being Doric hexastyle with a column at each side of the cella entrance, it was perhaps inspired by the Theseum in Athens. In October 1758 Lord Lyttelton wrote to Mrs. Elizabeth Montagu: "Stuart is going to embellish one of my little hills with a true Attic building, a Portico of six pillars, which will make a fine effect to my new house, and command a most beautiful view of the country." Thus, the Greek Revival was conceived from the start as part of the Picturesque impact of contrived landscape scenery.

Six years after Hagley, Stuart began to develop in a quite extraordinary way this theme of reducing Greek architecture to garden ornaments. From 1764 on, at Shugborough, in Staffordshire, for another Whig landowner, Thomas Anson (a founder-member of the Society of Dilettanti), Stuart dropped a succession of Picturesque buildings based on the minor

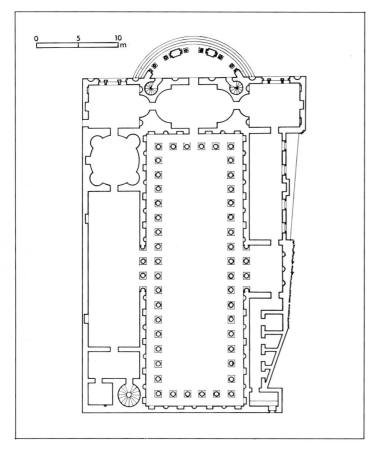

architecture of Athens into a park that had long been adorned with garden ornaments and ruins of different shapes and sizes, including Chinese.

In some ways Stuart was more successful at adapting his archaeological knowledge to modern design in furniture and interior decoration than to architecture. Soon after his return to England from Greece he was invited to design interiors for two Whig landowners who were to subscribe to the first volume of *Antiquities of Athens*. Stuart's tripod stands of about 1757 for Lord Scarsdale at Kedleston, Derbyshire, and a related pair of candelabra for Lord Spencer at Spencer House, London, of 1759–60, are based upon the tripod at the top of the Choragic Monument of Lysicrates, but develop it in a novel, beautiful, and functional way. Stuart's interiors for Kedleston were not executed, but his Painted Room of 1759 at Spencer House survives as the first "Etruscan" Revival room in Europe. It was conceived as a unity with its furniture, which included a set of four fantastic sofas and six armchairs with side pieces made up of gilt griffins. These derive from antique Roman marble seat furniture Stuart may have seen in the Vatican or in other Italian collections. Their flashy drama anticipates Regency and Empire style furniture and is astonishing for 1760.

Stuart's only remaining work of real consequence was his rebuilding and redecoration, after a fire, of Christopher Wren's chapel at the Royal Hospital, Greenwich. This was carried out with the assistance of Stuart's very talented Clerk of the Works, William Newton, between 1779 and 1788. Reflecting the impact of the mature Adam style, it is dominated by a rich but filigreed ornament, the details of which are Greek in origin though the overall impression is certainly not. The most imaginative feature of the chapel is the pulpit, obviously inspired by Stuart's favorite building, the Choragic Monument of Lysicrates.

It will have become clear that Stuart's career was marked by a certain failure of nerve and that he never created the new architecture for which his contemporaries were waiting. His procrastination delayed until 1789 the publication of the important second volume of the *Antiquities of Athens*, which illustrated the Parthenon. Nicholas Revett had in fact resigned his interest in the joint publishing venture even before the publication of the first volume. As a gentleman of leisure he certainly maintained his interest in Greek architecture and archaeology, and in 1764 was chosen by the Society of Dilettanti to go on an expedition to the coast of Asia Minor with Richard Chandler and William Pars. This resulted in his editorship of the *Antiquities of Ionia*, which appeared in two volumes in 1769 and 1797. The buildings depicted were of equal interest to those in the first volume of the *Antiquities of Athens*—in particular, the splendid Temple of Apollo at Didyma, near Miletus—but, rather unaccountably, they did not influence contemporary architecture as they could and perhaps ought to have done. One reason why they did not was that Revett himself used them in only one of his own buildings. His name can be connected with the design of only three important buildings, and in two of these he used the order based

on the Temple of Apollo at Delos, which he had illustrated in the first volume of the *Antiquities of Athens.* Revett adapted this late fourth-century Delian Doric style at Standlynch (now Trafalgar) House, Wiltshire (c. 1766), for his friend Henry Dawkins, and at the church at Ayot St. Lawrence, Hertfordshire (1778). At Standlynch the composition of the Doric portico is still basically Baroque and at Ayot St. Lawrence the whole composition, with a central pavilion linked to side wings by colonnades, is of Palladian origin. Evidently Revett could not think in a really Greek way, though at West Wycombe Park, Buckinghamshire, in 1770, he provided for Sir Francis Dashwood, a founder-member of the Society of Dilettanti, an undeniably impressive western portico, based on the Temple of Dionysus at Teos, of the second century B.C., which he had included the year before in the *Antiquities of Ionia.*

Other important archaeological publications that influenced taste were Robert Wood's *Ruins of Palmyra* and *Ruins of Balbec.* Thus, a late-Palladian building such as Henry Flitcroft's west front of Woburn Abbey, Bedford-shire (1757–61), incorporates in the State Bedroom a version of the ceiling of the vestibule at the south end of the cella of the Temple of the Sun at Palmyra of the early first century A.D., as illustrated in Wood's book. It is interesting to compare Flitcroft's straightforward imitation of antiquity with Adam's more fanciful adaptation in the drawing room at Osterly Park, begun in the 1760s and completed in 1773. The ceiling of Adam's Great Drawing Room at Syon House of the 1760s is an imaginative mingling of Wood's illustrations with Raphael's and Giovanni da Udine's decorations in the vaulting of the loggia of Villa Madama, Rome.

The engravings for Wood's *Ruins of Palmyra* were prepared in London in 1751 by Giovanni Battista Borra, a Piedmontese architect, after drawings he had made at Palmyra. From 1752 to 1755 he incorporated Palmyrene themes in the ceiling of his State Bedchamber at Stowe House, Buckingham-shire. In 1775 the painter-architect Vincenzo Valdrè (c. 1742–1814), of Faenza, created the magnificent oval saloon at Stowe, flanked by sixteen, freestanding columns supporting a full Doric entablature and a crowded frieze depicting a Roman triumphal procession. This hermetic, monumental interior, windowless, domed, top-lit, leads into a richly Pompeian music room of 1777, also by Valdrè. In the drawing room the Greek Corinthian order was adapted by Valdrè from that of the Choragic Monument of Lysicrates as illustrated in Stuart and Revett; the Bacchic frieze in the south portico was also taken from Stuart and Revett.

A decade after the Pompeian music room at Stowe another Italian-born architect working in England produced a room of greater archaeological accuracy. This was the Pompeian Gallery at Packington Hall, Warwickshire, designed for Lord Aylesford by the eccentric Joseph Bonomi (1739–1808). Bonomi, a Roman, was a pupil of Clérisseau who had been engaged in 1765 by Robert Adam as tutor, guide, and companion. In 1767 Bonomi came to England to work for Adam and married the niece of Angelica Kauffmann,

one of Adam's decorative painters. On the collapse of the Adam brothers' Adelphi speculation (a development of terraced houses on the Thames), Bonomi left their office, possibly in 1774, for that of Thomas Leverton (1743–1824). The project for decorating the Long Gallery at Packington, initiated in 1782, seems to have been Bonomi's first independent commis-sion. Lord Aylesford was a remarkable figure, a gifted painter, an architect manqué, a traveler and connoisseur, a friend of the Picturesque theorist Sir Uvedale Price and of the collector Sir George Beaumont. He was the dream patron for any neoclassical architect. The Pompeian Gallery that Bonomi created for him at Packington was the work of one English and three Italian craftsmen: Benedetto Pastorini, a painter and engraver who had been employed by Robert and James Adam to make the plates for their *Works in Architecture;* Domenico Bartoli, a scagliola manufacturer; Joseph Rose, Jr., Adam's plasterworker; Giovanni Borgnis, a fresco painter; and, perhaps most important, John Francis Rigaud, a painter from Turin who came to England by way of Paris in 1771. The lower part of the walls up to the shelf of the chimneypiece was of scagliola, imitating panels of porphyry surrounded by borders of Siena marble: This arrangement corresponds with

what had been discovered at Pompeii. The strong black and terra-cotta coloring recalls the Greek vases that Lord Aylesford enthusiastically collected, although the real source for the decoration was neither Greek nor Pompeian but Roman. It was taken from the plates either in Ludovico Mirri's and Giuseppe Carletti's *Antiche camere delle terme di Tito e loro pitture* (1776) or in Vincenzo Brenna's, Ludovico Mirri's, and Franiszek Smugle-wicz's *Vestigia delle terme di Tito* (c. 1780), which were both later used by Nicolas Ponce in his *Description des bains de Titus; ou, collection des peintures trouvées dans les ruines des thermes de cet empereur* (1786). As interesting as the bold archaeological decoration of the gallery is the design of a set of eight Greek Revival chairs that still adorn it. Bonomi based the klismos form of these—a type subsequently popularized by Thomas Hope—not on Roman furniture but on the chairs depicted in Greek vase paintings.

After his tour de force in the gallery Bonomi turned his attention to the design of a new church in the park at Packington. The plans were prepared in 1788 with the active assistance of Lord Aylesford, and the foundation stone was laid in April 1789. This grim, gaunt building is Revolutionary in the manner of Ledoux's *barrières,* which Bonomi presumably knew. Its interior is no less remarkable for its confident use of the still-revolutionary Greek Doric order. It seems to be based on the Temple of Neptune at Paestum, which had been illustrated in T. Major's *The Ruins of Paestum* (1768), though without the entasis so prominent at Packington. Lord Aylesford's etchings of Greek ruins can be seen in the fourth volume of Henry Swinburne's *Travels in the Two Sicilies* (1783), and it may be that the addition of entasis is due to him rather than to Bonomi. The Doric groin-vaulted interior seems to have influenced several interiors by Sir John Soane and James Wyatt in the 1790s: Soane's Tyringham Hall, Buckinghamshire; Bentley Priory, Middlesex; an unexecuted House of Lords project; and Wyatt's remarkable chapel at Dodington Park, Gloucestershire, designed some time between 1798 and 1805.

The stark and deliberately unprecedented air of the exterior of the Packington church is also echoed in the Berlin Mint (1798–1800; demolished 1886), by Heinrich Gentz (1766–1811). Gentz was a pioneer in the introduction of the Greek Doric style to Germany. He visited Paestum and Sicily, and also traveled in England, Holland, and France. He was a friend of the artist Asmus Jakob Carstens and the publisher Wilhelm Tischbein and he married the sister of Friedrich Gilly (1772–1800), the most original architect of late eighteenth-century Germany. Although so many German architects looked to the Paris of Ledoux for inspiration at this time, it was English neoclassical architecture, with its archaeological interest in the revival of the Greek Doric, that was closest in spirit to German architecture at the end of the century. Indeed, it was in Germany—not in England, and least of all in France—that the first building based on the Athenian Propylaea was erected. This was the Brandenburg Gate (1789–91) by Carl Gotthard Langhans (1732–1808), the gateway not only to Berlin

98. Robert Adam, Kedleston Hall,
Derbyshire, hall, 1760–70

99. *Joseph Bonomi, church in the park at Packington, Warwickshire, 1789*

but also, in a sense, to German neoclassicism itself. It was probably inspired by Le Roy's striking reconstruction of the Athenian Propylaea published in his *Ruines des plus beaux monuments de la Grèce*. Langhans had visited Italy in 1768–69, and Holland, France, and England in 1775. He became director of the Royal Office of Public Buildings in Berlin in 1788, and his striking Greek Revival gateway has always impressed visitors to that city. In December 1794, for example the influential connoisseur, patron, and designer Thomas Hope was so much affected by the gateway when he saw it that ten years later, when he came to write a pamphlet on the style he believed ought to be adopted at Downing College, Cambridge, he recommended it as a model for the entrance to the college. And sure enough, Hope's protégé, the dutiful William Wilkins, provided designs in 1806 for a more than usually extensive porter's lodge à la Propylaea. Whereas Wilkins's Greek Doric style was accurate and based on firsthand study of the originals in Greece—his *Antiquities of Magna Graecia* was published at Cambridge in 1807—Langhans had merely employed a sort of stripped Roman Doric style. His overattenuated columns have bases, unlike the Greek Doric order, and are unequally spaced in the side pavilions; also, there are demi-metopes at the ends of the frieze, whereas the Greeks ended their friezes firmly with a triglyph.

The examples of Langhans and Wilkins were followed by the architect Thomas Harrison (1744–1829) in his gateway at Chester Castle (1810–22), the design of which he had been cogitating since the 1780s. The theme was brought to a triumphant and imaginative conclusion by Leo von Klenze (1784–1864) in his Propylaeon, of 1846–60, on the west side of the Königsplatz in Munich. The project was first proposed in 1817, and Klenze's early sketches followed the Athenian prototype more closely than his final scheme with its powerful pylons.

Greek Doric was employed with varying degrees of accuracy by Benjamin Latrobe, James Wyatt, and Joseph Gandy. Shortly before embarking on his successful career in North America in 1796, Latrobe designed Hammerwood Lodge, Sussex, with Paestum-style Doric capitals. In the 1790s Wyatt transformed an unremarkable house, Stoke Poges Park, Buckinghamshire, into a neoclassical fantasy by surrounding it with stocky Greek Doric colonnades; similar stylistically was Storrs Hall, Westmorland, of 1808, by the eccentric Joseph Gandy, who later turned a temple inside out for the design of Doric House, Sion Hill, Bath (c. 1810). One of the noblest of all antique-inspired English houses is Belsay Hall, Northumberland. An austere product of the collaboration between 1806 and 1817 of three men—its owner Sir Charles Monck, the connoisseur Sir William Gell, and the architect John Dobson—Belsay Hall is the quintessence of what everyone in Europe had learned to feel about Greek art since Winckelmann first praised its noble simplicity and calm grandeur. The striking Villa Giulia at Palermo, Sicily (1789–92), by the French architect Léon Defourny (1754–1818), is close in form to Belsay, but Dobson's building has a quality

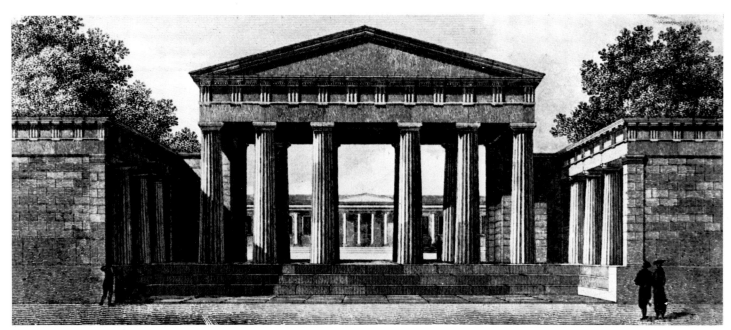

104. Leo von Klenze, Propylaeon, Munich, 1846–60

105. Sir Charles Monck, Sir William Gell, and John Dobson, Belsay Hall, Northumberland, detail of the exterior, 1806–17

and an air of absolute authority that made it unique in Europe for its time. Karl Friedrich Schinkel gave his buildings the same stamp of conviction, as can be seen in his first important commission, the Royal Guard House in Unter den Linden, Berlin (1816). Two years later came an even greater masterpiece in the center of Berlin, the State Theater, of which Schinkel wrote: "I tried to emulate Greek forms and methods of construction insofar as this is possible in such a complex work." Apart from the Greek Ionic portico, the most memorable feature of the building is the frequent use of a kind of functionalist pilaster strip. For these Schinkel cited a Greek source, the Choragic Monument of Thrasyllus (illustrated in the second volume of Stuart's and Revett's *Antiquities of Athens,* 1789, and since destroyed), and also argued that, when used in windows, these pilasters admitted the maximum amount of light. Schinkel's theater was imitated by Sir Charles Barry in his Royal Institution, Manchester, now the City Art Gallery (1823–35).

C. R. Cockerell is in some ways the most characteristic of archaeologist-architects. His staggeringly successful seven-year tour of Greece, Turkey, and Italy resulted in the discovery of the pediment sculpture at Aegina, the Bassae frieze, and the use of entasis at the Parthenon. His early buildings show the difficulty he experienced in trying to incorporate this new knowledge of what Greek architecture was like into the classical tradition as practiced then in England. His staircase hall, of 1823, at Oakly Park, Shropshire, includes casts of the Bassae frieze with a version of the unique Ionic order from Bassae and details taken from the capitals of the Tower of the Winds in Athens. (However, Cockerell increasingly relied on Italian Renaissance and Mannerist sources to enliven his classical vocabulary, and will thus be considered later in the book).

Two buildings of the greatest archaeological interest are Wilkins's Grange Park, Hampshire (1809), and, exactly contemporary with Oakly Park, St. Pancras church, London (1819–22), by William Inwood (c. 1771–1843) and his son Henry William (1794–1843). Henry Inwood had traveled to Greece to study Athenian architecture in 1819 and had formed a small collection of Greek antiquities which was later given to the British Museum. In 1827 he published *The Erechtheion at Athens, Fragments of Athenian, Architecture and a Few Remains in Attica, Megara and Epirus.* Meanwhile, at immense expense, he and his father produced their own version of the Erechtheum—St. Pancras church, which, with its astonishing caryatid-flanked porches, has never failed to surprise generations of visitors.

Equally surprising is Wilkins's Grange Park, the grandest temple-like house in Europe. Its vast portico, alas only of brick and plaster, was based on the Theseum in Athens, and the monumental piers on the sides of the building are developed from those on the Choragic Monument of Thrasyllus. The effect was rather like a stage set, although beneath the Athenian drama Wilkins left the original seventeenth-century red-brick house more or less intact. Blending into its beautiful Hampshire landscape,

106. Sir Charles Monck, Sir William Gell, and John Dobson, Belsay Hall, Northumberland, interior, 1806–17

VII. James Stuart, Spencer House, London, Painted Room, 1758

107. Friedrich Gilly, project for a
monument to Frederick the Great,
gateway, 1797

108. Thomas Hamilton, Royal High
School, Edinburgh, 1825–29

richly wooded and watered, Grange Park epitomizes the archaeological and the Picturesque side of English neoclassicism. It is thus a fulfillment of what Stuart initiated at Hagley Park fifty years earlier with his little Greek garden temple described by Lord Lyttelton as "a true Attic building . . . which will . . . command a most beautiful view of the country." That image of a Greek temple set in a high place remained powerfully in men's minds from the mid-eighteenth to the early nineteenth century. Nowhere was it more powerful than in Germany. Friedrich Gilly's entry of 1797 in the first of the many competitions for a monument to Frederick the Great in Berlin, though it departed from the terms of the competition, inspired a whole generation of architects with its solemn Doric temple set in a sacred precinct. The passionate desire to erect an adequate monument to Frederick's glory was linked to the process of establishing German national unity and self-identity, so that, in a sense, the real monument to Frederick was the foundation of the German Empire in 1871.

The competition for the monument to Frederick the Great did not, in fact, result in the erection of any single building. Curiously, something of the mood of Gilly's influential design can perhaps best be sensed in Scotland and in the north of England. In Edinburgh, for example, there are the Royal High School (1825–29) by Thomas Hamilton (1784–1858), the Royal Scottish Academy (1822–35) by W. H. Playfair (1789–1857), and Cockerell's and Playfair's uncompleted National Monument, or Walhalla, of 1821. The grim but dramatic Penshaw Monument in County Durham, modeled on the Parthenon (as was the Scottish National Monument), was erected in 1830 from designs by Benjamin Green (died 1858). As a bizarre but undoubtedly impressive footnote we should add that hybrid combination of Parthenon and Pantheon situated high up in the mountains above the village of Possagno, the Tempio del Canova (1819–33), designed by Antonio Canova (1757–1822) himself, possibly with help from Giannantonio Selva. The Walhalla near Regensburg in Bavaria (1830–42) is surely the culmination of the Picturesque vision of setting a temple on high and endowing it with that ennobling power with which Winckelmann had credited Greek art. But before examining this masterpiece by Leo von Klenze, we will turn again to France, since the design of the Walhalla was influenced by a new wave of archaeological discovery and debate, largely about polychromy, that was emanating from Paris.

During the early years of the nineteenth century a doctrinaire classicism was fostered in France, in particular by Antoine-Chrysostome Quatremère de Quincy (1755–1849), an unsuccessful sculptor who became *Secrétaire Perpétuel de l'Académie des Beaux-Arts* in 1816, a position he was to retain for twenty-three years, to be succeeded by a classicist of almost equally limited outlook, Désirée-Raoul Rochette (1790–1854).

Quatremère de Quincy upheld Winckelmann's ideals, though he was prepared to adapt them at times to accommodate new discoveries as they occurred. When he traveled to London in 1816 to see the Elgin Marbles,

97

which he viewed with C. R. Cockerell, he was greatly moved, and thereafter altered his canons somewhat. But such small flexibility in his outlook was to destroy almost the image of classical rectitude for which he labored throughout his life. Already in 1815 he had produced a major study, *Le Jupiter Olympien; ou, l'art de la sculpture antique,* in which he had indicated that the great cult statues of the Greeks might not be of pure white marble, but might incorporate gold and ivory, lapis lazuli and semiprecious stones. He scarcely intended to evoke a colorful image of antiquity, but was following, rather, the scholarly lead of such men as Edward Dodwell—who had noticed traces of color on Greek fragments in Sicily in the early years of the century—and, more important, of that great French scholar and enthusiast of the Doric, Léon Dufourny—architect of the marvelously robust early essay in the Greek Revival, the Villa Giulia, in the Orto Botanico, Palermo. Dufourny had reported his findings directly to Quatremère de Quincy, whose rash interpretation of this discovery was to be taken up many years later by Jacques-Ignace Hittorff, who, as we have already seen would attempt to revise totally the accepted image of antique architecture, to present it in the most vivid array of colors, as a basis for a livelier and more colorful contemporary style. This was the last occasion on which archaeological study was to make a fresh and vital impact on current design.

In Rome, in 1823, Hittorff encountered Thomas Leverton Donaldson (1795–1885), later to become president of the Royal Institute of British Architects, who had just written a brief essay on the discoveries of a group of young English scholars and architects—William Kinnaird, Joseph Woods, C. R. Cockerell, and Charles Barry—who had noticed traces of color on Greek buildings. Hittorff was hoping to make an archaeological discovery on his own account, and when he heard that William Harris and Samuel Angell had made similar observations in Sicily, he dashed there at once, overtaking Leo von Klenze, who was on the same trail. At Selinunte and at Agrigento Hittorff put eighteen excavators to work. He found what he wanted there and wrote at once to the editors of learned journals to stake his claim. When Hittorff returned to France, in 1824, he started a campaign to publicize his notions of a colorful image of antiquity. He believed that Greek temples had been covered completely with yellow paint, the sculpture and moldings heightened with lively patterns of bright blue, green, red, and gold paint. His short manifesto *De l'architecture polychrome chez les grecs; ou, restitution complète du temple d'Empédocle dans l'Acropolis d'Empédocle* was printed both in Italy and in France in 1830, starting an active and most acrimonious debate. Rochette defended the orthodox position; Antoine-Jean Letronne, professor of classical archaeology at the Collège de France, argued on Hittorff's behalf. Soon the debate became widespread. In 1834 Gottfried Semper voiced his theory that vapory red, rather than yellow, had served as the base color, and Franz Kugler produced his less fanciful reconstructions in the following year. In England a select committee was set up in 1837 to inspect the Elgin Marbles for traces of color, and Donaldson, Francis

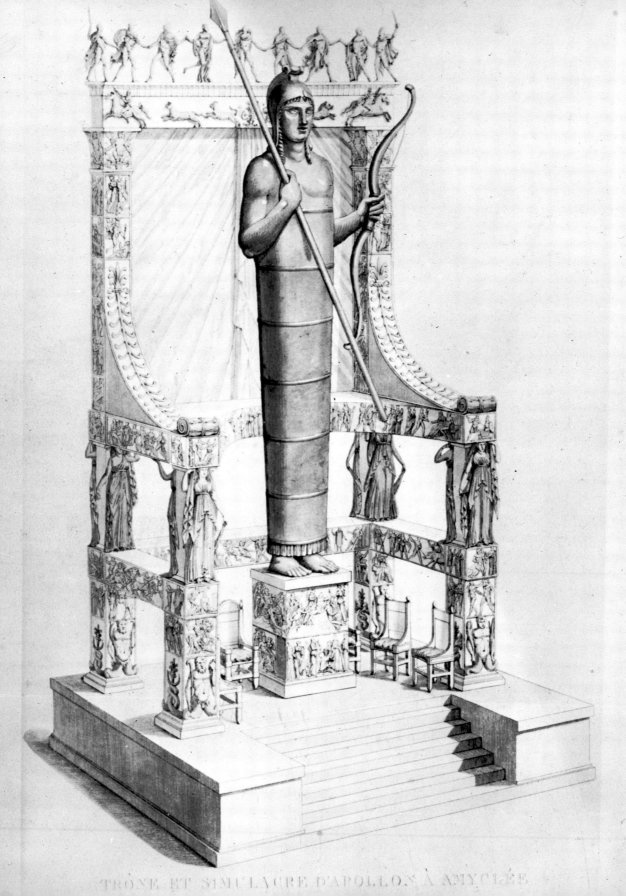

TRONE ET SIMULACRE D'APOLLON À AMYCLÉE

112. Antoine-Chrysostome Quatremère de Quincy, reconstruction in gold, ivory, and lapis lazuli of the throne of Apollo, from his Le Jupiter Olympien, *1815*

113. A. A. Jal, Jollivet House, 11 Cité Malesherbes, Paris, 1858. Majolica decoration

Cranmer Penrose, and Cockerell were to continue afterward to take a very active interest in the subject, though it was not until 1854 that Owen Jones and Sir Matthew Digby Wyatt erected the highly colored Greek court at the Crystal Palace at Sydenham. The influence of their ideas was enormous, especially in the field of decorative design. In France Hittorff, too, had attempted to infuse his ideas into contemporary design: His colorful portico for the Cirque Nationale, set up on the Champs-Élysées, Paris, in 1840, was one such experiment. Later, in 1852, he was to build another at the Cirque d'Hiver; it still stands in the Boulevard des Filles-du-Calvaire, though its present appearance is now toned down. His most important demonstration of architectural coloring, however, was the church of St.-Vincent-de-Paul, Place Lafayette, Paris, which was begun in 1824, though Hittorff took over only in 1830. Sixteen years later he began to cover the external portico wall with brightly colored enamel plaques depicting scenes from the Bible, but they were soon removed at the request of the clergy, who were incensed by the color and by the nudity of Adam and Eve.

The internal decorative scheme—a variant of that of the Norman cathedral in Monreale, Sicily—was also not begun until the 1840s. Something of Hittorff's intentions, though in muted form, was realized in the house built in 1858 by the architect A. A. Jal for the artist Pierre-Jules Jollivet at 11 Cité Malesherbes. But though Hittorff's own attempts to give expression to his ideas were of no great consequence, and though his final summation of his theories, the *Restitution du temple d'Empédocle à Selinonte; ou, l'architecture polychrome chez les grecs,* was probably not much read when it finally came out, between 1846 and 1851, there can be no doubt that he vitally influenced a whole range of architects, as disparate as Henri Labrouste and Charles Garnier, and showed them that a reassessment of antiquity was possible and most desirable. Hittorff was an indifferent archaeologist and an awkward, lackluster designer, but, almost unaided, he broke the spell of the doctrinaire classicists in France and prepared the way for the exuberance of the architecture of the Second Empire.

Leo von Klenze, Hittorff's rival in Sicily, was also influenced by the debate about polychromy, as is clear from the rich use of color, particularly colored marbles, in his Walhalla near Regensburg, and from its elaborate openwork roof, which resembles that of Hittorff's St.-Vincent-de-Paul. In 1833 Klenze designed the temple in the English Garden in Munich, which was described at the time as the "first example of lithochromy in the present day." The notion of the Walhalla was initially suggested to Crown Prince Ludwig of Bavaria by the defeat of Napoleon at Leipzig in 1813. The competition was announced in 1814 and its terms demanded Greek forms because, it was argued, the Parthenon had been closely linked to the Greek victory over the Persians from which Greek unity derived. In 1815 the architect Haller von Hallerstein (1774–1817) submitted a project from Athens, where he was visiting Greek sites in the company of C. R. Cockerell. In 1829 the competition was reframed and Klenze's plan for a monumental temple on

an enormous substructure was chosen. What exactly is the Walhalla? In
Norse mythology it is the place in which the souls of slain heroes feast,
having been brought there by the Valkyrie. For Ludwig it was also to be
"to excellent Germans a monument, hence a Walhalla," and he emphasized
that one was intended to be more German on leaving it than upon entering.
It was a pantheon of political and intellectual portrait busts of, for example,
Leibnitz, Schiller, Gluck, Mozart, Mengs, Thomas à Kempis, and Blücher.
The Valkyrie also appear inside, but in the form of Greek caryatids wearing
Nordic bearskins! Outside, one sculptured tympanum shows the defeat of
Napoleon at Leipzig, the other the defeat in A.D. 9 of Augustus's legions
by the united tribes of central and north-western Germany, who thereby
saved the country from Roman domination.

Faced with a building, so classical yet so Romantic, so archaeological yet
so much a part of nineteenth-century Germany, we are reminded forcibly
of the paradox that neoclassicism can justly be regarded as one aspect of
the Romantic movement. That point is neatly underlined by the fact that
the painter J. M. A. Turner chose as the subject of and entitled one of his
most remarkable paintings *The Opening of the Walhalla* (1842).

115. Joseph Mallod William Turner,
The Opening of the Walhalla,
detail, 1842. London, Tate Gallery

*116. Leo von Klenze, Walhalla, near
Regensburg, 1830–42*

*117. Giovanni Niccolò Servandoni,
design for the west front of St.-Sulpice,
Paris, with the addition of a third
order, c. 1752*

FRANCE: *From Gabriel to Ledoux*

The ideas that were to condition the changes in the form of architecture in late eighteenth-century France were generated early, by Perrault, Frémin, Cordemoy, and others; by 1753 these had been encapsulated and expressed with the utmost lucidity in the Abbé Laugier's *Essai sur l'architecture.* But the vital visual inspiration that was to make precise and alive the new style emerged but fitfully. L.-J. Le Lorrain's three designs for the Festa della Chinea of 1745, 1746, and 1747—borrowing motifs from Perrault's Louvre facade and also from Piranesi's *Prima parte*—provided the key for much that was to follow. Many formal devices and details can be traced to Le Lorrain's designs, but for a new boldness of massing, sudden changes of scale, contrasts of richness and stark wall surfaces, architects were to be indebted directly to Piranesi. His vision was to dominate architecture. The ruins of Rome, or rather an interpretation of them, were the mainspring of the new style.

Fittingly, the first architect who was to capture something of the new spirit, Giovanni Niccolò Servandoni (1695–1766), was trained in Rome by Piranesi's own forerunner G. P. Panini, and also by the Florentine architect Giuseppe Ignazio Rossi; he began his career as a stage designer, and he traveled in this capacity throughout Europe to Lisbon and London, Brussels, Stuttgart, and Vienna. Far too little is known of his designs, but he appears to have made his debut in France (whence came his father, coachman from Lyons) in 1726, with lavish sets for *Pyramus and Thisbe.* By 1732 he had won a competition for the west front of the church of St.-Sulpice in Paris. His design was not advanced—indeed, it had less to recommend it in the way of geometrical clarity than one drawn up six years earlier by Gilles-Marie Oppenordt—and was evidently derived from the west front of St. Paul's in London. But as work went slowly ahead the detail was modified and changed. In 1742 Servandoni engraved a variant that showed the entablature above the first order extending unbroken across the facade; by 1752 the entablature at the second level had also become an unbroken line across the facade. At this stage a third order was erected between the towers and a square planned in front of the church. Only the robust house that Servandoni designed and built for himself on the square from 1752 to 1757, on the corner of the Rue des Canettes, Paris, survives. The third order was taken down after Servandoni's death in 1766 and a giant pediment put in its place; this was struck by lightning in 1770 and replaced in turn by the simple balustrade that stands today—a reversion to the initial project by Oppenordt.

The north tower was then finished off by Jean-François-Thérèse Chalgrin, a pupil of Servandoni. "Plein des beautés de l'antique," Blondel wrote of Servandoni in his *Cours d'architecture,* "il a su soutenir le style grec dans toutes ses productions, tandis que Paris, de son temps, n'enfantoit guère que des chimères" (vol. 3, p. 351). No exaggeration surely was intended, for when it was finished in 1777 the west front of St.-Sulpice seemed to contempo-

118. Giovanni Niccolò Servandoni,
design for the west front of St.-Sulpice,
Paris, 1732

119. Giovanni Niccolò Servandoni,
St.-Sulpice, Paris, west front,
1732–77

raries to have the firmness of geometry, the regularity, and the columnar
rhythms of a Greek temple. Certainly it was one of the starkest and most
startling buildings in Paris. But its design had been evolved over a long
period and by many architects, Chalgrin no less than Servandoni.

The chief architects of the years of transition were Pierre Contant d'Ivry
and J.-G. Soufflot, whose designs for churches—especially Soufflot's
Ste.-Geneviève—first suggested the form that the new architecture might
take. But Contant d'Ivry did not visit Rome, and Soufflot was first there
in the 1730s, before that interlude of enterprise and interaction between
the French *pensionnaires* and the Italian painters of views, the *vedutisti*. In
consequence, Soufflot's vision was to include little of novelty. The two
architects took over an established tradition: Contant d'Ivry one that was
French, Soufflot a late Renaissance formula. Neither was in any case greatly
interested in novel formal devices. The spur to their architecture was
structural finesse. The focus of interest in Contant d'Ivry's churches—at
Condé-sur-l'Escaut, Arras, and, even more, the Abbaye Royale de Penthémont (106 Rue de Grenelle, Paris), of 1747 to 1756, and his unfinished
project for the Madeleine, designed in 1761—is the refinement of
construction. He experimented continually to reduce the mass of his
structures and to make more daring his vaulting techniques.

Soufflot's concern for the way in which a building was made and how
it might operate efficiently was evident from the start in the theater he began
in 1754 in Lyons, in which the shape of the auditorium was conditioned
by the sight lines and acoustics already tested in the theaters of Italy—though
he went further than the Italians in introducing heating systems, tanks of
water for fire fighting, and new lighting devices. His facades were creditable
but dull. And at Ste.-Geneviève itself, as we have seen, though he was greatly
concerned with the formal geometry, building the whole up from a regular
grid, and slowly developing the design of the dome so that it became more
and more pure in form, it was the manipulations of structure that drew forth
his best energies and his delight—and led also, it was said, to his death (from
worry). Considering that he presented himself as a reformer of architecture,
and operated with the fullest support of the Marquis de Marigny, how
disappointing is his output—in particular, those buildings in which structural
experiment could play but a small part: the sacristy of Notre-Dame, of 1756;
the École de Droit, facing Ste.-Geneviève, of 1771–83; and the buildings
for Marigny himself, which included a house in the Faubourg du Roule,
of 1769, notable for its Palladian window, and the orangery and nymphaeum
at the Château de Ménars. Soufflot relied too readily on what he had learned
in Italy.

The first architect to provide a model for a new and reformed classical
style and to infuse into it the well-considered grace and décorum of the
French tradition, which—despite the rococo irruption—had continued
strong from the reign of Louis XIV onward, was Ange-Jacques Gabriel
(1698–1782). He did not go to Italy, but trained with his father, *Premier*

120. Pierre Contant d'Ivry, Abbaye Royale de Penthémont, Paris, interior of the dome and vaults, 1747–56

Architecte du Roi, and succeeded to that title (as well as to *Directeur de l'Académie d'Architecture*) with the fullest confidence in his ability, in 1742; he retained the title until he retired, in 1774. He worked only at the king's command: Far too much of his time and energy was to be taken up with complex and futile schemes of alteration and extension to the royal palaces at Versailles, Fontainebleau, Compiègne, and Choisy. His *grands projets* no less than his *petits appartements*—and certainly the splendid and now beautifully restored theater that he built at Versailles for the dauphin's wedding in May 1770—are all deserving of study, and no doubt served to influence the course of architecture, but it was rather the succession of small and comparatively simple buildings that he erected for the court in the 1750s that was to indicate to his contemporaries how architecture might be reformed—Mme. de Pompadour's Pavillon Français (1749–50) at the Petit Trianon, Versailles, and her Ermitage (1749) at Fontainebleau, and the hunting lodges of Le Butard (1750), St.-Hubert (1755-57), Les Fausses-Reposes (1756; virtually unrecorded), and La Muette (1764), in the forests around Versailles. They were all neat and restrained in treatment. The culmination of his career was the Petit Trianon itself, promised to Mme. de Pompadour in 1761, begun in 1762, but not taken up in earnest until 1764, one year after the Seven Years' War, and the year of her death. The interiors, with paneling by Honoré Guibert, were not completed until 1769. This is a perfect example of the most refined taste of the period, the forerunner of the architecture of Boullée, Ledoux, and others. All admired Gabriel's work, but it was in Paris that its impact was to be most forcibly felt, once again on the initiative of Mme. de Pompadour. Even before her brother became *Directeur Général des Bâtiments,* in 1751, Gabriel had been called upon to design the imposing École Militaire, begun that year, greatly revised in 1765, and continued by a succession of architects until 1788.

In 1748 architects had been asked to submit proposals for a townplanning venture to frame a commemorative statue of the king. About one hundred fifty projects were sent in for sites all over Paris. But the king, alarmed at the cost of acquiring the sites proposed, ceded a large area of ground at the end of the Tuileries gardens and ordered another competition in 1753. Only nineteen architects submitted on this occasion. Gabriel's design was finally chosen in 1755 and work was begun —and continued until 1775—to provide Paris with the noblest and also the most unusual square in Europe, the Place Louis XV (today the Place de la Concorde). The rectangular space was defined by ditches and balustrades, with small pavilions, topped with statues, to mark the cutoff corners. The whole was dominated by two majestic colonnaded buildings, fittingly commemorating Perrault's example at the Louvre. "On aurait beaucoup mieux fait," Laugier carped in his *Observations,* of 1765, "de retrancher l'énorme soubassement de ces deux façades, d'établir la péristile au rez-de-chaussée sur un perron, élevé de plusieurs marches, et de lui donner toute la hauteur du bâtiment" (p. 35). But Ledoux, less intractable, wrote in his *L'architecture,* "Voyez les colonnes

121. Pierre Contant d'Ivry, Palais-Royal, Paris, grand staircase, 1756–70

122. Pierre Contant d'Ivry, St.-Vaast, Arras, interior, designed 1754

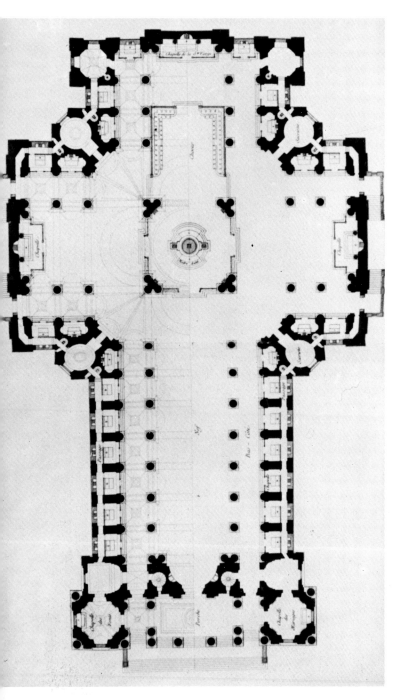

de la place Louis XV . . . on les aperçoit du quai du nord, à plus de trois cent toises; elles sont si bien conçues qu'elles s'effacent aux yeux, pour laisser à la pensée sublime idéal qui tient du prodige. C'est là, c'est dans ce fastueux édifice que brille le sentiment inépuisable de l'architecture française" (vol. 1, 1804, p. 108). One cannot be altogether sure that no sarcasm was intended here, for, like Laugier, Ledoux ridiculed the fussines of the detail. Yet Gabriel's influence on later generations of architects was enormous. He was the exact counterpart of Jacques-François Blondel, a man of moderation and common sense in all things, wanting restraint and no great novelty, balance without violent movement or contrast. Together they provided a sound basis for the future.

With the signing of the Treaty of Paris in 1763 and the ending of the Seven Years' War, building activity began once again in Paris on an unprecedented scale. Whole new quarters sprang up within a few years on the site of the northern ramparts, where the new boulevards were laid out. Farther to the north toward Montmartre, to the west bordering the Champs-Élysées, and in scattered pockets to the south, a succession of small and elegant villas was built in imitation of Italian casinas, Vitruvius's *aedes pseudourbanae*. These marked the beginnings of a suburban development and were termed *folies*, not to account for any whimsicality—though many were bizarre enough—but because they were intended as retreats, hidden by foliage and trees. A new generation of architects emerged, then, to take control and impose their ideas, a generation inspired by Blondel, Gabriel, and Soufflot, but aiming at something different, something more severely classical, more starkly monumental and large in scale.

"La plupart de nos élèves s'y trompent-ils tous les jours," Blondel wrote in the fourth volume of his *Cours d'architecture*, in 1773, "il leur parât plus aisé d'arriver aux compositions gigantesques, qu'aux proportions de la belle architecture" (p. lxx). Yet he was able to appreciate the largeness of scale and the simple geometry of the circular Halle aux Blés that Nicolas Le Camus de Mézières was to build right in the heart of the Marais, on the site of the old Hôtel de Soissons, between 1763 and 1767. This was not, strictly, a classically inspired work though contemporaries did liken it to an antique amphitheater and Laugier himself was moved to write, in 1765, even before its completion, that it was likely to become the finest building in Paris. When, in 1782 and 1783, Jacques-Guillaume Legrand (1743–1808) and Jacques Molinos (1743–1831) covered the circular central court with a giant dome, thirty-nine meters (one hundred twenty-nine feet) in diameter, of a light timber construction—similar to that proposed by Philibert de l'Orme for a nun's dormitory at Montmartre—the building appeared the most complete expression in France of the current liking for bold geometrical form. It was referred to as an equivalent of the Panthéon, which it almost equaled in size, and was to be inordinately admired by architects of the new generation.

The architects with whom we will deal first, Peyre, de Wailly, and

124. Pierre Contant d'Ivry, the
Madeleine, Paris, interior, begun
1764

125. Jacques-Germain Soufflot, design
for the Hôtel de Marigny, Faubourg
du Roule, Paris, 1769

126. Jacques-Germain Soufflot,
nymphaeum for the Marquis de
Marigny, Château de Ménars (Loire),
1764

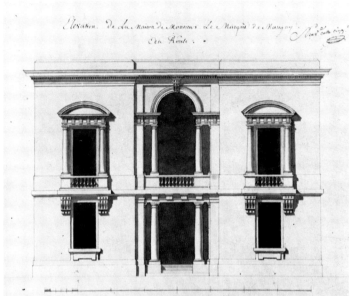

127. Ange-Jacques Gabriel, Pavillon Français, garden of the Petit Trianon, Versailles, 1749–50

128. Ange-Jacques Gabriel, Le Butard, a hunting lodge near Marly, 1750

129. Ange-Jacques Gabriel, Place de la Concorde

130. Ange-Jacques Gabriel, building on the north side of the Place de la Concorde, Paris, 1758–75

Moreau-Desproux, had all been to Rome, though only two had won the Grand Prix. The most advanced was Marie-Joseph Peyre (1730–1785), an innovator of great power. His influence flashed suddenly into the international sphere with the publication, in 1765, of his *Oeuvres d'architecture,* dedicated to the Marquis de Marigny, and was instantly absorbed and lasted longer than that of most of his contemporaries. He was a pupil of Blondel, Denis Jossenay, and Louis-Adam Loriot. In 1571 he won the Grand Prix with a design for a public fountain, a grand affair with projecting side pavilions made up of Doric columns *in antis* supporting unadorned entablatures and pediments. The skyline is enlivened with statues and a dome, topped with a feature that looks something like an antique sarcophagus. But it is in no sense a design in the antique spirit; it is very characteristically a product of Blondel's school. In the spring of 1753 Peyre reached Rome, where he was to find at least one fellow pupil, William Chambers, and was to be joined within eighteen months by two more, Charles de Wailly (1730–1798) and Pierre-Louis Moreau-Desproux. Together with them Peyre was to explore the monuments of the city and measure the thermae, the circuses, and, in particular, Hadrian's Villa.

He soon put these studies to use. Not long after his arrival in Rome he entered and won a competition at the Accademia di San Luca for a cathedral and two related palaces, one for an archbishop and the other for the canons. His designs show that, though he had studied carefully both Michelangelo's and Bernini's work at St. Peter's, he was also incorporating aspects of antique architecture into his work. From this period dates his extraordinary fondness for freestanding columns. His cathedral, a Greek cross surmounted by a great dome with four subsidiary cupolas, is set in a circular colonnade circumscribed by a circular space and an even larger colonnade, copied directly from Bernini. The two palaces, square buildings planned around open courtyards, are set laterally on either side of the circle thus formed. The scheme is vast. But it is no less vast, though perhaps less advanced, than that for an academic center he prepared a few years later, in 1756. The main building this time is square in plan, though diminished in area by the inclusion of two grand semicircular courts. It is far more overtly antique in conception in that it contains a variety of rooms and halls of different geometrical shapes, all toplit, cleverly counterpointing one another and derived for the most part from Hadrian's Villa, but also no doubt from Piranesi's own variations on this theme. The main building, topped by a colonnaded drum, is again encompassed by columns, and is placed in a square court delimited by a range of buildings screened by more freestanding columns. This court is flanked by a "cirque . . . pour les révolutions militaires" and a naumachia, modeled, naturally, on Roman circuses, but terminating in hemicycles of serried columns.

The giant formality of these designs—though not at all unusual within the context of the competitions of the Accademia di San Luca—profoundly affected the future of architecture when they were published, together with

131. Ange-Jacques Gabriel, Place
Louis XV (now Place de la
Concorde), Paris, designed 1753,
executed 1755–75. Engraving by
G. L. Le Rouge

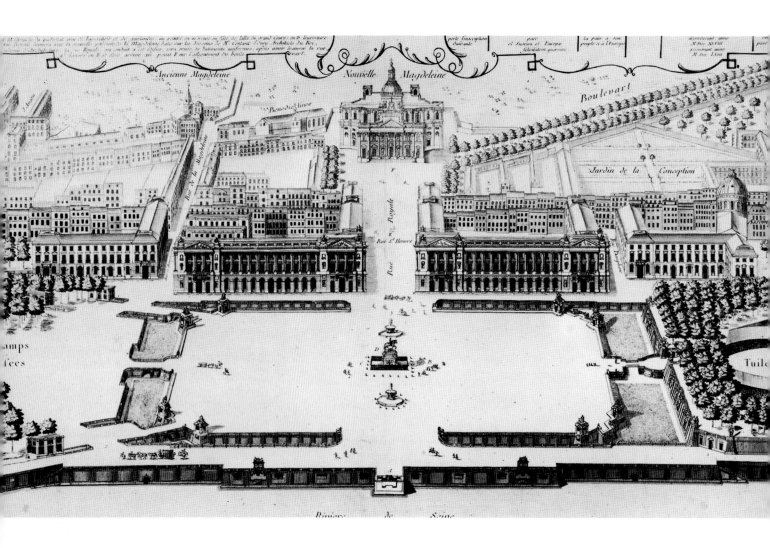

a similar though slightly more commonplace project for a sovereign's palace, in the *Oeuvres d'architecture,* in 1765. They had no doubt exercised their potent influence on a number of architects even before their publication. Certainly their sheer magnificence of scale finds its parallel in the drawings of the Grand Prix winners of the early 1760s. And Peyre's insistence on the use of columns, so that all architecture appears as a sequence of columnar episodes (calling to mind Frézier's horrified comment on Cordemoy, "Il nevoulait partout que des colonnes, isolées et dégagées"; *Mémoires de Trévoux,* 1704, p. 161), can be traced in the works of such architects as Jacques Gondoin and Robert Adam long before it served to transform the late eighteenth-century architecture of France and England. Peyre's strong liking for toplighting was also to be echoed in the undertakings of Gondoin, Adam, and George Dance, the younger, before the end of the 1760s. Peyre wrote several articles at this time for the *Mercure de France* (reprinted in the second edition of his *Oeuvres d'architecture,* in 1795), one of which dealt with the planning arrangements of the ancient Romans, upholding for imitation their single-story buildings, with service areas below, made up of rooms of different shapes and sizes packed together and lit from above. "Les romaines," he wrote, "étaint si persuadés de l'effet et de la beauté des grandes pièces éclairées par les voûtes, que, non seulement ils les pratiquaient dans les palais de leurs empereurs et dans les monuments publics, mais aussi dans les maisons des particuliers, et on y voyat toujours quelques salles principales dans ce genre" (p. 11).

In only a handful of buildings in Paris, however, all of a fanciful kind, were the vastness of scale, the complexity of planning, and the experimental lighting effects to be realized. The most ambitious was the Colisée, built between 1769 and 1771 to the designs of Louis-Denis Le Camus, at the top end of the Champs-Élysées. This pleasure dome soon deteriorated and was demolished within fifteen years, though its spectacular effects were recorded in sketches by Gabriel de Saint-Aubin. In 1770 Victor Louis proposed a similar, if less elaborate, layout for a vauxhall in the Bois de Boulogne, which was never built, although a related enterprise, the Cirque Royal, designed by Nicolas Lenoir le Romain or Jacques Cellerier (1742–1814), was opened on the boulevards in 1775. Between 1774 and 1785 Henri Piètre (c. 1725–after 1785), a pupil of Jean-Silvain Cartaud, together with A.-T. Brongniart, completed a smaller, though private and permanent and thus more remarkable, pavilion for the Duc d'Orléans in the Rue de Provence, adjoining the house that Brongniart had built for the duke's morganatic wife, Mme. de Montesson. The Pavillon d'Orléans, an altogether charming work, was closest in appearance to Peyre's ideal, especially as illustrated—no doubt inaccurately—by J.K. Krafft and P.-N. Ransonnette in the *Plans, coupes, élévations des plus belles maisons et des hôtels construits à Paris et dans les environs,* iu 1802.

Although Peyre had returned to Paris from Rome in 1756, it was not until 1762 that he was called upon to build his first—but very remarkable—

135, 136. Ange-Jacques Gabriel,
Salle de l'Opéra, Versailles, 1748–70

work, a *folie,* the Hôtel Leprêtre de Neubourg, at Clos Payen, south of Paris. This was built in the same year in which Gabriel produced the revised design for the equally remarkable but more elegant and less reserved Petit Trianon, and four years after Stuart's Doric temple at Hagley Park in Worcestershire was completed. Unlike Stuart, however, Peyre was not concerned with imitating antique architecture, but, following Palladio, he wished to distill its effects and infuse them into his work. The Hôtel Leprêtre de Neubourg is, in essence, neoclassical. It is, perhaps, the first strictly neoclassical building in France (though in appearance it is not at all unlike William Kent's Wakefield Lodge, at Potterspury in Northamptonshire, built about 1745 or soon after). Like many of Jules Hardouin Mansart's houses, it rests on a stylobate and consists broadly of two pedimented blocks joined by a rectangular mass to which a portico of six Doric columns, carrying a horizontal entablature, is appended. Leading up to the portico is a divided flight of stairs. The composition is compact, with unadorned wall surfaces— apart from a few niches—and well-spaced door and window openings, without surrounds; despite all its symmetry, there is a true neoclassical reluctance to emphasize the center. The principal entrance itself is placed not on the main axis of the house but at the side, and the planning reflects this fondness for underemphasis. The stair is enclosed and played down, as Peyre had noted was usually the case in antique architecture. The entrance and stair hall, decorated with columns, lead to the dining room, which opens in turn on to the salon and then to the principal bedchambers and dressing rooms. There are no passages. Gone is the marvelous complexity and refinement of arrangement that Blondel had lauded as the great French contribution to architecture. Here is a baldly empirical arrangement, almost antique in character, suggesting that Peyre's innovations were applicable on even the smallest of domestic scales.

137, 138. Nicolas Le Camus de
Mézières, Halle aux Blés, Paris,
exterior and interior, 1763–67.
Drawings by Maréchal

Extérieur de la Halle au Blé

Peyre's next design was less severe. In April 1763 he drew up the plans of a house for the Prince de Condé, intended for a site opposite the Palais du Luxembourg, delimited today by the Rue de Condé, the Rue Monsieur-le-Prince, and the Rue de Vaugirard. The exaggerated aspect of his Roman projects is at once apparent in the perspective sketch (illustrated in the *Oeuvres d'architecture*), though the plan has none of that novelty. It is, indeed, not unlike that for an ideal château that Blondel drew for his pupils, though the central feature of Peyre's design—a low-domed rotunda containing a freestanding circle of columns behind which four symmetrical flights of stairs rise, preceded by a flat-topped portico—is an updated and purified version of the Panthéon. The most striking feature, however, is a columnar screen, with a triumphal arch enclosing the entrance court. This theme can be traced back to Cordemoy, and to Delamair'sa Hôtel de Soubise of the same period, and it was to be illustrated with flourishes by both Blondel and Neufforge in the 1750s. It was taken up in 1764 by Gabriel for the château at Compiègne, and a few years later suitably flattened, by Gondoin at the École de Chirurgie, Paris. The most direct transcription from Peyre, however, was the derivative masterpiece of Nicolas-Marie Potain's son-in-law, Pierre Rousseau (1751–1810), the Hôtel de Salm (now the Palais de la Légion d'Honneur), at 64 Rue de Lille, Paris, built between 1782 and 1785. In England, Robert Adam introduced the idea for the Admiralty Screen at Whitehall in 1759, soon after his return from Italy, but missed the point in placing a blank screen-wall immediately behind the colonnade.

From the first, Peyre was conscious of himself as an innovator. His purpose, he declared in the *Oeuvres d'architecture,* was to show how the works of the ancient Romans might be imitated to counteract the established French tradition, yet after the publication of his book he did very little work of importance. He became *Contrôleur* at Choisy. In 1767 he was admitted to the Académie, and throughout the rest of his life he submitted a number of schemes for reconstructions and new buildings (at least two of his houses in Paris survive today: the Hôtel de Nivernais, 10 Rue de Tournon, and the adjoining 11 Rue Garancière). But his only significant work was the Théâtre-Français (later Théâtre de l'Odéon, new Théâtre de France), designed in collaboration with his friend Charles de Wailly.

A pupil of Legeay and Blondel, de Wailly won the Grand Prix in 1752 with a design for a facade for a vast palace with a concave central feature screened with giant Corinthian columns, the whole preceded by a triumphal arch and a much lower curved colonnaded screen adapted from Bernini's at St. Peter's. Clearly, Peyre was to be indebted to this design for his *grands projets.* De Wailly generously offered to share his prize with his friend Pierre-Louis Moreau-Desproux, who, for three successive years, had come was a man of no great talent: He built, as we have seen the Hôtel de Chavannes (1756–58), the Théâtre de l'Opéra at the Palais-Royal (1763–70), and the Pavillon Carré de Beaudouin, on the heights of Ménilmontant (1770). All these works are of interest, and show promise, but all are

139. *Marie-Joseph Peyre, competition project for a cathedral submitted to the Accademia di San Luca, Rome, 1753*

140. *Marie-Joseph Peyre, project for an academy, designed at Rome in 1756*

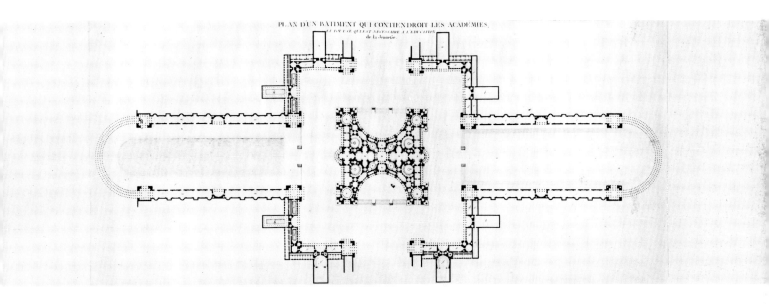

PLAN D'UN BATIMENT QUI CONTIENDROIT LES ACADÉMIES, *ET TOUT CE QUI EST NÉCESSAIRE À L'ÉDUCATION de la Jeunesse.*

unsatisfactory in that they lack tension of design. Moreau-Desproux was sustained by the family post he inherited in 1763, the *Maître des Bâtiments de la Ville de Paris.* He was the last to hold that title. De Wailly, however, was a challenging man. On his return from Rome he opened an *atelier* where he taught a number of architects—among them the Russians Vasili Ivanovich Bazhenov (1737–1799), Ivan Yegorovich Starov (1743–1808), and Fiodor Ivanovich Volkhov (1755–1803). In 1767 de Wailly became *Contrôleur* at Versailles under Gabriel, and in the same year he was literally forced into the *première classe* of the Académie Royale de Peinture et de Sculpture by Marigny, who greatly admired his work. Four years later he was elected to the Académie Royale de Peinture et de Sculpture, the only architect to achieve this distinction apart from that maverick recorder of ruins Clérisseau.

Charles-Louis Clérisseau (1722–1820) was the painter of the Ruin Room at S. Trinità dei Monti, in Rome, that was so admired by Piranesi, designer of the early arabesque decorations for Grimod de la Renière's salon in the Rue Boissy-d'Anglas (1774/75), and architect of the Palais du Gouverneur (now the Palais de Justice), in Metz (built between 1776 and 1789). De Wailly's activity was almost as diverse but his development was less consistent. Indeed, his ouput is baffling. In Rome, for instance, he made drawings of the ceiling of Il Gesù and of Bernini's *Throne of Saint Peter* with an obvious interest in the richness of form and the atmospheric qualities of lighting. Many of his interiors, such as the *salone* of the Palazzo Spinola in Genoa (1772–73), the Chapelle de la Vierge in St.-Sulpice (1777–78), and even the rooms of the old Hôtel d'Argenson (redecorated in 1784), are overabundant and exuberant in a Baroque sort of way. For the Marquis d'Argenson's country house, Les Ormes, he designed an elaborate stair in about 1771 (with which Sir William Chambers was in some way involved), derived from that by G. B. Piacentini, built in 1695 into the Palazzo dei Ranuzzi (now di Giustizia) in Bologna, where de Wailly had been made a member of the Academy in 1755. For the Marquis de Marigny, at the Château de Ménars, he designed a garden pavilion in 1768 or 1769, with partially fluted Doric columns like those of the Temple of Apollo at Delos, the only direct imitation of the Greek Doric in France, and for the crypt of St.-Leu-St.-Gilles, in Paris (1773–80), he used columns derived from the temples at Paestum, but with a square base and reeding rather than concave fluting—Gothic in effect rather than classical. In his whole manner of composing buildings there is this same discordance of vision: Some are made up of small, contrasting elements of divergent shapes and scale; others consist of large, simplified geometrical masses. Yet his major works, if not always as hard and stark as those of his contemporaries, are undeniably neoclassical.

The first and boldest of de Wailly's country houses, Montmusard, on the outskirts of Dijon, was designed in 1764 for Olivier Fyot de la Marche, first president of the Parlement of Burgundy. The plan was marked by a complex yet wonderfully lucid geometry and was consciously antique in spirit; it was to be the first secular building in eighteenth-century France to be dedicated as a temple, a temple to the muses. This was clearly expressed in its arrangement. Only a fragment was built, but de Wailly's original plan survives, as does a painting by Panini's pupil Jean-Baptiste Lallemand (1716–1803), to convey the architect's intention. The plan is rectangular, almost square, with just the suggestion in the articulation of four corner pavilions. On the garden side a domed circular salon projects to form a semicircle; at the entrance front an open colonnaded temple is formed, cutting into the mass of the building. The detailed planning was more intricate than usual. The facades, though, were treated as single story, with an attic above and a balustrade over, the whole unified by an overall pattern of rustication. There were no moldings around the window and door openings. Had it been completed in this form, the house would have been the most daring yet noble in France. But money ran out in 1772, long before the building was finished. In the following year de Wailly exhibited a design at the Salon for an even grander variant on the theme for Catherine the Great, dedicated this time to Minerva. Much later, in 1812, J. K. Krafft was to publish an altogether different design for the Château de Montmusard, consisting of a cylinder linked to two cubic blocks. The *raison d'être* of this arrangement was the domed open circular *salon d'été* at first-floor level, surrounded by two rows of columns with the staircase rising between them. This, no doubt, was derived from Peyre's stair hall for the Hôtel de Condé, though it may be distantly linked also to Balthasar Neumann's oval stair at the Episcopal Palace at Bruchsal, in Baden-Württemberg, built in 1731. Such central focus on the stair hall is unusual in France. In England experiments with a circular domed and colonnaded stair hall began with a design of 1759 for York House, Pall Mall, by Sir William Chambers; he, as we have seen, seems to have collaborated in 1774 with de Wailly on the latter's more complex variation at the Château d'Ormes. The most notable of these stair halls, however, was that designed in 1770 by James Paine for Wardour Castle, in Wiltshire.

The five town houses that de Wailly planned for the Rue de la Pépinière, Paris (only two were built—the sculptor Augustin Pajou's in 1776, and his own, in 1778—and a third was begun in 1779), consist of an array of simple blocks, some of them surmounted by small pediments, others by rounded gables; they were evidently intended to form a unified architectural panorama of lively interest. The handling of the forms is wonderfully resourceful, if we are to judge by the illustrations in Krafft's and Ransonnette's *Plans . . . des plus belles maisons . . . à Paris.* Another circular colonnaded stair hall is introduced to give a central focus. But the constant setbacks in the composition, made up of small and varied elements, would have weakened the total effect.

In 1767 de Wailly was called upon with Peyre to design his greatest work, the Théâtre-Français (later Théâtre de l'Odéon, today Théâtre de France), on the site of the Hôtel de Condé. In the following years he traveled to England, Germany, and twice to Italy in order to study theaters. The history of the building is complex, with many changes of site and client and much rivalry involving a takeover at one stage by Moreau Desproux, who had not only benefited from de Wailly's friendship, as a student, but was by then the brother-in-law of Peyre. But the building that was started in May 1779 on the foundations set down by Moreau-Desproux (to be completed in 1782) was in most respects similar to his and de Wailly's joint project approved in 1770. The circular auditorium is contained entirely within a rectangular block, rusticated all over, with arcades on the ground floor along the sides and the rear, rectangular windows on the second floor, and circular openings in the attic story. The whole is surmounted by a high pyramid roof. In front of the building is a Doric portico with a horizontal entablature, at one time intended to carry two reclining figures and a lyre, a symbolic dedication to Apollo. Later, in 1786, when the theater was to be converted into an opera house, de Wailly prepared a design in which two lodges and, further back, a pavilion with a Venetian window, niches, and sculptural decorations were to be set above the portico, providing a trinity of features in a different key from the rest. But the building that was erected, sober and severe in form, was made only marginally more severe when, after a fire in 1799, it was rebuilt by Chalgrin.

The bare account offered of the careers of Peyre and de Wailly gives some indication of the dramatic changes that took place in domestic architecture after 1763: changes in massing and the treatment of wall surfaces; changes in planning, from reliance on the simple *enfilade* to a complexity of

interlocking rooms of different shapes and sizes; and changes also of detail. In the whole range of building types there were similar significant developments. More public buildings were erected than ever before. Theaters, which multiplied throughout France in this period, provide a particularly fruitful field for study. The practical demands of acoustics, sight lines, lighting, fire precaution, and construction resulted in notable departures from the norm. A progression—indeed, a progress—may be traced, starting with the new theater at Metz, or, more properly, with Soufflot's theater in Lyons begun in 1754, and including no less than twenty in Paris, dominated by Peyre's and de Wailly's designs for the Théâtre-Français. The building of theaters extended also to the provincial centers: to Amiens, where Jean Rousseau built a theater in 1778; to Besançon, where Ledoux was active from 1775 to 1784; and especially to Bordeaux, where the most magnificent theater in all of France, a great rectangular block preceded by a portico of twelve giant Corinthian columns, was erected between 1773 and 1780. This, containing a stair hall that is one of the splendors of eighteenth-century architecture, is still virtually intact. The designer was Louis-Nicolas-Victoire Louis (1731–c. 1807), a pupil of L.-A. Loriot, who called himself Victor Louis after he won the equivalent of the

Grand Prix in 1755 and went to Rome for three years. Upon his return to France he established an extremely fashionable practice, first under the protection of Mme. Geoffrin, as architect to the king of Poland, then as designer of a majestic temporary ballroom for the Spanish ambassador's reception in honor of the dauphin's marriage in 1770 (Chalgrin set up an equally noble ballroom for the Austrian ambassador). But Louis made a name and a living for himself chiefly in Bordeaux, where he built a number of *hôtels* in the new quarters adjoining his theater—the Hôtels Saige (1774–80), Fontfrède (1774–76), Legrix, de la Molère, de Rolly, and de Nairac (begun 1775). He was also responsible for several country houses, such as the Château de Virasel, near Marmande. The most ambitious by far was the Château de Bouilh, at St.-André-de-Cubzac, for the Marquis de la Tour du Pin, begun in 1786 but realized only in part. Even the unfinished fragment reveals it as one of the grandest country houses of the century. Louis's project of 1785 for the Place Louis XVI, on the site of the Château Trompette (now the Place des Quinconces), Bordeaux was of an equivalent heightened scale: a hemicycle of linked houses, 400 meters (1, 320 feet) in diameter, was to open on to and extend along the Garonne River, but they were never begun. In 1772, while still busy in Bordeaux, he planned

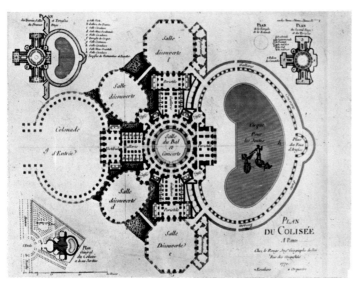

143. Louis-Denis Le Camus,
Colisée, Champs-Élysées, Paris, plan,
1769–71

144. Gabriel de Saint-Aubin, La
Fête du Colisée. London, Wallace
Collection

145. Henry Piètre with Alexandre-
Théodore Brongniart, or, more likely,
Brongniart alone, Pavillon d'Orléans,
Paris, elevation and plan, 1774

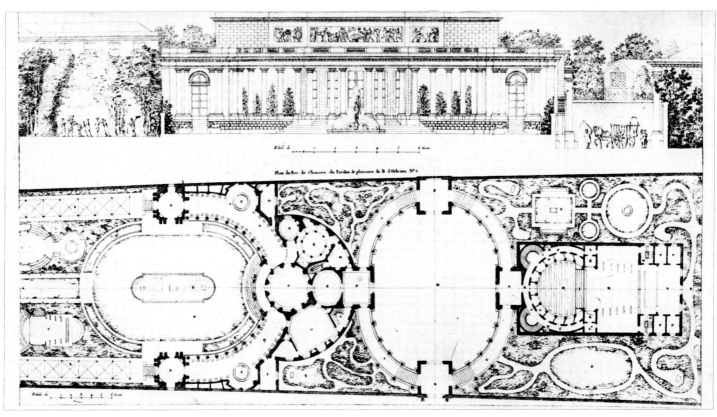

the Hôtel de l'Intendance (now the Préfecture) in Besançon, to be carried out faithfully during the next four years by a pupil of Blondel, Nicolas Nicole (1702–1784). Later, Louis was to return to Paris, upon which he conferred his expansive vision in 1781 in the form of the Galeries du Palais-Royal and a related theater, rebuilt by Julien Guadet in 1902, after a fire. The theater was notable for its cast-iron trusses and reinforcements, all lovingly phototraphed by Guadet's son Paul in their ruined state.

One of Louis's earliest works, the Chapelle des Âmes du Purgatoire in the church of Ste.-Marguerite-de-Charonne, Paris, designed in 1763, was no less distinctive a contribution to the evolution of church design than his theaters. The chapel—seemingly flanked by rows of Ionic columns supporting a horizontal entablature, without a projecting cornice, designed in imitation of a frieze from a sarcophagus, and carrying a coffered barrel vault—was, in fact, a *trompe l'oeil* painting by Paolo Antonio Brunetti, who, together with his father, Gaetano, and Charles-Joseph Natoire, had painted the scene of ruins on the walls of the chapel in Boffrand's Enfants-Trouvés (1746–51). It was a startling novelty, hailed by the Abbé Laugier in his *Observations* as "un des plus beaux dessins d'architecture que nous ayons à Paris" (p. 115). The revolution in church design that Louis thus acknowledged, proclaimed first by the Perraults with their project for Ste.-Geneviève and later by Cordemoy and Laugier, and culminating at just this time *en grand* with Soufflot's Ste.-Geneviève and Contant d'Ivry's Madeleine, was given convincing form a year or two later in the designs of three basilican churches: St.-Philippe-du-Roule, in Paris; St.-Symphorien, at Versailles; and St.-Louis, at St.-Germain-en-Laye. These, one should note, were preceded by St.-Vincent-des-Augustins, in Lyons—built in 1759 by Léonard Roux (1725–c. 1794), an associate of Soufflot—which was finished only in 1789 and was thus not to achieve the fame or the influence of the Parisian exemplars of the genre.

The most famous of these, of course, is St.-Philippe-du-Roule, the work of another pupil of Loriot and also of Boullée, Jean-François-Thérèse Chalgrin (1739–1811).

He won the Grand Prix at the age of nineteen, and traveled to Rome the following year. From Rome, he corresponded with Soufflot. On his return to France he became *Inspecteur des Travaux de la Ville de Paris,* under Moreau-Desproux, and in this capacity supervised the building of the Hôtel de Saint-Florentin, just off the Place Louis XV, according to the designs of Gabriel. Chalgrin himself designed the gateway and entrance door. He was commissioned in 1764 by the Comte de Saint-Florentin, as *Ministre de la Maison du Roi,* to design a new church. But the site was not acquired until May 1767, the plans approved by the Académie only in August 1768, and work finally begun in 1772, to be completed in 1784. The arrogant novelty of the design—with its freestanding Ionic columns ranged down the nave and continuing around the curve of the apse, a coffered barrel vault above, and a squat Tuscan portico outside—was thus not to be appreciated until

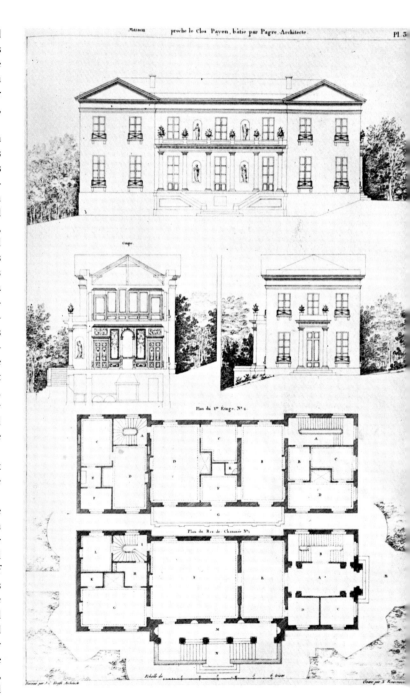

very late in the century. Today the church has lost the coherency and the feeling for classical unity so evident in old engravings, for it has twice been altered, once in 1846 by Étienne-Hippolyte Gode—who introduced windows into the vaults and built the Chapelle de la Vierge at the east end, opening up a vista through the screen of the apse—and in 1853 by Victor Baltard, who added the Chapelle des Catéchismes. Some of the initial quality was captured, however, by Chalgrin's pupil Jean-Baptiste Kléber (1753–1800), the future general, who copied the arrangement in 1774 for the Capuchin chapel at Strasbourg. Indeed, Kléber's version was even closer to Chalgrin's original intentions, for he retained the vault of stone complete with its flying buttresses that was omitted at St.-Philippe-du-Roule when a timber and plaster vault was built instead for economy.

Long before Chalgrin's church was complete, a similar basilica, designed in 1764 with partially fluted Doric columns supporting a horizontal entablature and surmounted by a coffered barrel vault (broken to accommodate windows), and preceded by a portico with freestanding Tuscan columns, was erected at Versailles. This was the church of St.-Symphorien de Montreuil, consecrated in 1770. The architect was Louis-François Trouard (1729–1794), once again a pupil of Loriot, who won the Grand Prix in 1753, arrived in Rome in the autumn of 1754, and spent three years there before returning to work at Versailles, where he was responsible for the barracks of the Gardes-françaises and other large and unremarkable

buildings. He became architect at Orléans cathedral and at the Économats Royaux (an administration that spent the income from vacant bishoprics and estates confiscated from Protestants). In this capacity he was to design both St.-Symphorien and the Chapelle des Catéchismes at the east end of St.-Louis, in Versailles, in 1764–70. This chapel, divided with screens of columns, appears to have been derived directly from a plate in Piranesi's *Prima parte*. Another Italian-inspired church once attributed to Trouard but now more convincingly shown to be the work of Étienne-François Legrand—Trouard's successor at both the Économats Royaux and Orléans cathedral—is St.-Louis, in Port Marly (Yvelines), dating from 1778, the year in which Nicholas Revett built a comparable church at Ayot St. Lawrence, in England.

Legrand's successor at Orléans, in turn, was Trouard's pupil Pierre-Adrien Pâris (1747–1819). Pâris did not win the Grand Prix, but nonetheless traveled to Rome in 1770–71, in the company of Trouard's son; he returned to France in 1774 and four years later joined the Menus-Plaisirs, the administration responsible for royal fêtes, festivities, and spectacles, and to serve the world of fashion as well with designs for neat, precise, and altogether charming town and country houses. Pâris's chief claim to distinction, though, derives from his larger works—a vast Italianate palace at Porrentruy, for the Prince Bishop of Basel, begun in 1776 but never completed; the town hall at Neuchâtel, erected between 1784 and 1790 by the local builder Raimond; and the hospital at Bourg-en-Bresse. When he died in 1819 he left to his native Besançon an unrivaled collection of drawings by such artists as François Boucher, Jean-Honoré Fragonard, and Hubert Robert, together with an even more extensive array of his own drawings done on his early visit to Italy. He made other drawings during later visits to Rome in 1783, and with his students, after 1806, when he became director of the Académie de France à Rome. These illustrate all the buildings he studied, whether antique, Renaissance, or later, and include not only Palladio's works and those of Giulio Romano and the Sangallos but also Pirro Ligorio's buildings and other oddities such as the Collegio Elvetico, in Milan (so admired by Gondoin), and the Certosa, at Ema (which would prove so exciting to Le Corbusier). All Pâris's original designs are still in Besançon, demonstrations of the exotic range of his sources, and, as such, urgently requiring investigation.

The third of the basilican churches being considered here, St.-Louis, in St.-Germain-en-Laye, was, like St.-Symphorien, also designed in 1764, though work was not begun for two years; it was interrupted and resumed only in 1787, just before the Revolution, and was finally built in 1823–24 by Alexandre-Jacques Malpièce and A.-J. Moutier. The original architect was Nicolas-Marie Potain (1713–1796), a man of Soufflot's generation, who had won the Grand Prix in 1738 and had remained in Rome until 1744, where, like Soufflot, he measured St. Peter's, and then traveled through Italy studying theaters. The result, in 1763, was an unusual project for a theater on a corner site. The auditorium, with its axes on the diagonals, was

149. Pierre Rousseau, Hôtel de Salm
(now Palais de la Légion d'Honneur),
Paris, entry colonnade, 1782–85

150. *Pierre Rousseau, Hôtel de Salm*
(now Palais de la Légion d'Honneur),
Paris, facade on the Quai Anatole
France, 1782–85

151. *Charles de Wailly, Grand Prix*
design for a palace, 1752

elliptical in plan, with receding tiers or seats. The wide proscenium opening, divided up by columns, was to be recalled by Peyre and de Wailly. The elevations, however, are less striking: Two prostyle porticos of Ionic columns with balustrades above give the building an air of boldness, but the pattern of window openings and the decoration betray a fondness rather for Gabriel's brand of classicism. Potain was to work as Gabriel's assistant on the Place Louis XV from 1754 to 1770. His work was, not altogether surprisingly, much admired by Marigny. When, therefore, in 1762, Soufflot's fullest energies were required in Paris on Ste.-Geneviève, Marigny decided on Potain to replace him as architect of the new cathedral in Rennes. Soufflot's appointment dates from 1754; Potain's designs for the cathedral, based on those of Soufflot, were submitted to the Académie on July 26, 1762. They were revised the following year, and approved by the king on May 9, 1764. The surviving plan shows freestanding columns along the nave, on the foundations of a destroyed Gothic church. The nature of the vaulting is not indicated. Construction was started in 1786, to be stopped by the Revolution. Although the cathedral as it stands today was built between 1811 and 1844, it is tempting to think that this exemplary basilica, with its Ionic columns alongside the nave and continuing around the apse, its horizontal entablatures, and its coffered barrel vault, reflects Potain's early designs and thus, indirectly, Soufflot's first project (1754). Certainly this plan would have provided a prototype for all three basilicas designed about 1764, and would in some measure account for their simultaneous conception.

A number of churches of this type were to be built in the years that followed. One of the least visited, but the most elegant, is St.-Symphorien, at Gy, by the engineer Henri Frignet and the local architect Charles Colombot, constructed between 1769 and 1785 for the Bishop of Besançon. By the early nineteenth century the pattern was ubiquitous, accepted as as

159. Charles de Wailly, crypt,
St.-Leu-St.-Gilles, Paris, 1773–80

160. Charles de Wailly, Château de
Montmusard, Dijon, elevation and
ground-floor plan as illustrated
by J. K. Krafft, 1812

161. Charles de Wailly, Château de
Montmusard (now part of the École
St.-Dominique), Dijon, 1764–72

162. Detail of a painting of c. 1770
by Jean-Baptiste Lallemand, showing
the Château de Montmusard as
Charles de Wailly designed it in
1764. Dijon, Musée des Beaux-Arts

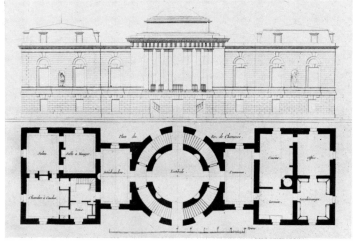

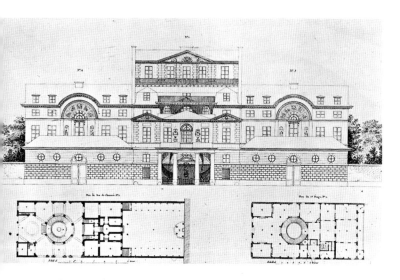

trite and well-tried formula; no one then cared about, or was aware of, the play of Gothic that had been so important an aspect of the eighteenth-century experiment.

Peyre, de Wailly, Louis, and Chalgrin have been presented as the first true representatives of the revised classical style of late eighteenth-century France, but no less important are Boullée, Jacques-Denis Antoine, Ledoux, Gondoin, Brongniart, and Bélanger—not one of whom was to win the Grand Prix, though Gondoin did travel to Italy. They made their debuts in the 1760s. Not all, though, were innovators. The youngest members of the group, Alexandre-Théodore Brongniart (1739–1813) and François-Joseph Bélanger (1744-1818), were indeed fashionable exponents rather than precursors of the new style. Heirs to Gabriel, excellent planners, and designers of taste, they managed to capture much of the elegance and grace of his best mid-century work and to infuse it into their new, more sober—if sometimes even grander—Parisian manner.

Brongniart, a pupil of Blondel and Boullée, began his career in 1765, when he built the theater at Caen, a building of little enough merit, which shows a liking for the works of Soufflot and, naturally, Blondel. The numerous houses that he built in Paris in the years following, however, reflect the influence of de Wailly and the smooth and flattening tastes of advanced classicism. All his *hôtels* are restrained in outline and pure in form, beautifully planned, with most of the rooms rectangular or square but a few of a circular or other geometrical shape to provide a degree of variety. The facades of the houses are, almost invariably, composed with regular roundheaded openings on the ground floor and rectangular bas-relief panels or windows above, each unit separated by giant pilasters. The roof line is always horizontal. Later he was to forego the pilasters, retaining only the most restrained and even rustication. His first mature work, the Hôtel de Montesson, of 1770 to 1771, in the Chaussée-d'Antin, thus has affinities with the late buildings of Gabriel, though it is understandably more reserved and crisply geometrical. This has now been demolished, along with his most ambitious work, the Hôtel de Sainte-Foix, of 1775, on the Rue Basse-du-Rempart, but many of his later *hôtels* survive, if only in part, and may easily be visited—the Hôtel de Monaco (now the Polish Embassy), of 1775–77, at 57 Rue St.-Dominique, and a nearby group: the Hôtel de Mlle. de Bourbon-Condé, of 1780–81, at 12 Rue Monsieur (now minus Clodion's relief panels); the Hôtel de Montesquiou, of the following year, at 20 Rue Monsieur; his own house, of the same date, at 49 Boulevard des Invalides; the Hôtel Chamblin, of about 1789, at 3-5 Rue Masseran; and the Hôtel Masserano, dating from 1787, at 11 Rue Masseran.

Before the Revolution Brongniart built only two important buildings outside the domestic range: the church of St.-Germain-l'Auxerrois, at Romainville, Paris, of 1785–87, recalling St.-Philippe-du-Roule in its internal arrangement but with far sturdier Doric columns in the nave, and the Couvent des Capucins de la Chaussée-d'Antin (now the Lycée Condorcet

165, 166. *Marie-Joseph Peyre and Charles de Wailly, Théâtre-Français (later Théâtre de l'Odéon, now Théâtre de France), Paris, section and view of the foyer and staircase showing the design of 1770*

167. *Marie-Joseph Peyre and Charles de Wailly, Théâtre-Français, Paris, 1779-82. Rebuilt after a fire in 1799. The house on the left, for the sculptor Augustin Pajou, was begun in 1776*

INTÉRIEUR DE LA NOUVELLE SALLE DE COMEDIE FRANÇAISE DE L'ANCIEN PROJET.

168. Jacques-Germain Soufflot,
Grand Théâtre, Lyons, plan, 1753
169. Jean Rousseau, theater, Amiens,
facade, 1778

170. Victor Louis, Grand Théâtre,
Bordeaux, cross section, 1773–80
171. Victor Louis, Grand Théâtre,
Bordeaux, view of the auditorium

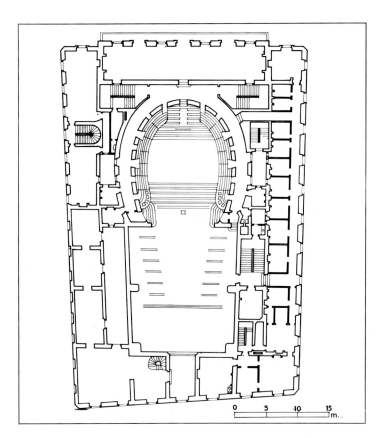

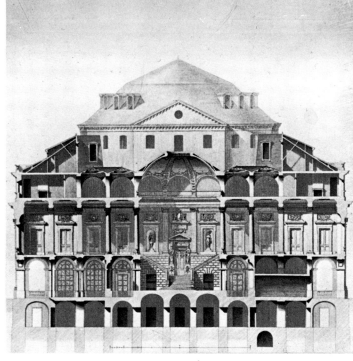

172. *Victor Louis, Grand Théâtre,*
Bordeaux, perspective view
173. *Victor Louis, Grand Théâtre,*
Bordeaux, longitudinal section

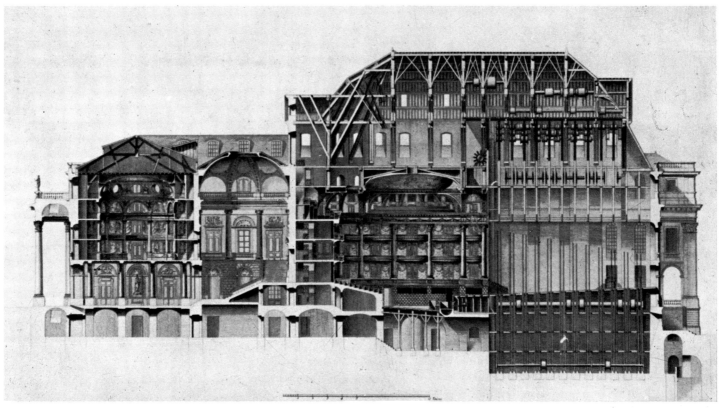

174. *Victor Louis, Grand Théâtre, Bordeaux, exterior, 1773-80*

175. *Victor Louis, Grand Théâtre, Bordeaux, staircase, 1773–80*

1/6. *Victor Louis, project for the Château de Bouilh, St.-André-de-Cubzac, begun 1786*

177. *Victor Louis, project for the Place Louis XVI, on the site of the Château Trompette (now Place des Quinconces), Bordeaux, 1785*

and the church of St.-Louis d'Antin), of 1780–83, where he showed for the first time an original temper of mind. In the courtyard he introduced columns of the Paestum type, but with smaller capitals and without fluting. The main facade is also more robust and geometrical. Two pedimented pavilions linked by a lower mass, each with its own doorway, are otherwise sparsely punctuated with no more than empty niches and two elongated bas-relief panels. The whole, however, is inclined to be precise rather than powerful.

His great post-Revolutionary work, the Bourse, designed in 1807 when he was sixty-eight, was likewise not the creation of a man fitted for design in the grand manner. Yet it seemed to contemporaries to embody many of their ideals, and even Perrault's and Cordemoy's theories find their fullest expression there. Giant Corinthian columns supporting a simple entablature and cornice surround the solid rectangle of a structure pierced by regularly spaced, arched rectangular openings. Even before it was transformed into a Greek cross in 1903, the building did not convey an impression of either magnitude or magnificence. It lacked the weight needed for success.

Bélanger, taught by Le Roy and Contant d'Ivry, began his career in 1767, when, at the age of twenty-three, he was appointed *Dessinateur aux Menus-Plaisirs.* The previous year he had perhaps traveled to England, recording some of his impressions in a notebook that is today in the library of the old École des Beaux-Arts. He was certainly in England in 1778, when he prepared a design—he was one of a succession of such designers, from Robert Adam in 1773 to Robert Smirke in 1819—for Lord Shelburne's gallery in Lansdowne House, off Berkeley Square. But, for the rest, his activity and work were to be concentrated in Versailles and Paris; through the Menus he came into contact with the Comte d'Artois, whose architect he became, and also with the great singer Sophie Arnould, whose lover and architect he became. During the next twenty years he designed almost exclusively for her distinguished group of admirers, thus earning the title "faiseur à la mode." But he was an architect of the highest competence and finesse. He established himself early, in 1769, with the Pavillon Lauraguais in the garden of the Hôtel de Brancas, in the Rue Taitbout—a dazzling temporary confection in which he was assisted by Clérisseau—but his most spectacular feat was the Pavillon de Bagatelle, designed, erected, and furnished between September 21 and November 26, 1777, the result of a wager between the Comté d'Artois and Marie Antoinette. The famous *jardin anglais* there was laid out from 1778 onward, with the advice of the Scotsman Thomas Blaikie, who had been employed first by the Comte de Lauraguais in Normandy. But Bélanger was soon to prove adept at this genre, too, notably at the Folie Saint-James in nearby Neuilly-sur-Seine (also begun with the help of Blaikie in 1778), and later, starting in 1784, on the grandest of scales, on the estate of the court banker Jean-Joseph de Laborde at Méréville, near Étampes. Here he would be succeeded by Hubert Robert, who was to claim the garden as his own.

X. *Victor Louis, Grand Théâtre, Bordeaux, staircase, 1773–80*
180. *Victor Louis, Chapelle des Âmes du Purgatoire. Ste.-Marguerite-de-Charonne, Paris, 1763–65 (painted by Paolo Antonio Brunetti)*

181. *Jean-François-Thérèse Chalgrin, St.-Philippe-du-Roule, Paris, interior, approved 1768, built 1772–84. Engraving by J.-N.-L. Durand*

182. *Jean-François-Thérèse Chalgrin, St.-Philippe-du-Roule, Paris, approved 1768, built 1772–84*

183. *Louis-François Trouard, Ste.-Symphorien de Montreuil, Versailles, east facade, 1764–70*

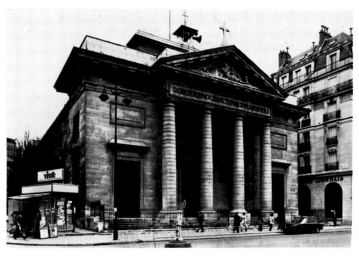

184. Louis-François Trouard,
St.-Symphorien de Montreuil,
Versailles, west façade, 1764–70

185. Louis-François Trouard,
St.-Symphorien de Montreuil,
Versailles, interior, 1764–70

Boullée, Ledoux, and Gondoin were not all as adept and as busy but they were innovators of influence and power. All three were pupils of Blondel, though Boullée intended a career as a painter and studied first with Jean-Baptiste Pierre and later with the architects Pierre-Étienne Lebon and Jean-Laurent Legeay; Ledoux worked also for Louis-François Trouard. Not one of them won the Grand Prix; Gondoin, however, the son of a skillful gardener at Choisy, was sent to Rome in 1761 at the instigation of the king, and during his stay of two years he became—and remained—a close friend of Piranesi. Rome, in the imaginations of Boullée and Ledoux, remained the pretentious place of Piranesi's assembled engravings, although the exaggerated fantasies for which they are held today in such uncritical esteem were not done, as one might expect, in their young and student days when Piranesi's influence was at its highest, but in the years that immediately preceded the Revolution and, in particular, in the idle years that followed. Their early works were, in comparison, almost restrained.

Étienne-Louis Boullée, by far the oldest member of the group, built little of importance. He made his reputation and demonstrated his ability as a teacher. At the early age of nineteen, it seems, he began to teach at the École des Ponts et Chaussées. Later he opened an *atelier* of his own from which emerged such distinguished architects as Brongniart, Chalgrin, J.-N.-L. Durand, N.-C. Girardin, Jacques-Pierre de Gisors, Antoine-François Peyre, Pâris, and Jean-Thomas Thibault. Though he taught for over fifty years, Boullée was not merely a pedagogue. His career began in 1752, when, together with his master, J.-B. Pierre, and the sculptor Étienne-Maurice Falconet, he began work on a dramatic *trompe l'oeil* decoration, greatly admired by Soufflot, in the Chapelle du Calvaire at St.-Roch, in Paris. But the works that first served to establish his reputation were the redecoration of the Hôtel de Tourolle (some of his *boiserie* survives) and a design for the entrance to the Hôpital de Charité, in the Rue Jacob, both dating from 1762. Thereafter, in quick succession, came eight *hôtels* in Paris—the Hôtel Alexandre (1763–66), the two Hôtels de Monville (1764), the Hôtel de Pernon (1768–71), the Hôtel de Thun (1769–71), the redecoration of the Hôtel d'Évreux (1774–78), the Hôtel de Brunoy (1775–79), and a speculative venture in the Rue Royale (1777–78). He worked on four houses near Paris: the financier Nicolas Beaujon's house at Issy-les-Moulineaux (1760–73), the Château de Perreux (begun 1761), the Château de Chaville (1764–66), and an extension to the Château de Chauvry (1783). Of these, only the first, the Hôtel Alexandre, at 16 Rue de la Ville-l'Évêque, survives, but drawings for the larger Hôtel de Brunoy enable us to imagine their effect. The planning is straightforward, consisting largely of rectangular rooms in *enfilade*. The compositions are of unusual rectangularity and compactness, the masses, packed tightly against each other, related by continuous cornices and stringcourses. The facades of the *corps de logis* (main building) are articulated, as a rule, with giant Ionic pilasters, each bay thus formed being punctuated with a rectangular or round-headed doorway and

186. *Jean-Baptiste Kléber, design for the Chapelle des Capucins, Strasbourg, 1774*

188. *Plate from Giambattista Piranesi's* Prima parte di architetture e prospettive, *1743, showing a Doric atrium*

187. *Louis-François Trouard, Chapelle des Catéchismes, St.-Louis, Versailles, 1764–70*

189. *Étienne-François Legrand, St.-Louis, Port Marly, west façade, 1778*

190, 191. Pierre-Adrien Pâris, design
for a palace for the Prince Bishop of
Basel, Porrentruy, details of exterior
and plan of the ground floor

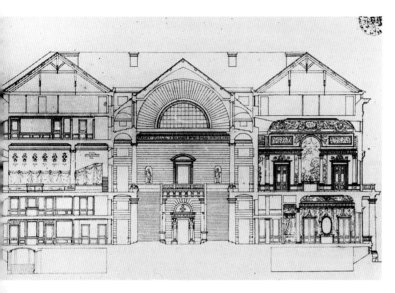

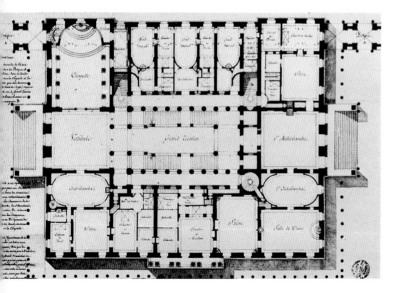

a bas-relief panel above. The result is a closely woven surface pattern, the grid of pilasters overlying the stringcourses and moldings—a theme to be taken up soon enough by Brongniart. The entrance fronts of the Hôtel Alexandre and the Château de Chaville offer a variation in the format of a portico with freestanding columns *in antis,* flanked by rectangular openings, each with a wreathed oval medallion above. But the effect is not much different. Only on the garden front of the Château de Chaville is something novel attempted, an overall pattern of rustication punctured by rectangular openings. The handling of the detail is not at all unlike that of de Wailly's exactly contemporary Château de Montmusard.

During the first phase of his career Boullée was also responsible for a series of projects for the Hôtel des Monnaies, starting in 1755 and continuing until 1767, when the commission was awarded to Jacques-Denis Antoine (1733–1801). Antoine, the son of a joiner who had gained his knowledge of architecture from a building contractor, was to take up Boullée's proposals with considerable success, to produce that noble structure, more than three hundred meters (almost one thousand feet) long, on the Quai de Conti, its regular pattern of close-set openings broken only by a slightly advancing central pavilion, with a giant Ionic order on an arcuated and rusticated ground floor, and, above, a heavy cornice with a high attic and statues in front. The effect, however, is one of monotony rather than monumentality. As Le Camus de Mézières was to remark, the architecture was too well-ordered to face the sunless north; it lacked movement. The only entirely satisfactory feature was the triple-arched vaulted entry, with coupled columns, and the great stair hall, which led from the entry to an equally magnificent salon above. In 1764 Boullée prepared a scheme for the conversion of Giovanni Giardini's Palais-Bourbon into an establishment for the Prince de Condé, a design that M.-J. Peyre, who also submitted a plan, was to describe to his nephew as "une machine immense," though today it does not seem particularly shocking but rather a suitably enlarged version of his early domestic projects. In 1775 Boullée became *Intendant des Bâtiments* to the Comte d'Artois, for whom he designed a sumptuous suite in the Enclos du Temple, including a room in the Turkish style. Two years later he resigned this position, but in 1780 he prepared drawings for the Comte d'Artois for a palace on the site of the Pépinières du Roule. This was an immense affair, whose giant formality and colonnaded vistas presaged the phantasmagoria to come. Yet it was the Hôtel de Brunoy rather that marked the change both in his approach and in his activity. Though his earlier works are clear and consistent in design, they are lacking in the vigor of this composition, where a raised central feature, screened by a portico of six Ionic columns, is integrated with perfect fluency and restraint with a lower arcaded range, and is topped with a curious stepped roof terminating in a statue of the goddess Flora, recalling Pliny's description of the Mausoleum at Halicarnassus. This was Boullée's self-conscious archaeological twist. The house was, of course, known as the Temple de

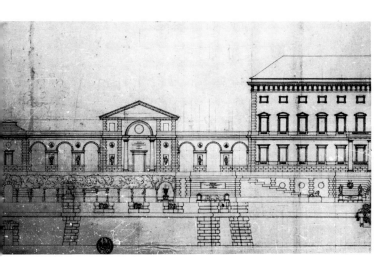

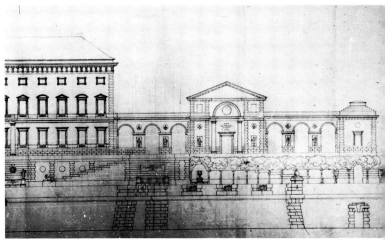

195, 196. *Pierre-Adrien Pâris, Hôtel de Ville, Neuchâtel, 1784–90*

Flore. Thereafter Boullée designed in a new key, overblown and arrogant. He decided, it seems, to become a genius, or, at very least, to resume his early interest in painting. He virtually forsook domestic work. In October 1778 he became *Contrôleur des Bâtiments à l'Hôtel Royal des Invalides;* two years later he was appointed to a similar post at the École Militaire. He thus embarked on an official career in architecture, the aim of most members of the profession. Unaccountably, however, he resigned both positions in 1782. He continued with other minor official commissions, but he was more intent to indulge his fantasies. Unfortunately, as we shall see, they were of the histrionic kind. They were to ensure that his influence was enormous—in particular, in post-Revolutionary France. Almost all architects of the period derived something of their style from his sophisticated and superbly rendered designs. No one, however, endowed his work with Boullée's spectacular spirit as successfully as Ledoux.

Yet the early buildings of Claude-Nicolas Ledoux (1736–1806) are not unconventional. A pupil of Blondel and an assistant to Trouard, he competed unsuccessfully for the Grand Prix and, like Boullée, he did not travel to Rome. In 1762, at the age of twenty-six, he started his career with the design of the *boiserie* for a military café, the Café Godeau, once in the Rue St.-Honoré (now in the Museé Carnavalet), made up of panels supporting trophies divided by wreathed clusters of spears topped with plumed helmets. The design and execution, though of a seventeenth-century kind, are exceptionally bold. For the next four years, however, Ledoux was to be active in the provinces, in Champagne, Franche-Comté, and Burgundy, working for the Service des Eaux et Forêts, building and supervising the execution of bridges, fountains, schools, and five small churches, none of particular distinction. By 1766 he was able to return to Paris to rebuild the Hôtel de Bouligneux, at 28 Rue Michel-le-Comte, for the Comte d'Hallwyl, a building of note—in particular, for the cononnades that flank the walls of the garden, and, in *trompe l'oeil* perspective, terminate the garden on the wall of a property beyond, thus imitating Jacques Rousseau's seventeenth-century perspective on the wall of the Hôtel de Dangeau—but one that, on the strength of engravings in the second, greatly enlarged edition of *L'architecture considérée sous le rapport de l'art, des moeurs et de la législation* (published only in 1847, as *L'architecture de Claude-Nicolas Ledoux*), has generally been thought to have been more advanced than it was. The heavy unbroken cornice shown in his engraving of the street facade gives an unusual coherence and tension to the architecture and reinforces the importance of the recessed central portion. But on the building as it stands today the cornice is more conventionally designed to follow the outline of the plan, which has two end pavilions with a setback in the center. The effect is altogether unlike Ledoux's Hôtel d'Uzès, based once again on an existing structure and designed a few months later in competition with two other architects, Pierre-Noël Rousset and Mathurin Cherpitel, and similarly lacking in vigor. The building is composed of rectangular masses, but

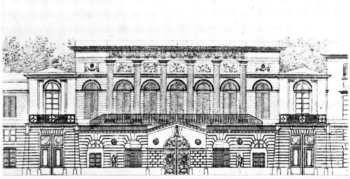

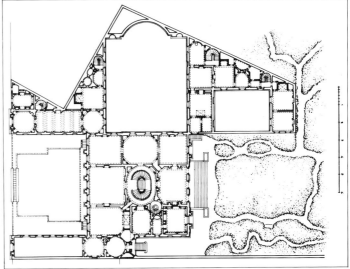

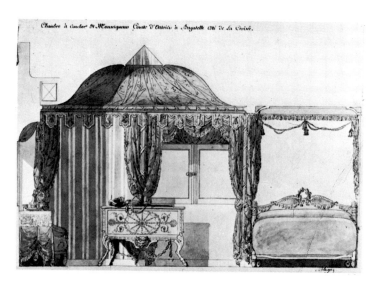

dramatic tension is lost with the use of close-set openings—some rectangular, some roundheaded, all in the same run—and an uneasy pattern of overall rustication. The forecourt, however, with its portico of four giant Corinthian columns supporting a far-projecting cornice and heavy balustrade, illustrates forcibly the boldness inherent in his powers of composition. These were more successfully displayed in the interior paneling, carved in 1769 by Jean-Baptiste Boistou and Joseph Métivier, some of which is now also in the Musée Carnavalet. Ledoux's first country house, the Château de Bénouville (Calvados), also a remodeling—begun in 1770 and completed in 1777—is once again similar in treatment. It consists of a number of rectangular elements broadly composed to create a horizontal mass. The whole is pierced with very narrowly proportioned windows and is screened in part by a portico of giant Ionic columns. His engraved design of the building, not published until 1804, is, as before, bolder in conception than the executed work. There is no doubt that Ledoux updated his designs for publication. The great stone stair hall within, however, even as it stands, compares favorably with Antoine's contemporary stair at the Hôtel des Monnaies.

Ledoux's maturity begins with his next group of Parisian *hôtels,* starting in 1770 with the Hôtel de Montmorency, entered, exceptionally, on a corner (Boulevard de Montmorency and Rue de la Chaussée-d'Antin). The building is a cubic mass reinforced with a screen of Ionic columns on each of the two street facades, which suggests an unusual derivation from Potain's theater project of 1763, though it relates rather to the equal claims to the Montmorency lineage of the prince and princess, whose independent suites of rooms are thus expressed on the facades. The interior contains a succession of spaces, circular, oval, and some less straightforwardly geometrical, all brilliantly planned around a diagonal. Ledoux surpassed this tour de force in the same year with a pavilion nearby for the dancer Marie Madeleine Guimard. Here he scored a triumph. The open, semidomed apse of the porch, screened by four Ionic columns carrying an entablature, and, above, a statue of Terpsichore, provides an altogether successful and ingenious focus for the design. The conception was inspired, no doubt, by the measured studies of Roman Baths carried out by Peyre and de Wailly, but the parallel between the Temple of Venus at Stowe—dated as early as 1732 and usually ascribed to William Kent—and Robert Adam's similar themes in the interiors of Syon House, Kenwood, and Newby is suggested irresistibly, the more so as Ledoux is known to have traveled to England, where he is said to have designed a house for Lord Clive. The attracting feature was used a year later, but in a slightly different form, for the pavilion Ledoux designed at Louveciennes for Mme. du Barry. The exedra of the entrance porch is screened as before by four Ionic columns, but the semidome rises up instead behind the entablature and balustrade of the facade. The planning here, though exemplary, is also less adventurous than in the Guimard pavilion.

204. *François-Joseph Bélanger, project for the gallery of Lord Shelburne in Landsdowne House, London, longitudinal section, 1778*

205. *François-Joseph Bélanger, Pavillon Lauranguais, in the garden of the Hôtel de Brancas (Hôtel de Lassay), Rue Taitbout, Paris, facade elevation, 1769*

206. *J. Métivier, Hôtel Gouthière, Paris, entrance on the courtyard, 1780*

207. *François-Joseph Bélanger and Thomas Blaikie, plan of the* jardin anglais, *Parc de Bagatelle, Paris, 1778–80. Engraving by Le Rouge*

208. *François-Joseph Bélanger, Folie Saint-James, Neuilly-sur-Seine, 1778–84*

209, 210. *Étienne-Louis Boullée, Hôtel Alexandre, Paris, elevation and ground-floor plan 1763–66*

211. *Étienne-Louis Boullée, Hôtel Alexandre, Paris, 1763–66*

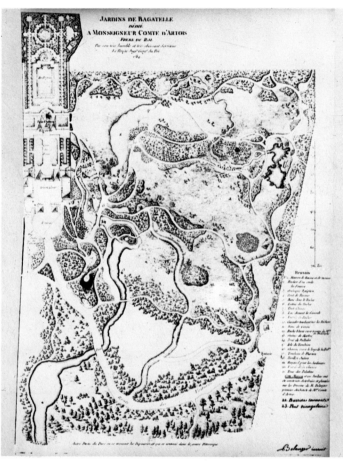

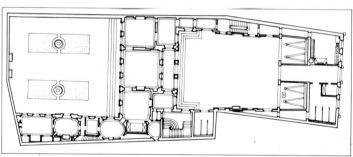

212, 213. Étienne-Louis Boullée,
Hôtel de Brunoy, Paris, plan and
elevation of the garden facade,
1775–79

214. Jacques-Denis Antoine, Hôtel des
Monnaies, Paris, principal facade,
begun 1767

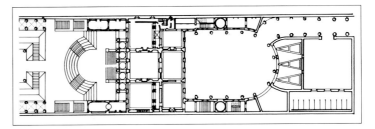

From this period dates a whole succession of small and costly *hôtels*, wonderfully resourcefully planned and with much variation in design, often of a Palladian sort, beginning with the Hôtel Tabary, in the Faubourg Poissonnière, in 1771—which may be compared with Soufflot's slightly earlier handling of the same themes for Marigny's house in the Faubourg du Roule—and culminating in the magnificent and altogether overindulgent Hôtel de Thélusson in the Rue de Provence, dating from 1778 to 1783. This was approached through a triumphal arch, designed as if half-buried, as in Piranesi's Roman views.

All Ledoux's great works date from his middle years. In 1771 he was appointed *Inspecteur des Salines de la Franche-Comté,* as adjunct to Perronet, and within three years had designed and started to build his famous project for the Salines d'Arc-et-Senans; both the remaining heavily rusticated buildings of the saltworks, completed in 1779, and the outlandish unexecuted designs that he was to evolve later show him to have been at once an admirer of the reserved and dignified architecture of Louis XV's reign and an unbridled experimentalist with a pronounced liking for a conglomeration of heavy simplified masses and unadorned wall surfaces. This aspect of his character was to find its fullest expression in the *barrières,* or tollhouses, for Paris, built between 1785 and 1789, which seem at first sight supremely monumental in the traditional French manner, though on inspection reveal that the characteristic forms and measures of classical architecture have been interpreted with a waywardness and a willful wrong-headedness peculiar to Ledoux. They are the most powerful architectural works of the century. The promise of Piranesi finds its fulfillment here. However, when Ledoux attempted something of the sort on a larger scale the result was less immediately successful. At Aix-en-Provence he began a Palais de Justice and related prison in 1786. Work progressed slowly, and was stopped altogether in 1790; the structure was replaced in the nineteenth century by M.-R. Penchaud's Maison d'Arrêt. But Ledoux's engraved drawings show one of the buildings, the prison, as a solid simplified mass that is deliberately top-heavy. The roofs of the four corner pavilions dominate the whole, and all the richness and incident in the architecture, the curious squat porticos apart, are concentrated at the eaves. Nothing quite like it was to be built in eighteenth-century France. Yet many of the remarkable and altogether surprising projects that Ledoux prepared from 1786 onward (in particular, in the idle years that followed his fourteen-month stay in the prison of La Force, beginning in December 1793, when he was suspected of undermining the Revolution), and that he published, in part, together with his equally idiosyncratic theories, in 1804, in *L'architecture,* all exemplify his notion of architectural beauty as something large in scale, simple and lumpish, enclosed and amplified by a clear-cut, if broken, outline. It was an ideal that many of his contemporaries shared and one that they derived, most probably, from Boullée; though more strictly classical in spirit, Ledoux tended to prefer continuous masses and

unbroken outlines. Ledoux may thus have been the forerunner of much of
the turgidity of nineteenth-century architecture.

Neigher Boullée nor Ledoux, however, would have come to his early
understanding of continuity and the unbroken line without Gondoin.
Jacques Gondoin (1737–1818) was nine years younger than Boullée, one
year younger than Ledoux, and he made his architectural debut about five
years after the latter, yet he appears to have remained throughout his life
a strict and consistent classicist. Indeed, he is remembered for one building
and hardly any other, the École de Chirurgie in the Rue de l'École de
Médecine in Paris, which might be said to epitomize the classical movement
of the late eighteenth century: "Un seul mot doit faire l'éloge de ce
monument," that upholder of classical orthodoxy, Quatremère de Quincy,
was to write in the early nineteenth century. "Il est le monument classique
du dixhuitième siècle" ("Notice sur . . . M. Gondoin," 1821, in *Recueil de
notices historiques . . . ,* Paris, 1834, p. 201).

Commissioned, designed, and begun in 1769, three years after Gondoin
had returned from Italy—via Holland and England—the École de Chirurgie
was finished by 1775. The problem of planning a surgical college in 1769
called for no great ingenuity, and the detailed arrangements are of little
interest. But the semicircular lecture hall, with its rising tiers of seats, its
blank curved wall, and its coffered half-dome and demi-oculus, was a
creation of genius and not surprisingly was reflected in all the assembly halls
of the Consulate and Empire periods—the Chambre des Députés, built
between 1795 and 1797 by J.-P. de Gisors and Étienne-Chérubin Leconte;
the Salle du Sénat at the Palais du Luxembourg, designed in 1804 by
Chalgrin; and the Salle du Tribunat, installed a few years later by C.-E. de
Beaumont in the Palais-Royal. Yet it was rather Gondoin's conception of
a facade composed of a triumphal arch embedded in a continuous screen
of Ionic columns, some engaged, some freestanding, and at the far end a
giant Corinthian portico—in short, the dramatic interpenetration of continuous columnar screens—that makes the École de Chirurgie so remarkable
and so stunning a work. The notion had been a part of French architectural
thought from Perrault onward, and had recently been reinforced by Peyre,
yet the liberating stimulus came from Italy, from the arrangement of the
Temple of Isis at Pompeii—the École de Chirurgie was conceived as a
Temple of Aesculapius—and, more surprisingly, from the first court of the
Collegio Elvetico in Milan, begun in 1608 by Fabio Mangone. There,
freestanding columns are used with even greater uniformity and obsession,
while the continuous, unbroken line of the cornice and the columns running
the entire length of the facade, which seemed so rude a departure from the
French tradition of composed elements, also came from Italian sources—
perhaps from the Raphaelesque Palazzo Vidoni-Caffarelli, in Rome, begun
in 1515 but greatly extended in the mid-eighteenth century, when it was
engraved by Piranesi for his *Varie vedute di Roma.* But to Gondoin's
contemporaries the design of the École, with its related yet contrasting

218. Claude-Nicolas Ledoux, Hôtel
d'Hallwyl, Paris, elevations of the
street and garden facades, 1766–67
219. Claude-Nicolas Ledoux, Hôtel
d'Hallwyl, Paris, 1766–67

220. Claude-Nicolas Ledoux, Hôtel
d'Uzès, Paris, cour d'honneur,
1767-68

221. Claude-Nicolas Ledoux,
boiserie for the Hôtel d'Uzès, Paris,
1769 (panels carved by J. B. Boistou
and J. Metvier, 1769). Paris, Musée
Carnavalet

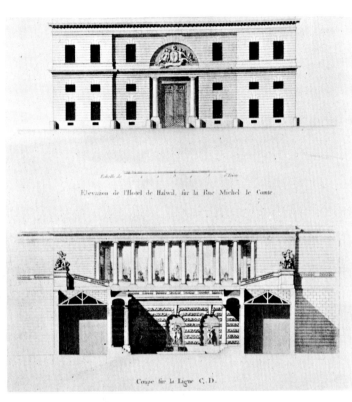

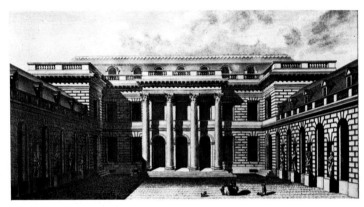

square and fountain in front, was a revelation and altogether original. Many attacked it. Blondel reluctantly recognized its peculiar antique power and Peyre defended it with vigor. J.-G. Legrand wrote of it in C.P. Landon's *Annales du musée* in 1803: "Tout le système de la vieille architecture française fut renversé par cet exemple inattendu, et les partisans de la routine furent stupéfaits de voir une façade sans avant-corps au milieu, sans arrière-corps, et dont la corniche suivant d'un bout à l'autre sans ressaut ni profil, contre l'usage reçu en France, et dont les Contant, les Gabriel, les Soufflot, venaient de donner de si récens et si dispendieux exemples dans l'École Militaire, dans la Madeleine, et dans la nouvelle Sainte-Geneviève. Cependant l'opinion publique se prononça en faveur du nouveau système, la critique se tut, et l'École de Chirurgie fut proclamée par tous les gens de goût, le chef-d'oeuvre de notre architecture moderne" (vol. 5, p. 127).

The success of this work won many commissions for Gondoin. In 1769 he became *Dessinateur du Mobilier de la Couronne* and started at once to design furniture for Marie Antoinette; he is said to have built a number of town and country houses, though only minor works such as the Hôtel Saint-Léonard, at 12 Rue Victor Hugo, Falaise (Calvados), and the Hôtel de Ville in the same town can yet be attributed to him. He also began a house for himself on the banks of the Seine, near Melun, in the late 1780s, and building continued in the years that followed the Revolution. He became wealthy. When, in 1775, he traveled to Italy for the second time, he sought to buy Hadrian's Villa at Tivoli. This proved impossible, as too many disputatious individual landowners were involved. He was thus forced to content himself with making measured drawings of the villa, which he gave to his friend Piranesi, who had been excavating there for several years with Gavin Hamilton and Clérisseau. Gondoin's drawings presumably served as the basis for the great site plan issued after Piranesi's death in 1781.

The classical movement of the eighteenth century was, as Quatremère de Quincy insisted, "une communauté d'instruction et de connaissance, une certaine égalité du goût et du savoir . . . entre toutes les contrées de l'Europe" (L. Hautecoeur, *Rome et la renaissance de l'antiquité à la fin du XVIIIᵉ siècle*, 1912, p. 224).

ENGLAND: *From Chambers to Wyatt*

The architects at whom we shall be looking in this section—principally Sir William Chambers, Robert Adam, James Wyatt, and Henry Holland—are more famous and were more prolific than those who figured in the earlier chapter on the influence of the antique. It is not that Chambers, Adam, Holland, and Wyatt were not interested in the antique—far from it—but they did not allow either archaeology or theory to interfere with their large and successful practices: They were ambitious, fashionable, popular, and stylistically omnivorous. Again we should begin by appreciating the pioneering achievements of the architects in the Palladias tradition, in particular of two second-generation Palladian architects, Sir Robert Taylor

224. Claude-Nicolas Ledoux,
Château de Bénouville (Calvados),
facade, 1770–77

225. Claude-Nicolas Ledoux,
Château de Bénouville, grand
staircase, 1770–77

226. Claude-Niocolas Ledoux, Hôtel
Guimard, Paris, principal facade,
designed 1770, built 1773–76

227. Claude-Nicolas Ledoux, Hôtel
Guimard, Paris, plan, 1770

228. Claude-Nicolas Ledoux,
Pavillon de Mme. du Barry,
Louveciennes, 1770 onward

229. Claude-Nicolas Ledoux,
Pavillon de Mme. du Barry,
Louveciennes, plan

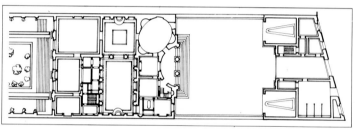

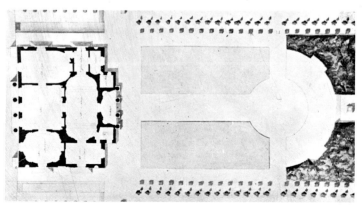

(1714–1788) and James Paine (1717–1789). Adhering basically to the Palladian canon, Paine created such powerful buildings as Stockeld Park, Yorkshire (1758–63), with its great arched facade and superb staircase, and Brocket Hall, Hertfordshire (1760s onward), where a dull exterior contains another remarkable staircase and a great saloon in which the painted historical and allegorical decoraration by John Hamilton Mortimer offers a substantial alternative to the lighter Adam style. At Wardour Castle, Wiltshire, Paine created, in the 1770s, his most breathtaking interior—a centrally placed pantheon containing a circular staircase.

Sir Robert Taylor also created a pantheon at the Bank of England, in 1765, which he flanked by four identical transfer offices inspired by the Early Christian church of S. Costanza in Rome, believed in the eighteenth century to be an ancient Roman temple of Bacchus. In the late 1760s, at Purbrook, Hampshire, whose plan was similar to that of Paine's Kedleston Hall, Derbyshire (1757), he placed a Roman atrium in the center, perhaps the first reconstruction of its kind. But Taylor is particularly associated with the creation of a series of beautiful villas, of which the dramatically situated Sharpham, Devon (c. 1770), may stand as an example, where the Palladian tradition is enlivened by imaginative planning with interlocking rooms of contrasting shapes. Although Taylor had initiated this tradition at Harleyford Manor, Buckinghamshire, as early as 1755, it was not fully exploited until the end of the century by Sir John Soane, John Nash, and James Lewis.

Paine and Taylor scarcely traveled abroad, but the career of Sir William Chambers (1723–1796) reveals the essentially cosmopolitan character of the style we call neoclassicism, which emerged in the 1740s and 1750s. As a pupil of J.-F. Blondel in Paris in 1749–50 he came into close contact with the brilliant group of designers who were developing a new Franco-Italian style, anti-rococo and neoclassical: men like L.-J. Le Lorrain and J.-L. Legeay, Charles de Wailly and M.-J. Peyre. From Paris Chambers moved naturally to Rome, where he spent the years 1750 to 1755, and learned much from Piranesi and Clérisseau. The outcome of all this learning and activity is clearly seen in the designs he made in Rome in 1751–52 for a mausoleum for Frederick, Prince of Wales. In some ways these designs, Chambers's first architectural production, constitute the beginnings of English neoclassical architecture, but they also represent a point from which Chambers subsequently retreated stylistically. Combining elements from such antique Roman buildings as the Tomb of Caecilia Metella and the Pantheon with features based on the Festa della Chinea designs of the 1740s by Frenchmen such as Le Lorrain and E.-A. Petitot, Chambers's mausoleum was too heady to be acceptable in England in the early 1750s. On his return from Rome in 1755 he prepared designs in an ill-digested Grand Prix manner for Harewood House, Yorkshire. When these were turned down by Edwin Lascelles in 1756 Chambers finally lost his nerve and retreated for the rest of his career into a safe, second-generation Palladianism inspired by Isaac Ware and enlivened with pretty motifs culled from the work of French

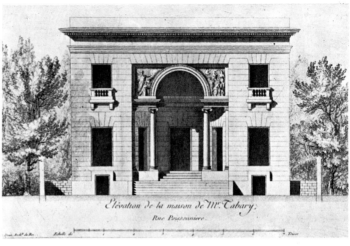

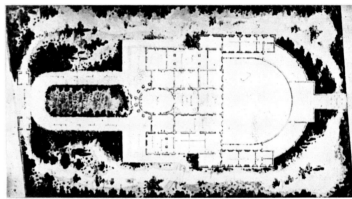

233. Jacques Gondoin, project for a square in front of the École de Chirurgie, Paris, 1769. Important features for the plan included a new facade for the church of St.-Come and a fountain against the wall of the adjoining destined monastery

234. Jacques Gondoin, École de Chirurgie (now École de Médecine), Paris, anatomy theater, 1769–75

235. Jacques Gondoin, École de Chirurgie (now École de Médecine), Paris, plan, 1769–75

236. Jacques Gondoin, École de Chirurgie (now École de Médecine), Paris principal facade, 1769–75

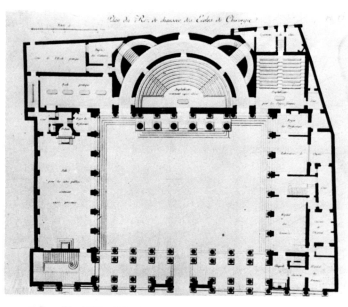

architects ranging from A.-J. Gabriel (born 1698) to J.-G. Soufflot (born 1713) and J.-D. Antoine (born 1733). On a small scale, as at the Casina at Marino near Dublin (begun 1758), this was enchanting, but it was quite inadequate for a major public building such as Somerset House, London (1776–96). Like a number of English eighteenth-century architects, Chambers was perhaps at his best with staircase design. His *Treatise on Civil Architecture* (1759), expanded in a third edition to *A Treatise on the Decorative Part of Civil Architecture* (1791), was widely influential in England and France as a scholarly and broadly based survey of the use of the orders in antique and Renaissance architecture. Chambers's pupil James Gandon (1743–1823) was in some ways more successful than his master in creating a monumental architecture inspired by French neoclassical precedent. At the Four Courts in Dublin, which he took over from Thomas Cooley (1740–1748) in 1785, Gandon produced a powerful building, which, if it has Peyre for a father, has Sir Christopher Wren for a grandfather. Cooley, an assistant of Robert Mylne, was also a better architect than Chambers. His masterly and original Dublin Exchange (1769–79) reveals a close knowledge of contemporary French work and is one of the finest buildings of its date in Europe.

Cooley and Gandon worked almost exclusively in Ireland, and their buildings had little impact in England. But if Chambers lacked the flair to create a new language out of the architectural experiments he had witnessed in Paris and Rome, there was one architect who was determined to achieve that very synthesis, Robert Adam. In 1754 he left his native Scotland for France and Italy, where, like Chambers, he became intimate with Piranesi and Clérisseau. With the assistance of Clérisseau and two other draftsmen in 1757 he prepared measured drawings of the great late Roman palace at Split in Dalmatia, which he published in sumptuous form in 1764 as *Ruins of the Palace of the Emperor Diocletian at Spalato.* The speed with which Adam worked was characteristic of him—he spent only five weeks at Split—as also was an ability to rouse public interest in a Picturesque and arresting manner. The captivating engravings by Francesco Bartolozzi and others were in a rhetorical style inspired by Piranesi that Adam used again in the depiction of his own buildings, published in 1773 and 1779 as *The Works in Architecture of Robert and James Adam, Esquires.* This gift for self-advertisement, this determination to achieve success, explains much about his eye-catching, all-inclusive, yet individual style. He could not afford to be doctrinaire. Greek, Roman, Palladian, neo-Palladian, neoclassical, Picturesque, all were grist to his mill. He had a quick eye for everything that was going on around him and assimilated his observations into a style of unique loveliness, which matured rapidly from Harewood House, Yorkshire (begun 1759); Kedleston Hall, Derbyshire (1760 onward); Osterley Park, Middlesex (1761 onward); Syon House, Middlesex (1762–69); Luton Hoo, Bedfordshire (1766–70); Newby Hall, Yorkshire (1767–85); and Kenwood House, Hampstead (1767–69). The desire to please, which is so strong in the

240. James Paine, Brocket Hall,
Hertfordshire, staircase, 1760 onward

241. James Paine, Brocket Hall,
Hertfordshire, saloon, 1760 onward
242. Sir Robert Taylor, Bank of
England, London, rotunda, 1765

243. Sir Robert Taylor, Bank of
England, London, Transfer Office,
1765

244. *James Paine, Wardour Castle,*
Wiltshire, stair hall, 1770–76

245. *Sir Robert Taylor, Harleyford*
Manor, Buckinghamshire, plan,
1755
246. *Sir William Chambers, Casina,*
Marino, near Dublin, begun 1758

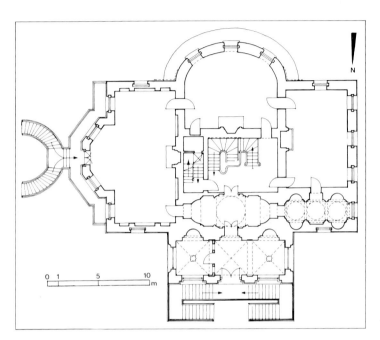

enchanting series of rooms contained in these houses, is frankly not an ambition that one particularly associates with the neoclassical movement, although those in search of the characteristically neoclassical interest in archaeology will find many hints from the Roman Baths, particularly at Syon. The essential adaptability of the Adam style is clearly conveyed in the preface to Part 2 of his *Works in Architecture,* where he writes of the orders, for example, that the Tuscan is needlessly austere, the Composite needlessly elaborate, the "great size of the volute of the Grecian Ionic [is] much too heavy," while those used by the Romans "border on the other extreme." "We have therefore," he concluded, "generally taken a mean between them." So perhaps the English *via media,* the comfortable compromise, must be taken into account in considering Adam's success. From the Grecian Ionic he adopted what he called the "double fillet" in the volute, which "far exceeds in grace and beauty that used by the Romans." Indeed, he claimed that he favored Greek profiles because Roman moldings were "considerably less curvilinear than those of the ancient monuments of Greece." An example of his empirical approach is his refusal to fix a definite entablature for each order: "A latitude in this respect is often productive of great novelty, variety and beauty."

What this meant in practice can be well appreciated in the celebrated anteroom at Syon of the mid-1760s. The volutes and moldings of the capitals here were taken from the Erechtheum as illustrated in J.-D. Le Roy's pioneering publication of 1758, *Les ruines des plus beaux monuments de la Grèce.* However, for the necking of the capitals he drew on a purely Roman source, familiar from the Baths and subsequently illustrated in Charles Cameron's *Description of the Baths of the Romans* (1772). The decoration of the Erechtheum necking he daringly and attractively transposed to the frieze of the entablature. Elsewhere in the room the gilded martial trophies anticipatory of the Empire style are derived from Piranesi's illustrations of the trophies of Octavian Augustus on the Campidoglio in Rome, which had already been imitated at the Villa Madama. The ceiling design, on the other hand, looks back to an English Palladian precedent established at Houghton Hall, Norfolk, by Colen Campbell in the 1720s. But the room recalls yet another period, for the twelve superb blue verde columns were antique Roman ones, said to have been excavated from the bed of the Tiber, and were dispatched by James Adam in April 1765 from Civitavecchia. In this one room, then, all the known historical boundaries are transcended by Adam's brilliant classical synthesis. This synthesis is not intellectual in origin but scenic and Picturesque, as already shown in Chapter 2.

The immediately recognizable style that Adam established in the 1760s, when remodeling the great Whig country houses put up by the first- and second-generation Palladian architects, was transferred in the 1770s to London, where, on a smaller scale, he created some of the most refined if rather mannered interiors of the century: No. 20 St. James's Square (1771–74); Derby House, No. 23 Grosvenor Square (1773–74; demol-

248. James Gandon, Four Courts,
Dublin, 1786–1802
249. Thomas Cooley, Royal Exchange
(now City Hall), Dublin, 1769–79

250. Robert Adam, harbor elevation
of the palace of Diocletian at Split
(Spalato), Dalmatia, 1757

ished 1862); and No. 20 Portman Square (1775). This exquisite style was not transported to the Continent, perhaps because it depended on a highly trained group of craftsmen, led by the plasterer Joseph Rose, Jr., who moved from house to house.

It should not be thought, however, that Adam's genius was limited to the creation of these pastel boudoirs. His colonnaded Admiralty Screen in Whitehall, of 1759, points forward to the bolder open screens of Jacques Gondoin at the École de Chirurgie, Paris (1769–85); Holland at Carlton House, London (c. 1794); and Karl Friedrich Schinkel at the palace for Prince Albrecht, Berlin (1829–33). At Bowood, Wiltshire, in 1761–64, he erected a chaste Tuscan mausoleum, domed and barrel-vaulted, which an architect like Gondoin might have envied. There is a ruthless originality about his twin-towered church at Mistley, Essex (1776; partially demolished 1870), which may have inspired Soane's Dulwich Gallery (1812). The garden front of Adam's Kedleston Hall, Derbyshire, takes its place in the long line of applications of the Roman triumphal-arch motif from Alberti to C. R. Cockerell, while at the Register House (1774–92) and University (1789–93) at Edinburgh, he created some of the most successful monumental public buildings of the century.

Adam was rarely short of commissions or publicity, though the flashy innovatory aspect of his style made him unpopular with Sir William Chambers, pillar of the academic tradition, who acquired for himself many of the official appointments of the day and prevented Adam from being elected to the Royal Academy. Adam also had to face difficulties of a different kind—imitation—by an architect very different from Chambers, James Wyatt. Nearly twenty years younger than Adam, Wyatt rocketed to fame as a very young man with his Pantheon in Oxford Street, designed in 1769 and opened in January 1772 as an unprecedented setting for entertainment. The brilliant and wholly unexpected plan led from a fairly simple street front past elegant but small vestibules and card rooms into the breath-taking rotunda. The disposition should be compared and contrasted with Lord Burlington's Assembly Rooms at York. Whereas Burlington's main room was an austere archaeological reconstruction based on Vitruvius and Palladio, Wyatt's was essentially a scenic composition modeled not on the all-too-familiar Pantheon in Rome (from which the building took its name) but on the less familar and more exotic Hagia Sophia in Constantinople. This Byzantine source was somewhat unorthodox, but it lent itself to Picturesque adaptation that clearly caught the mood of the day. In any other country in Europe Burlington's Assembly Rooms would have been sufficiently novel if erected in 1769–72, but by then, England, having enjoyed a proto-neoclassicism during the Palladian Revival at the beginning of the century, needed something more hotly spiced to whet her jaded appetite. The feverishly excited reaction to Wyatt's display at the Pantheon is perfectly conveyed in Horace Walpole's account of his own impressions: "It amazed me myself. Imagine Balbec in all its glory! . . . There has been

255. Robert Adam, mausoleum,
Bowood, Wiltshire, detail of the
interior, 1761–64

256. Robert Adam, Syon House,
London, anteroom, 1762–69

257. Robert Adam, Syon House,
London, entrance hall, c. 1765

261. *Robert Adam, University, Edinburgh, 1789–93; dome by Sir R. Anderson, 1887*

entrance hall with two tiers of columns, rather like his atrium at Purbrook, in Hampshire, but Wyatt decided that the height of the hall should speak for itself and allowed no columns to interfere with the flow upward into the wonderful barrel vault with its curious Gothic, concave fan vaults. It is instructive to compare the room with its ultimate source, Adam's library at Kenwood House, Hampstead, London (1767–69), whose plan and screen of columns based on the Roman Baths, and its remarkable curved vault decorated by the plasterer Joseph Rose, Jr., and the painter Antonio Zucchi, were revolutionary for their time. If anything, Wyatt's room is more of a unity. There is a logical relationship between the placing of the ribs of the vault, the pilasters on the wall, and the red and black marble bands across the floor. The foundation color of the walls and ceiling is apple green, with pilasters of yellow Siena scagliola, and capitals and enrichments in white. The seating furniture was also designed by Wyatt *en suite* with the whole room. Though this hall is the tour de force of the house, there are also an Etruscan room, library, and drawing room, all of high quality.

At Castle Coole, County Fermanagh, Wyatt was once more called in at the beginning to modernize and make fashionable what another architect had begun. The plans for the house are by Richard Johnston, dated Dublin, 1789, but before they could be executed Wyatt had waved the wand of London taste over them. On the facade, as executed by Wyatt, all superfluous ornament was eliminated, the unmolded window surrounds lack an entablature, and Johnston's Roman Doric was transformed into a bastardized Greek Doric of Wyatt's own invention. These Greek colonnades lead to pavilions inspired by Chambers's Casina at Marino. Inside Castle Coole, the two-storied entrance hall with its tiers of Doric columns was perhaps inspired by the interiors of Greek temples, but the most splendid interior is the great oval saloon in the middle of the garden front, with scagliola work by Domenico Bartoli and plasterwork by Joseph Rose, Jr. The whole production of the house was unusual, since it is doubtful that Wyatt ever saw it. His patron, Lord Belmore, was his own contractor and saw to it that Wyatt sent careful drawings for everything from ceilings to curtains and furniture. Once the joiners had finished the doors and windows they were set to work on Wyatt's furniture, which still survives in the rooms for which it was designed. The house cost more than double the original estimates, partly because of the decision to build it in Portland stone, necessarily imported from England. In June 1790 there was a total of sixty stonecutters and masons at work on the site. The whole house—design, materials, furniture, and plasterwork—is in every sense an importation from England. It was an extraordinary fantasy made reality, the quintessence of what one means by the Ascendancy in Ireland.

The Chambersian note, hinted at in Castle Coole and developed at Dodington Park, was frequently struck in Wyatt's works. In the mausoleum at Cobham Hall, Kent (1783), he was able to realize some of Chambers's early neoclassical ambitions. The canted corners with coupled columns are

XV. Robert Adam, Syon House, London, Red Parlour. 1762–69

262. James Wyatt, Heaton Hall,
Lancashire, Cupola Room, 1772
263. Robert Adam, Osterley Park,
Middlesex, dining room, 1775–79

264. Robert Adam, Kenwood House,
Hampstead, London, library,
1767–69

265. James Wyatt, Castle Coole,
County Fermanagh, saloon,
1790–97

266. *James Wyatt, Pantheon, Oxford*
Street, London, plan, 1769

267. *William Hodges,* Interior of
the Pantheon in Oxford Street,
c. 1771. Leeds City Art Galleries,
Temple Neusam House

268. *James Wyatt, Heaton Hall,*
Lancashire, garden front, 1772
269. *James Wyatt, Heveningham*
Hall, Suffolk, hall, 1778–84 ▷

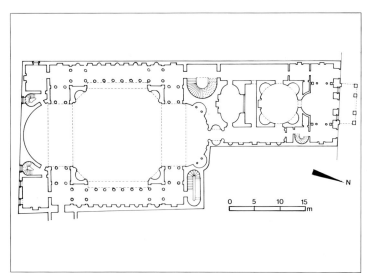

echoes of Chambers's design for a temple for the earl of Tylney, while the pyramid on top reminds one of designs by Neufforge. Wyatt's even more sumptuous mausoleum at Brocklesby Park, Lincolnshire (1787), recalls Chambers's mausoleum for the Prince of Wales, and also, interestingly enough. Nicholas Hawksmoor's at Castle Howard, Yorkshire (1728). Both are based ultimately on the Tomb of Caecilia Metella on the Appian Way, but whereas Hawksmoor's columns are set closer together than classical precedent allows, and thus create a crowded, restless, Baroque effect, Wyatt's intercolumniation is the correct one for the Doric order. He has further enlivened the building with references to the Temple of Vesta in Rome and the temple to the same deity at Tivoli. Inside, Hawksmoor placed his order on a tall pedestal; Wyatt's rests directly on the floor.

Of Wyatt's many country houses, the last at which we shall look is Dodington Park, Gloucestershire, commissioned in 1796. By this date, however, he was far better known for his Gothic than his classical houses. He had made this style fashionable in the early 1780s with such buildings as Sheffield Place, Sussex; Sandleford Priory, Berkshire; Pishiobury Park, Hertfordshire; Lee Priory, Kent; and Slane Castle, County Meath. He continued to erect houses of this type right up until his death in 1813 but, with the exception of the astonishing Fonthill Abbey, Wiltshire, they do not rival in interest his classical work.

Dodington, designed after Adam's death, represents a new departure. Strikingly different from the tight symmetry of Castle Coole, the west front of Dodington is freely disposed like the elements in a Capability Brown landscape. The quadrant greenhouse, with a picture gallery following its curve behind it, stretches out lazily toward the remarkable domed cruciform church built by Wyatt on the site of the medieval church. In powerful contrast is the immense entrance portico on the west front of the house, Greek in spirit but Roman Corinthian in detail. Different again is the south front, which reverts to a Chambersian mode of composition, its pilasters and attic reminiscent of Somerset House. The east front is simple to the point of inadequacy, enlivened only by curved end bays. These three facades are completely different and unrelated; their seemingly casual asymmetry is continued on the east front by the office wing (demolished 1932), culminating in the elegant minor axis of the dairy with its Greek Doric tholos, or rotunda. Both the designing and the building of Dodington were slow processes. The plans were initiated in 1796 but the details of the facades were not settled until 1800 and building work was carried on until 1813. More than seven hundred drawings survive but few are signed or dated—this is typical of a certain slaphappy note about Wyatt's method of work.

The grandeur of the entrance portico is sustained by the scale of the interiors, particularly of the double-cube entrance hall, which runs its full length of twenty meters (sixty-five feet). In scale, originality, and quality this ranks with his hall at Heveningham as one of the best neoclassical

272. James Wyatt, Dodington Park,
Gloucestershire, stair hall, c. 1798

273. James Wyatt, Dodington Park,
Gloucestershire, entrance hall,
c. 1798

interiors in England. Wyatt had now moved away from the Adam-inspired interpretation of the antique that characterized Heveningham to a more sober version of the Roman atrium. The heavily gilded, coffered ceiling of the central space is reflected in the patterning of the floor in black marble, red Scottish stone, and cream Painswick stone enriched with thin strips of brass between the flagstones. Porphry scagliola columns, which have lighter lozenge-shaped coffering inspired by the Basilica of Maxentius in Rome, screen off raised areas at each end of the room. Visiting the house in the 1820s the young architect C. R. Cockerell could not help admiring the hall, but felt obliged to record in his diary: "I should say it is very injudicious to have scagliola oriental granite & gilt capital and ceilings in the Hall. If you begin thus, what can you end in? Nothing you can put in the drawing rooms & others can ever keep pace with such a commencement." In fact, Cockerell was too hard on Wyatt, for the staircase hall undoubtedly maintains the grandeur and drama of the entrance hall. In true Picturesque manner it is not approached axially but from one corner of the entrance hall, so that the first view of it is obliquely through the trio of arches in shadow. Behind them light flows down from the as-yet-concealed dome. The source for this magnificently architectural staircase hall and its arched colonnade is Chambers's staircase at Gower (sometimes called Carrington) House, Whitehall (1765–74; demolished 1886), itself inspired by Baldassare Longhena's staircase at S. Giorgio Maggiore, Venice (1643).

Dodington had a powerful influence on James Wyatt's nephew, Lewis William Wyatt (1777–1853), who was helping with the designs for it by 1801–2. In 1817 Lewis was called to Tatton Park, Cheshire, to complete the house begun about 1785 by another of his uncles, Samuel Wyatt. His proposals of 1807 included a giant, hexastyle, Corinthian portico identical to that at Dodington. This was not executed. The new entrance hall, carried out to Lewis Wyatt's designs with screens of porphyry Ionic columns carrying a segmental coffered vault, was also a variant of the hall at Dodington. The real fruit of Dodington, however, was not Tatton but Willey Park, Shropshire. Here in 1812 Lewis Wyatt produced the final synthesis of Burlingtonian Palladianism as successively developed by Paine and James Wyatt. As befits its late date, the house is both more Picturesque and more antique than would have been the case in the eighteenth century. It is superbly related to a Picturesque park and contains an interior more temple-like than that of any other English neoclassical house.

We should look finally at the work of an exact contemporary of James Wyatt's, Henry Holland (1745–1806). Though undoubtedly attracted stylistically to the Adam-Wyatt synthesis, which was the great achievement of the second half of the eighteenth century in England, he also pursued a calm, agreeable path, with one eye firmly fixed on the Louis XVI style in France, which gave most of his work a flavor of uncontroversial but elegant consistency unruffled by any real interest in the Greek Revival, the Picturesque, or antiquity.

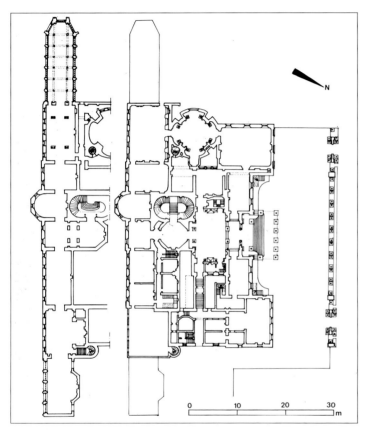

His first significant commission was for Brooks's Club in St. James's Street, London, in 1776. Behind a yellow brick facade of still basically Palladian disposition, on the first floor, lies the Subscription Room, in which Holland kept the Adam-like decoration to a minimum. The commission was one of extreme importance for Holland since the club was one of the most fashionable in London, patronized by the Prince of Wales and his intimate circle. The discreetly elegant interiors were popular with the club's members, so that not only was Holland commissioned to design Carlton House for the Prince of Wales, but other members followed the prince's example by patronizing Holland: notably the duke of Bedford at Woburn Abbey, Lord Spencer at Althorp, Samuel Whitbread at Southill House, and R. B. Sheridan at the Drury Lane and Covent Garden theaters.

In 1778 Holland began work on Berrington Hall, Herefordshire, where his partner from 1771, and father-in-law from 1773, the celebrated landscape designer Capability Brown, had been engaged from 1775. The exterior of Berrington is memorable, with its gaunt, emphatic portico and its monumental office courtyard laid out geometrically behind the house. The magnificent staircase hall is the richest surviving interior by Holland since the destruction of Carlton House. Its mood is not, perhaps, one we tend to associate with Holland, but it helps us to understand what it was that the Prince of Wales saw in him. The hall at Berrington has a dramatic double or ambiguous axis, with a coffered, arched recess which, in fact, leads only to the back staircase. Thus, as one enters from the entrance hall one has a dramatic view in perspective of the underbelly of the segmental arch. This painterly, Piranesian atmosphere, which is sustained as one mounts the cantilevered staircase beneath its glazed dome, had affinities with the staircase of a year or so later at Woodhall Park, Hertfordshire, by Thomas Leverton. Holland's drawing room, library, and boudoir at Berrington are also extremely fine, though their debt to Adam is clearer. The increasing richness in the decoration of these rooms reflects the marriage of Mr. Harley's daughter and co-heir to the son and heir of Admiral Lord Rodney in 1781.

The commission for Holland's most important work, Carlton House, came in 1783, the year in which the Prince of Wales, whose London residence it was to be, came of age. The site was occupied by a muddle of buildings put up in 1709 for Lord Carleton and partially remodeled in 1733 by Henry Flitcroft. Holland's extensive transformations were not completed until 1789, though the celebrated north front with its entrance portico and open screen-wall to Pall Mall were not ready until 1794. In 1785 Holland had visited Paris, where he would have seen such buildings as Rousseau's Hôtel de Salm, Ledoux's Hôtel de Thélusson, the Palais-Royal, the Hôtel de Condé, and Godoin's École de Chirurgie, which would have given him a number of ideas, particularly for the open Ionic screen along the road. The complex, interlocking plan of smallish rooms is probably French in origin, though the idea of the central octagonal tribune on which the whole plan seems to pivot is perhaps derived from Adam—in particular, from his similarly placed circular tribune at Luton Hoo, Bedfordshire. To help him in the design of decoration and furniture, Holland employed a number of French craftsmen, of whom two are of special interest. They are Alexandre-Louis Delabrière and Dominique Daguerre, who in 1777 had been involved in the decoration of one of the most exquisite Parisian houses of the century, the Pavillon de Bagatelle in the Bois de Boulogne, designed for Louis XVI's brother, the Comte d'Artois, by F.-J. Bélanger. Contact between England and France reached a peak in exactly these years with the signing of the Anglo-French Treaty of Commerce in 1786. Moreover, after the Revolution many goods and much furniture were smuggled out of France and sold in England, with Daguerre acting as an important medium. The large scale of Carlton House and the enthusiasm of the Prince of Wales enabled Holland to develop a style of his own with the strong French influences that appealed to the Whig circle at the moment. We know the Carlton House interiors principally from the magnificent aquatints published in the second volume of William Henry Pyne's *Royal Residentes* (1819), though by that time they had been considerably enlivened by the architect John Nash and the decorator Walsh Porter with rather flashy draperies and seating furniture. The granite-green entrance hall seems to have remained much as Holland left it, as did the lovely lavender and blue circular saloon flanked by Greek Ionic columns with silvered capitals.

In 1794–96 Holland employed the architect Charles Heathcote Tatham (1772–1842) to make sketches in Italy of antique decorative fragments, including antique furniture, which Holland could use as a model. Tatham shipped back numerous antique ornamental and architectural fragments, which were subsequently bought (about 1821) by Sir John Soane, who utilized them in a characteristically claustrophobic way in the tiny study and dressing room leading from the dining room of his house-*cum*-museum in Lincoln's Inn Fields. In this way Holland exercised an important influence over the development of Regency furniture styles.

For the immediate influence of Carlton House in the late 1780s we need look no further than Dover House, Whitehall. When, in his early twenties, Prince Frederick, younger brother of the Prince of Wales, needed a London house, it was natural to look to Holland. The house chosen for him had been built in the 1750s by James Paine and stood some way back from Whitehall. Holland increased its accommodation and its privacy by filling in the courtyard with a beautiful domed circular vestibule inspired by French plans such as those in Neufforge's *Recueil élémentaire d'architecture* (9 vols., 1757–72). He further concealed the house from public view behind a blank rusticated screen-wall. This was punctuated by Greek Ionic columns with an order based on that of the Temple on the Ilissus, as illustrated in Stuart and Revett, but engaged against the wall in a manner inspired by a Hellenistic building also illustrated in Stuart and Revett, the so-called Library of Hadrian in Athens.

In December 1786 Holland was called to Althorp, Northamptonshire, by the Whig grandee Lord Spencer. Holland's remodeling of this basically Elizabethan house resulted in one of the most convincing late Louis XVI interiors in England; the dressing room was painted in 1790–91 by the French artist T. H. Pernotin, whom Holland was at the time employing at Carlton House. Holland's work at Woburn Abbey, Bedfordshire, for the duke of Bedford, was more eclectic. Apart from some characteristically restrained interiors in his Anglo-Parisian manner, he provided a deep porte cochere in a style verging on the Greek Doric (demolished 1950); a Chinese dairy, after plates in Sir William Chambers's *Chinese Designs* (1757); and, in 1801, an exquisite little Temple of Liberty at one end of the sculpture gallery. Based on the Greek Ionic order of the Temple on the Ilissus, it was built to contain busts of the duke's favorite political heroes and was presided over by Joseph Nollekens's bust of the arch-Whig Charles James Fox, whose bust also presides over Brooks's Club.

Holland's last major commissions came in 1795 from the brewer Samuel Whitbread for the remodeling of his mid-eighteenth-century residence, Southill House, Bedfordshire. Mrs. Whitbread's drawing room and boudoir, painted by Delabrière with delicate white and gray coloring set off by a few chaste, Pompeian-style decorations, were finished by April 1800. The same artist painted some of the furniture, which still survives at Southill. The drawing room and dining room also contain furniture designed by Holland in a style moving away from Louis XVI to Regency. The large scale and rich gilding of this furniture create an opulent, almost royal, atmosphere, which contrasts with the refined and understated design of the rooms themselves. Holland's thoughtful Gallic manner separates him from his contemporaries, yet no one could deny that—like the better-known Adam and Wyatt—he formed a successful synthesis out of the myriad stylistic sources about which information had been accumulating so rapidly during the eighteenth century: Greek, Hellenistic, Roman, Renaissance, and neoclassical.

280. Henry Holland, Southill House, Bedfordshire, drawing room, 1795

281. Henry Holland, Southill House, Bedfordshire, fireplace in the painted study, 1795

FRANCE: *Boullée and Ledoux*

The largeness of scale, the delight in formal geometry that are associated, as a rule, with the visionary architecture of the late eighteenth century are evident even in the earliest years of the century in the drawings, in particular, submitted to the Accademia di San Luca in Rome. The annual competitions organized there were a vital feature of architectural activity, even before G. P. Panini became *Principe* of the Accademia in 1754, serving to focus all aspiration and experiment in architecture, international rather than local. Many young architects visiting Rome thought to establish a reputation for themselves by winning one of its prizes. Marie-Joseph Peyre, as we have seen, started off with a grandiose cathedral (and two related palaces) and went on to design his equally vast *envoi de Rome,* an academic center, both of which he illustrated in 1765 in his *Oeuvres d'architecture.* The impetus that these gave to students in France was considerable. But, already, if we are to judge by the entries for the Prix de Rome dating from the 1750s, the overblown, intoxicating visions of the Accademia had become an established part of the French academic tradition. Blondel, as we know, did not approve. Whatever his reservations, they were not heeded by the students. The designs of the Prix de Rome winners of the late eighteenth century became consistently more and more grand. Even the members of the Académie grew alarmed. In August 1787, in a letter signed by de Wailly, Pâris, and Boullée, they complained to the director of the Académie de France à Rome, "Les projets envoyés à l'Académie ont très rarement répondu à son attente; la pluspart étoient plutôt des compositions gigantesques d'une éxécution impossible, que les productions d'architectes qui, mettant le dernier sceau à leur instruction, sont prêts à revenir dans leur patrie réclamer la confiance de leurs concitoyens" (*Correspondance des directeurs,* vol. 15, p. 161). Boullée himself, somewhat compromised by this pronouncement, later found it necessary to draw a distinction between "gigantesque" and "colossale." After the Revolution this largeness of vision was to be regarded as a positive need of resurgent citizens, a means of asserting their rights and their very existence. In his *Discours sur les monuments publics* addressed to the Conseil du Département de Paris in December 1791, Armand-Guy Kersaint declared, "Affermissons la liberté et tout deviendra facile; pour y parvenir joignons aux instructions de la parole le langage énergique des monuments: la confiance qu'il est nécessaire d'inspirer sur la stabilité de nos nouvelles lois, s'établira, par une sorte d'instinct, sur la solidité des édifices destinés à les conserver et à en perpétuer la durée." Architects in the years that followed were to produce an endless series of projects for vast public buildings, but the successive administrations of the Revolution were to leave nothing tangible—even their *fêtes* to the *Être suprême* were ephemeral manifestations.

A great many architects may be adduced to give evidence of the visionary splendor in late eighteenth-century France—Jean-Nicolas Sobre, J.-P. de Gisors (1755–1818), Pierre-Jules-Nicolas Delespine (1756–1825), An- toine-Laurent-Thomas Vaudoyer (1756–1846), J.-T. Thibault (1757–1826), J.-N.-L. Durand, and Jean-Jacques Tardieu (1762–1833) are some of them—but the two men who were most inspired and inspiring were Boullée and Ledoux. Their work was quite distinct, though there was clearly some interaction between them. Boullée seems to have been the first to break from the traditional bonds of architecture to produce a new visionary style, though it is just possible that Ledoux initiated the genre; both, however, grounded their first experiments on actual projects, even commissions.

The completion of the Hôtel de Brunoy in 1779 marks the vital change in Boullée's style; it became at once more solemn and splendid, and also more pretentious. In 1780 he prepared a series of designs for the rebuilding of Versailles of which only the last, the *grand projet,* survives. This shows a vastly extended building of dreadful uniformity and dullness. Boullée cannot have expected that it would be built. Gabriel's work at Versailles had been in abeyance for five years, finances were low, and the king was not greatly interested in large architectural projects. Similarly, the theater and church that Boullée designed immediately after, though ostensibly based on definite programs, were not in any sense realistic. They were *exercices de style.* His theater of 1781 for the Place du Carrousel, Paris, though related to an earlier project by Soufflot, is fitted unconvincingly into a vast colonnaded drum with a flattened dome above. The church (in a series of projects of the same year) was intended, he said, to stand on the foundations of Contant d'Ivry's unfinished Madeleine, but successive drawings show that he was slowly transforming Soufflot's Ste.-Geneviève rather into a building of unearthly grandeur. Absolutely it is beyond the bounds of eighteenth-century resources. The vaults are empyreal, the colonnades unending. Three thousand columns would have been required in the interior alone. Boullée's project of 1783 for a museum is an even grander and more purified variation on the columnar theme. But the innumerable columns, the interminable steps, and the great barrel vaults are on this occasion conspicuously and ostentatiously useless; the whole serves only a symbolic purpose. Even his projected library, which was formally commissioned in 1784—first for the site of the Couvent des Capucines, then, when that scheme was found to be too expensive, for the old Palais Mazarin—was grossly impractical.

There is no evidence that Boullée considered how a library might work. The limitations imposed by the site were no less willfully ignored. The celebrated perspective of the interior of the library can only with the greatest difficulty be related to the courtyard of the Palais Mazarin, which it was to enclose. The figures, moreover, were shown in togas, recalling, Boullée explained, Raphael's *School of Athens*—a conceit in which de Wailly had first indulged in his perspective of the foyer of the Théâtre-Français exhibited in 1771 (see illustration 166). The very meaning of the word *monument,* it is not surprising to find, was extended, at this time, from "a commemorative edifice" to a "public building of symbolic connotation." Boullée was, in effect, designing temples. His museum was manifestly inspired by

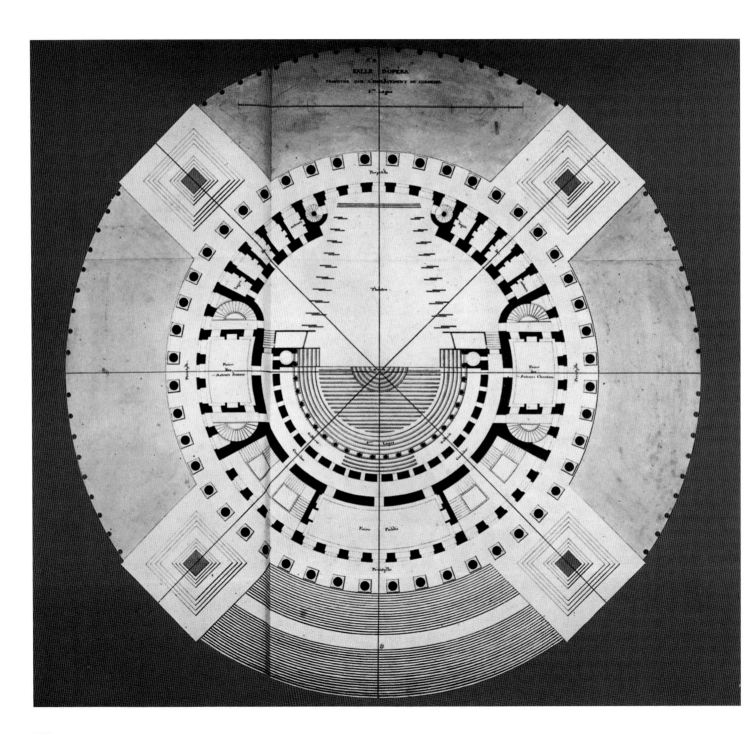

282. Étienne-Louis Boullée, project for
a theater for the Place du Carrousel,
Paris, plan, 1781

283. Étienne-Louis Boullée, project for
a theater for the Place du Carrousel,
Paris, 1781

284. Étienne-Louis Boullée, project for
a large church, perspective view, after
1781

283. Étienne-Louis Boullée, project for
a theater for the Place du Carrousel,
Paris, 1781

284. Étienne-Louis Boullée, project for
a large church, perspective view, after
1781

285. Étienne-Louis Boullée, a large
metropolitan church during Evensong,
interior view, c. 1781

286. Étienne-Louis Boullée, project for
the new hall of the Bibliothèque
Nationale, Paris, 1784

Alexander Pope's *Temple of Fame*. The dreadful pretension of his designs became more marked. Human conditions had ceased to be relevant. People were mere decorative adjuncts. "Jaloux enfin d'offrir le tableau le plus agréable," he wrote of his theater (or temple of pleasure), "j'ai cru y parvenir en disposant les spectateurs tellement que ce fussent eux qui décorassent ma salle et en formassent le principal ornement" (J. M. Pérouse de Montclos, ed., *E. L. Boullée: Architecture, Essai sur l'art,* 1968, p. 107). Human figures served only to increase the apparent size of his architecture. By 1784 he was able to epitomize his ideals in a great empty sphere designed as a cenotaph to Newton. "O Newton! Si par l'étendue de tes lumières et la sublimité de ton génie, tu as déterminé la figure de la terre, moi j'ai conçu le projet de t'envelopper de ta découverte" (ibid., p. 137). Boullée seems to have confused Newton and Galileo, but it scarcely mattered. His aim was to conjure up a vision of the immensity of the universe, to indulge celestial sensations. Thereafter, and particularly after the Revolution, his designs for even more magnificent public buildings, triumphal arches, gateways, towers of light, tombs, and pyramids pass into the realm of the truly sublime. He had sacrificed all reality and had determined to approach architecture as a painter; his motto, "Ed io anche sono pittore," was borrowed from Correggio, but he had reduced architecture to pictoral representation—little more. Drawing was all.

Boullée published nothing during his lifetime. However, his random notes and his *Essai sur l'art*—begun about 1780, but set down, for the most part, between 1790 and 1793 when he retired, ill, to the country—serve to illuminate his drawings and indicate something of his teachings. He had studied the works of Perrault—"Étant jeune, je partageais l'opinion publique; j'admirais la façade du péristyle du Louvre et regardais cette production comme tout ce qu'il y avait de plus beau en architecture" (ibid., p. 154)—but he found, in time, that he could not accept Perrault's contention that architecture was based, even in part, on an arbitrary system of rules. Boullée wanted an absolute, fixed and all-embracing. He sought to find it in nature: "Je ne saurais trop le répéter, l'architecte doit être le metteur en oeuvre de la nature" (ibid., p. 73). Nature was not to be too clearly defined, but he saw at once that forms and shapes served to conjure up thoughts and ideas.

"C'est par les effets que produisent leurs masses sur nos sens que nous distinguons les corps légers des corps massifs et c'est par une juste application, qui ne peut provenir que de l'étude des corps, que l'artiste parvient à donner à ses productions le caractère qui leur est propre. Les corps circulaires nous sont agréables par la douceur de leurs contours; les corps anguleux nous sont désagréables par la dureté de leurs formes; les corps qui rampent sur la terre nous attristent; ceux qui s'élèvent dans les cieux nous ravissent et ceux qui s'étendent sur l'horizon sont nobles et majestueux" (ibid., p. 35).

There was thus a direct relationship between forms and the sensation they

288. Étienne-Louis Boullée, project
for a funerary monument
289. Étienne-Louis Boullée, project
for a monument to Newton, 1784

290. Étienne-Louis Boullée, project
for a monument in the form of a
truncated Egyptian pyramid

aroused. This was the basis of his theory—*la théorie des corps.* He chose for study the regular solids, for the despised irregularity in all things. He sought order desperately—not to be wondered at in the years of the Terror. Symmetry, his very image of order, was the inviolable rule. He built up his designs with cubes, cylinders, pyramids, and cones (always shown truncated, it should be remarked), but his ideal was the sphere, for not only was it the most regular of figures but, under the effects of light, it was capable of exhibiting the most infinite variety, from the darkest of shades to the sharpest brilliance. Light was an essential component in Boullée's ideal architecture.

"Le corps sphérique," he wrote, "sous tous les rapports, est l'image de la perfection. Il réunit l'exacte symétrie, la régularité la plus parfaite, la variété la plus grande; il a le plus grand développement; sa forme est la plus simple, sa figure est dessinée par le contour le plus agréable; enfin ce corps est favorisé par les effets de la lumière qui sont tels qu'il n'est pas possible que la dégradation en soit plus douce, plus agréable et plus variée. Voilà des avantages uniques qu'il tient de la nature et qui ont sur nos sens un pouvoir illimité" (ibid., p. 64).

In his design for a theater Boullée was already attempting to give form to this idea; in his monument to Newton he might be said to have achieved it. Ledoux, it is worth noting, was to outdo him in sheer boldness of conception in his shepherds' house for the park at Maupertuis, as was his pupil Sobre—using the device of a reflecting pool—in his Temple of Immortality. But Boullée was concerned not only with the finite beauty of forms; he saw that their effects might change under different conditions, at different times of the year, at different times of the day, in sunlight or in moonlight, and even in relation to the spectator's mood.

"Toutes nos idées, toutes nos perceptions," he remarked, quoting John Locke or his French disciple Étienne Bonnot de Condillac," ne nous viennent que par les objets extérieurs. Le objets extérieurs font sur nous différentes impressions par le plus ou le moins d'analogie qu'ils ont avec notre organisation" (ibid., p. 61).

Symbolism was thus of the highest importance in suggesting the character of each of Boullée's monuments: Certainly it was more important than practical considerations. The techiques of fortification were irrelevant to military architecture, Boullée said; the aim was "l'image de la force." Often his symbolism was overt, as with his trophies and shields applied to town gateways, or the text of the Constitution chiseled into the walls of his Palais National; more often it was obscure. For though his architecture might seem bland and formal, it was a distillation of a teeming esoteric knowledge. Like most French architects of the period, he was a Freemason. He was also an avid reader of travelers' tales. In his library he had James Bruce's account of the search for the source of the Nile, William Patterson on the Kaffirs and Hottentots, William Robertson's stories of the ancient American civilizations, and other tales of journeys to Siberia, China, and the South

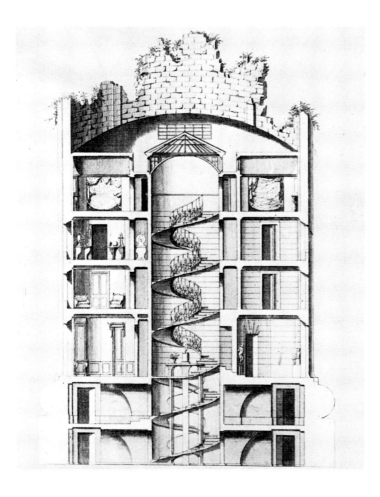

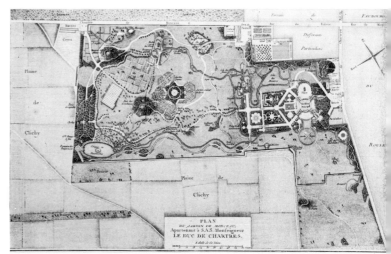

Seas. He himself scarcely moved out of Paris. This taste for the exotic was
not to be overtly displayed in his designs. Everything was sublimated and
given its purest form, for he aspired to the poetry of architecture. He aimed
to elevate it above mere building (he despised Vitruvius for his humdrum
mechanical interests) to a point beyond even the bounds of reason. His
architecture was to be that of the sublime.

"La seule manière dont les artistes doivent s'entretenir entre eux," he
wrote, "c'est de rappeler avec force et énergie ce qui excite leur sensibilité;
c'est par cet attrait qui leur est propre qu'ils peuvent se stimuler et échauffer
leur génie. Qu'ils se gardent bien d'entrer dans des explications qui tiennent
trop au raisonnement, car l'impression d'une image sur nos sens s'attiédit
quand nous nous appesantissons sur la cause que produit son effet. Com-
menter sur ses plaisirs, c'est cesser de vivre sous leur empire, c'est cesser

295. *Richard Mique,* hameau, *Petit Trianon, Versailles, 1778–82*

296. *Richard Mique,* hameau, *Petit Trianon, Versailles, the mill, 1778–82*

297. *François-Joseph Bélanger and Hubert Robert, the park at Méréville, near Étampes, 1784 onward*

298. *Painting by Hubert Robert of the park and the château at Méréville by François-Joseph Bélanger and Hubert Robert (Sceaux, Musée de l'Ile de France)*

d'en jouir, c'est cesser d'exister'' (ibid., p. 164).

Boullée was no unbridled enthusiast. He founded his vision on study and careful thought. He worked beneath portraits of Copernicus and Newton. He possessed books on physics and astronomy. He read Francis Bacon and the Comte de Buffon and had clearly studied to advantage Condillac's *Traité des systèmes et des sensations* (1754). There are close links between his theory of forms and Jean-Baptiste-Louis Romé de l'Isle's *Cristallographie; ou, description des formes propres à tous le corps du regne minéral* (1738). Knowledge is at the root of his activities. Identifiable prototypes may be adduced for each of his visionary projects, giving evidence of a wide erudition. The most obvious are the buildings of the ancient Romans—the Colosseum, the Pantheon, the Pyramid of Cestius, the Tomb of Caecilia Metella, the mausoleums of Hadrian and Augustus, and that at Halicarnassus—all of which he stripped bare and rendered more noble and ethereal. He borrowed from Athanasius Kircher, from Fischer von Erlach, and even from Hubert Robert.

The liberating stimulus for Boullée's excursus, as for many of his contemporaries, was Jean-Jacques Rousseau and even his disciple Jacques-Henri Bernardin de Saint-Pierre, but the specific factor that served to alter the pattern of thinking on architecture was the introduction into France of the *jardin anglais.* Boullée himself was among the first to design one of these, possibly at the Château de Chaville, in 1765, certainly at Issy-les-Moulineaux a few years later. But the frenzied fashion for Picturesque gardening in France dates rather from the 1770s, when a spate of wonderfully resourceful but largely frivolous gardens was designed in something of an English manner: Simon-Charles Boutin's Tivoli at Montmartre (completed by

299. *François-Joseph Bélanger, the dairy at Méréville, now in the park of the Château de Jeurre*

300. *Chinese pavilion, Parc de Cassan, near L'Isle Adam*

301. *Chinese pavilion, Parc de Cassan, near L'Isle Adam*

302. René de Girardin, the gardens
at Ermenonville, with the tomb of
Jean-Jacques Rousseau. Engraving by
Merigot

303. René de Girardin, Temple of
Fame, pavilion in the gardens at
Ermenonville

1771); L. Carrogis de Carmontelle's Monceau (1773–78); François Barbier's Désert de Retz (1774–84), for Boullée's own client Racine de Monville, where for the first time the house itself became a garden ornament—a simulacrum of a ruined column; then the *hameau* at Chantilly (1775) by Jean-François Leroy, and that at the Petit Trianon (1778–82) by Richard Mique (1728–1794); and also F.-J. Bélanger's gardens at Bagatelle (1780), the Folie Saint-James (1778–84), and Méréville (1784), this last finished off by Hubert Robert, who worked also at Betz with the Duc d'Harcourt and at Rambouillet, after 1783. The success of these, from an English point of view, varied greatly. "There are three or four very high hills," Horace Walpole wrote to his friend John Chute about Tivoli, on August 5, 1771, "almost as high as, and exactly in the shape of a tansy pudding. You squeeze between these and a river, that is conducted at obtuse angles in a stone channel, and supplied by a pump; and when walnuts come in, I suppose it will be navigable" (*Letters,* vol. 8, p. 64). Carmontelle's garden at Monceau was so flagrantly frivolous—a succession of *tableaux vivants* designed to ensure a maximum of conversational stimulus with a minimum of fatigue—that even its designer sought to distinguish it from the more serious English attempts to give order to nature: "Ceci," he wrote on the wall, "n'est point un jardin anglais" (F. A. de Frémilly, *Souvenirs,* 1909, p. 7).

But there were, of course, many gardens in which noble aims were pursued, moral and uplifting aims. The finest of these were the gardens at Ermenonville, belonging to the Marquis René de Girardin. The hermit here was no less a man than Rousseau. And it was from Girardin that one of the most important theoretical studies was to come, *De la composition des paysages,* of 1777. "Ce n'est donc ni en architecte ni en jardinier, c'est en poète ou en peintre qu'il faut composer des paysages," he counseled (p. 8). Within six years this work had been translated into English. However, the first book of this sort to appear in France was, as one might expect, English—Thomas Whately's pioneering study on the theory of the Picturesque garden, *Observations on Modern Gardening,* of 1770, which F.-P. de Latapie translated into French the following year. Walpole was quick to notice this, too: "They have translated Mr. Whateley's book," he told Chute in his same letter, "and lord knows what barbarism is to laid at our door." This was followed by two French works, C.-H. Watelet's *Essai sur les jardins,* of 1774, and Jean-Marie Morel's *Théorie des jardins,* issued two years later. Walpole's own study, *The History of the Modern Taste in Gardening,* first printed in 1771, was translated into French in 1785 by the Duc de Nivernois.

Morel had worked with Girardin at Ermenonville as early as 1766, but they had quarreled furiously as to the propriety of littering a landscape garden with buildings. He departed, piqued, to design no fewer than forty other gardens to his own liking. His writings make it clear that he did not object to building as such; cottages and barns or sheds that served a useful purpose and were designed in the traditional manner were altogether

304. Pierre-François-Léonard
Fontaine, funerary monument for the
ruler of a great empire, Grand Prix
design, 1785

305. Antoine-Laurent-Thomas
Vaudoyer, house for a cosmopolitan,
1785

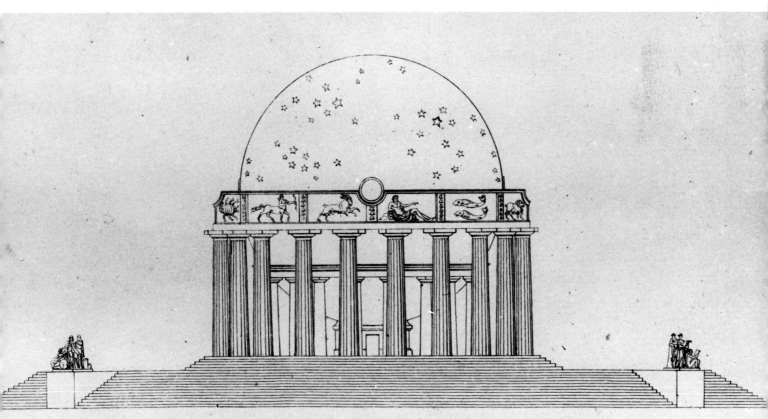

187

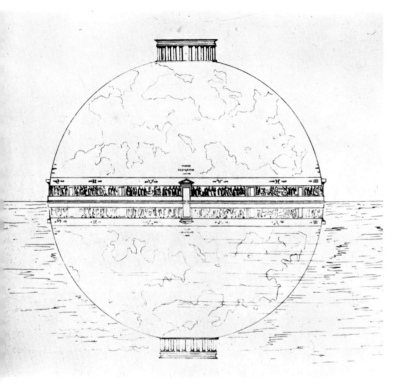

306. *Jean-Nicolas Sobre, project for a Temple of Immortality*

une seule ligne, un simple contour suffisent pour l'exprimer" (p. 3). Le Camus's ideas are less well developed than those of Boullée, the language certainly less elevated; his dogged insistence on indicating at length how his analogies might be incorporated into the routines of planning and detail design serve to set his book in an altogether different category from that of the *Essai.* But throughout there are parallels and similarities, for the preoccupations of both men were the same: "Un édifice très éclairé," Le Camus writes, "bien aeré, lorsque tout le reste est parfaitement traité, devient agréable et riant. Moins ouvert, plus abrité, il offre un caractère sérieux: la lumière encore plus interceptée, il est mystérieux ou triste" (p. 43). It is scarcely necessary to trace at further length the connection between the ideas of Boullée and ideas regarding composition introduced into France by gardening theorists in the 1770s.

Even at the most humdrum level one can note his borrowings from gardeners: His biographer Jean-Marie Pérouse de Montclos has suggested that his great theater is no more than an enlarged Temple of Love, while the monument to Newton itself, though it accords with a description in Pope's *Temple of Fame,* may equally be an illustration of the Miau Ting, or the Halls of the Moon, described in Sir William Chambers's *Dissertation on Oriental Gardening* (1772), available in French by 1773. The French, inspired by the visions of Panini and Piranesi and then the English, were learning to accept visual criteria alone.

The authority of the Picturesque theorists and of such men as Boullée was enormous. For though Boullée published nothing, he was active as a teacher. Indeed, many of his designs seem to have been prepared as a direct result of his teaching; they are based on the Grand Prix programs and incorporate, moreover, ideas that appear first in his students' submissions: magisterial corrections, as it were, to their hesitant essays. Not that they were slow to learn. Even outside Boullée's classes his works must have been known. Antoine-Laurent-Thomas Vaudoyer, a pupil of A.-F. Peyre, claimed to have produced his design for a *maison d'un cosmopolite,* a house in the form of a globe, in 1785, the year after Boullée designed his monument to Newton. And Pierre-François-Léonard Fontaine, a student of Jean-François Heurtier and A.-F. Peyre, who was awarded the second Grand Prix in 1785—but only after the students rioted when they heard that he had failed to win because the Académie feared to recompense so fine a draftsman—showed in his proposed "Monument sépulcral pour les souverains d'un grand empire" that he was in all things a true follower of Boullée. Boullée's influence was paramount.

Ledoux's impact as a visionary architect was not, at first, made through the mediums of teaching, drawing, and writing. He had very few students, but he liked to build. The forty *barrières* encircling Paris that he began in 1785, when he was already fifty, and built rapidly during the following four years—in part, under the supervision of J.-D. Antoine and Jean-Arnaud Raymond—showed that by changing the scale and measures of traditional

acceptable, as were old and rambling manor houses, but he wanted nothing new, nothing that might obtrude in the landscape. He liked best nature unadorned, and he described at great length the way in which he composed by natural means, making open expanses or enclosures, solids and voids. There should be no great insistence on logic, he explained, for the aim was poetry. His raw materials were grass and trees, rock, and water—still or running; he was alilve to the effects of running water, the rustle of wind, and, of course, the play of light. Four successive chapters in his book were devoted to the changing effects of the four seasons. His interests, it is evident, are much the same as Boullée's, though Morel, it must be stressed, unlike Boullée, did not care much for symmetry. The transposition of these ideas into architectural theory, however, was probably not made by Boullée himself. His *Essai* was preceded by Le Camus de Mézières's *Le génie de l'architecture; ou, l'analogie de cet art avec nos sensations,* issued in 1780. Le Camus was spurred on by the landscape gardeners; indeed, he dedicated his book to Watelet. "Mon zèlè," he wrote, " s'est soutenu en fixant mon attention sur les ouvrages de la nature. Plus j'ai examiné, plus j'ai reconnu que chaque objet possède un caractère qui lui est propre, et que souvent forms, and by assembling these simplified geometrical forms in a bolder, if more complex, arrangement than usual, applying ornament only sparingly and then in a new relation to the surface or mass, an architecture of extraordinary novelty and power could be fashioned. Ledoux was a potent innovator. Most of the *barrières,* which continued to be built even after the Revolution, were torn down in the mid-nineteenth century, but four remain—the Barrière d'Enfer, Place Denfert-Rochereau; the Barrière du Trône, Place de la Nation; the Rotonde de la Villette, Place de Stalingrad; and the Rotonde de Monceau, Place de la République Dominicaine. The last shows Ledoux at his least adventurous, but the monumental building at the head of the Bassin de la Villette embodies his boldest aspirations. A giant arcaded drum is placed four-square on a solid, rectangular mass. At the core is a circular court. The silhouette is hard and sharp; and, though the detailing is strong, it is totally subservient to the geometry of the whole. Its air of primordial splendor is overwhelmingly impressive.

The extraordinary projects for which Ledoux is famous were not published as a group until 1804, two years before his death, when the first volume of *L'architecture considérée sous le rapport de l'art, des moeurs et de la législation* was issued. This contained his writings and one hundred and twenty-five plates illustrating the extant buildings and his project for an ideal city centered on the saltworks at Arc-et-Senans, on the edge of the forest of Chaux. Not until 1847 did his supposed son, Daniel Ramée, issue the second edition, containing two hundred and thirty extra plates, relating to Ledoux's realized work and unfulfilled commissions. Other isolated engravings exist—many of the plates included in the published volumes may have been distributed separately. The earliest dates from 1771, but this is unremarkable. Some of the designs for the buildings erected at Arc-et-Senans are dated 1776, just after the work there had begun; others are from 1780; but the first dated engraving for a design that is odd and altogether unconformable by contemporary standards is that of 1778 for an imagined hunting lodge for the Prince de Bauffremont. Later commissions—the Château de Maupertuis (c. 1780); the house for M. de Witt (1781); the Bishop's Palace at Sisteron (c. 1781); the Château d'Éguière, which must also be contemporary; and even that remarkable group of fifteen houses in the Rue St.-Georges, Paris, for M. Hosten (four were built from 1792 until 1795, just after Ledoux was released from prison)—are all unusual enough, but are not really so extraordinary. They are lacking in the brutal harshness of composition that makes so startling the prince's lodge, and, especially, the other famous designs for the Utopian city of Chaux—among them the Maison d'Éducation; the Cénobie (or commune) for sixteen families; the Panarethéon (or Temple of Virtue); the Oikema (or Temple of Love); and the cemetery. The last, not unlike Boullée's monument to Newton, may date from the late 1770s, though this seems unlikely; all were probably designed and engraved only after Catherine the Great's son, in the guise of the Comte du Nord, visited Paris in 1782 and accepted the dedication

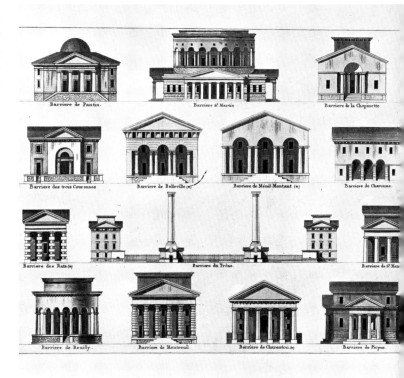

of the book (it was to be dedicated, in the end, to his son, Alexander I). Ledoux was probably most active designing in the idle years that followed his release from prison in 1795. He built nothing then. From this period, also, must date the revisions to the works built early in his career, which make his engravings such telling evidence of his activity as an architect. The prospectus for his book did not come out until 1803.

For all the arbitrary nature of his refashioning, Ledoux's executed buildings from the late 1770s onward, and all his subsequent projects, reveal him as a designer of unparalleled power and vision, although his vision was less elevated than that of Boullée. He had a livelier imagination, clearly well-stimulated by knowledge of the odd and curious in architecture—and inspired also by the curious in literature, if we are to judge by a comparison of his account of a traveler to his ideal city with that of the hero in Tiphaigne de la Roche's *Giphantie* (1760), who discovers a new land where nature continues still to create new plant and animal species. Boullée, of course, responded also to the exotic, but he was careful always to distill such interests.

Ledoux introduced minarets into the design of a country house without

308. Claude-Nicolas Ledoux, Barrière
du Trône, Paris, 1785–89
309. Claude-Nicolas Ledoux, Rotonde
de la Villette, Paris, 1785–89

qualm. Like Boullée, he was intrigued by symbolism and mystery. He was, not surprisingly, a Freemason and seems so have been involved in an abortive initiation ceremony with William Beckford, possibly at Maupertuis. But whereas Boullée subordinated such rich and varied interests to a consistent and completely coherent vision of architecture, Ledoux was altogether erratic. He evolved no sustained or sustaining theory. His writings reveal him at his most wayward: He offered notions, not a philosophy. His style is rhapsodic and hortatory. Often, when his ideas can be connected to known facts or realities, he is revealed as commonplace enough, but his overblown language serves to distort and confuse. His text is a farrago. There is no clear organization, no argument, and much is already familiar. "Vous qui voulez devenir architecte," he wrote, "commencez par être peintre" (L'architecture, 1804, p. 113). His criteria throughout are not unlike those of Boullée: For example, his overwhelming responsiveness to nature, evident, in particular, in the natural and pleasant settings in which he placed his designs; his insistence on symmetry; his feeling for the qualities of solid geometry, light and shade, and poetry in architecture. "L'architecture," he wrote, "est à la maçonnerie ce que la poésie est aux belles-lettres: c'est l'enthousiasme dramatique du métier, ne peut en parler qu'avec exaltation" (ibid., pp. 15-16). He was fearful also of too much reason or knowledge: "L'érudition," he warned, "cette souveraine empesée, conduit rarement à l'heureux délire" (ibid.).

He aimed to be an inspired genius, and consciously thought of himself as the revolutionary prophet, both the architectural and moral kind. There is more social concern evident in his writings than in Boullée's. Indeed, he is often regarded as an early socialist, but most of his exhortations belong to the realm of post-Revolutionary cant. There is little evidence of sustained thinking. He dedicated his book to the czar of Russia, sent two hundred and thirty-seven of his drawings to the czar just before the Revolution, and was proud to recount his dealings with the king: "De tous temps," he wrote, "les souverains ont donné le ton" (ibid., p. 26). His hints as to the organization of the ideal city indicate that he envisaged an authoritarian regime, while his paean to the riches of nature as sufficient unto the needs of the poor, though it may recall Rousseau and Bernardin de Saint-Pierre, makes embarrassing reading. One may doubt at times that Ledoux was even a humanitarian. Yet he did design and build the saltworks at Arc-et-Senans as a noble architectural enterprise, which was unusual enough at the time, and in his visionary designs showed that canon forges could be conceived as elevating works of art; even the humblest dwellings, shepherds', coopers', and woodmen's houses, are of no less exalted an architecture than the house of the Directeurs de la Loue, or even the house of the Directeur de la Saline itself. This last had an altar in the center, dramatically lit, approached from a giant flight of steps. Everything was grist to Ledoux's creative mill and could be endowed with greatness and nobility. God, of course, was the supreme architect.

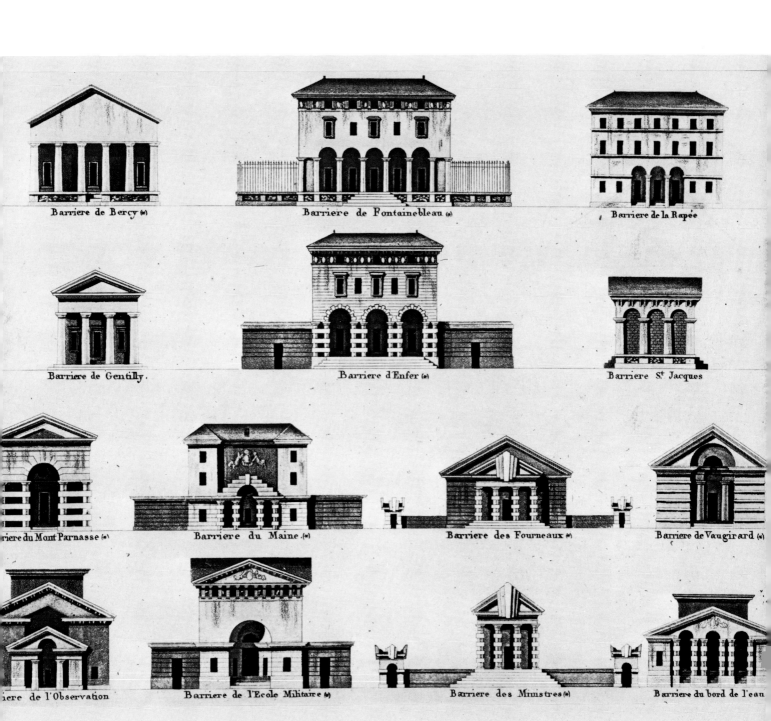

Barriere de Bercy (*)

Barriere de Fontainebleau (*)

Barriere de la Rapée

Barriere de Gentilly.

Barriere d'Enfer (*)

Barriere St. Jacques

riere du Mont Parnasse (*)

Barriere du Maine .(*)

Barriere des Fourneaux (*)

Barriere de Vaugirard

iere de l'Observation

Barriere de l'Ecole Militaire (*)

Barriere des Ministres (*)

Barriere du bord de l'eau

311. Claude-Nicolas Ledoux, Barrière
d'Enfer, Paris, 1785–89

312. Claude-Nicolas Ledoux, Barrière
d'Enfer, Paris, detail, 1785–89
313. Claude-Nicolas Ledoux, project
for barrières, Paris, 1785–89

311. Claude-Nicolas Ledoux, Barrière
d'Enfer, Paris, 1785–89

312. Claude-Nicolas Ledoux, Barrière
d'Enfer, Paris, detail, 1785–89

313. Claude-Nicolas Ledoux, project
for barrières, Paris, 1785–89

Ledoux, though, was infinitely less solemn than Boullée; he was livelier and less gloomy. "L'art sans éloquence," he wrote, "est comme l'amour sans virilité" (ibid., p. 16). Boullée produced endless projects for cenotaphs and cemeteries; indeed, most of his visionary designs have sepulchral overtones. All have a funerary ostentation and are set in desert landscapes. Ledoux concentrated rather on communal buildings and houses in attractive surroundings. His designs are undoubtedly more engaging than Boullée's, and all his works offered more possibilities for adaptation, but Ledoux was not often imitated. His architecture was thought to be undisciplined. Yet, much as Piranesi had set the tone and style that inspired Ledoux, so Ledoux suggested to architects how they might break from the classical norms to produce a new and radical architecture. Boullée provided the highest ideal; Ledoux offered a practical model. Together they were responsible for the profound change in architecture that is characterized as Revolutionary.

ENGLAND: *Dance and Soane*

In his *Description of the House and Museum on the North Side of Lincoln's Inn Fields*, of 1835–36, Sir John Soane wrote of the Breakfast Parlour in his house: "The view from this room into the Monument Court and into the Museum, the mirrors in the ceiling, and the looking-glasses, combined with the variety of outline and general arrangement in the design and decoration of this limited space, present a succession of those fanciful effects which constitute the poetry of architecture."

The same sentiments and the same language occur, as we have seen, in Boullée's *Architecture, Essai sur l'art*, written in the 1780s and 1790s as part of his bizarre retreat from reality. In these years his long-suppressed ambition to be a painter finally surfaced in the form of demands for a poetic architecture of a vague ennobling symbolism, recalling the immutability of death, light, dark, and the stark geometry of the sphere, cube, and pyramid: "Nos édifices," he declared, "surtout les édifices publics, devroient être, en quelque façon, des poèmes. Les images, qu'ils offrent à nos sens, devroient exciter en nous des sentiments analogues à l'usage, auquel ces édifices sont consacrés" (see H. Rosenau, *Boullée and Visionary Architecture*, 1976, p. 118). But the buildings he most enjoyed designing were, ironically, the most functionless, as is the horrifying empty sphere of the celebrated Newton cenotaph. It is interesting to speculate to what extent Soane may have been aware of Boullée's obsession with "the poetry of architecture." Although Boullée's *Essai sur l'art* was not published until 1953, he was an energetic teacher of architecture, and through his pupils Soane may have learned of Boullée's ideas. In his Royal Academy lectures, first delivered in 1809, Soane observed: "The 'lumière mystérieuse,' so successfully practised by the French Artist, is a most powerful agent in the hands of a man of genius, and its power cannot be too fully understood, nor too highly appreciated. It is, however, little attended to in our Architecture, and for

Elévation de la Maison du Directeur

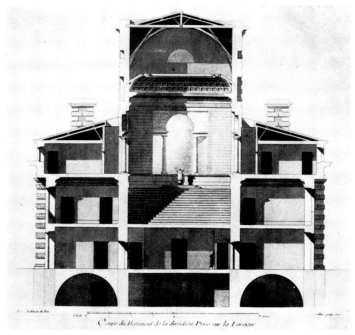

Coupe du Batiment de la direction Prise sur la Largeur

316. *Claude-Nicolas Ledoux, Saline de Chaux, Arc-et-Senans, principal gate, 1775–79*

317. *Claude-Nicolas Ledoux, ideal city of Chaux, Arc-et-Senans, aerial view, from his* Architecture, *1804*

318. *Claude-Nicolas Ledoux, ideal city of Chaux, Arc-et-Senans, perspective view, from his* Architecture, *1804*

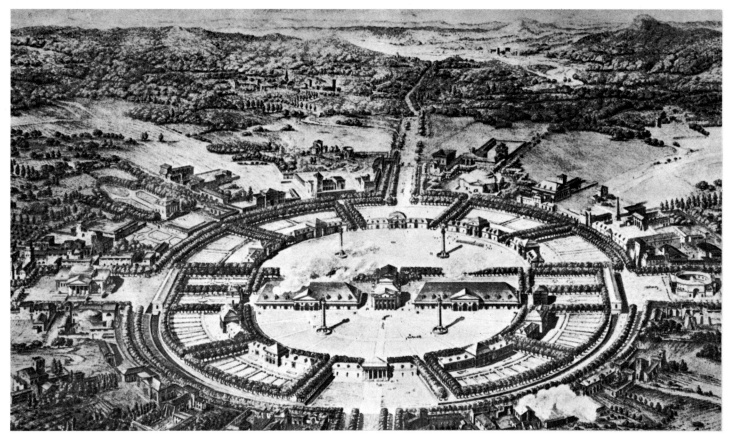

319. Claude-Nicolas Ledoux, project
for a hunting lodge for the Prince de
Bauffremont, 1778

320. Claude-Nicolas Ledoux, project
for the shepherds' house in the park
at Maupertuis, 1780

321. Claude-Nicolas Ledoux,
Château d'Éguière, c. 1780

this obvious reason, that we do not sufficiently feel the importance of Character in our buildings, to which the mode of admitting light contributes in no small degree."

It is from Le Camus de Mézières's book *Le génie de l'architecture,* of 1780, that Boullée and Soane derived their belief in the creation of architectural character by means of the mysterious effect of light that creates an architecture "mystérieux ou triste," and Boullée observed: "C'est la lumière qui produit les effets. Ceux-ci nous causent des sensations diverses et contraires, suivant qu'ils sont brillans ou sombres. . . . Si je peux éviter que la lumière arrive directement, et la faire pénétrer sans que le spectateur aperçoive d'où elle part, les effets résultans d'un jour mystérieux produiront des effets inconcevables, et en qualque façon, une espèce de magie vraiment enchanteresse" (see H. Rosenau, *Boullée and Visionary Architecture,* p. 126).

This could surely stand as an evocation of the effects aimed at and achieved by Soane in such interiors as the Breakfast Parlour at Lincoln's Inn Fields, the Bank of England, and the Law Courts. Soane, indeed, was able, as Boullée was not, to forge within the classical tradition a personal style that was both poetic and practical. As Sir John Summerson has observed (*Sir John Soane,* 1952, p. 15): "In 1792, when [Soane's] style arrives suddenly at maturity, there was not, anywhere in Europe, an architecture as unconstrained by classical loyalties, as free in the handling of proportions and as adventurous in structure and lighting as that which Soane introduced at the Bank of England in that year." The sources of this style are to be found both in France and in England. Soane had been profoundly influenced by the Abbé Laugier's demand for a new architecture that would reconstitute the lightness and grace of Gothic structure in a purified and reformed version of the classical language. We know that Soane possessed eleven copies of Laugier's *Essai sur l'architecture.* What is less well known is that a manuscript survives of Soane's translation of the book from which many of Laugier's ideas were taken, Cordemoy's *Nouveau traité de toute l'architecture.* But Soane's sources were also English. He had worshiped at the shrine of his old master, George Dance, the younger (1741–1825), to whose work we now give our attention.

Adam, Chambers, and Mylne all arrived in Rome, the melting pot of early neoclassicism, in 1754–55, and the eighteen-year-old George Dance followed in 1759. He had been sent there by his architect father in order to join his brother Nathaniel, a painter, who had arrived four years earlier. Soon George Dance met Piranesi, and together they made the first accurate measured drawings of the Temple of Castor and Pollux in the Forum. In 1762 he entered the competition for a design for a public gallery for statues and pictures organized by the Accademia at Parma. The design with which he won the Gold Medal in 1763, characterized by stone domes and bleak rusticated walls, shows how much he had absorbed of the emergent neoclassicism of the French Grand Prix projects. This was the style of heroic grimness that M.-J. Peyre was to encapsulate in his *Oeuvres d'architecture,* of

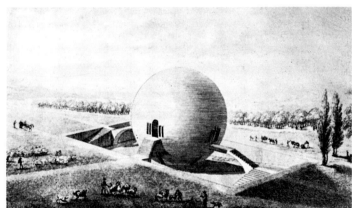

322. *Claude-Nicolas Ledoux, Hosten
Houses, Rue St.-Georges, Paris,
elevation, 1792–95*

323. *Claude-Nicolas Ledoux, Hosten
Houses, Paris, elevation, section*

324. *Claude-Nicolas Ledoux, the
Cénobie, ideal city of Chaux, Arc-et-
Senans, from his* Architecture, *1804*

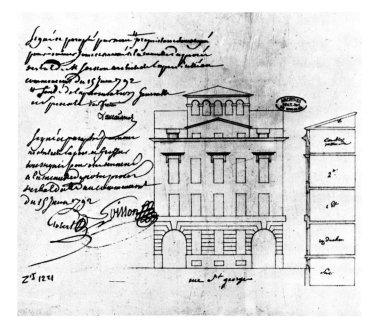

1765, and that also inspired the dreams of the young Soane, Dance's junior by twelve years.

Dance returned to England late in 1764 and by the following spring was at work on his first commission, the church of All Hallows, London Wall, in the City of London. Inspired by the Roman Baths, and roofed with a barrel vault—not the coffered ellipse used by Inigo Jones and James Gibbs—the church has an internal Ionic order that lacks a full entablature and has instead a highly enriched frieze. This not very daring novelty, which was due to Dance's reading of Laugier's *Essai sur l'architecture,* we know shocked Soane when he first saw it. Dance's next building was Newgate Gaol (designed in 1768–69), which combines themes derived from Peyre with a Mannerist handling of rustication inspired by Giulio Romano. Elements from the powerful style of Vanbrugh also appear in the centrally placed Keeper's House, where they help reinforce the dramatic "narrative" content of the building, which was evidently intended to be expressive of its grim function. In the *Cours d'architecture,* which J.-F. Blondel began delivering to his students in 1743 (it was not published until 1771), the prison was upheld as the sole permanent building type for the style later described as "architecture parlante." This seems to relate not only to Newgate Gaol but also to Burke's category of the Sublime, of which he wrote: "Whatever is fitted in any sort to excite the ideas of pain and anger . . . whatever is in any sort terrible . . . is a source of the sublime."

In the late 1770s Dance remodeled a country house, Cranbury Park, in Hampshire, for a family friend, providing a top-lit ballroom that contains the seeds of the mature Dance-Soane style. This vast room has semi-domes to east and west derived from the Roman Baths, but in the center is a beautiful, shallow cross vault in a starfish pattern that was adapted from a

XXIII. *George Dance, design for the*
library of Lansdowne House, London,
1788–91

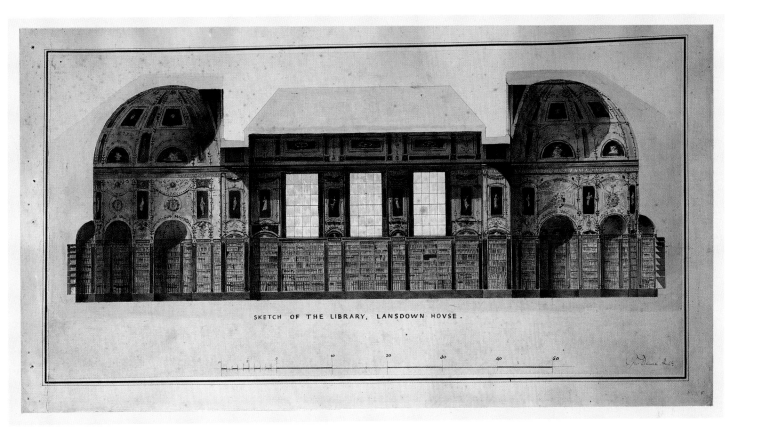

SKETCH OF THE LIBRARY, LANSDOWN HOVSE.

XXIV. Sir John Soane, No. 13
Lincoln's Inn Fields (Sir John Soane's
Museum), London, Breakfast Parlour
1812

325. Claude-Nicolas Ledoux,
cemetery, ideal city of Chaux,
Arc-et-Senans, section, from his
Architecture, 1804

326. Claude-Nicolas Ledoux, project
for a cooper's house, ideal city of
Chaux, Arc-et-Senans, from his
Architecture, 1804

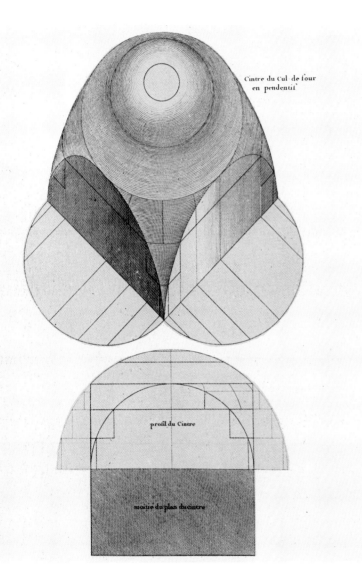

327. Plate from Jean-Baptiste de La Rue's Traité de la coupe des pierres, *1728*

328. George Dance, Cranbury Park, Hampshire, detail of the ballroom ceiling, c. 1778

329. George Dance, Newgate Goal, London, 1768–80

198

plate in Pietro Santi Bartoli's *Gli antichi sepolcri ovvero mausolei romani* (1697; new edition 1757). This important book, which was almost certainly known to Adam and was later owned by Soane, played a decisive role in disseminating knowledge of ancient Roman interior decoration. The groin vault in a starfish pattern, first imitated by Dance at Cranbury, became the hallmark of Soane's interiors, beginning with the study of his first house at Lincoln's Inn Fields, begun in 1792. The influence on Dance and Soane of this "sepulchral" architecture is particularly interesting in light of Boullée's obsession with the romantic effects of "buried architecture."

Dance developed the Cranbury theme in two interiors at the Guildhall in London, from 1777 to 1779. In the Common Council Chamber the dome and its pendentives are all parts of the same sphere, a device that may have been inspired by Jean-Baptiste de la Rue's *Traité de la coupe des pierres* (1728): Plate XXXIV shows the construction of a "cul-de-four en pendentifs sur un quarré." This is an attack on the Renaissance and Baroque conception of a domed space in which the dome is a separate handsome entity resting on clearly defined piers. At the Guildhall the dome is reduced to its essence. The whole room becomes a kind of dome, a basic tent or covering. This primitivist tent- or umbrella-like aspect is emphasized by the scalloped curves of decorative and nonstructural origin. The fluting applied to the dome is perhaps derived from the ruin of the Serapeum at Hadrian's Villa, which Dance may have seen and which was illustrated in the 1760s by Piranesi in *Vedute di Roma.* This type of fluting also became a feature of Grand Prix designs as, for example, in Sobre's Maison de Plaisance (1782). Another novelty of the Council Chamber was the space at the east and west ends that rose higher than that in the center, thus enabling the western end to be illuminated by two largely invisible windows casting light from a hidden source. This "lumière mystérieuse" was also a characteristic of the library that Dance designed within an uncompleted shell constructed by Adam at Lansdowne House, London, at the end of the 1780s. Dance remodeled Adam's vaults, creating semi-domes at each end of the long central space. The overall form of these domed spaces may derive from the Temple of Minerva Medica in Rome, but the sliced-off semi-domes, with their concealed Diocletian windows, were inspired by a French Grand Prix precedent. We find them in Pierre-Nicolas Bernard's project for a *palais de justice,* of 1782, and in Sobre's *hôtel de ville,* of five years later.

A related obsession of Dance's was top-lit octagonal halls in a stripped Gothic style, such as those at St.-Bartholomew-the-Less, London (1789); at St. Mary, Micheldever, Hampshire (1808); and at the house he built for the great patron and collector Sir George Beaumont at Coleorton, Leicestershire (1804). The combination of a kind of reductionist Gothic with Romantic toplighting echoes the ambitions of both Laugier and Boullée. In a very different interior at a London lunatic asylum, St. Luke's Hospital, Old Street (1781), Dance provided a nightmare-like, seemingly endless repetition of arches that anticipated the extreme shrill attenuation,

331. George Dance, St. Luke's
Hospital, London, interior, 1781
332. George Dance, project for No. 6
St. James's Square, London, after
1815

both horizontal and vertical, of Bernard Poyet's Rue des Colonnes, Paris (1798), and Friedrich Weinbrenner's Kaiserstrasse, Karlsruhe (1808). Again we are reminded of Burke, who, in defining the delightful horrors of the Sublime, analyzed the effect of "infinity and things multiplied without end."

The abstraction and linearity that we also find in Dance's work make him an architectural counterpart to John Flaxman. Dance reduced both Gothic and classical styles to a strange disembodied synthesis that recalls Flaxman's depiction of the Greek world in his illustrations of Homer and Aeschylus, and of medieval Catholicism in his illustrations of Dante. But before we consign Dance to that chill vacuum let us recall what C. R. Cockerell said of him in his Royal Academy lectures in the 1840s: "Dance showed himself the most complete Poet Architect of his day—no one can doubt that Newgate is a prison, that St. Luke's is an asylum, prison or place of milder confinement for the unhappy and bewildered in mind, or that the front of the Guildhall, though anything but Gothic, is still the metropolitan and magnificent place of Government and civil authority."

What we have said of Dance is, in general, true of Soane, for never were two artists more mutually dependent on each other in the development of a common style. Dance, as the older man, often provided the motifs first, although the last design by him—of which we have a record—shows a definite dependence on Soane. This is his unexecuted project, dating from some time after 1815, for a house for Lord Bristol at No. 6 St. James's Square, London. It is basically a kind of warehouse, a three-storied glass box that was inspired by Soane's ruthlessly novel Loggia in the Waiting Room Courtyard at the Bank of England, of 1804–5. Soane was appointed Surveyor to the bank in 1788, succeeding Sir Robert Taylor. His extensive additions to and remodelings of Taylor's work occupied him on and off for the next thirty-six years and undoubtedly represent the apotheosis of his unique architectural style. His first task was to rebuild completely Taylor's Stock Office immediately north of the Bartholomew Lane vestibule. Rain had seeped in through Taylor's lead roof and had decayed the principal roof timbers. Soane therefore concentrated his attention on a new roof set on stone piers with brick arches springing from them, replacing Taylor's interiors of lath and plaster and timber, which had been susceptible to both fire and water. Soane's vault was constructed of what he called cones—tapering hollow blocks of terra-cotta based on those used in the Byzantine buildings of Ravenna. He chose them for their fireproof qualities as well as for their lightness. Soane's floating, disembodied space—marked by sharply incised lines, ribs, and grooves—owes something, as Summerson has shown, to the Baths of Diocletian, Dance's Common Council Chamber at the Guildhall, Taylor's Reduced Annuities Office (1782–88) at the Bank of England, Piranesi's engravings, and to Laugier's emphasis on considerations of structure and utility through analogy to the primitive hut. As an indication of the daring step Soane took at the Bank Stock Office we may

compare it with a related interior of 1791–93, his Yellow Drawing Room at Wimpole Hall, Cambridgeshire. In this extraordinary, domed, T-shaped room Soane evidently went as far as he dared in adapting to domestic purposes the radical novelties pioneered by Dance at the Common Council Chamber, in 1777. At the bank he allowed himself more freedom. When he turned his attention, in 1794, to Taylor's Rotunda, also in need of repair, it emerged wondrously transformed. Where Taylor's space (see illustration 242) had been a pale echo of the Pantheon, Soane's is an imaginative re-creation of the spirit—not the letter—of an antique domed space. With Dance's help he provided an abstract synthesis in which the classical orders were reduced schematically to geometrical incised lines, the whole saved from totally chill austerity by the romantic lighting effects, the "lumière mystérieuse" of Le Camus de Mézières.

In the same style as the Bank Stock Office and Rotunda, Soane went on to turn Taylor's Transfer Office immediately north of the Rotunda into the Old Shutting Room. This dates from 1794–96, and was followed, in 1797–99, by the adjacent Consols Office, with its startling ring of caryatids, which, according to the original design, was to have been decorated even more richly. The development south of the Rotunda came much later, in 1812–23, but the stylistic consistency was remarkable. The caryatids of the Consols Office, greatly increased in height, turn up in the lantern of the Old Dividend or Four Percent Office, and are replaced by a noble Ionic colonnade in the Old Colonial or Five Percent Office, both completed in 1818. From 1804 to 1805 Soane provided a new western entrance to the bank in the newly realigned Prince's Street. The Picturesque vista from the barrel-vaulted Greek Doric entrance vestibule toward the dramatic open Loggia along the north side of the Waiting Room Courtyard is one of the most brilliant realizations of Soane's belief in the "poetry of architecture." Indeed, the whole bank could be seen as an embodiment of that belief. The way in which it grew slowly and haphazardly, with Soane obliged to combine and retain all manner of heterogeneous fragments of earlier buildings, and even to remodel his own, meant that the planning was empirical and not neoclassical. None of the grand gateways really led anywhere; nothing was related to anything else in a way that an ancient Roman or a modern Frenchman would have understood. In its piecemeal, haphazard growth and plan it was thoroughly English and thoroughly Picturesque, yet in actual design no building in Europe was more neoclassical. Its poetry has never been better captured than by Sir Osbert Sitwell in his autobiographical volume *Great Morning* (1948), where he describes how in the evening "this one-storey building emptied altogether of life, and with its garden-courts and cloisters, resembled a monastery or a deserted temple rather than the most famous financial institution in the world. By one of the passionate paradoxes of its creator—surely the most original of all English architects—it seemed to offer a quiet, leafy, well-kept retreat from the world."

335. *Sir John Soane, Bank of England, London, Lothbury Court, detail of the colonnade, 1797*

336. *Sir John Soane, Bank of England, London, entrance vestibule to the Waiting Room Courtyard, 1804–05*

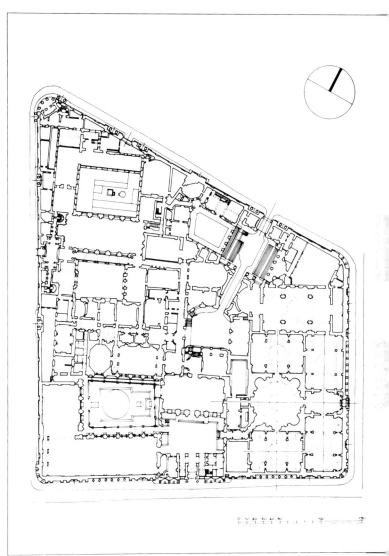

337. *Sir John Soane, Bank of England, London, 1788–1833, ground-floor plan as in 1924*

One type of interior not fully exploited at the Bank of England, but particularly associated with Soane's mature style, is that dominated by a kind of hanging ceiling or domed canopy. Its first tentative appearance is in the Front Parlour of Soane's own house, Pitzhanger Manor (1800–1802), at Ealing, near London. Of markedly funereal appearance, with sarcophagi in tomblike recesses and much other antique sculpture, this room must originally have been close in spirit to Thomas Hope's contemporary house-*cum*-museum in Duchess Street, London. The shadowy and funereal overtones of Soane's room were certainly not accidental and forcibly recall Boullée's ambition to create an "architecture ensevelie." Indeed, Boullée declared in his *Essai sur l'art* that the "Temple of Death" was the type of building that, more than any other, calls for the "poésie de l'architecture," so as to convey "l'image de l'architecture ensevelie, en n'employant que des proportions basses et affaissées et enfouies dans la terre, former enfin par les matières absorbant la lumière, le noir tableau de l'architecture des ombres dessiné par l'effet d'ombres encore plus noires. Ce genre d'architecture formé par des ombres," he proudly added, "est une découverte d'art qui m'appartient. C'est une carrière nouvelle que j'ai ouverte" (see H. Rosenau, *Boullée and Visionary Architecture,* pp. 124, 135). However, in such interiors as the Breakfast Parlour (1812) at Lincoln's Inn Fields, the National Debt Redemption Office, Old Jewry, City of London (1817), the Privy Council Chamber, Downing Street (1824), the Freemasons' Hall, Great Queen Street (1828), and the Law Courts at Westminster (1820s), Soane's obsession with toplighting and with high side lighting creates an eerie and mysteriously subterranean effect—occasionally inspired by Gothic vaulting and lighting arrangements—that represents the final and uniquely personal synthesis of the "lumière mystérieuse" of the visionary architecture of France and the Picturesque tradition of eighteenth-century England.

342. Sir John Soane, No. 13
Lincoln's Inn Fields (Sir John Soane's
Museum). London, Breakfast Parlour,
1812

343. Sir John Soane, Privy Council
Chamber, London, 1824

PART II

The chronological span of this book is 1750 to 1870. We have avoided reliance on the misleading descriptive term neoclassicism *and have emphasized the importance of both the rationalist theory developed in France and the Picturesque movement in England. The book is primarily a history of architecture and thus does not cover many of the important developments that took place during the years in question in town planning, transport, and engineering. We also felt it impossible, in a single volume, to give equal attention to each period and country. Thus, the reader will find less on England than on France, for English architecture has been examined by such historians as John Summerson, Henry-Russell Hitchcock, and Nikolaus Pevsner, whereas French architecture—particularly of the nineteenth century—has been much less extensively investigated. Architecture rests on intellectual as well as material foundations, and we hope that fresh light will be shed on the period by our emphasis on the theories and ideas that so often lay behind the new movements.*

Robin Middleton
David Watkin

Chapter Six
LATER CLASSICAL AND ITALIANATE ARCHITECTURE

FRANCE: *Percier and Fontaine to Garnier*

Building continued sporadically after the Revolution in France, but it was scarcely an auspicious time for architecture. There was little opportunity and a conspicuous lack of vigor in design. Arrangements and patterns evolved earlier in the eighteenth century were repeated to produce an array of neat, charming, and altogether well-planned and ornamented houses on the outskirts of Paris. But this was not the sort of activity to stimulate new talents. Architects turned to other occupations. Charles-Pierre-Joseph Normand (1765–1840) and Théodore Ollivier became engravers; others served as surveyors and military engineers in Napoleon's endless campaigns. Only Napoleon was able to act as a great patron, but not until after the coup d'état of 1799 that brought him finally to power. Most of the architects he employed on his larger projects had already made names for themselves before the Revolution. Rondelet restored once again the church of Ste.-Geneviève (now renamed the Panthéon). Chalgrin, who had started work on the Palais du Luxembourg in 1787, transformed its interior completely between 1803 and 1807 for the use of the Senate. The Salle du Sénat (disastrously redesigned in 1836 by Chalgrin's pupil Alphonse-Henri de Gisors) and the great extended stair with which Chalgrin replaced Rubens's gallery were unquestionably dramatic in a late eighteenth-century sort of way, but they were by then in the nature of established solutions. Chalgrin's Arc de Triomphe, the foundation stone of which was laid on August 18, 1806, was finer, though not as first conceived. He aimed, then, at the accepted grandeur of ancient Roman buildings, incorporating freestanding decorative columns, statues, and bas-relief panels. His projects of 1810, however, were more austere, and, as were all Chalgrin's works, faultless in proportion. Later Blouet was to complete the attic story of the Arc, destroying in the process the balance of Chalgrin's restrained classicism. Bélanger provided a design for an ambitious cast-iron dome for the court of the Halle aux Blés in 1805, two years after Legrand's and Molinos's timber dome burned down. He also began a very noble *abattoir* at Rochechouart in 1809, while Brongniart, as we have seen, started on the Bourse in the year before. Between 1806 and 1810 Gondoin, together with Jean-Baptiste Lepère (1761–1844), erected his most famous, if least enterprising, work, the Colonne Vendôme.

There were newcomers, though their architecture was even less precise and alive than that of the established practitioners. After much fuss and intrigue and no little competition, Ledoux's pupil Alexandre-Pierre Vignon (1763–1828) was commissioned in 1807 to build the Madeleine, incorporating some of the foundation of Contant d'Ivry's church. The result was a lifeless paraphrase of an antique Roman temple. The interior, in which the theme of the Roman Bath was developed with dogged determination and success of a kind, was the work of Jean-Jacques-Marie Huvé (1783–1852), who took over in 1828 and completed most of the building twelve years later, though decoration continued until 1845.

344. *Jean-François-Thérèse Chalgrin, Palais du Luxembourg, Paris, Salle du Sénat, 1803–7*

345. *Jean-François-Thérèse Chalgrin, Palais du Luxembourg, Paris, grand staircase, 1803–7*

211

he passed it on to Hittorff. Hittorff added brightly painted porticos to his Rotonde des Panoramas (1838-39) and, as we have seen, to the Cirque National—both on the Champs-Élysées—and elaborately decorated the Cirque d'Hiver, Boulevard des Filles-du-Calvaire. However, his real opportunity to demonstrate how the studied and serious classical style of the early nineteenth century might be transformed, but in conformity with antique precedents, came with the completion of St.-Vincent-de-Paul, overlooking the Place Lafayette, Paris. This church was sketched first, in 1824, by Hittorff's father-in-law, Lepère, who had worked with Gondoin on the Colonne Vendôme. But building was not begun in earnest until 1830, by which time Hittorff had revised the design completely. It is the largest basilican church of the period, with two tiers of columns inside supporting an open, timber-trussed roof. Externally it is preceded by a large pedimented portico set against a flat masonry wall with a central projection, and is flanked by two square towers. The site and the setting lend some grandeur to the composition, but all feeling for mass is lacking and the detailing is disappointingly thin. Internally the same criticisms would apply were the interior not transformed into a riot of strong color: The columns are apricot; above, there are frescoes by a host of Ingres's pupils, including Jean-Hippolyte Flandrin; the roof trusses are brilliant blues and reds, all scattered with gold, in imitation of those at Monreale cathedral, which Hittorff saw as a latter-day expression of what he had imagined as the colorful architecture of Greek antiquity. Even today this interior is vibrant. For the outside Hittorff proposed something parallel. In 1846 he started to cover the wall of the portico with large, brightly colored enameled plaques, painted by Gros's pupil Jollivet. This panorama of biblical scenes was intended to extend over the entire surface. Seven of these were eventually put up, but the clergy was scandalized by the nudity of Adam and Eve—and everyone else by the blaze of color—and in 1861, at the clergy's behest, the plaques were taken down, though they still survive in a depot at Ivry-sur-Seine.

Hittorff built a great deal besides. Between 1836 and 1840 he flattened out Gabriel's Place Louis XV, by then renamed the Place de la Concorde, topped the pavilions with heavy statues, and added the obelisk, the fountains (of cast-iron), and the lamp standards. These were all originally gilt. He embellished the Champs-Élysées with an array of fountains, shelters, restaurants, and the circus and panorama already mentioned. Then in 1855 he designed the houses around the Place de l'Étoile and began what is now the Avenue Foch, leading to the Bois de Boulogne, where he began excavating the lakes. To the east of the Place de la Concorde he extended the Rue de Rivoli, designing the first of the large-scale *hôtels* in Paris on the American pattern, the Grand Hôtel des Chemins de Fer (now the Grands Magasins du Louvre). Opposite Perrault's Louvre facade he built the ungainly Mairie du 1er between 1855 and 1861, as a pendant to St.-Germain-l'Auxerrois, which he was forced to paraphrase. He found no

that was both fastidious and coarse. He employed a great many sculptors and painters, and the church became at once a focus of artistic attention—an attention, when related to the ideas put forward in the *Jupiter Olympien,* that was to undermine, if not destroy, much that Quatremère de Quincy had stood for.

Hittorff, the exponent of a highly colored image of Greek antiquity, was the agent of change. In 1834, ten years after his return from Italy, and at the height of the quarrel concerning the application of color in Greek architecture, he designed two side altars for Notre-Dame-de-Lorette, gilded, pedimented affairs that incorporated panels of vividly colored enamel. The commission had been offered first to Jean-Auguste-Dominique Ingres, but

XXVI. Charles Percier and Pierre
François-Léonard Fontaine, Château
de Malmaison (Rueil-Malmaison),
music room, 1799–1803

354. Charles Percier and Pierre-
François-Léonard Fontaine, Palais
Royal, Paris, Galerie d'Orléans,
1829

enjoyment in this task, for he loathed the Gothic style. But he was no favorite of Baron Haussmann, the all-powerful *Préfet de la Seine,* who was intent to embarrass him. They were involved soon enough in bitter litigation about the works in the Bois de Boulogne and the payment of fees. Hittorff won, but Haussmann had his revenge. By changing the alignments of the streets he saw to it that Hittorff's greatest work, the Gare du Nord, designed in 1859 and started two years later, did not act as a terminal feature to a main boulevard.

The Gare du Nord was a fitting conclusion to Hittorff's career. It reflected faithfully the disparities of his approach to architecture. The planning was excellent and sufficiently flexible to allow for the gradual transformation from a mixed goods and passenger terminal to one for people alone. The construction of the sheds was simple, economical, daring, and successful—A.-R. Polonceau's newly developed gable trusses were used, and all the ironwork was made in Glasgow. But the architecture of the facade was an assorted medley of classical motifs, all of unrelated scale, used neither correctly nor with sufficient panache to transcend the lack of convention. Hittorff was not a creative architect. Not one of his buildings is resolved. He applied decoration, usually of a meager kind, in an attempt to disguise his failure to compose convincingly, but even here he appeared to be fiddling. He was, however, wonderfully adventurous in other respects, especially as a technical innovator. In 1828 he introduced safety curtains of iron into the Théâtre de l'Ambigu Comique (demolished 1966). For the roof of his Rotonde des Panoramas he adapted the principle of the suspension bridge; for that of the Cirque National he employed an extremely elegant lattice timber truss, and repeated this with an even greater refinement at the Cirque d'Hiver. His prowess in this respect was always acclaimed and was slowly emulated. And his archaeological theories, too, though they had little enough to do with archaeology, opened the eyes of a whole generation of architects in France to the possibility of breaking from the established classical routine and developing a new architecture. The use of applied color in architecture after 1830 was a sign of rebellion.

The rebels of the 1830s are usually accounted as Guillaume-Abel Blouet, Émile-Jacques Gilbert, Félix-Jacques Duban, Henri Labrouste, Louis-Joseph Duc, and Léon Vaudoyer. But their contributions to architecture were very different and quite distinct.

Blouet (1795–1853) and Gilbert (1793–1874) emerged first. Blouet trained with Delespine, Gilbert with Durand at the École Polytechnique and then with Vignon at the École des Beaux-Arts. They both won the Grand Prix, Blouet in 1821, Gilbert in the year following; they worked together in Rome and again, after their return, when Blouet was appointed architect to the Arc de Triomphe in 1831, with Gilbert as his *Inspecteur.* Blouet, a protégé of Quatremère de Quincy, had been sent on an official mission to Greece in 1828; when his restoration studies of the Doric temple on Aegina were published in 1838, the temple was revealed in bright color, primarily

blue and red. Gilbert made his attestation in the brilliantly colored interior of the chapel that forms the focus of his vast and very austere Asile d'Aliénés at Charenton, on the edge of Paris, built between 1838 and 1845. But Blouet's and Gilbert's idea of reform in architecture was based on nothing so superficial as the application of color.

They thought to enrich architecture by making moral and social aims determine its arrangement, as never before. Like many intellectuals of their generation, they were sustained by the humanitarian ideas of Saint-Simon and Charles Fourier. Saint-Simon was not at first much interested in architecture or even in art—"Il n'y a aujourd'hui d'hommes qui se vouent à la poésie que ceux qui ne peuvent pas réussir dans les travaux de l'intelligence," he wrote in 1813 in his *Mémoire sur la science de l'homme.* But by the year of his death, in 1825, when he wrote *Le nouveau christianisme,* he had reserved a place for architects among the leaders of society, alongside the engineers and the factory owners. He made no positive proposals himself, although his disciples, led by Émile Barrault, were to propound a doctrine at both the Saint-Simonist expositions of 1828 and 1830, and, especially, in the pamphlet *Aux artistes: du passé et de l'avenir des beaux-arts,* issued in 1830, which held that the history of the arts followed a succession of "organic" and "critical" periods, the organic being identified as pre-Periclean Greek and that of the Middle Ages, expressive both of a unity of religious belief and social aspiration. The early Greek temple and the Gothic cathedral were thus seen as embodiments of integrated societies. Victor Hugo's architectural ideas, contained, in particular, in the second edition of his *Notre-Dame de Paris,* of 1832, were a direct response to such propaganda. But the Saint-Simonists themselves did not pursue these ideas to any consequence, nor were they to interpret them with any resounding success. Under the leadership of Barthélemy-Prosper Enfantin, a group of Saint-Simon's followers did set out in 1834 to build a city for the workers digging the Suez Canal. The plan of the city was in the shape of a human figure, the buildings corresponding to the functions of the body, administrative buildings and scientific institutes at the head, academies and temples at the heart, and so on. But the disciples did not get far with their plans. They were decimated by cholera. Fourier, however, suggested an architectural form for his ideas, at first reluctantly, but by 1829, when he published *Le nouveau monde industriel et sociétaire,* he included a sketch plan for one of his communes, which he called a *phalange.* This appeared as a bird's-eye perspective on the title page of *Le phalanstère* in June 1832, the year in which an attempt was made to found such a commune at Condé-sur-Vesgre, near Rambouillet. Victor Considerant was to depict his *phalanstère* as a palace of Versailles in 1834 in *Considérations sociales sur l'architecture.* But the opportunity for building such a community was to be rare. Only one was built in France, André Godin's *familistère* at Guise, begun in 1859, still standing and still working. No architect was involved. Godin employed a former art student, E. André, to prepare the drawings. The type was to

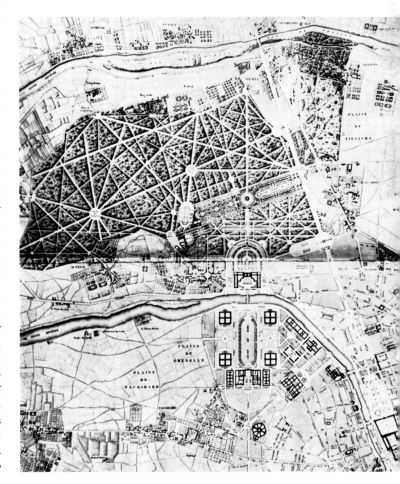

become familiar in America—where Godin himself financed a phalanstery in Texas in 1853—but in France such experiments were so isolated and of so specific a nature that they had only an indirect influence on architecture. Later low-cost houses for workers, notably those built by Émile Müller for the Société Mulhousienne des Cités Ouvrières, beginning in 1853, and even his pupil Émile Cacheux's minimal houses, put up in Auteuil (Villa Émile Meyer and Villa Dietz Monnin) and elsewhere in Paris in the 1880s, all aimed to provide single dwellings with gardens, not collectives. The workers were to buy their houses and to become respectable members of the propertied classes.

Gilbert's and Blouet's model was provided by C. B. Beccaria in Italy and John Howard in England, who in the late eighteenth century had initiated

362. Louis-Hippolyte Lebas, Notre-Dame-de-Lorette, Paris, 1823–36
363. Louis-Hippolyte Lebas, Notre-Dame-de-Lorette, Paris, interior, 1823–36

364. Étienne-Hippolyte Godde, St.-Pierre-du-Gros-Caillou, Paris, interior, 1822–30

365. Jacques-Ignace Hittorff and Jean-Baptiste Lepère, St.-Vincent-de-Paul, Paris, 1824, 1830–46

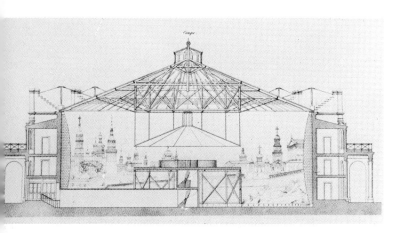

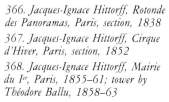

366. *Jacques-Ignace Hittorff, Rotonde des Panoramas, Paris, section, 1838*

367. *Jacques-Ignace Hittorff, Cirque d'Hiver, Paris, section, 1852*

368. *Jacques-Ignace Hittorff, Mairie du Ier, Paris, 1855–61; tower by Théodore Ballu, 1858–63*

369. *Jacques-Ignace Hittorff and Jules Jollivet, project for the decoration of the portico of St.-Vincent-de-Paul with enameled panels, one of which was painted in 1846, with six more to follow in 1852, all being taken down in 1861*

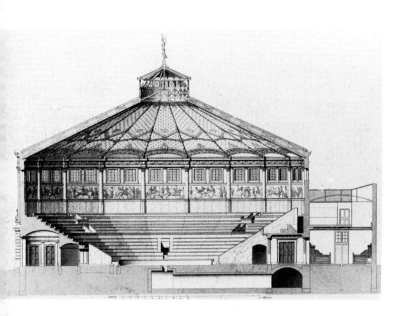

370. Jacques-Ignace Hittorff and
Jean-Baptiste Lepère, St.-Vincent-de-
Paul, Paris, interior, 1830–46

371. Jacques-Ignace Hittorff, Gare
du Nord, Paris, 1861–65

372. Jacques-Ignace Hittorff, Gare
du Nord, Paris, detail of the sheds,
1861–65

a series of penal reforms that resulted in the gradual separation of criminals from the sick and the insane. Criminals, in turn, were categorized according to sex, age, and the nature of their crimes, so that by degrees the only means of ensuring that they did not adversely influence one another was to provide each with an individual cell—a self-contained unit, fully serviced, that might ensure total isolation and thus opportunity for moral redemption. Many prisoners went mad under these conditions and regrouping began once again. The architectural image that embodied these ideals was Jeremy Bentham's Panopticon. Though never realized, this was reflected in the arrangement of the ill-fated penitentiary erected at Millbank in London, between 1812 and 1821. The aim was the continuous surveillance of all prisoners from a single observation post; the obvious expression of this was the radial plan. This was introduced into France in 1825, when Lebas, architect of Notre-Dame-de-Lorette, won a competition for a model prison on the site of La Roquette in Paris. Though he had visited Millbank, it is evident that he had not grasped its rationale. He produced a plan of giant formality, a hexagon with six wings linked to the center. There, he placed a chapel. Prison reformers soon realized that the building was unlikely to prove satisfactory. In 1830 a magistrate, G. de Beaumont, was sent with Alexis de Tocqueville to study prisons in America, where remarkably efficient systems of organization were being evolved, especially in Philadelphia. De Tocqueville spent too much time collecting material for *La démocratie en Amérique* (1835, 1840). By 1836 another tour of American prisons was needed; on this occasion the magistrate F. A. Demetz was provided with Blouet as his companion. At the same time Gilbert was appointed to design La Nouvelle Force at Mazas, together with Jean-François-Joseph Lecointe (1783–1858), an early associate of Hittorff. Work there started in 1843. The great period of prison reform had begun, and an architecture embodying the new humanitarian ideals was initiated.

Gilbert continued always to use the patterns of organization and the stylistic details that he had inherited from Durand, and so the change was not so much in any alteration of form or details as in a careful consideration of their use in relation to the function they were to perform. Nothing in Gilbert's architecture was done for effect. Everything had a straightforward raison d'être. His prison, which was opened in 1850, consisted of an administrative block linked to a domed rotunda—an observation post on one floor, a chapel on the next—from which radiated six wings at a forty-five-degree angle to one another, containing three floors of individual cells. Each cell was fully serviced with hot and cold water, a WC, and a heating and ventilation system. The organization of life in the prison determined the architecture in every way, as it had in that even more strictly utilitarian structure from which Gilbert derived many ideas, the Pentonville prison, put up in London between 1840 and 1842 by Major Joshua Jebb. But the prison at Mazas was not looked upon simply as a solution to some readily defined problem. "Le prison de Mazas," Adolphe Lance wrote in

373. *Victor Considerant, project for a*
phalanstère, *1834*
374. *André Godin and E. André,*
familistère, *Guise, begun 1859*

375. *André Godin and E. André,*
familistère, *Guise, interior court,*
begun 1859

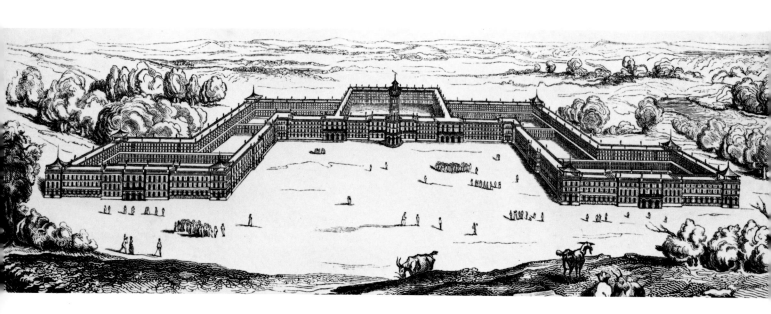

376. *Louis-Hippolyte Lebas, house of detention for juvenile offenders, Place de la Roquette, Paris, plan, 1825*

377. *Guillaume-Abel Blouet, penal farm colony, Mettray, near Tours, plan, designed 1839*

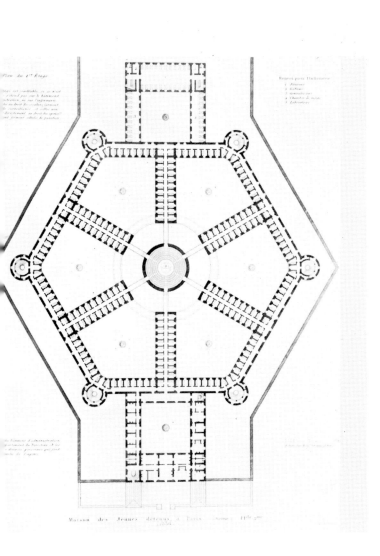

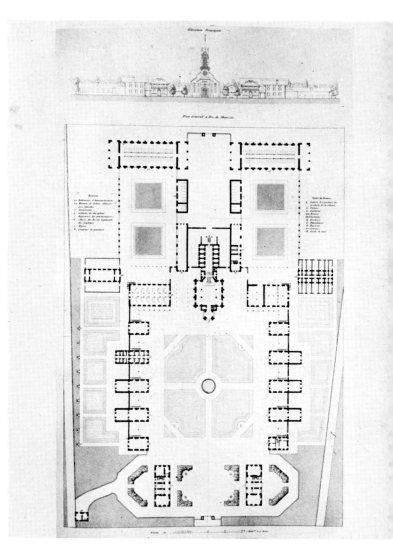

378. Émile-Jacques Gilbert, Asile
d'Aliénés, Charenton, chapel,
1838–45

379. Émile-Jacques Gilbert, Asile
d'Aliénés, Charenton, courtyard,
1838–45

the *Encyclopédie d'architecture* in December 1853, "n'est pas exclusivement une bâtisse bien entendu et un instrument administratif, c'est une oeuvre d'art" (pp. 175–82).

Gilbert's other buildings were all expressions of humanitarian reform in administrative guise, often of the most repressive if well-meaning kind. The new theories on the treatment of the insane led to his appointment in 1838 as architect of the Asile d'Aliénés, built during the next seven years on the hillside at Charenton, to the east of Paris, in a series of long, terraced pavilions, linked by colonnades, with a chapel, as we have seen, forming the focus. The different types of madmen were isolated here within the individual pavilions, men to one side, women to the other. Police reforms resulted in Gilbert's Préfecture de la Police on the Île de la Cité in Paris, of 1862 to 1876. Hospital reforms produced his Hôtel-Dieu nearby, put up between 1864 and 1876 with the aid of his son-in-law, Arthur-Stanislas Diet (1827–1890), who also completed Gilbert's asylum and prefecture. By the time the Hôtel-Dieu was completed, the simple geometrical ideals of Durand had proved inadequate to such a building. Even before it was finished part was dismantled and much redesigned. The doctors were never to be satisfied. But the sheer regularity of the architecture, the elegance even of the colonnaded courts, are undeniably impressive. Gilbert's only other building was the morgue erected on the Pont St.-Michel, Paris, opposite the east end of Notre-Dame, from 1861 to 1863. This has long since been demolished.

Blouet pursued his utilitarian aims largely through teaching. In 1846, when L.-P. Baltard died, a change in approach was at last possible in the training at the École des Beaux-Arts, and Blouet was appointed to succeed him as *Professeur de Théorie de l'Architecture.* The following year he began publication of his *Supplément à la traité théorique et pratique de l'art de bâtir de Jean Rondelet,* which, as we have remarked, was largely a catalogue of early nineteenth-century engineering achievements. He was responsible for only one noteworthy work of architecture—a church at Fontainebleau and the attic story of the Arc de Triomphe apart—a penal farm colony at Mettray, near Tours, designed in 1839, finished a few years later. The architecture here consists of no more than a series of dull utilitarian dormitory pavilions set formally on either side of a nondescript church, mildly medieval in inspiration, with the farm buildings behind. Yet Michel Foucault has recognized the system of reform that was enacted within as the ultimate limit of coercion on humanitarian grounds. Blouet became thereby the accepted authority on prison architecture.

The remaining members of the group of reform, Duban, Labrouste, Duc, and Vaudoyer, were less doctrinaire in their attitudes: They upheld the ideals of Durand, Rondelet, and the Saint-Simonists but did not allow them full play in their architecture; they were more concerned to infuse them into a renewed classical tradition. All were Grand Prix winners, starting with Duban in 1823 and continuing to 1826, when Vaudoyer was awarded the

380. Émile-Jacques Gilbert and
Arthur-Stanislas Diet, Hôtel-Dieu,
Paris, 1864–76

381. Émile-Jacques Gilbert and
Arthur-Stanislas Diet, Hôtel-Dieu,
Paris, courtyard, 1864–76

prize. In Rome, Duban and Labrouste met Hittorff and Blouet; all of them met Gilbert, who served as their mentor. They formed a close-knit group and continued through life to collaborate and support one another. But their architecture revealed them as very different. Félix-Jacques Duban (1797–1870), who had trained under Percier, had a passion for intricate and lively surface decoration, though it is fair to note that he integrated it far more successfully into his compositions than did Hittorff. In 1832 he took over the building of the École des Beaux-Arts from his brother-in-law François Debres. The foundations were already laid, but the great building facing the court on the Rue Bonaparte is his. It is a compression of all his Italian learning. The triumphal arches of Rome, the Colosseum, and the Cancelleria are all hinted at in the facade; inside, the frescoes of Pompeii no less than those of Raphael are recalled. The glass-covered courtyard with its cast-iron columns was conceived and designed by Duban but put up only between 1871 and 1874 by Ernest-Georges Coquart. The court in front and at the side was equally an assemblage, of fragments of medieval and Renaissance buildings rescued by Alexander Lenoir for the Musée des Monuments Français. The whole was inordinately admired when it was completed, in particular the attic floor (for which Labrouste served as *Inspecteur*) and the treatment of the roof, which was regarded as something of a novelty. This was hipped with a prettily detailed iron ridgepiece. Duban's reputation was made. But he did not build much else of consequence, though his superb Italianate house at 7 Rue Tronchet, Paris, for the Swiss collector the Comte Pourtalès, is deserving of study. Duban was active largely as a restorer, starting with the Ste.-Chapelle in 1837, tackling then in turn the Château de Blois, that at Fontainebleau, and then the Louvre, where some richly modeled and gilded rooms survive to attest to his activity, together with some forlorn railings in the corners of the courtyard, for which he was ridiculed and therefore resigned. But in 1858 he did design a building of some nobility and largeness of scale, the extension to the École des Beaux-Arts on the Quai Malaquais. Curiously, critics who had spent years castigating him for the fussiness of his details thought this too bald and bold.

Pierre-François-Henri Labrouste (1801–1875) was an architect of greater consistency and refinement, and of far greater stature. The beginning of his active career, however, was to be long delayed. He was a student of Lebas and A.-L.-T. Vaudoyer but was not prepared to accept their academic ideals without the most painstaking independent investigation. In 1824 he won the Grand Prix with a design for a *tribunal de cassation.* In 1828 he sent, as his fourth-year *envoi* from Rome, a restoration study of the three Doric temples of Paestum. His meticulous measurements proved that C. M. Delagardette's *Ruines de Paestum,* of 1799, was altogether untrustworthy. This was an affront to academic dignity. Labrouste went further: He developed a theory on the history of the people who had built the temples and showed how their social aspirations were reflected in their architecture. One of the buildings, he argued, was not a temple, but a civic structure.

382. *Félix-Jacques Duban, Hôtel*
Pourtalès, Paris, 1836

383. *Félix-Jacques Duban, Hôtel*
Pourtalès, Paris, staircase, 1836
384. *Félix-Jacques Duban, École*
des Beaux-Arts, Paris, forecourt,
1832–40

385. Félix-Jacques Duban, École des
Beaux-Arts, Paris, façade on the Quai
Malaquais, 1858–62

386. Félix-Jacques Duban, Galerie
d'Apollon, the Louvre, Paris,
1848–52

He illustrated this, hip-roofed—decked with large paintings, trophies, and
inscriptions—as Jean Houel had done many years earlier, in 1787, in a
restoration study of one of the Doric temples of Agrigento, illustrated in
the fourth volume of his *Voyage pittoresque des îles de Sicile, de Malte, et de Lipari.*
But Labrouste went further; he added graffiti. He wished to penetrate to
the reality of the architecture, to present the buildings as they might really
have existed. Naturally, he applied color. Many of his assumptions were
wrong, but what roused the members of the Académie to fury was his
deliberate dismissal of the ideal. And he compounded this rude rejection
of established criteria in the following year, sending in as his fifth-year *envoi*
a design of a frontier bridge between Italy and France that was modeled
on a coarse Roman provincial work, the Flavian bridge at St.-Chamas, near
Marseilles. For almost ten years the members of the Académie saw to it that
he received no major commission. He became a student idol, and for
twenty-six years from 1830 directed the most austerely intellectual *atelier*
in Paris. Not one of his students won the Grand Prix. During this time he
entered and won a number of competitions for utilitarian buildings, a
Hospice d'Aliénés at Lausanne in 1837, a prison for Alessandria, Italy, in
1840, and an *abattoir* in Provins in 1841. None of these was built. His
opportunity came in October 1838, when he was appointed architect to the
new Bibliothèque Ste.-Geneviève, facing Soufflot's great church. There
were difficulties over the acquisition of the site, but in January 1840
Labrouste's initial scheme was approved in principle, though the revisions
were not settled for another two years and money not voted until 1843.
A final plan was approved in July 1844 after work on the foundation had
begun. The building, completed in December 1850, is very simple in
arrangement. It is a long rectangle, entered on the ground floor, with stack
rooms to the left, offices and rare books to the right. At the rear of the
building is a separate stair hall leading up to the reading room, which
occupies the whole of the upper level. This is a room of great dignity. The
effect is achieved by means of a completely independent system of cast-iron
columns and arches arranged to provide two long narrow naves, a spine
down the center, hinting at the "civic" temple at Paestum and also at the
medieval refectory at the former Abbaye de St.-Martin-des-Champs, Paris,
which his pupil Lassus had recently measured and which his friend Léon
Vaudoyer was about to turn into a library for the Conservatoire des Arts
et Métiers—an echo, one must assume, of Saint-Simonist theory. There is,
of course, nothing overtly Gothic about Labrouste's detailing. This, if
anything, recalls his visits to Pompeii. The exterior is even more noble and
purified. The arches inside are reflected in the arched openings of the upper
floor—windows above, infilling panels below, each of which is, in turn,
punctured by a small window to light the small workrooms arranged on the
perimeter within. The ground floor is pierced by a row of round-headed
windows and an equally reticent rounded doorway, decorated only with
lamps of learning. The division between the two floors was at first marked

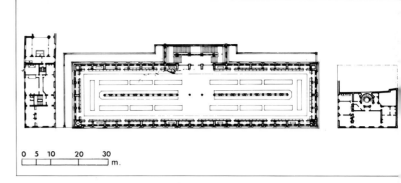

by no more than a strong horizontal molding, but the members of the *Conseil Général des Bâtiments Civils* thought this too sharp. When the stack rooms were raised nineteen centimeters (seven and one-half inches) Labrouste introduced the frieze of garlands, which echoes that on the Panthéon opposite and, more important, provides just that degree of movement required to render the facade less static. The silhouette is strong and square. On either side Labrouste designed two buildings that show how he could vary his arrangements to relate to their functions and yet ensure a unified whole. To the east are the staff quarters (1847–48); to the west the Collège Ste.-Barbe (1845–47), his old school, of which one of his brothers was head. Another brother, Théodore Labrouste (1799–1885), collaborated with him here as architect.

The facade of the Bibliothèque Ste.-Geneviève is altogether Labrouste's own—though it should be remarked how closely it relates to that of the École de Dessin, nearby, at 8 Rue Racine, designed and built between 1841 and 1844 by Simon-Claude Constant-Defeux (1801–1871), soon to be appointed *Professeur de Perspective* at the École des Beaux-Arts. Labrouste's facade, however, contains mnemonic references to many others that he had admired: Sir Christopher Wren's library at Cambridge; Leon Battista Alberti's Tempio Malatestiano in Rimini; Michelozzo's Banco Mediceo in Milan; and Jacopo Sansovino's Biblioteca Marciana in Venice. Even Egyptian temples are said to be embodied therein. This distillation of knowledge, which we have seen to lie also at the heart of Duban's work, was to be regarded as Labrouste's great contribution. From it, Neil Levin has suggested, was to spring that movement known somewhat inaccurately as the *néo-grec.* This flourished in France in the 1870s, though as late as 1911 the English architect A. E. Richardson was writing of it in the *Architectural Review* as the basis of renewal: "The true *néo-grec* style is the epitome of design, its interest a reflection of the tireless mind of the designer, who, having obtained a great many ideas on his subject, melts these very ideas in the crucible of his imagination, refining them again and again until the minted metal gleams refulgent. All material is the same to such a one. By these means and these alone, is original design possible" (July 1911, p. 28).

Labrouste did indeed succeed in restoring to nineteenth-century architecture some of the classic wholeness of that of the Greeks, but he aimed at a larger synthesis. He used his lifts, his heating and lighting systems, and his cast-iron columns not for utilitarian reasons alone, nor even to shock (though he did), but in order to relate his building organically to a nineteenth-century industrialized society, of which it was to be a noble expression. He intended it to represent the moment of achievement in a third organic period of architecture (the Saint-Simonists, as we have seen, had recognized two others, the Doric Greek and the Gothic). Neil Levine has recently shown that to make quite explicit his aim he decided in August 1848—just after the riots of July that marked the end of the July Monarchy, and just after the publication of the *Discours sur l'ensemble du positivisme* by

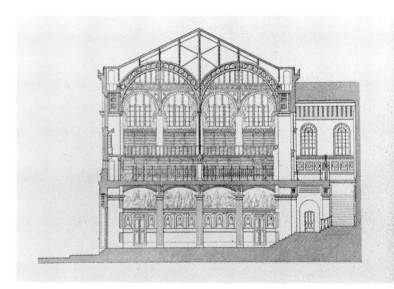

233

391. Pierre-François-Henri Labrouste,
Bibliothèque Ste.-Geneviève, Paris,
entrance vestibule, 1842–50

392. Pierre-François-Henri Labrouste,
Bibliothèque Ste.-Geneviève, Paris,
detail of the facade, 1842–50

Auguste Comte, Saint-Simon's renegade disciple—to inscribe the names of the authors whose works were contained within the library on the panels of the facade, arranging them in chronological order from Moses to Berzelius (a Swedish chemist much admired at the time, to whom Michel Eugène Chevreul, for instance, had dedicated his book on color theory), illustrating the progress of humanity from monotheism to scientism. The name of Psellus in the center just over the door, marking the meeting of east and west, the central stage in the history of metaphysics as outlined by Comte. The carving was completed in two months. The Bibliothèque Ste.-Geneviève thus became, demonstrably, a temple of all learning, a beginning of the new way. The letters were painted red.

Three years after completion, in 1853, Labrouste was appointed to succeed L.-T.-J. Visconti as architect at the Bibliothèque Nationale. He tidied up the existing conglomeration with skill and ruthlessness; then, in

1859, he began work on the main reading room, filling part of the court for which Boullée had prepared his designs. This was Labrouste's second masterpiece. But magnificent as it is, it represents no more than an extension of ideas already worked out to perfection at the Bibliothèque Ste.-Geneviève. Only his stack room, tiered galleries of cast iron, built between 1862 and 1867, shows him grappling to renewed effect with his initiatory themes. This, to early twentieth-century eyes, was his greatest creation. Even his contemporaries admired it, and for much the same reasons. "Tout," Louis-Auguste Boileau wrote in 1871 in *Le fer,* "jusqu'au moindre boulon et rivet, devient un objet d'art de nouvelle création."

Labrouste's other works need not detain us: a handful of tombs; a farm colony at Mesnil-St.-Fermin (1845–48); a large and dull seminary at Rennes (1854–72; now the Faculté des Lettres), whose construction he did not supervise; a house for the banker Louis Fould (1856–58; now gone), another for M. Vilgruy (1860–65; still standing at 9 Rue François 1er, Paris), and the Hôtel Rouvenat (1861; now gone) at Neuilly-sur-Seine, all three disappointing pastiches of the architecture of Louis XIII's reign; a small boxlike villa for a jeweler, M. Thouret (1860; still standing, though altered, at 68 Boulevard Bourdon, Neuilly-sur-Seine); and the Hôtel de l'Administration du Chemin de Fer PLM, Paris (1861–63; 44 Rue Neuves-des-Mathurins), which he did not complete and which was torn down in part within a few years.

Louis-Joseph Duc (1802–1879) and Léon Vaudoyer (1803–1872) were, like Labrouste, to pour their energies into no more than one or two buildings. On his return from Rome in 1831, Duc became *Inspecteur* of the July Column, in the Place de la Bastille, under Jean-Antoine Alavoine (1778–1834). Soon he succeeded to the commission and at once started to apply decoration to Alavoine's sheer shaft. For the inauguration, in 1840, he designed some temporary pavilions, Greek in inspiration, brightly painted in yellow and red. In the same year he took over the work of completing the Palais de Justice in Paris. He did a great deal there, but the focus of all his effort was the Salle des Pas Perdus, referred to also as the Vestibule d'Assises, on the Rue de Harlay. This was started in 1857 and finished eleven years later, though much rebuilt and changed internally after damage suffered in 1870. Its hipped and heavily encrusted roof relates it at once to Duban's first building at the École des Beaux-Arts; its rhythmical bays, glazed above and filled in below with panels bearing inscriptions, link it to the Bibliothèque Ste.-Geneviève. But Duc wanted no fusion of structure, form, and expression. The structure—the arched vaulting within, the enclosing walls pierced with flattened arched openings—was to be seen and expressed as a humdrum working part of the architecture; the poetry, and all that mattered, were to arise from the artistic handling of an independent system of decoration, set in contradistinction to the rest. An array of columns derived from the Doric order, the highest form of expression in architecture, was thus set as a sculptural element in front of

ITZ   ISAAC DE BEAUSOBRE   LESAGE   FONTENELLE
ZE   J-ALB.FABRICIUS   VAUVENARGUES   MONTESQUIEU
ON   BOERHAAVE   FRÉRET   MOSHEIM
TON   DOM EDM. MARTENE   MURATORI   RÉAUMUR
EURY   MONTFAUCON   D'AGUESSEAU   RICHARDSON
S CANTEMIR   ROLLIN   CORMONTAIGNE   CRÉBILLON
ON   J-B.ROUSSEAU   HOLBERG   J-CHR.WOLFF
    HALLEY   FIELDING   RAMEAU

TAYLOR   MASSILLON   LA CAILLE
TROUIN   VICO   CLAIRAUT
    POPE   STERNE

393. Pierre-François-Henri Labrouste,
Bibliothèque Ste.-Geneviève, Paris,
reading room on the second floor,
1842–50

the wall. There was much more to Duc's composition—recollections of the
Temple of Hathor in Egypt, details borrowed from the Temple of Athena
Nike—but they need not be discussed. He aimed, clearly, to separate the
practical and the expressive elements in architecture. And he was acclaimed.
Viollet-le-Duc himself sat on the committee that awarded him the Prix de
Cent Mille Francs in 1869 for the greatest work of art produced in France
during the century.

Léon Vaudoyer made no such startling contribution to the development
of architecture. He was closer to Labrouste, with whom he had been at
school, and was said to be an intellectual, though we have little evidence
of this. In 1838 he began work with his father, A.-L.-T. Vaudoyer, on the
transformation of St.-Martin-des-Champs into the Conservatoire des Arts et
Métiers. Work continued for years, right up to 1897, but it is of no great
distinction or interest. The effects are contrived and awkward. But in 1845,
the same year in which he took over from his father at St.-Martin-des-
Champs, he prepared the first designs for his most important work, the
cathedral at Marseilles. Its horizontal banding appeared on his drawings only
in 1852, a year after John Ruskin had published the *Stones of Venice.* Ruskin's
influence here would be unlikely, though the cathedral is an extraordinarily
eclectic work. Vaudoyer's range of sources here was wider, and also more
overt in expression, than that employed by his friends. The plan is
thirteenth-century Gothic; the forms and many of the details are Byzantine.
But the most notable influence of all is that of the Florence cathedral.
Vaudoyer, less self-sure perhaps than Labrouste, aimed to provide an
exemplar of a new architecture on the very threshold of an "organic period,"

at the end of an age of transition. He built on the basis of a Gothic plan because it was typically French. He selected Byzantine details because that style was a prelude to Gothic (he saw the pointed arch as a simple development of the arcade) and early Renaissance architecture because it marked the transition from an ecclesiastical authority to that of classical humanism. He had added, it seems, the Renaissance to the succession of "époques organiques" recognized by the Saint-Simonists. The result of all this thought and learning is not particularly impressive. Vaudoyer had insufficient feeling for the forms he was handling and assembled them without conviction. The building up of the docks alongside the cathedral has not enhanced its splendor, though in the interior something of the grand and thoughtfully—often brightly—colored architecture that he envisioned may still be experienced. The cathedral, finished only in 1893, was not much imitated in France, although echoes of it occur in the French colonies on the southern shores of the Mediterranean. And in Marseilles itself, Vaudoyer's pupil and assistant Henri-Jacques Espérandieu (1829–1874) took it as the point of departure for his first independent work of importance, the ungainly Notre-Dame-de-la-Garde (1853–64), which dominates the hill on the other side of the port. Vaudoyer's precepts, if we are to judge by Espérandieu's later buildings, all in Marseilles, were not of the stirring kind, nor were they sustaining. In 1858 Espérandieu started to design the Bibliothèque Municipale; four years later he began the flamboyant and highly ostentatious Palais de Longchamp, taking over ideas suggested a few years earlier by the sculptor Frédéric-Auguste Bartholdi. There was an ugly court case, but Espérandieu was exonerated. He went on, in 1862, to build the École des Beaux-Arts, which was a coarsened and undisciplined variant of Duban's; then followed the observatory and the *abattoir*. His works were florid and attractive only from afar; they give evidence of neither skill in design nor sustained intellectual effort.

Vaudoyer was no doubt aware of his inability to give convincing form to his ideas. He avoided building as long as he could—traveling at length in Germany, England, Spain, and Algeria, refusing many commissions—and was equally hesitant in expressing himself in writing. All his friends were agreed that he had thought long and hard about architecture, but he published no book on the subject, though he did contribute to such Romantic journals as the *Journal des artistes* and *Le magasin pittoresque* and, after its founding in 1840, to the *Revue générale de l'architecture et des travaux publics*. Indeed, his chief claim to fame is to have coined the term *architecture parlante* to describe the works of Ledoux, which he reviewed in *Le magasin pittoresque* in December 1852 (p. 388). He was intrigued, but did not approve. Ledoux's symbolism was to him too blatant by far.

The influence of the architects we have been considering was strongly felt in the second half of the century, in instigating both a more thoughtful eclecticism and a greater concern for precision in planning, engineering, and the design of details. Inevitably these became richer and, in the hands

399. Pierre-François-Henri Labrouste,
Hôtel Vilgruy, Paris, 1860–65
400. Louis-Joseph Duc, Palais de
Justice, Paris, facade on the Rue de
Harlay, 1857–68

401. Louis-Joseph Duc, Palais de
Justice, Paris, Salle des Pas Perdus,
1857–68

of the less strictly trained architects, were debased and vulgarized. Espérandieu is a case in point. However, the career of Charles-Auguste Questel (1807–1888), a pupil of both Blouet and Duban, who himself worked on the largest scale at Nîmes (where he first noticed Espérandieu), at Grenoble, and at Paris, may be adduced to show a contrary process at work. On the whole, however, the extent and the pace of building during the Second Empire served to degenerate architecture; the rational tradition was disastrously weakened. But a few—very few—architects were able to turn this to their advantage. It became in their hands a liberating stimulus.

The greatest period of activity in the history of French architecture was initiated on June 22, 1853, when Baron Georges-Eugène Haussmann (1809–1891) succeeded Amédée Berger as *Préfet de la Seine.* On June 29, seven days after his appointment, Haussmann was called to St.-Cloud and shown a plan with the emperor's personal proposals for the remaking of Paris marked down in blue, red, yellow, and green, according to their relative urgency. It was this plan that Haussmann carried out in the years that followed. Paris was to be "la capitale des capitales." The city was virtually rebuilt. Streets and boulevards were opened up and lined with regular facades. The destruction was terrible. At intersections and focal points great public buildings and churches were erected; within the first ten years of Haussmann's administration more than fifteen large churches had been begun, and ten more were to follow. Almost all the old bridges over the Seine were rebuilt and five new ones begun. Markets were erected, including the great Halles Centrales. The latter were started afresh as an iron construction in 1853 by the architects Victor Baltard (1805–1874) and Félix-Emmanuel Callet (1792–1854). The Bois de Boulogne (1853–58), the Bois de Vincennes (1858–60), the Parc Monceau (1860–62), the Parc des Buttes-Chaumont (1864–67), the Parc de Montsouris (1867–68), and no fewer than thirty new squares were laid out and embellished with pavilions, railings, and appropriate street furniture. The streets were lighted by gas and the drainage system extended. Water in quantity was brought into the city. By the end of the Second Empire there were sixty public fountains in Paris. Paris itself was extended. On January 1, 1860, Passy, Auteuil, Les Batignolles-Monceau, Montmartre, La Chapelle, La Villette, Belleville, Charonne, Bercy, Vaugirard, and Grenelle were formally incorporated within the city. A few years later the building of *mairies* in these new *arrondissements* was begun. But from all this ferment only one or two names of interest emerge.

Haussmann, like his patron Louis-Napoleon, was a man of much common sense but less than common sensibility. Moreover, he mistrusted architects. He chose as his collaborators Eugène Belgrand (1810–1878), Maillebiau, and Jean-Charles-Adolphe Alphand (1817–1891), members all of the École des Ponts et Chaussées. Baullet-Deschamps, the only trusted architect, acted as surveyor of roads. Victor Baltard, who had won the Grand Prix in 1833, was appointed *Architecte en Chef de la Ville de Paris* and in that capacity

redecorated and rebuilt a host of churches; but apart from the Halles Centrales and the church of St.-Augustin (1860–71), with cast-iron columns inside, he has little claim to architectural recognition. Hector-Martin Lefuel (1810–1880), a pupil of Jean-Nicolas Huyot (1780-1840), was employed to reconstruct the Louvre and to link it finally to the Tuileries. He started in 1854, modestly enough, executing the plan that Visconti had left, but within a few years was piling sculpture and ornament onto the building with an exuberance that would have shocked Visconti. Lefuel's work was hurried and ill considered, but much appreciated in court circles. In 1853 he was commissioned to build the theater at Fontainebleau—which he designed in the eighteenth-century style that he had already introduced into the Salle des États in the Louvre.

Haussmann appointed Antoine-Nicolas-Louis Bailly (1810–1892), a pupil of Debret and Duban, to design the Tribunal de Commerce (1858–64), adapted at the emperor's request from the town hall at Brescia. Bailly's other important building of the period, the Mairie du IVe (1826–67), is no less pompous, if more prosaic. Théodore Ballu (1817–1885), a contractor's son and a disciple of Lebas, emerged also at this time. He completed Franz Christian Gau's Gothic pastiche Ste.-Clotilde, restored the Tour St.-Jacques, and, between Hittorff's Mairie du 1er and St.-Germain-l'Auxerrois, built that absurd tower that won for the ensemble the nickname of "porte-huilier." In 1861 he began work on La Trinité, a well-sited and richly adorned but not in the least impressive church. The Renaissance vaulting is all of *papier-mâché*. Bally built several other churches. But of all the new architects employed by Haussmann only one produced anything of more than marginal worth, Gabriel-Jean-Antoine Davioud (1823–1881). His buildings are well considered and possessed always of some straightforward merit, though they are undeniably dull. He studied for three years at the École de Dessin, perhaps under Viollet-le-Duc, then in 1841 entered the *atelier* of Vaudoyer. His studies completed, he began work with Victor Baltard on the Halles Centrales, and on his recommendation was made *Inspecteur des Promenades* and put in charge of the Service des Fontaines. For Alphand he put up a host of pavilions and lodges in the Bois de Boulogne between 1855 and 1859, all intentionally Picturesque in an English sort of way, with an admixture of the Swiss-chalet style (one chalet was brought direct from Berne). Equally ambitiously, he worked at the Bois de Vincennes, the Parc des Buttes-Chaumont, and the Parc Monceau, where his showy grilles, inspired by those of Emmanuel Héré at Nancy, are particularly deserving of praise. For the Champs-Élysées, in 1857, he designed a new circus and panorama, still standing, a building of less structural quality than Hittorff's. Then in the following year, he designed the first of his four great fountains, the Fontaine St.-Michel at the beginning of the Boulevard St.-Michel, a mass of metal and stone that was both praised and rudely dismissed. Charles Darcel remarked in the *Gazzette des beaux-arts* in 1860, "C'est une oeuvre banale, sans signification et sans caractère" (p.

44), but César-Denis Daly (1811–1893), influential editor of the *Revue générale de l'architecture,* thought far too much of it. Later came the Fontaine de Château d'Eau (1867–74); the Fontaine de l'Observatoire (1870–75), with figures by Jean-Baptiste Carpeaux; and the Fontaine de la Place du Théâtre-Français (1872–74). In 1860 Davioud started on two mammoth theaters, the Théâtre du Châtelet and the Théâtre Lyrique (now Théâtre de la Ville), both completed within two years. Darcel was as brutal in his comments as before; Daly published a magnificent monograph on the buildings. They are undeniably grand and were not uncomfortable, but as architecture they are altogether indigestible.

The Magasins Réunis, on the Place de la République, begun in April 1865 and completed in January 1867, are likewise adequate up to the point they reached and are distinguished by their planning and structural organization above much of the architecture of the time; but that is all. As such later works as the Mairie du XIXᶜ (1876–78) and the vast Palais du Trocadéro (1876–78) attest, Davioud was a thoughtful and extremely industrious architect who gave a great deal of attention to fine, finished detail. But he was incapable of communicating through architecture the feelings that had originally impelled him to take it up.

Many of Haussmann's architects were uninspired. Yet men such as Davioud were influential and widely imitated. And it would be a mistake to think that they achieved nothing in the field of architecture and landscape design. The Parc des Buttes-Chaumont is a wonderfully rich amalgam of the traditional Picturesque and the railway age. The train tracks running alongside the park are integrated with perfect fluency into the landscape design, as is the vast panorama of the industrialized city. The new vistas and spaces that Haussmann gave to Paris, moreover, demanded a new breadth of scale and a grandness of public performance that one architect at least was able to perceive and respond to. This man was Jean-Louis-Charles Garnier (1825–1898). He expressed both the ostentation and the power of the Second Empire with such intensity and candid freshness when he built the Opéra that it is almost impossible not to be enthralled by it. Certainly he changed thereby the direction of French architecture.

For two years Charles Rohault de Fleury worked under the emperor's personal direction on the design of the new opera house; then in 1860 he was suddenly dismissed, in order, it was widely thought, that the empress's favorite, Viollet-le-Duc, might be appointed architect. We may be thankful that Viollet-le-Duc proposed a competition instead. One hundred and seventy-one sentries were submitted, including one from the empress. Early in 1861 the winners in the first stage were announced. Paul-René-Léon Ginain was first; second came Botrel and Adolphe-Nicolas Crepinet, then Antoine-Martin Garnaud and Louis Duc. Garnier was fifth. In the second stage of the competition Garnier was unanimously acclaimed. Garnaud died soon after, of grief, it was said. Ginain never forgave Garnier. The empress was furious. When he went to the Tuileries to show her his project, she

exclaimed, "Qu'est cela, ce n'est pas un style; ce n'est ni du Louis XIV, ni du Louis XV, ni du Louis XVI." Garnier had his reply. "Madame," he said, "c'est du Napoléon III, et vous vous plaignez" (*Bulletin de la Société de l'Histoire de l'Art Français,* 1941–44, p. 83). Garnier thus gave a name to the style but, though the empress became reconciled, the building was not much admired by Louis-Napoleon, who visited it only once, in 1862, when he laid the foundation stone. The gala opening did not take place until January 5, 1875, more than four years after the battle of Sedan.

The most illuminating comments on the building were made by Garnier himself, first in *Le théâtre,* published in 1871, in which he outlined his aims, then in the texts to the two magnificently colored folios of *Le nouvel Opéra de Paris,* issued in 1878 and 1881, in which he judged of his success. He was clear and frank in all his explanations, sometimes facetious, never pretentious. He saw the Opéra as the embodiment of man's most primitive instincts: that of gathering together in ceremony around the campfire to share thoughts and dreams, to hear and to see and be seen. The spectacle was thus not to be enacted on the stage alone; theater involved all encounters, all actions. The spectators themselves were actors. And Garnier described in detail how he had fashioned his architecture with these ideas in mind. The Opéra was the entire society of the Second Empire. There were, of course, distinctions between different categories of people—those who paid more and those who paid less—and the part of each in the ritual was clearly assessed and defined. If one came by carriage or foot there was a sequence prepared, and also a place for intermingling—even though this might be at a distance. Even the act of queuing for tickets was considered a part of the ceremony. Care was lavished on every detail. In the main foyer there were mirrors set into the columns so the women might glance at themselves and make last minute adjustments to their dress or expressions before entering the great stair hall, a climax to the architecture. Here all excitement, all passion was stirred. Here society disported itself in its splendor; people saw and were seen as they passed in procession up the stairs—which were copied, Garnier happily admitted, from Victor Louis's at Bordeaux. The lesser members of society watched from on high. The spectacle, the stuffs, the scents, and the diamonds were no less part of the architecture than the marbles, the draperies, and the chandeliers. "La lumière qui étincelera," he wrote in *Le théâtre,* "les toilettes qui resplendiront, les figures qui seront animées et souriantes, les rencontres qui se produiront, les saluts qui s'échangeront, tout aura un air de fête et de plaisir, et sans se rendre compte de la part qui doit revenir à l'architecture dans ce effet magique, tout le monde en jouira et tout le monde rendra ainsi, par son impression heureuse, hommage à ce grand art, si puissant dans ses manifestations, si élevé dans ses résultats."

The flights of Garnier's stairs soar with perfect fluency through the stair hall, they are at once easy and satisfying, yet they provide just that degree of surprise and excitement needed in all artistic success. There is a tension

413. Antoine-Nicolas-Louis Bailly,
Tribunal de Commerce, Paris,
1858–64
414. Antoine-Nicolas-Louis Bailly,
Mairie du IV, Paris, 1862–67*

415. Gabriel-Jean-Antoine Davioud,
Théâtre du Châtelet, Paris, 1860–62
416. Gabriel-Jean-Antoine Davioud,
Théâtre Lyrique (now Théâtre de la
Ville), Paris, 1860–62

417. Jean-Charles-Adolphe Alphand
and Gabriel-Jean-Antoine Davioud,
Parc des Buttes-Chaumont, Paris,
1864–67

418. Jean-Charles-Adolphe Alphand
and Gabriel-Jean-Antoine Davioud,
Parc des Buttes-Chaumont, Paris,
suspension bridge

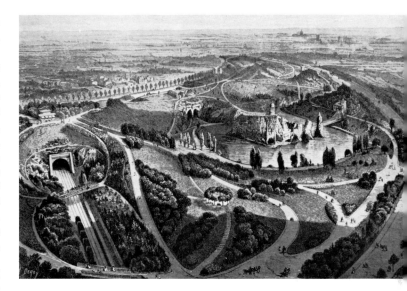

in every form. With their related corridors and foyers, the stairs seem to provide the best of all possible ceremonial approaches to the auditorium, itself, sadly, one of the least remarkable features of this remarkable building. Garnier agreed, but, as always, he had his explanation. The auditorium, he said, would seem to be the natural climax for the architecture, yet when it was most in use attention was necessarily directed at the spectacle on the stage. The auditorium was then in semidarkness. Only for relatively short periods was it brilliantly lit and vibrant, but the audience was then static, and when the people moved they moved inevitably to the foyers and stairs, where they could enact their communal ceremonies with greater freedom. The lobbies and corridors were thus made larger than ever before, with areas for sitting, and with smoking rooms for the men (with fire and sun motifs) and ice cream parlors for the women (with lunar motifs). The decoration throughout was sumptuous. There was color everywhere, inside and out. Salviati the glassmakers' fortune was soon made. "Alors," Garnier wrote in *Le nouvel Opéra,* "vous ferez vos maisons moins blanches . . ." (vol. 1, p. 18).

Garnier rejoiced in his achievement. It expressed, he said, as all good architecture should, his entire personality: "J'ai beau chercher en parcourant le grand vestibule du nouvel Opéra, si je verrai quelques défauts à signaler: ma recherche est vaine, et je ne trouve vraiment rien à regretter dans cette partie du monument" (*Le nouvel Opéra,* vol. 1, p. 215). This, like other such pronouncements by the architect, is no more than a statement of fact. Garnier well knew how to satisfy practical requirements: He dismissed the heating and ventilating engineers who had worked on the Châtelet theaters because they thought of the Opéra only as a duct, and designed all this part himself, as well as the stage machinery and structure; and he searched France until he found marble blocks large enough for the maximum possibilities of architecture. He knew exactly when to be extravagant with space, with form, or with decoration. There is nothing coarse or vulgar about his building, as some of his contemporaries thought and as many people since have declared who believe themselves to have good taste. Le Corbusier detested it. Garnier could play with consummate mastery and gusto with most of those sacrosanct essentials of architecture—mass, rhythm, texture, and outline—and achieve a splendidly unified character. The silhouette of the Opéra when viewed from the Avenue de l'Opéra is superb. Even Haussmann admired it to the extent of eliminating the trees that were planned to line the avenue. The facade itself, massive and heavily decorated and gilded, is yet monumental in the best possible sense of the word: it possesses, as Garnier himself remarked, a considered dignity. "C'est l'art qui y séjourne," he wrote in *Le nouvel Opéra,* "et l'art ne doit pas être entaché de pruderie; il faut seulement que la richesse soit quelque peu digne, parce que si l'art peut danser la gavotte ou le menuet, il doit se garder du cancan" (vol. 1, p. 23). He did not even object to bad taste if there was in it passion and warmth.

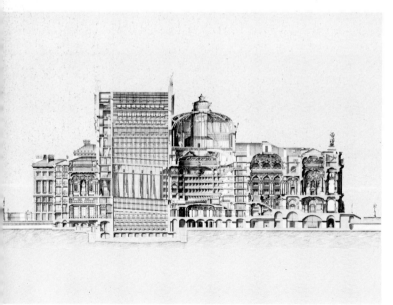

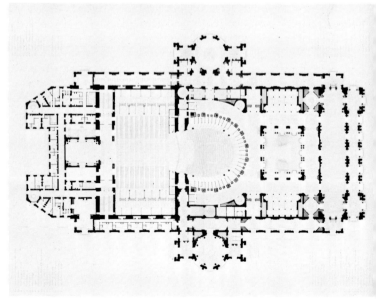

252

All that Garnier did and admired was conditioned by his classical training. As a young man, a pupil of Lebas, he had won the Grand Prix with a design for a Conservatoire des Arts et Métiers, similar in style to the buildings Questel was later to build at Grenoble. He had developed these quattrocento and cinquecento tastes in Florence itself, where the Académie de France had moved from Rome under threat of attack from Garibaldi's army. But he undertook Roman studies as well—Trajan's Column and the Temple of Vesta—and later traveled to Sicily with the Duc de Luynes. In 1852, at the end of a three-year stay in Italy, when still a young man of twenty-eight, he traveled to Greece with Théophile Gautier and with Edmond About, who was later to write his account of the journey in *La Grèce contemporaine*. In Greece, Garnier felt, he perceived for the first time the true quality of classical architecture. He saw that there was emotion and human life latent in it, and a harmony and meaning not present in mere building: "Plaine de l'Attique, rocher de Minerve," he wrote in 1869 in *À travers les arts*, "c'est en vous voyant que j'ai compris la puissance magique de l'art et la majesté de l'architecture antique . . ." (p. 268). But his vision of Greek architecture was not that of Winckelmann. His restoration study of the Temple of Jupiter Panhellenius at Aegina was vibrantly colored, the colomns in yellow, the walls of the cella and the architraves and friezes all bright red, with the metopes picked out in blue. There was, he admitted, no justification for this, other than that it pleased him. Between the columns were rich bronze grilles, once again no part of archaeological study.

Garnier always remained faithful to his Mediterranean inheritance; it was part of a world of smiling intelligence, unruffled by calculation and hardheaded need. In all his buildings he sought to stir this sense of buoyant ease and success. It is apparent in the Cercle de la Librairie (1878–79) at 117 Boulevard St.-Germain and, further along, in No. 195, the Maison Hachette (1882), a lavishly planned block of apartments; even more in those buildings he put up along the Riviera—a hotel, a school, a church, the Villa Bischoffsheim, and his own house at Bordighera; in the observatory at Nice; but most especially in the theater and casino at Monte Carlo, begun in 1878. This, before its gradual alteration, was another radiant masterpiece.

As a student, even before he entered the École des Beaux-Arts, Garnier had studied under Viollet-le-Duc at the École de Dessin (where he met Carpeau, who was to design *Les Danseuses* for the Opéra). Later he worked as an assistant to Viollet-le-Duc, but he came, as must be already evident, to reject all that Viollet-le-Duc stood for. He dismissed his architecture readily enough, together with that of all Viollet-le-Duc's followers: "On hésite dans l'appréciation de ses oeuvres plus personelles. Est-ce un souvenir du passé? Est-ce un essai de novation? Cela est difficile à dire" (*À travers les arts,* p. 48). And he went much further even in rejecting his theories: "Le raisonnement *a priori* est donc inutile, puis qu'il se produit inconsciemment. Il serait nuisible s'il voulait remplacer le sentiment et prendre la première place au detriment de la main qui opère et les yeux qui jugent.

C'est pour cela que je repousse instinctivement et volontairement l'école utilitaire qui, voulant remplacer l'école de l'impression, part du raisonnement seul et, mal guidée dans son choix, repoussant le contrôle du sentiment, tombe à tout instant dans le faux et produit sous le spécieux prétexte de logique, des oeuvres bâtardes et incohérentes'' (*Le théâtre*, p. 414). This was a theme he returned to again and again. He saw no future in an architecture based on rationalism, on science, on engineering, least of all on new materials: "Je le dis tout de suite, c'est là une erreur, et une grande erreur: le fer est un moyen, ce ne serait jamais une principe" (*À travers les arts*, p. 75). But if he was thus rejecting Viollet-le-Duc and his admirers, he was renouncing also that framework of reason, that particular thoughtfulness and concern, that had sustained the classical tradition in France. With Viollet-le-Duc were eliminated Durand, Rondelet, Gilbert, Blouet, and Labrouste. Certainly, Garnier did not expect that an artist should have moral or political convictions, or, if he had, that they should be allowed to inflect his work. One could not, he said, begin with fixed ideas, with any theory at all. The imagination must be allowed free play in works of creation. The rationale, if such was required, could be invented later.

If Garnier's works had not been so obviously successful, such statements would not have mattered. But the example of his easy mastery served, effectively, to destroy the thoughtful tradition of French architecture. His buildings were widely imitated, both inside and out. Opera houses all over the world commemorate his. An Italian, Squadrelli, conflated it with the Monte Carlo casino, throwing an admixture of Secessionist ironwork on top,

to provide the local casino for San Pellegrino at the turn of the century. The result, as may be expected, was dreadful. Very few men possessed Garnier's talents. In France careful and serious architects did make a determined attempt to restore to the classical tradition its measured dignity and its system of belief: among them, E.-G. Coquart (1831–1902), Henri-Adolphe-Auguste Deglane (1855–1931), P.-R.-L. Ginain (1825–1898), Charles-Louis Girault (1851–1932), Julien-Azais Guadet (1834–1908), Victor-Alexandre-Frédéric Laloux (1850–1937), Paul-Henri Nénot (1853–1934), and Jean-Louis Pascal (1837–1920). Guadet, Nénot, and Pascal, incidentally, trained at the Opéra. But they were no longer sustained by a faith, even of a specious sort. Architecture in France had for the moment lost its sap and its savor.

ENGLAND: *C.R. Cockerell to Barry*

It cannot be denied that in nineteenth-century England most of the finest minds and the most brilliant designers, with the exception of Cockerell, were drawn to the Gothic not the Classical Revival. There is simply no classical parallel to the astonishingly rich concatenation of Gothic Revivalists—A. W.N. Pugin, John Ruskin, William Morris, William Butterfield, George Edmund Street, and George Frederick Bodley. Harvey Lonsdale Elmes and George Basevi came close to matching them in achievement, but since they both died young, they appear as late Georgian rather than as Victorian architects. Sir James Pennethorne and Sir Charles Barry lacked imaginative

greatness, while Alexander ("Greek") Thomson, though a brilliantly individual exponent of the classical tradition, somehow remains a figure of Scottish rather than of European importance.

With Charles Robert Cockerell English classicism achieved a new level of scholarship and imagination. During his remarkable *grand tour* of 1810–17 he became not only one of the leading archaeologists in Europe but also a greater expert on antique architecture than any English architect before or since. Excavating the late Archaic Temple of Jupiter Panhellenius on the island of Aegina with a group of English and German colleagues in 1811, Cockerell was involved in the discovery of the pedimental sculpture now housed in the Glyptothek in Munich. In the same year he was responsible for discovering the sculptured frieze of the fifth-century Temple of Apollo Epicurius at Bassae, and in 1813 he helped conduct the arrangements by which this sculpture was purchased by the British government. He incorporated casts of it in several of his buildings, notably the Ashmolean Museum, Oxford; the highly independent Ionic order of the temple also recurs with powerful effect in a number of his works. Indeed, his discoveries in Greece gave him a sense of the sculptural basis of Greek design, which influenced the development of his own architecture by enabling him to see the weaknesses of the current Greek Revival. We can trace this process in his diaries of the 1820s, where he criticizes not only the work of his contemporaries but also his own. Of his Literary and Philosophical Institution at Bristol (1821), he noted that the portico, based on the Temple

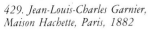

428. *Jean-Louis-Charles Garnier,*
Cercle de la Librairie, Paris,
1878–79

429. *Jean-Louis-Charles Garnier,*
Maison Hachette, Paris, 1882

430. *Jean-Louis-Charles Garnier,*
Maison Hachette, Paris, plan of the
second floor, 1882

431. *Jean-Louis-Charles Garnier,*
Maison Hachette, Paris, elevation,
1882

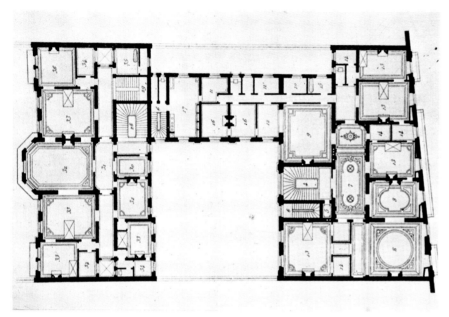

of Vesta at Tivoli but with Corinthian capitals that imitate the one he had discovered at Bassae, was "inharmoniously attached" to the main building. An even more revealing self-criticism is that of Lough Crew, a Greek Revival mansion that he built in Ireland from 1820 to 1825. In 1823 he already found it "very plain, too bald . . . its squareness left me an unpleasant impression . . . it would have been well to rusticate between the pilasters." Finding the Athenian Ionic capitals of the portico too minuscule to enliven a monumental building, he decided "never again [to] use Athenian order except in small scale."

One of the first buildings in which Cockerell began to realize his own stylistic ambitions was the Westminster Life and British Fire Office, in the Strand, London (1831; demolished 1908). Its Greek Doric order was not applied in the form of the usual attached portico but was deeply embedded in the facade. The depth and richness of articulation, the sense of layers within layers, are reminiscent of Italian Mannerism, particularly two buildings by Palladio: the Villa Barbaro at Maser (c. 1555–59) and the Loggia del Capitaniato at Vicenza (1571). Once formulated, this allusive style was soon used to create a series of highly independent yet highly classical masterpieces: Cambridge University Library (only partly executed), the Ashmolean Museum, Oxford, and the Royal Exchange, London (unexecuted), all of the late 1830s, and the branches of the Bank of England at Bristol, Manchester, and Liverpool, of 1844–45. Such a composition as his St. Giles's facade of the Ashmolean blends Greek, Roman, Renaissance,

and Baroque vocabulary into a language "the study of which," as one critic observed of the Liverpool Bank of England, "is a liberal education" (H. H. Statham, *A Short Critical History of Architecture,* 1912, p. 527). What immediately strikes the visitor to any building by Cockerell, whether it be a major public building like the Cambridge University Library or the lodge to a country house, as at Wynnstay, Denbighshire (1827), is the sheer largeness of scale of the parts and of the whole. We feel at once that we are in the presence of a man possessed of a profound intelligence, who thinks architecturally with a persuasive conviction and authority. Exactly the same impression is given by the work of C.-N. Ledoux—both large buildings, such as the Rotonde de la Villette, Paris, and smaller ones, such as the *grenier à sel* at Compiègne. We know that Cockerell was an admirer of Ledoux, in particular of his Hôtel de Thélusson in Paris (see D. J. Watkin, *The Life and Work of C. R. Cockerell, R. A.,* 1974, p. 124).

In the early 1850s Cockerell designed the interiors of St. George's Hall, Liverpool, following the premature death of the architect of the building, Harvey Lonsdale Elmes (1814–1847). Cockerell's exquisite Concert Hall, in which the fine calligraphy of his rich classical ornament is demonstrated at its best, is an admirable foil to the harder sobriety of Elmes's exterior. St. George's Hall, of which the final designs were settled by Elmes in 1841, is in plan a brilliant imaginative re-creation of the *tepidarium* of the Baths of Caracalla, which Elmes seems to have known from Blouet's *Restauration des thermes d'Antonin Caracalla à Rome* (1828). It is in no sense a mere

432. Jean-Louis-Charles Garnier, Casino, Monte Carlo, 1878–79

433. Paul-René-Léon Ginain, École de Médecine, Paris, facade on the Boulevard St.-Germain, 1878–1900

434. Paul-Henri Nénot, Nouvelle Sorbonne, Paris, the great amphitheater, 1885–91

435. Charles Robert Cockerell, Westminster Life and British Fire Office, London, 1831

436. Charles Robert Cockerell, University Library, Cambridge, project for the west side of the courtyard, c. 1837

archaeological restoration and ranks as one of the finest neoclassical public buildings in Europe.

The death of the gifted young Elmes in 1847 was a tragedy for the classical tradition in England. So, too, was that two years earlier of the fifty-one-year-old George Basevi. The latter was a favorite pupil of Soane, and his masterpiece was the Fitzwilliam Museum, Cambridge, a commission he was awarded after an open competition held in 1834–35. Like St. George's Hall, this massive building was inspired by the public architecture of the Roman Empire, in this case the Capitolium at Brescia, dating from the third quarter of the first century A.D. From this source comes the method by which Basevi's monumental Corinthian portico is extended on each side so as to form a colonnade and thus integrated powerfully into the body of the building in a way that one is tempted to call Baroque, although Basevi's stylistic sympathies are shown to be different by his architectural use of casts from the Bassae and Parthenon friezes in the interior.

For a variety of reasons, some of which seem to be accidental, the Gothic Revival was particularly associated with a religious, architectural, and intellectual tradition centered in Oxford, Cambridge, London, and the south of England generally. The classical tradition, by contrast, tended to flourish in Scotland and in the north of England. Thus, the "hyper-Corinthian luxury" (H. S. Goodhart-Rendel's apt characterization) of the Fitzwilliam Museum was echoed in the magnificent Town Hall, of 1845, at Leeds, Yorkshire, by Cuthbert Brodrick (1822–1905) and in William Hill's Town Hall at Bolton, Lancashire, of 1866. Liverpool also reflected a classical bias, from 1823, when John Foster designed St. Andrew's Church of Scotland, Rodney Street, manifestly inspired by Cockerell's Hanover Chapel, Regent Street, London (1821), to 1875, when Cornelius Sherlock (d. 1888) designed the Picton Reading Room, with its spectacular semicircle of Corinthian columns. In Edinburgh, the "Athens of the North," a more sternly Greek note was retained, as can be seen in Thomas Hamilton's Royal College of Physicians (1844–46) and in W. H. Playfair's National Gallery of Scotland (1850–57). In Glasgow a more masterly architect, Alexander Thomson (1817–1875), provided an astonishingly rich and powerful interpretation of the late international neoclassicism of Schinkel and Cockerell. His Caledonia Road Free Church of 1856 is a characteristic example of his work, which, confined to Glasgow, exercised little or no influence on his contemporaries elsewhere.

In London the one architect who seemed capable of perpetuating the intellectual classicism of Cockerell was Sir James Pennethorne (1801–1871). He was a pupil of John Nash, who told him, when Pennethorne was setting out on his *grand tour* of France and Italy in 1824, to seek the advice of Cockerell. Pennethorne later noted that "by Cockerell's urgent advice I paid more attention to the palaces and modern architecture of Italy than to the works of ancient art." The significance of this can hardly be overemphasized.

Perhaps Pennethorne's most important work was his Museum of

437. *Charles Robert Cockerell,*
Ashmolean Museum, Oxford, view
from the southeast, 1839–41

438. *Charles Robert Cockerell, Bank*
of England, Bristol, 1844

439. *Charles Robert Cockerell,*
Concert Hall, St. George's Hall,
Liverpool, detail of a caryatid,
1851–54

441. Harvey Lonsdale Elmes,
St. George's Hall, Liverpool, 1841
442. Harvey Londsale Elmes,
St. George's Hall, Liverpool, plan,
1841
443. George Basevi, Fitzwilliam
Museum, Cambridge, 1834
444. Cuthbert Brodrick, Town Hall,
Leeds, 1853

441. Harvey Lonsdale Elmes,
St. George's Hall, Liverpool, 1841

443. George Basevi, Fitzwilliam
Museum, Cambridge, 1834

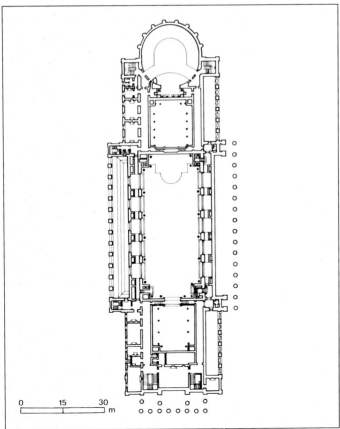

442. Harvey Londsale Elmes,
St. George's Hall, Liverpool, plan,
1841

444. Cuthbert Brodrick, Town Hall,
Leeds, 1853

446. *Cornelius Sherlock, Picton
Reading Room, Liverpool, 1875*
447. *Thomas Hamilton, Royal
College of Physicians, Edinburgh,
1844–46*

448. *Alexander Thomson, Caledonia
Road Free Church, Glasgow, 1856*

Economic (or Practical) Geology, in Piccadilly, London, designed between 1844 and 1846, the first cultural monument of the Victorian age to be sponsored by the state. A building of great earnestness, sobriety, and authority, it showed what architects in the classical tradition were capable of when, assured of that tradition's refinement, logic, and dignity, they did not feel obliged to compete with the more immediately eye-catching effects of the fashionable Gothic and Italianate revivals. The museum's monumental but undemonstrative facades, in cream Colchester brick and Ancaster stone, concealed a dense and subtle plan that exploited interlocking volumes with a sophistication lacking in many later Gothic Revival buildings. Along the second story ran the great top-lit exhibition gallery, forty-seven meters (one hundred fifty-five feet) long, with a large rectangular opening in the floor that illuminated the Doric Hall below. The gallery, in which the horizontal and the vertical supports were of cast iron, was a space both formed and frankly defined by its construction. In this it differed from the two other great contemporary buildings in London that employed cast-iron construction: Robert Smirke's British Museum (1824–47), where the presence of cast iron is completely hidden, and J. B. Bunning's Coal Exchange (1847), where it is boldly exposed. Pennethorne adopted the perhaps more attractive solution of revealing that cast and wrought iron helped determine the shape of the room but then moderating the disclosure by covering the surface of the metal with plasterwork.

Pennethorne's geological museum was demolished in 1935, and his important interiors at Buckingham Palace (1852–58) were mutilated in 1902. His somewhat grim but constructionally interesting Public Record Office (1851–66) survives, as does his west wing (1856) at Sir William Chambers's Somerset House, where he brilliantly and modestly adapted Chambers's style. As architect to the Office of Works, Pennethorne enjoyed the kind of settled civil-service position that some other architects of the period, including Schinkel, occupied. He was thus preserved from the embarrassment of entering the scandalously conducted architectural competitions of the nineteenth century, which so impeded Cockerell's career. One of the fruits of Pennethorne's official position was the commission for buildings for the University of London in Burlington Gardens in 1866. However, he became a pawn in the "Battle of the Styles," which was being played so absurdly between Liberal and Conservative politicians in the 1860s. He was thus obliged to present designs in both Gothic and Italianate modes in 1866–67, and the result is a dour piece of classicism with strongly French overtones. It is symptomatic of the failure of English architects to maintain the classical tradition in the face of competition from the Gothic and Italianate revivals.

The master of the Italianate Revival was Sir Charles Barry. Though comparatively of humble birth, he forged a career for himself that was one of the spectacular successes of the nineteenth century. His early work was varied, ranging stylistically from a Gothic manner reminiscent of Wyatt's

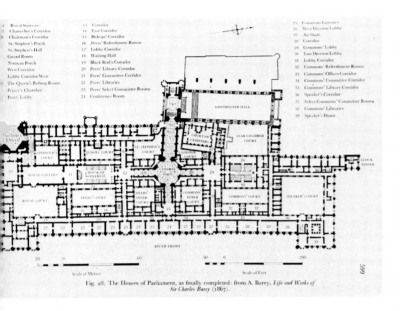

Fig. 28. The Houses of Parliament, as finally completed: from A. Barry, *Life and Works of Sir Charles Barry* (1867).

Fonthill Abbey (St. Peter, Brighton, 1823–28), via the Schinkelesque trabeation of his Royal Institution, Manchester (1823), and Nos. 16–17 Pall Mall, London (1833–34; demolished 1913), to the early Italian Renaissance manner of Brunswick Chapel, Hove, Sussex, (1827) and two important buildings of 1829, the Attree Villa, Brighton, and the Travellers' Club in Pall Mall. He shot to fame in 1836 when he had the extraordinarily good fortune to be selected as architect of the New Palace of Westminster. The terms of the competition, in keeping with the sentimental and literary romanticism of an increasingly nationalist age, called for a "Gothic or Elizabethan" style in order to emphasize the supposed medieval roots of English government. Barry's complex masterpiece, with its essentially classical disposition (despite the elaborate Gothic detail provided by A. W. B. Pugin), was a curiosity that exercised no significant architectural influence but that has undoubtedly continued to color, up to the present day, the Englishman's notion of the political framework within which he expects his country to be governed.

Barry's choice of a Cinquecento Palazzo style for the Travellers' Club was fraught with consequences for the nineteenth century. It suggested that the Palladian Revival of early eighteenth-century England had returned, though the architects and styles that had come to be admired were not those that had appealed to Lord Burlington and his circle. Burlington had been interested in Palladio as an exemplar of order, harmony, and the antique, not as a representative of Italian culture; the Victorians were interested in the warmth and color of the Renaissance as an Italian phenomenon. The Travellers' Club was in some sense the culmination of Englishmen's obsession with the *grand tour,* an institution that had persisted without interruption from at least the time of the foundation of the Society of Dilettanti. The club members were anxious to build a noble mansion in which those who had made the *grand tour* could meet each other and return hospitality to the foreign gentlemen who had entertained them on their travels. It was not, therefore, inappropriate that its architecture should be a tangible memorial of this *entente cordiale.* Barry chose as his model Raphael's Palazzo Pandolfini in Florence, though in execution he abandoned the elaborate rusticated surrounds to the ground-floor windows that had appeared in his first proposals for the Pall Mall facade. For the much larger Reform Club of 1837, farther along the same street, Barry chose as his model the grander Palazzo Farnese by Antonio da Sangallo and Michelangelo. But neither of Barry's clubs was in any sense a copy. The planning of both was extremely novel, particulary at the Reform Club, whose great central *cortile* became a recurrent theme in different Victorian building types. In tribute to the classical impetus that gave rise to these buildings, the Morning Room of the Reform Club was adorned with a cast of the Parthenon frieze, the Library of the Travellers' with a cast of the Bassae frieze (the latter doubtless on the recommendation of Cockerell, who was a founder-member).

Barry developed his Italianate style in a series of spectacular country

houses: for example, Trentham, Staffordshire (1833 onward), Shrubland Park, Suffolk (1849–50), and Cliveden House, Buckinghamshire (1850). Others were quick to follow his lead. Thomas Cubitt provided mansions in this style during the 1840s for George Hudson, the railway king, at Albert Gate, London, and for Queen Victoria and Prince Albert at Osborne House on the Isle of Wight. Far more distinguished that anything by Cubitt and much by Barry was Dorchester House, Park Lane, London (1850–63), by Lewis Vulliamy (1791–1871). It was designed in close collaboration with its owner, R. S. Holford, the art collector and shipping magnate, who was evidently trying to rival Barry's Bridgewater House of 1846–51 for Lord Ellesmere. Based on Baldassare Peruzzi's Villa Farnesina, Rome (1509–11), Vulliamy's Dorchester House was one of the great buildings of the nineteenth century, and its destruction in 1929 was a major loss to British architecture. It expressed the culmination of those opulent, aristocratic Mediterranean sympathies that had developed in the 1830s and 1840s at the end of the long Georgian and Whig heyday. The sumptuously decorated interior reached a climax in the second-floor ballroom, or saloon, which, by a brilliant theatrical stroke, opened through three archways directly into the upper spaces of the stair hall. The whole house thus became alive with sound and movement on evenings when great balls and receptions were held. The dining room was designed by Alfred George Stevens (1817–1875), a pupil of Bertel Thorvaldsen and undoubtedly the finest of the Victorian sculptors. He was in deep sympathy with the cinquecento, particularly with Michelangelo, and was, of all nineteenth-century designers, the closest in temperament and talent to Cockerell. His Willington Monument in St. Paul's cathedral (1856), a great triumphal arch of marble, is one of the noblest memorials to the nineteenth-century Italianate Revival. His magnificent chimneypiece in the dining room at Dorchester House took ten years to design and construct (1859–69). Its incredible cost of 1,778 pounds shocked even the millionaire Holford.

To remind us of what we have lost at Dorchester House is a building in the same vein, though perhaps of even greater quality and originality: the Free Trade Hall, Manchester (1853), by Edward Walters (1808–1872), who had worked in the offices of both Cubitt and Vulliamy. William Bruce Gingell (1819–1900) was another talented architect in the Italianate manner. His West of England and South Wales District (now Lloyds) Bank at Bristol (1854) is a stylish variation on the theme of Pietro Sansovino's Libreria Vecchia, Venice. Samuel Angell (1800–1866) had also made a special study of cinquecento architecture; he lectured on Giacomo da Vignola at the Royal Institute of British Architects in 1850, and in 1856 produced the sumptuous Clothworkers' Hall, Mincing Lane, London (destroyed 1940). An interesting offshoot of the taste for things Italian was the vogue in the 1840s for the "round-arch style" in church architecture, which included every kind of variant from Early Christian and Byzantine to Italian Romanesque and Norman. The most elaborate example of this

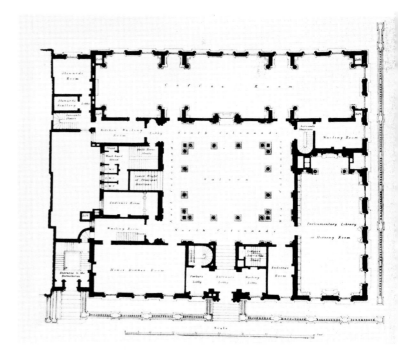

453. Sir Charles Barry, Reform
Club, London, saloon, 1837–41
454. Sir Charles Barry, Shrubland
Park, Suffolk, gardens, 1849–54
455. Thomas Cubitt, Osborne House,
Isle of Wight, aerial view, 1845–48
456. Thomas Cubitt, Osborne
House, Isle of Wight, drawing room,
1845–48

taste is afforded by the church of St. Mary and St. Nicholas at Wilton, Wiltshire (1840–46), by Thomas Henry (1807–1880) and David Brandon. In a rich Italian Romanesque style, with a campanile over thirty meters (one hundred feet) high, it contains ancient Roman columns of black marble from the Temple of Venus at Porto Venere. A building of rare quality in the round-arch style is the museum of Trinity College, Dublin, of 1852–57, by Sir Thomas Newenham Deane (1828–1899) and Benjamin Woodward (1815–1861). Though organized around a central glazed courtyard, rather like Barry's Reform Club, the building has naturalistically carved capitals inspired by Ruskin and details in a Venetian early-Renaissance mode.

The Palazzo style was agreed upon as appropriate, for a variety of practical and associational reasons, for commercial premises and private clubs, but when it came to the style in which a great building of national and symbolic importance should be built, the latent battle between the exponents of the classical and the Gothic came with some violence to the surface. The particular victim of the strife was Sir George Gilbert Scott (1811–1878), who between 1856 and 1861 was forced more than once to remodel his Gothic design for the Foreign Office to suit the Renaissance tastes of the Prime Minister, Lord Palmerston. Ironically, the result was one of Scott's best buildings, though it must be said that he had much help from Matthew Digby Wyatt (1820–1877).

After the 1860s the classical tradition lost impetus and the best architects worked in other veins. It was revived, together with an interest in Cockerell, between 1890 and 1910 with some surprisingly impressive results.

GERMANY

There were many similarities between the development of German and English architecture between 1790 and 1840; thus, a number of the major designs and buildings by Gilly, Schinkel, and Klenze have already been mentioned in the course of our discussion of the Greek Revival and the Picturesque. Certainly the intensely eclectic work of the greatest German architect of these years, Karl Friedrich Schinkel, reminds us immediately not of France or Italy but of England. Schinkel also developed a "functional" interpretation of classicism, which was successfully revived in Germany between 1900 and 1940 as a reaction against both the Wilhelmine Baroque and Bauhaus bleakness. Schinkel particularly appealed to his countrymen during the first half of the twentieth century in part because of what they saw as his essential "Germanness." As head of the Public Works Department, Schinkel became identified with the creation of the new Germany between the Napoleonic Wars and the foundation of the empire in 1871. Indeed, so much was he seen as part of its reforging that the royal family walked behind his coffin in his funeral procession.

He provided the center of Berlin with a number of striking monuments in different styles: Greek Revival for the Royal Guardhouse (1816–18),

462. Alfred George Stevens, Wellington Monument, St. Paul's cathedral, London, 1856

463. Sir Thomas Newenham Deane and Benjamin Woodward, Trinity College Museum, Dublin, stair hall, 1852–57

464. Sir Thomas Newenham Deane and Benjamin Woodward, Trinity College Museum, Dublin, 1852–57

465. Samuel Angell, Clothworkers' Hall, London, 1856

466. Thomas Henry Wyatt and
David Brandon, St. Mary and St.
Nicholas, Wilton, Wiltshire,
1840–46

467. Sir George Gilbert Scott and Sir
Matthew Digby Wyatt, Foreign
Office, London, 1856–73

468. Samuel Angell, Clothworkers' Hall, London, interior, 1856
469. Sir George Gilbert Scott and Sir Matthew Digby Wyatt, Foreign Office, London, stair hall, 1862–73

State Theater (1818–21), and Altes Museum (1822–28); Gothic for the grim brick Friedrich-Werdersche church (1821–30) and the cast-iron Kreuzberg War Memorial (1818); and a cross between Functional and North Italian quattrocento for the School of Architecture (1831–36). Despite the claims that have been made for his ability as a town planner (H. G. Pundt, *Schinkel's Berlin: A Study in Environmental Planning,* 1972), it must be confessed that, unlike John Nash in London, he was not able to make a coherent impact on the city of Berlin, which remained dominated by its Baroque and eighteenth-century planning and monuments.

One of the most prolific and eclectic architects of all time, Schinkel is difficult to sum up, to generalize about, to fit into a pattern. It is possible that his important study-tour of England in 1826 influenced the development of his "functional" style, with its prominent use of iron. He was both appalled and attracted by the architecture of the Industrial Revolution in England, and it seems that it was after observing the giant cotton mills that he conceived the idea of a fireproof architecture whose gridlike brick skin would wrap around an iron frame. The various explorations he made of this after his return from England include two unexecuted proposals—a bazaar for Unter den Linden (1827) and a State Library (1832–39) nearby—the Royal Customs Warehouses (1829), the School of Architecture, and the spectacular cast-iron staircases in two of the palaces in the Wilhelmstrasse that he remodeled for the king's sons, Prince Karl (1827) and Prince Albrecht (1829–33).

We have touched elsewhere on Schinkel's work in a Picturesque vein that, too, has English overtones: Schloss Glienicke, Schloss Charlottenhof, and Schloss Babelsberg. It culminated later in the 1830s in two unexecuted fantasies: a palace on the Acropolis for the king of Greece (Otto von Wittelsbach of Bavaria) and a palace at Orianda, in the Crimea, for the empress of Russia, who was a daughter of King Friedrich-Wilhelm III of Prussia. Both display a rich polychromy inspired by the researches of Hittorff, a great admirer of Schinkel; both are examples of Schinkel's special gift for distributing symmetrical Grecian forms in an asymmetrically landscaped composition; and both give the impression of sumptuous film sets. The palace on the Acropolis, which turned the Parthenon into a kind of glorified garden ornament, is the apotheosis of what some scholars have called Romantic classicism.

Leo von Klenze (1784–1864), like Schinkel, was a North German who turned to architecture after meeting the visionary and influential young Friedrich Gilly. He studied in Paris in the opening years of the nineteenth century under Percier and Fontaine and also under J.-N.-L. Durand at the École Polytechnique. After working from 1808 to 1813 as court architect to Napoleon's youngest brother, Jérôme, who had been elevated to the throne of Westphalia, Klenze met Crown Prince Ludwig of Bavaria, in 1814. The young prince, who had purchased the Aegina Marbles in 1811, shared Klenze's passion for antiquity and in 1816 persuaded his father, Maximilian

470. *Karl Friedrich Schinkel, Altes Museum, Berlin, 1822–23*
471. *Karl Friedrich Schinkel, Altes Museum, Berlin, hall, 1822–23*

472. *Karl Friedrich Schinkel, School of Architecture, Berlin, 1831–36*

473, 474. *Karl Friedrich Schinkel, project for a palace, Orianda, Crimea, atrium and courtyard, 1838*

XXXIV. *Karl Friederich Schinkel,*
project for a palace on the Acropolis,
Athens, 1834

XXXV. *Eduard Gärtner,*
Bauakademie *by Karl Friederich*
Shinkel. Berlin, Nationalgalerie

XXXVI. Karl Friederich Schinkel, project for a palace, Orianda, Crim, atrium, 1838

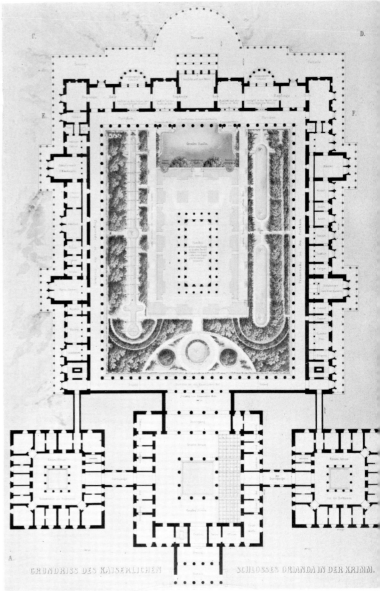

GRUNDRISS DES KAISERLICHEN SCHLOSSES ORIANDA IN DER KRIMM.

I, to appoint Klenze as supervisor of court buildings in Munich. This royal support in architectural endeavor finds a close parallel in the relationship between Schinkel and the crown prince in Berlin, between Percier and Fontaine and Napoleon in Paris, and between Nash and the Prince Regent in England. Klenze and the crown prince made the same kind of sweeping impact on Munich that Nash did on London, though the German architect and his patron worked in a style rather different from Nash's. Their principal contributions were the great Ludwigstrasse, running north from the royal Residenz, and the Königsplatz, which lay to the west of the Ludwigstrasse on the route into the city from the royal palace of Nymphenburg.

In 1816 Klenze designed two major buildings that reflect the influence of his French masters. The Glyptothek in the Königsplatz is notable as the first public sculpture gallery ever erected. It was commissioned by the crown prince, who wished to house the Aegina Marbles suitably. In contained Roman as well as Greek antiquities, and its Grecian portico is flanked by Roman aedicules. From the same year dates the very different Leuchtenberg Palace, off the Ludwigstrasse, designed for Napoleon's stepson, Eugène de Beauharnais, who had married the crown prince's sister. Perhaps the first major monument of the Renaissance Revival, it was inspired, like Barry's Reform Club of twenty-one years later, by the Palazzo Farnese. Klenze doubtless knew the engravings of Italian domestic architecture of the fifteenth and sixteenth centuries that Percier and Fontaine had published in their *Palais, maisons, et autres édifices modernes dessinés à Rome* (1798). The fifteenth-century Florentine style chosen by the crown prince for much of Klenze's street architecture in Munich may also owe something to the plates in *Architecture toscane,* published in 1815 by Auguste Grandjean de Montigny, Klenze's predecessor as architect to King Jérome. Klenze's Pinakothek, or Picture Gallery, in Munich (designed 1822–25; built 1826–36) antedates both Smirke's British Museum and Schinkel's Altes Museum and, unlike either of these, reflects a neo-Renaissance vocabulary. In 1823–24 Klenze visited Sicily and Paestum with the crown prince, and there he made detailed drawings of the Greek temples while the prince fell in love with the Palatine Chapel at Palermo. In 1824 he became director

492. Matvei Feodorovich Kazakov,
Senate Building, Kremlin, Moscow,
1771–85

493. Giacomo Antonio Domenico
Quarenghi, Matvei Feodorovich
Kazakov, and Ivan Petrovich
Argunov, Sheremetev Palace,
Ostankino, near Moscow, 1791–98

it was not executed. His highly ornamental Pashkov Palace (now the Lenin Library) of 1784–86 maintained links with the Baroque. The work of his assistant Matvei Feodorovich Kazakov (1733–1812), more than that of any other architect, gave the new Moscow its classical character. Kazakov's mighty triangular Senate Building in the Kremlin (now the Council of the Ministers of the USSR), of 1771–85, was a fulfillment of Bazhenov's Kremlin project. Its great Doric rotunda is flanked internally with impressive freestanding Corinthian columns, as is his Hall of the Noblemen's Assembly of 1784–86 (now the Hall of Columns, House of the Trade Unions). Kazakov, who had traveled in France and Italy, was an admirer of Palladio, as can be seen in both his public buildings (Golitsyn Hospital, 1796–1801) and his private palaces (Demidov House, 1789–91; and Batashev House, 1798–1802). He was also interested in reviving ancient Russian forms and mingling them with Gothic details, as he did with bizarre effect in the Petrovsky Palace (1775–82; altered 1840). Like Bazhenov's church of Our Lady of All Sorrows, Kazakov's Moscow churches of the 1780s and 1790s—SS. Cosmas and Damian, St. Philip the Metropolitan, Ascension, and St. Martin the Confessor—are asymmetrical in composition. The familiar Russian rotunda and tall campanile create a staccato effect oddly reminiscent of E.-M. Gauthey's church at Givry-sur-Saône (1770–91) and George Steuart's New St. Chad, Shrewsbury (1790).

A number of Moscow buildings of the turn of the century are associated with Quarenghi. He remodeled the Catherine (Golovin) Palace, incorporating a Tuscan colonnaded hall, and added a startling hemicycle of Tuscan columns to the facade by Yelezvoi Nazarov of the Sheremetev Pilgrims' Refuge. One of the grandest private palaces of the period was built at Ostankino in 1791–98 for Count Sheremetev by Quarenghi, Kazakov, and Ivan Petrovich Argunov. With its superbly ornamented theater and, on the grounds, the Italian and so-called Egyptian pavilions, Ostankino has something of the quality of Cameron's work for Catherine the Great at Tsarskoe Selo.

In the early nineteenth century the principal Muscovite architects who followed Kazakov were the Italian-born Domenico Gilardi (1788–1845), Afanasy Grigoryev (1782–1868), and Osip Beauvais (1784–1834). By Grigoryev and Adam Menelaws is the Razumovsky House (1801–3). Its powerful facade is based on the motif by now familiar to us in the work of Kent, Adam, and Ledoux: an open screen of columns in front of a coffered apse. Gilardi's Khrushchev House (1814) and Lopukhin House (1817–22) are Palladian in theme, enlivened with crisp Empire decoration. Gilardi, however, did inject a more astringent note into Muscovite classicism, and his influence was, in some ways, comparable to the impact of Gilly in Germany. Strikingly reminiscent of Gilly are his adaptation of Kazakov's Music Pavilion of the Equerry on the Kuzminki estate (1819) and his completion in the late 1820s of Quarenghi's and Kazakov's Suburban Palace (begun 1788). Between 1809 and 1818, with his father, Giacomo, Gilardi

XXXVII. Leo von Klenze, Glyptothek, competition project in Greek style, Munich, 1815

XXXVIII. Leo von Klenze, Glyptothek, competition project in Palladian style, Munich, 1815

494. *Giacomo Antonio Domenico Quarenghi, Matvei Feodorovich Kazakov, and Ivan Petrovich Argunov, Sheremetev Palace, Ostantkino, near Moscow, view of the park, 1791–98*

495, 496. *Giacomo Antonio Domenico Quarenghi, Matvei Feodorovich Kasakov, and Ivan Petrovich Argunov, Sheremetev Palace, Ostankino, near Moscow, views of the interior, 1791–98*

built the Widows' House, and from 1823 to 1826 the Guardianship Council Building. The former is notable for a great octostyle portico of unfluted Greek Doric columns, the latter for a similar portico of Greek Ionic columns and a superb vaulted stair hall with two tiers of unfluted marble columns. His most impressive private house is the Lunin House (1818–23), on Nikitsky Boulevard, but his major work was the reconstruction, in 1817–19, of Kazakov's Moscow University of 1786–93. For Kazakov's elegant Ionic order on the entrance portico he substituted a powerful Greek Doric and also reworked the side pavilions in a harder, chunkier style. In a similar fashion, Menelaws remodeled the English Club (now the Museum of the Revolution of the USSR) with a Greek Doric portico. Greek Doric also are Osip Beauvais's squat, truncated columns set in a rusticated arch in the grotto of the Alexandrovsky Garden.

Beauvais's name is particularly associated with the planning in Moscow carried out after the disastrous fire of 1812, for he was director of the commission for rebuilding the city. In front of his Bolshoi Theater (1821–24) the Theater (now Sverdlov) Square merges with the Resurrection (now Revolution) Square. At the Tverskaya Zastava he built a splendid triumphal arch (1827–34), based on the Arch of Titus in Rome, to mark the spot where the victorious army had returned to Moscow from the Napoleonic Wars. It has now, unfortunately, been moved to the Mozhaiskoye Highway.

During the 1830s German influence penetrated where French and Italian had for so long held sway. In 1838, following the fire at the old Winter Palace in St. Petersburg in December 1837, Leo von Klenze was called from Munich by Nicholas I to design the New Hermitage Museum. Klenze's vast building on the banks of the Neva next to the Hermitage Theater is an impressive amalgam of French, Russian, and German classicism: The monumental porch supported by giant *atlantes* carved by Alexander Ivanovitch Terebenev has a Russian grandiosity; the principal staircase echoes the one of 1803–7 by Chalgrin at the Palais du Luxembourg; the restrained Grecian trabeation of the facades was inspired by Schinkel, as was the careful layout of the galleries, with pictures hung on low side screens and with rooms allotted to the different schools of painting.

In Moscow the classical tradition came to an end in two great buildings by the German-born architect Konstantin Andreevich Ton (1794–1881): the Great Kremlin Palace (1838–49) and the huge church of the Redeemer (1839–83), whose odd, half-Byzantine, half-classical style points forward to the nationalistic Slav Revival of the later nineteenth century.

SCANDINAVIA

In the early nineteenth century the capital cities of Scandinavia—Copenhagen, Helsinki, and Christian (Oslo)—produced a rich harvest of public buildings in the classical style that had been developed since the mid-

497. Caspar Frederik Harsdorff, mortuary chapel for Frederik V, cathedral, Roskilde, 1768–78; completed by Christian Frederik Hansen, 1821–25

498. Christian Frederik Hansen, Vor Fruc Kirke, Copenhagen, 1811–29

499. Christian Frederik Hansen, courthouse and prison, Copenhagen, 1803–16

500. Christian Frederik Hansen, Vor Fruc Kirke, Copenhagen, interior, 1811–29

501. M. Gottlieb Bindeshøll, Thorvaldsen Museum, Copenhagen, courtyard, 1837–48

502. Johann Carl Ludwig Engel,
cathedral, Helsinki, 1830–51
503. Johann Carl Ludwig Engel,
Senate, Helsinki, 1818–22

504. Johann Carl Ludwig Engel,
University Library, Helsinki, reading
room, 1836–45

eighteenth century in France, England, and Italy and that was to be so strikingly codified by Schinkel in Germany. Indeed, there is a strong German flavor to Scandinavian classicism in these years. However, the new style had been imported very early from France by two French architects, Nicolas-Henry Jardin (1720–1799), who lived in Denmark from 1755 to 1771, and Jean-Louis Desprez (1743–1804), who was employed by Gustavus III of Sweden beginning in 1784. Jardin's dining room of 1755–57 for Count A. G. Moltke in what is now the Amalienborg Palace in Copenhagen has been described as "the earliest surviving room decorated entirely in the Neo-Classical taste by a French architect" (S. Eriksen, *Early Neo-Classicism in France*, 1974, p. 57). Caspar Frederik Harsdorff (1735–1799), first a pupil of Jardin at the Royal Academy in Copenhagen, later studied under Blondel in Paris. His mortuary chapel for Frederick V in the cathedral at Roskilde, built in the 1770s, is a cool and beautiful blend of Blondel's and Adam's styles. Desprez, who was principally a stage designer, built the Botanicum at Uppsala in 1788 with a long, low portico of eight Greek Doric columns. This Greek enthusiasm had already been expressed in the designs of the Swedish-born Carl August Ehrensvärd (1745–1800), whose visit to Paestum in 1780–82 had resulted in his primitivist Doric project of 1785 for a dockyard gate at Karlskrona. The most important Scandinavian architect to emerge in these years was Christian Frederick Hansen (1756–1845). In his architectural group composed of town hall, courthouse, and prison, with its attendant archways (1803–16), he brought to Copenhagen the Franco-Prussian style that Gilly had developed out of the work of Ledoux. Hansen's principal achievement is the cathedral at Copenhagen, the Vor Fruc Kirke (designed 1808–10; built 1811–29), with its Doric colonnades supporting an immense coffered barrel vault reminiscent of Boullée's celebrated project for the new hall of the Bibliothèque Nationale. Hansen's pupil M. Gottlieb Bindesboll (1800–1856) produced the memorable Thorvaldsen Museum in Copenhagen (1837–48), an idiosyncratic blend of styles borrowed from Egypt, Greece, and Schinkel. In his other works Bindesboll tended toward the Rundborgenstil ("round-arch" style), as did his follower J. D. Herholdt (1818–1902), for example, in the Copenhagen University Library (1855–61).

The foundation of a new capital in Norway after that country's separation from Denmark in 1814 created great opportunities for the architect Christian Heinrich Grosch (1801–1865), a pupil of Hansen. At Christiania he built the Exchange (1826–52), using a baseless Tuscan order *in antis,* the Norwegian Bank (1828), and, most important, the University (1841–52), which has a markedly Schinkelesque trabeation. Here, a Greek Ionic portico leads into a fine Greek Doric hall.

Perhaps the most attractive project of the period in Scandinavia was the development of Helsinki after the city became a Russian gran duchy in 1809. The plan of the newly chosen capital of Finland is the work of the architect Johan Albrekt Ehrenström (1762–1847), but all the major public buildings

505. *Johann Carl Ludwig Engel,*
hospital, Helsinki, 1826

506. *Johann Carl Ludwig Engel,*
University Library, Helsinki,
staircase, 1836–45

507. *Alessandro Pompei, Museo*
Lapidario Maffeiano, Verona,
elevation and plan, 1739–c. 1746

and many private houses are by the German-born Johann Carl Ludwig Engel (1778–1840). He created the superb Senate Square, dominated by his cathedral (designed from 1818 onward; built 1830–51) at the top of a great flight of steps, and flanked by his University (1828–32) and Senate (1818–22). The University Library, with its magnificent colonnaded reading rooms, was designed in 1833 and later, and built from 1836 to 1845. Perhaps the most striking features of Engel's work are his Doric staircases: The massive, freestanding Paestum-Doric columns of the Senate staircase unexpectedly carry groin-vaulted ceilings, whereas two stories of fluted and unfluted columns create a complex web of trabeation in the staircase at the University Library.

ITALY

Italy was partially unified under the French from 1796 to the fall of Napoleon in 1814, but not until the late nineteenth century was it formally united under a single ruler, Victor Emmanuel II. For most of the period under consideration it was thus a conglomeration of odd and often opposing states, controlled for the most part by outside powers. Piedmont was completely oriented to France until the Treaty of Aix-la-Chapelle in 1748. Lombardy was a province of Austria until the arrival of Napoleon. Parma remained an outpost of French culture after 1748, when Louis XV's daughter married the Bourbon duke. Venice maintained a staunch independence until Napoleon dismissed the last doge. Trieste owed allegiance to Austria but became a free port in 1719, which inevitably changed things. And so one might continue. There was no common culture. From the middle years of the eighteenth century there was, in addition, very little money. Circumstances were not auspicious for architecture.

Early in the eighteenth century there was, indeed, a short but brilliant flowering of the late Baroque. In Piedmost Filippo Juvarra and Bernardo Antonio Vittone were busy; in Roma those monuments that still give pleasure without alloy—the Spanish Steps (1723–25), the Piazza S. Ignazio (1727–28), and the Fontana di Trevi (1732–62)—were being built. But in the middle years of the century this heady architectural splurge suddenly ceased. Activity continued in the south, where the Bourbon had taken over in 1738. Charles III summoned Ferdinando Fuga (1699–1782) and Luigi Vanvitelli (1700–1773) to Naples in 1751, and there they began some of the largest schemes ever devised for the Bourbons—Fuga's Albergo de' Poveri and the granary, Vanvitelli's royal palace at Caserta and the barracks. But inspiration was weak, and architecture in Italy entered the doldrums.

Even in Venice and on the nearby mainland, where building continued and the fiery Lodoli, as we have seen, was preaching his radical doctrines, little of interest was being done. Lodoli and his circle of intellectuals did not much influence the course of architecture, though Scipione Maffei's Museo Lapidario at Verona, completed about 1746 by Alessandro Pompei

293

513. *Raffaello Stern,*
Braccio Nuovo, Vatican Museum,
Rome, 1817–22

(1705–1772), must be regarded as a harbinger of neoclassicism, and Andrea Memmo's public-spirited works in Padua, the Prato della Valle and the hospital, both begun in 1775 by the local professor of architecture Domenico Cerato (1720–1792), were clearly intended to illustrate Lodoli's ideas. But architecture in the Veneto continued to be dominated by the influence of Palladio. Architects as diverse as the exuberant Giorgio Massari (1687–1766) and the over-fastidious Antonio Visentini (1688–1782), designer of the Palazzo Smith (now the Argentine Consulate), of 1751, and the Palazzo Coletti-Giusti, of 1766, both on the Grand Canal, used the elements and the compositional devices that Palladio had established. Ottavio Bertotti-Scamozzi, working in Vicenza on this same basis, was able to evolve an architecture of some power and conviction, but there was no fresh impulse. Yet a significant line of architectural descent can be traced in Venice, beginning with Massari's master, Andrea Tirali (1657–1737), and his nephew Giovanni Antonio Scalfarotto (1690–1764), designers, respectively, of the giant portico of S. Nicolò da Tolentino (1706–14) and of SS. Simeone e Giuda (1718–38), a high-domed, circular church, also fronted with a pedimented portico. Scalfarotto's nephew and disciple was Tommaso Temanza (1705–1789), architect of the small but robustly designed circular church S. Maria Maddalena (1760, 1763–78), but remembered chiefly as a stern teacher and propagandist, and especially as author of the *Vita dei più celebri architetti e scultori veneziani,* of 1778. Francesco Milizia was to derive much of his information from Temanza. Lodoli loathed him as an insufferable pedant. They were bitterly opposed, possibly in connection with the building of Temanza's first work, the Cappella dei Sagredo, in S. Francesco della Vigna, also in Venice. But Temanza was to attain success through his pupil Giannantonio Selva (1754–1819), who traveled to Rome, Paris, London, and, later, Constantinople, before he settled down to design a number of well-proportioned and clear-cut buildings based on one or two themes and no more, but so competently handled that they are of more than provincial interest: the Teatro La Fenice, Venice, built rapidly between 1790 and 1792, and much reorganized by G.B. Meduna after a fire in 1836, but still today resplendent; the Palazzo Dotti-Vigodarzere, in the Via Rudena, Padua, of 1796; and the two Venetian churches S. Maurizio, begun in 1806, and S. Nome di Gesù, of nine years later, both completed by Selva's assistant Antonio Diedo (1772–1847). With Diedo, Selva also designed the dull facade of the duomo at Cologna Veneta (1810–17) and that most famous and even more boring work associated with his name, the great mausoleum for Antonio Canova at Possagno, of 1819 to 1833 (however, credit—or the reverse—for this conflation of the Parthenon and the Pantheon has not yet been fixed). Selva's most celebrated pupil was Giuseppe Jappelli (1783–1852), the first of these Venetian architects to win international recognition—largely, it must be admitted, for that hydra-headed work, the Caffè Pedrocchi and the Pedrocchino in Padua—part Egyptian, part classical, begun in 1826, part

516. Giannantonio Selva and Antonio Diedo (attributed), mausoleum of Antonio Canova, Possagno, 1819–33

517. Giuseppe Jappelli, Caffè Pedrocchi, Padua, 1826–31

518. Giambattista Piranesi, S. Maria del Priorato, Rome, begun 1764

519. Lorenzo Santi, Caffè (now Air Terminal), Venice, 1815–38

524. Francesco Gurrieri Pasquale
Poccianti and Giuseppe Cacialli, Villa
del Poggio Imperiale, Florence, begun
1806

525. Francesco Gurrieri Pasquale
Poccianti, Sala d'Elci, Biblioteca
Laurenziana, Florence, 1816–41

Picturesque Gothic, begun in 1838, all completed by 1842. But Jappelli was also responsible for other equally arresting works, including the stern Doric meat market (1819–24), now the Scuola Pietro Selvatico, and the Villa Treves de' Bonfili, with its *giardino inglese* (now a public park), both in Padua; outside Padua, at Saonara, the far better preserved villa and garden of the Conti Cittadella Vigodarzere (begun 1816); the Villa Gera on the Via F. Benini at Conegliano (1827); and the Villa Manzoni at Patt di Sedico (1837), probably the largest in the province of Belluno. Altogether, Jappelli evolved a firm and competent style, one that impinges on international neoclassicism, even if it did not influence it.

When Napoleon reached Venice in 1807, he at once thought to make an impression by ordering large-scale works. Selva built the public garden at Castello for him, now greatly altered, and also the cemetery, also modified; but most of the major commissions went to outsiders. Giuseppe Maria Soli (1747–1823), from Vignola (though he had trained in Bologna under Malvasia), began the west side of the Piazza S. Marco in 1810. Lorenzo Santi (1783–1839), from Siena, also a pupil of Selva, designed the great stair and the ballroom inside Soli's Ala Napoleonica in 1822. Then he undertook that lively yet Doric-decked Caffè (1815–38), at the far end of the old Giardinetto Reale, now used as an air terminal, and finally the Palazzo Patriarcale tucked in at the side of the duomo (1837–50). There is nothing much to tell of architecture in Venice after this date.

In Rome, where the turmoil and intrigue occasioned by foreign visitors largely conditioned the form of international neoclassicism, there was even less sustained architectural activity. Piranesi, who arrived there from Venice in 1740, produced only the disappointing, if most intriguing, church of S. Maria del Priorato, high on the Aventine, begun in 1764. Quarenghi, who went in 1763 from Bergamo to Rome, where he met and studied with Selva, stayed long enough to rebuild the church of S. Scolastica at Subiaco (1771–77) before he was packed off to Russia in 1779 by Baron Friedrich Grimm. Carlo Francesco Giacomo Marchionni (1702–1786) was born in Rome but spent his early years in his family's native town of Montecelio, in the Marches. He was trained in Rome, under Filippo Barigioni, and in 1728 won first prize in the Concorso Clementino, at the Accademia di San Luca. By 1751 he had begun work on the Villa Albani, soon to become the mecca of Winckelmann and Mengs. This famous villa, heavily articulated both inside and out, with decorative details evidently influenced by Piranesi, was more or less complete by the end of 1762, though work in the interior continued until 1764, and on the terraces and garden buildings until 1767. It was a tour de force, but not one that had much influence. Nor indeed did Marchionni's other important work, the new sacristy of St. Peter's, erected between 1776 and 1784. This was viciously attacked by the only Italian critic of any acumen, Francesco Milizia (1725–1798), who had come from Otranto, via Naples, to Rome. He was hounded out of town for such effrontery. But his reputation had already been made with the publication

in 1768 of the first edition of the *Vita degli architetti più celebri,* to be followed four years after by *Del teatro* and in 1781 by the *Principii di architettura civile.* These were all to be translated abroad.

Neoclassicism came to Rome only after the death of Winckelmann in 1768. He was succeeded as *Commissario dei Musei e Soprintendente alle Antichità* by the archaeologist Giovanni Battista Visconti, who at once initiated the transformation of Innocent VIII's casina in the Vatican as a museum. The alterations to the octagonal court were begun by Alessandro Dori, but in 1772 Michelangelo Simonetti (1724–1781) took up the work, which was to be continued with real enthusiasm only after the election of Pius VI in 1775, when Simonetti was joined by Pietro Camporese (1726–1781). The Sala delle Muse, the Sala a Croce Greca, and the new access stairs are all theirs, while the Braccio Nuovo, built between 1817 and 1822, is by Raffaello Stern (1774–1820); together, these rooms make up a sequence of varied spaces, each based on an antique precedent, with the details also of unusual archaeological correctness. The result is indeed neoclassical, and most impressive, but not readily applicable to smaller-scale works.

A confident, easily imitated neoclassical style appeared in Rome only with the arrival of the French. Giuseppe Valadier (1762–1839), who had worked long and hard in the Papal States, and in particular at Urbino, where he had rebuilt the duomo, presented an initial project for the planning and development of the Piazza del Popolo and the Pincio in 1793. This ambitious scheme, with its ramps and carriageways climbing the hill, was at once taken up by the French. Alexandre-Jean-Baptiste-Guy de Gisors (1762–1835) and Louis-Martin Berthault were sent from France to supervise both it and the superb Casina at the top. The final project was not approved, however, until April 1813, and when Pius VII assumed control in 1816 further modifications were made, so that the full splendor of the whole was not to be experienced before 1820. By then Valadier had done several other works of a neoclassical kind: restorations to the Arch of Titus (1819–20) and the Colosseum (1820), but mostly large and pretentious villas. The grandest to be built at this time, the Villa Torlonia, on the Via Nomentana, was begun early in the nineteenth century to the designs of Valadier, who was succeeded within a few years by Giovanni Battista Caretti (1803–1878). He laid out the gardens and the first pavilions, but the later ones and the ruins were built from 1840 to 1846 by Jappelli, Antonio Sarti, and others.

In Rome there was little succession to these works, though Valadier's pupil Lorenzo Nottolini (1785–1851) set up in Lucca, where he designed a noble stairway and sculpture gallery for the Palazzo Ducale in 1818 and, in 1826, proposed a grand layout for the Prato del Marchese not unrelated to Memmo's town-planning venture in Padua. During these years he built a succession of bridges and aqueducts, town houses, and, in particular, the Specola (Observatory) and Rotonda, at Marlia nearby, that conferred something of cosmopolitan sophistication on this provincial outpost.

528. *Leopoldo Laperuta, Antonio*
de Simone, and Pietro Bianchi,
S. Francesco di Paola, begun 1809,
redesigned 1817, finished 1831

529. *Giuseppe Venanzio Marvuglia*
with Giuseppe Patricola, La Favorita
(or Palazzina Cinese), Palermo,
1799–1802

530. *Ennemond-Alexandre Petitot,*
La Venezia, Colorno, 1753–55

Clearly, the development of architecture in Venice and Rome was, at first, sluggish, and when the pace quickened it was owing largely to outside influence. Selva was probably more indebted to the English example than to the French (though in his obituary Diedo described Selva's early work as in the "gusto francese"), but most architects took their cue from Paris. This is not, of course, to suggest that the Italians themselves had nothing to offer, but rather to indicate that the style of 1800 was one the French had first fashioned and used—exploited, even—long before the Italians took it up and gave it their own particular twist. The French provided not only the ideas and the examples but also the authority and power. They were invaders intent to make their presence felt and seen. They were great builders. The same, to a lesser extent, was true of the Austrians. Throughout Italy the impetus for change came from outside.

In Trieste, Germanic influences were strong, starting with Matteo Pertsch, who had trained under Giuseppe Piermarini in Milan and adapted his master's La Scala for his first works of importance, the Teatro Grande (now Verdi), in 1798–1806. His mature works, too, relate to Milanese classicism: the vast Palazzo Carciotti (1799–1806), conspicuously and rather ridiculously domed; nearby, also on the Riva 3 Novembre, the front of S. Nicolò dei Greci (1818–19); and—still within the new quarter of the town then being developed—the Rotonda dei Pancera (c. 1818). The second and far more able architect active in Trieste was Pietro Nobile (1774–1854), from the Ticino area of Switzerland, who trained from 1803 to 1805 in Rome. But he was soon established in Trieste, where he designed the Fontana House in 1813–16 (built only in 1827–30) and the Accademia di Commercio e Nautica (now the Biblioteca Civica Hortis), of 1817. His major work was S. Antonio Nuovo (1825–49), a noble church, beautifully sited at the head of the Canal Grande, and of more spatial interest than anything else of the period. His Costanzi House, of 1840, trim and unadorned, is in a style that was by then long out of fashion in the rest of Europe. In 1817 he was called to Vienna, where he was to build the Theseus Temple in the Volksgarten, of 1822, and the nearby Burgtor, of 1821 to 1824, in a heavy classical style still coherent and strong.

In Genoa the spark was kindled by de Wailly. Work on his salon for the Palazzo Spinola, commissioned in 1772, was supervised by Emanuele Andrea Tagliafichi (1729–1811), who traveled two years later to Paris, where he was made a corresponding member of the Académie. His original contribution came in the stair hall and salon of the Palazzo Durazzo-Pallavicini, in the Via Balbi, begun in 1780. But the only Genoan architect of consequence was Carlo Francesco Barabino (1768–1835), designer of the Teatro Carlo Felice and the related Palazzo dell'Accademia (1825–28; badly damaged in 1944) and of the first project for the cemetery of Staglieno (1835, 1844–51). He had trained in Rome with Giuseppe Barberi.

In Florence, activity was stirred by the work of redecorating the Palazzo Pitti, from 1796 onward, by Gaspare Maria Paoletti (1727–1813). He was

303

533. Giuseppe Piermarini, Teatro
alla Scala, Milan, 1776–78

534. Simone Cantoni, hall on the
first floor, Palazzo Ducale, Genoa,
decorated in 1783

535. Giuseppe Piermarini, Villa
Ducale, Monza, 1776–80

536. Plate from Giocondo Albertolli's
Alcune decorazioni di nobili sale
ed altri ornamenti, 1787, showing
interior decorations

537. Simone Cantoni, project for the
Palazzo Pertusati, on the Naviglio,
Milan, 1789–91

538. Giovanni Perego and Innocenzo
Domenico Giusti, Palazzo Rocca-
Saporiti, Milan, completed 1812

responsible for the first design for the ballroom, while his pupils Giuseppe
Cacialli (1778–1828) and Francesco Gurrieri Pasquale Poccianti (1774–
1858) designed the highly articulated stairway in the garden wing. All were
involved also in the rebuilding of the Villa del Poggio Imperiale, outside
Florence, for Queen Marie Louise, whose kingdom of Etruria existed from
1801 to 1808. The powerful facade there was designed by Poccianti in 1806,
but he left the work to Cacialli, to return to Florence, to the Pitti and to
design the Sala d'Elci (1817–41) adjoining Michelangelo's Biblioteca
Laurenziana. He also took up the system of aqueducts, filters, and cisterns
in and around Livorno, which were to culminate in his Cisternone
(1829–42), a not unworthy successor to Ledoux's gateway at Arc-et-Senans
and certainly the most successful attempt in Italy, if not in all Europe, to
realize the dreams of French visionaries. Giovanni Antonio Antolini, it
seems, offered his advice, but Poccianti kept him at bay in Bologna by
sending him his favorite salamis. The Cisternino, which came later, between
1837 and 1848, is powerful, too, but without dramatic impact.

Poccianti's facade for the Villa del Poggio Imperiale must have impressed
deeply the young Antonio Niccolini (1772–1850), the stage designer, who
worked there and also at Livorno. He reached Naples in 1808 (two years
after the arrival of the French) and was commissioned one year later to
design a new facade for G.A. Medrano's Teatro S. Carlo; the result was a
tough Florentine (and French) leviathan, at odds with the sloppy Baroque
architecture that the Bourbons had cultivated until then, *pace* the Vanvitellis.
The facade was largely built in 1810. Six years later the old theater burned
down and Niccolini was employed with Antonio de Simone to erect a new
one behind it. For the Bourbons, who returned in 1815, he built extensively:
On the Vomero he put up the Villa Floridiana (1817–19) and the adjoining
Villa Lucia (1818) for Ferdinand I and his morganatic wife, Lucia Partanna;
in the Piazza dei Martiri he refaced and decorated the Palazzo Partanna.
Most of his energy was spent on designs for the reordering of the royal palace
itself, but he saw none of this built.

Outside Naples his chief works were in Bari: the Teatro Piccini (now part
of the Villa Comunale) and the church of S. Ferdinando, both projects
supervised by his son Fausto.

The second altogether surprising and successful building begun at Naples
under the French was the church of S. Francesco di Paola, enclosing the
Piazza Plebiscito with curved colonnades. The Foro Murat, as it was first
called, was established by a decree of February 1808; demolition was begun
at once but Leopoldo Laperuta's design was chosen only later in the year.
The colonnades were built and the church started with the assistance of
Antonio de Simone, but when the Bourbons returned they decided that it
should become a dynastic chapel, dominating the square, now named the
Foro Ferdinando. A competition for a new church was held. Eventually, after
much intrigue and trickery, Pietro Bianchi (1787-1849), a pupil of Luigi
Cagnola from the Ticino area, was commissioned to build it in 1817. It was

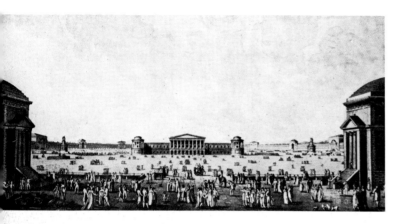

completed by 1831, the most carefully detailed and richly finished of all new churches in Italy.

Related to, but distinct from, the activity in Naples was that in Sicily, in Palermo, where the break from the late Baroque was occasioned by the Frenchman Léon Dufourny. He spent six years there, and between 1789 and 1792 built the Villa Giulia, a botanical institute, stiff and four-square, clearly inspired by the Doric temples of the island. This was soon extended by two pavilions in an even more consciously primitive style by Giuseppe Venanzio Marvuglia (1729–1814). He had studied under Vanvitelli in Roma and had pursued an active if undistinguished career in Palermo until, inspired by Dufourny, he began La Favorita, or Palazzina Cinese, in 1799, a curious but captivating confection, part classical, part Chinese. In the garden he built the Fontana dell'Ercole, a monstrous Doric column supporting a tiny statue of Hercules. His other late work, the Villa Belmonte, of 1801, high on the slopes of Monte Pellegrino, was less engaging and far more restrained. In 1805 he was elected a corresponding member of the Institut National des Sciences et des Arts (later the Académie des Beaux-Arts) in Paris.

Architectural activity, though fervid during the Napoleonic interlude, was, on the whole, sporadic. Only in Lombardy was it sustained and consistent over a long period. The *locus classicus* for reform, however, was not in Milan but in Parma, where an academy was established in 1752, to which, on the Comte de Caylus's suggestion, Soufflot's pupil Ennemond-Alexandre Petitot was invited in the following year. He introduced and cultivated the French tradition both in his teaching and by his example. As court architect he built the new facade of S. Pietro (1761) and the Palazzo di Riserva (1764), both painted yellow; he drew up plans for La Pilotta (1766), an extended palace that was not to be built but that served nonetheless as a point of reference for his pupils; and he altered and enlarged the Palazzo Ducale (1767 onward), known also as the Palazzo del Giardino. Neraby, in Colorno, he built La Veneria (1753–55) and S. Liborio (1775–91), both of which were thought to be very French: La Veneria on account of its round-headed windows, the church because of the freestanding columns inside, which were more in evidence in the initial scheme than in the one executed. Petitot's style was scarcely advanced, despite the evidence of his student projects. However, he was able to handle the elements of A.-J. Gabriel's style whith sufficient competence and confidence, and his academy became famous. When Catherine the Great decided to set up one of her own, she wrote to Petitot for advice. His pupils were legion: Agostino Gerli, Simone Cantoni, Carlo Felice Soave, Giocondo Albertolli, Carlo Antonio Aspari, and Faustino Rodi (1751–1835) among them. Gerli, who worked also in Paris, perhaps with Honoré Guibert, is often thought to have marked the beginnings of late eighteenth-century classicism in Lombardy with his decorations for the main salons of the Villa Longhi at Vialba, begun in 1769. But there was more to the new style than decoration.

Power in Milan was long the Austrian prerogative, but after 1796 it passed several times into the hands of the French, causing upheavals and changes in personnel. Both administrations, however, were efficient and ambitious, and their aims were not dissimilar. The pattern of architectural development, if not the personalities involved, continued throughout almost uninterrupted.

When Caylus visited Milan in the first half of the century he found it a miserable city, but with the building of canals in the Lombardy plain and the consequent spectacular expansion of agriculture, landowners became richer and thought to build both town and country houses. The Austrians, moreover, were able to collect taxes with greater success than ever before. Milan was slowly rebuilt. Roads were constructed and new areas opened up on the sites of the monastic establishments that had been suppressed—twenty-six were closed down in 1782 alone. In 1790 the old gates were torn down and the city limits increased. The building of houses continued apace. Under Napoleon's administration even larger planning proposals were instigated and much was built. The nature of the city was not, however, to be greatly changed until the middle of the nineteenth century, when silk and cotton mills were opened up and industrialization began. This is part of a later history.

Under the Austrians architecture in Milan was dominated by Giuseppe Piermarini (1734–1808), who had worked for twelve years in Rome and Caserta with Vanvitelli and was brought by him to Milan in 1769, when he was invited to rebuild the Palazzo Ducale. Soon after, Piermarini took the project over and was made *Architetto di Stato,* a position he held until he fled from the French in 1796. For twenty-five years he controlled all building; nothing was erected of which he did not approve. He also ensured a continuance of his tastes by presiding over the Brera Academy, founded in 1776. His first independent work was the Accademia Virgiliana in Mantua, designed in 1770, built between 1773 and 1775. This is uninspiring, with an uneasy relationship between plan and elevation indicative of Piermarini's weakness as an architect. Not that this seems to have affected his career. He began in Milan with the vast Palazzo Belgioioso (1772–81) on the piazza of the same name, with a facade that is heavily articulated, though each element, even the individual rustications, retains a curious isolation. Other houses followed, the best of which are the Palazzo Greppi (1772–78); the Palazzo Moriggia (c. 1775), in the Via Borgonuovo; and the Casnedi House (c. 1776), with facades made up, as it were, of thin layers of rectangular panels. They are, for the rest, unadorned: "Ces indignes façades à la Piermarini," Stendhal wrote in his guide to Rome, Naples, and Florence. But the major work of this period was the Palazzo Ducale, which he took up in 1773 and continued until 1778. Here he introduced for the first time the most famous of the seven Albertollis, Giocondo (1742–1839), who had taught design at Parma for ten years, before moving in 1772 to Rome and then to Naples to work with Vanvitelli. By 1774 he was in

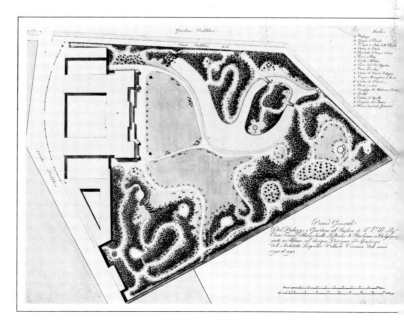

Neufforge. His only important independent building was the Villa Melzi (1805–15), at Bellagio, overlooking Lake Como. The facade, as in Piermarini's houses, is curiously flat.

Outside Milan, at Monza, Piermarini built the Villa Ducale (1776–80), once again decorated by Albertolli, though the chapel, still intact, was all to Piermarini's design. At Cassano d'Adda he erected a smaller variant in the extension to the Villa Borromeo (1780–85). Both these buildings are made up of cubic masses, the surfaces smooth and flattened, altogether without strength, as indeed was his last major work in Milan, the Teatro alla Scala (1776–78). The detail here is too lightweight. The interior has been many times altered. Yet within a year of laying the foundation stone Piermarini was busy on another theater in Milan, the Canobbiana (for those members of the aristocracy who had failed to get a box at La Scala), and was soon at work on others at Novara (1777), Monza (c. 1778), Mantua (1782–83), Crema (1783–85) and Matelica (designed 1803; built 1805–12). Those for whom he did not build imitated him: at Trieste, as we have seen; at Piacenza; and even as far afield as Lisbon, where J. Costa y Silva built the new opera house in 1792. Selva, who had been replaced as architect to the theater at Trieste by Piermarini's pupil Pertsch, disliked La Scala; it was, he noted, far too French. But there is really nothing particularly French about Piermarini's work. His contemporary Simone Cantoni (1739–1818), who had also worked for Vanvitelli but had trained between 1767 and 1768 in Parma and then with Tagliafichi in Genoa, was more French-inspired. Piermarini saw to it that he received no official commissions, but he built a great number of town and country houses and one public building, the Palazzo Ducale (1778–83) in Genoa. Milizia inspected the salon there and, even before its completion, conferred his approval. But the two works that reveal Cantoni at his most Gallic are the Palazzo Serbelloni (designed 1775; much revised and built 1779–94), 16 Corso Venezia, Milan, where Napoleon was received in 1796—though the grand salon was not complete until 1814—and the Palazzo Pertusati (1789–91), on the canal in Milan, now destroyed. The likes of these had not been seen in Italy. The first building has two attenuated Ionic columns set *in antis* within a central feature, topped by a steep pediment, screening a continuous bas-relief panel, a combination of motifs first used by Bélanger. The second was even more closely modeled on a Parisian *hôtel,* of the type of the Hôtel d'Argenson. But Cantoni was a wayward architect. For the Serbellonis he also built SS. Protasio e Gervasio at Gorgonzola (where in 1775 he had already designed the cemetery), a bold but broken composition consisting of a central portico linked by low arcades to two pavilions with great arched openings breaking into the pediments above. Behind the facade other features were piled up, topped by a lantern. The church, which shows Cantoni at his most idiosyncratic, was begun in 1802 and finished in 1842, when the campanile was completed by Giacomo Moraglia. Between these works came a long series of villas, starting with the Villa Olmo at Borgovico (1782–94), and

Florence, cooperating with Paoletti on the Sala della Niobe in the Uffizi, and also at the Villa del Poggio Imperiale, to which he later returned. Late in 1774 Piermarini invited Albertolli to Milan, where he began on the interiors of the Palazzo Ducale—"il primo esempio," he said, "di buon gusto"—now sadly charred. He soon took over all the decorative work in Piermarini's buildings and began teaching also at the Brera Academy. He showed his students how to isolate forms and motifs and then assemble them in geometrical patterns. His pupils were numerous; it has even been suggested that Percier and Fontaine are to be numbered among them. Selva certainly was. Albertolli's publications, the *Ornamenti diversi inventati* (1782), *Alcune decorazioni di nobili sale ed altri ornamenti* (1787), and *Miscellanea per i giovani studiosi del disegno* (1796), made his style even more readily available. This was of the heavy sort, not unlike that of Jean-Louis Prieur and of

including the Villa Giovio at Brescia (1790–95) and the Villa Gallarati-Scotti at Oreno (1790–93). Together they present an extraordinary medley of styles, some traditional, some more advanced, but having in common only Cantoni's consistent fondness for *atlantes* supported on attenuated pedestals in the attic story.

Piermarini's pupils Leopoldo Pollack (1751–1806) and Luigi Canonica (1764–1844) set the tone of a revised architecture more effectively. Pollack was trained in Vienna with his father, a builder, as was his younger brother Michael Johann, who was to become the most active architect in Budapest. In 1775 Pollack moved to Milan, where Piermarini at once set him to work on the Palazzo Ducale. Canonica, born in the Ticino, was trained by Piermarini at the Brera Academy and inherited thus his administrative skills. When the French arrived in 1796 and Piermarini fled to his native Foligno, Canonica assumed the title of *Architetto di Stato,* for which he was not forgiven: "Capace," Piermarini said of him, "della più nera ingratitudine." Canonica was trusted by the French, though, who invited him to Paris in 1805, and also by the Austrians, for he retained his position until 1807, when it was thought more democratic to set up a commission of five (the Commissione d'Ornato) to control building activity in Milan. Canonica was judicious and competent always. He laid out much of Milan and erected many public and administrative buildings, in particular, the enlargement of the Collegio Elvetico for the senate. Tact was one of his great qualities. This is evident in his own works, which merge into the street pattern: the Palazzo Brentani-Greppi (1829–31), in the Via Manzoni, for example, with its recessed roundels above the windows of the *piano nobile;* on the same street, the Palazzo Anguissola-Traversi (1829–30), with fluted Corinthian pilasters and a rich frieze. Behind, in the Via Morone, is the Anguissola House (1775–78), by Carlo Felice Soave (1740–1803), another Ticinese taught at Parma; its detailing is very much more lively and well thought out, especially on the garden front and in the interiors. Together, these buildings reveal the extraordinary homogeneity of the style developed in Milan at this period. Canonica designed only one building that stands out—and it can hardly have done otherwise—the vast Arena in the park, laid out between 1805 and 1807 and completed in 1824, with a triumphal gateway of 1813. This is very simple, but of a size and scale that lend it grandeur. The inspiration was not Canonica's alone but derives in part from the perfervid activity in Milan of both Giuseppe Pistocchi (1744–1841), who came from Faenza, and Giovanni Antonio Antolini (1753–1841), who came also from Faenza after a long stay in Rome, in 1800. In Milan they indulged themselves in a series of public-spirited projects for the area around the Castello Sforzesco, which, in effect, meant mammoth projects, of which Canonica's Arena was the only built result.

Pollack was a less dutiful follower of Piermarini; he had a style of his own. This was evident from the first, when he took over from Piermarini the building of the University of Pavia: In 1785 came the anatomy theater (Aula

Scarpa); in 1786 he began the third court; and by 1787 the physics theater (Aula Volta) was complete, all three in a fashionable French manner. The main stair, not greatly different, was built much later, in 1828, by Giuseppe Marchese. Petitot approved what he saw there: "Bon, bon," was his laconic comment. But Pollack's reputation was made, rather, by the Villa Belgioioso (later Reale), of 1790–96, in Milan. This hints, once again, at French sources, but has, in addition, that tight-packed quality of Piermarini's facades at the Palazzo Belgioioso. The rich interiors provide an odd setting today for the Galleria d'Arte Moderna. The garden, to which Selva and Carlo Amati also contributed, is one of the earliest in the city in a full-fledged Picturesque style, preceding by almost a decade the publication in 1801 of Ercole Silva's pioneering study *Dell'arte dei giardini inglesi,* though not, of course, antedating Silva's own garden at the Villa Ghirlanda Silva in

545. Rodolfo Vantini, Porta Venezia,
Milan, 1827–33

546. Luigi Cagnola, S. Lorenzo
(known as La Rotonda), Ghisalba,
1822–33

547. Luigi Cagnola, Villa Cagnola
(or La Rotonda), Inverigo, c. 1813–33

Cinisello Balsamo. Pollack's most distinguished works followed soon after, the Villa Casati at Muggiò and the Villa Villani Rocca-Saporini, known as La Rotonda, at Borgovico, in both of which the central oval salon plays a dominant part, though in neither instance is it an effective part of the planning arrangements. Pollack, like Piermarini and Canonica, was an indifferent planner. And, again like Canonica, his work in seen to best advantage in the context of contemporary architecture. This may still be done at Borgovico, on the western side of Lake Como, starting with the Villa Carminati (Resta Pallavicino), by Soave, arriving halfway along at La Rotonda, and ending at Cantoni's Villa Olmo and, down a side street, Soave's Villa Salazar. This architectural panorama is wonderfully varied, yet unified.

Only one architect of note succeeded these men, Luigi Cagnola (1762-1833). He represents the climax in the development from Piermarini, a development from a desiccated planar geometry applied to facades to a robust and very solid geometry of form. Cagnola had intended to be a diplomat and began his career in 1795 in Vienna. There he first dabbled actively in architecture, designing a gateway. His initial work in Italy was the Villa Zurla (Vimercati-Sanseverino) at Vaiano Cremasco, almost complete in 1802, when it was damaged by earth tremors. This low, colonnaded building was the outcome of a few years of study at the Academy in Venice and also of a particularly close inspection of the works of Palladio—not that Cagnola's borrowings were ever to be much in evidence. He was a rabid nationalist, which he thought the correct attitude for one of aristocratic descent at that time of unrest, and he turned thus to Italian sources for inspiration: to Palladio, to the Florentine Renaissance, and to ancient Rome. These sources conditioned even his earliest works. In Milan he built the Porta Ticinese (or Marengo), of 1801-14, a simple pedimented portico, and the Arco del Sempione (or della Pace), of 1806–38. Other gates built there in those years were the Porta Nuova (1810–13) by Giuseppe Zanoia (1752–1817);the Porta Comasina (now Porta Garibaldi), of 1826, by Giacomo Moraglia (1791–1860); and, best of all, the Porta Venezia (1827–33) by Rodolfo Vantini (1791–1856). Of these, Cagnola's Arco del Sempione was the one most deliberately based on ancient Roman precedents and executed with the richest of materials and sculptural details. The finest panels were carved by Pompeo Marchesi, Cagnola was to prepare a design for Malmaison after the dismissal of Percier and Fontaine, but his next executed work was his own house. Begun a year or two before 1816, when he married his cousin Francesa del Marchesi d'Adda, it was continued for seventeen years after that date. This was his masterpiece. It is a great inflated piece of architecture set high on a hill overlooking Inverigo, all columns and pedimented porticos approached up giant stairways on one side, all rustications pierced with round-headed openings on the others. In the center is a flattened dome covering a circular hall. A small portico halfway up the hill has giant *atlantes* by Pompeo Marchesi. Formal geometry is the

311

determining factor throughout. The internal planning and spatial organization are altogether inept. But having found his style, Cagnola stuck to it: at the Villa Cagnola at Verdello (c. 1820), which has surprisingly pretty floral frescoes in the rooms and romantic ruins in the garden; and the colonnaded church of Concorezzo (1818–58) and that mammoth Pantheon-like one at Ghisalba (1822–33). For neither of these churches did he design the campanile, though he was responsible for the very stylish one at Urgnano (1824–29), near Ghisalba, and another at Chiari (1832), further to the southeast. He built very little in the last years of his life, but he was long held in awe, both by his students and by architects throughout Italy and even abroad. He designed a mausoleum for Metternich and an imperial palace for Vienna, neither of which was built. He was, in fact, a very limited architect, but he appeared to provide a focus in Italy for a style that was based on national precedents demonstrably large in scale, and strong. His appeal to all those architects who prepared vast designs in 1813 for the Monumento alla Riconoscenza al Moncenisio—Selva, Cantoni, and Pistocchi among them—must have been hard to resist. His ability is at once apparent when his work is compared with that of such a follower as Carlo Amati (1776–1852), architect of S. Carlo al Corso in Milan, built, despite well-founded alarms as to its structural stability, between 1839 and 1847. This overscaled church brings to a close the classical movement in Milan, if not in Italy. The rest is gutless niceties. The next phase, beyond the scope of this book, is represented by the Galleria Vittorio Emmanuele II, built by English entrepreneurs with English capital, between 1865 and 1877, to the designs of Giuseppe Mengoni (1829–1877). This is an aspect of the late nineteenth-century process of industrialization and large-scale replanning in Italy, the most disastrous result of which was the destruction of the heart of Florence in 1888.

In all this history there has not been much evidence offered of intellectual endeavor. Much of what there was came during the eighteenth century from France. Milizia's debt has already been mentioned; other authors could be adduced: Paolo Frisi, whose *Saggio sopra l'architettura gotica* was published in Livorno in 1766, or Ermenegildo Pini, author of *Dell'Architettura. Dialoghi,* of 1770. But these are of no great moment. They offered compilations of French thought.

During the nineteenth century the intrusion of new ideas was owing to the activities of the Gothic Revivalists—as it was throughout most of Europe. The Gothic Revival came late to Italy; it began in the early nineteenth century as a foreign import, largely from England, and largely connected with garden decoration. The first structure of any significance was La Margheria at Racconigi, near Turin, of 1834–39, designed by Pelagio Palagi (1775–1860). On the other side of Italy, in Padua, Giuseppe Jappelli had completed his Gothic wing at the Caffè Pedrocchi by 1842. But these were essentially lighthearted, frivolous structures. Gradually, with the growth of Italian nationalism, an interest was stimulated in Italy's own Gothic past;

551. *Camillo Boito, Palazzo delle Debite Padua, 1872–74*

552. *Camillo Boito, Museo Civico, Padua, 1879*

553. *Pelagio Palagi, La Margheria, Racconigi, 1834–39*

554. Hans Christian Hansen and Theophilos Eduard Hansen, National Library, University, and Academy, Athens, 1839–91

555. Aerial view of Athens in 1932, showing the town as laid out in 1836 by Friedrich von Gärtner, with the principal neoclassical buildings: top right, the Royal Palace; grouped together on the left, The National Library, University and arcade

a serious revival was planned. The most influential exponents were Pietro Estense Selvatico (1803–1880) and Camillo Boito (1836–1914). Selvatico, from the Veneto, was no great revolutionary. He adopted ideas from Pugin, Ruskin, and Viollet-le-Duc, but added a few of his own. He did not build much of interest. However, he trained Boito. Boito, though born in Rome, was taught at the Brera Academy in Milan under Friedrich von Schmidt (1825–1891), who was there from 1857 to 1859 but resigned when Milan was finally lost to the Austrians. He devoted much of his later life to the completion of the cathedral at Cologne. It was from neither Selvatico nor Schmidt, however, that Boito borrowed his ideas; these came from the writings of Viollet-le-Duc, whom he may possibly have met when they acted as judges together at the competition for the facade of Florence cathedral. Boito taught in succession to Schmidt at the Brera Academy for no less than forty-eight years. He was thus of some influence in establishing a new and invigorated doctrine on the lines suggested by Viollet-le-Duc. Among his pupils were Giuseppe Brentano, Luca Beltrami, Gaetano Moretti, and Giuseppe Sommaruga. His own buildings, in a stripped, flattened, and very Italianate medieval style, are of more distinction than any others of this sort in Italy—though they are not in the least engaging. At Gallarate, north of Milan, are two of his early works, a cemetery built in 1865, when he was twenty-nine, and a hospital six years later. These are comparatively restrained, but Boito's Gothic was already becoming more flamboyant and Venetian. At Padua, between 1872 and 1874, he built the Palazzo delle Debite and, five years later, the local museum. But the climax to his career was in Milan, the Casa Verdi, of 1899–1913, on the Piazza Buonarroti, complete with Verdi's colorful tomb chamber. Verdi's librettist, the composer Arrigo Boito, was Camillo's brother.

There are a number of buildings of this sort in Italy, though few were so carefully detailed; for the most part they are funerary chapels. The real energies of the Gothic Revivalists went rather into the completion or rebuilding of the facades of medieval churches. Throughout Italy there were competitions, revisions, disputes, and finally long-drawn-out building programs to finish off the churches of the Middle Ages. There was also a handful of staggering Gothic houses built late in the century: Ernesto Pirovano's Villa Crespi at Capriate d'Adda, of 1890, and Gino Coppedè's Castello Mackenzie at Genoa, of a few years later; and there are many more, even in Sardinia. It was not these stylish extravaganzas, however, that were to be influential in the future but rather the writings and teachings of Boito. He encouraged architects to use a wide variety of materials chosen not for their visual interest alone but also for their appropriateness to the particular role they were to perform. Brick was very popular; sometimes it was plastered, though this was not considered to be "honest." Stone was chosen to trim window surrounds to give added stength to the openings. Only colored plaques and tiles were allowed a purely decorative role. Each element was to be made distinct and expressive. Though the buildings might

559. Benjamin Latrobe, Supreme
Court Chamber, Capitol, Washington,
D.C., 1815–17

be complete, the thinking behind them was direct and comparatively simple—simplistic, one might say. But Boito did provide the basis for the acceptance in Italy of Arts-and-Crafts ideas and, ultimately, of the Stile Florale—and thus of Futurism.

GREECE

Athens had shrunk to a settlement of less than ten thousand people by the end of the third decade of the nineteenth century. The revival of architecture, classical architecture in particular, was to start late; indeed, the movement was consolidated there only when it was already out of fashion in the rest of Europe. The style, paradoxical as it may seem, was a foreign import. It arrived in 1833 with the new monarch, Otto von Wittelsbach of Bavaria, likewise an import. The first plan for the renewed capital of Athens was drawn up by Stamatios Kleanthes—who had been trained by Schinkel in Berlin—together with Édouard Schaubert. But this plan was not accepted, nor was that sent to Greece to straighten things out by Otto's father, Ludwig I of Bavaria. Von Klenze proposed a vast palace in the Kerameikos district, not far from the Temple of Hephaestus. In the same year Schinkel, spurred by knowledge of this grand enterprise, proposed a royal palace on the Acropolis itself. It was a marvelous, Picturesque cluster of classic forms, mingled with the ancient temples. The interiors were to be richly colored. But Schinkel did not visit Greece and could not press his claims. The new town plan and the royal palace were finally undertaken in 1836 to the designs of a less ambitious and more practical man, Friedrich von Gärtner. These German architects, though they built little (and, indeed, von Klenze's only building in Athens, the Roman Catholic church of Aghios Dionysios, built between 1858 and 1887, was in Renaissance style), set the tone and the pattern for all major building to follow. Neoclassicism was adopted as the official style. This group of architects was succeeded, like the Bavarian dynasty, by Danes: Hans Christian Hansen (1803–1883) and his brother Theophilos Eduard Hansen (1831–1891). These men established neoclassicism in Greece, and set up an array of the most rigid, but also elegant and pristine, monuments to the style to be seen anywhere in the world today. Three of these are ranged together, the University (H. C. Hansen, 1839–49), the Academy (T. E. Hansen, 1859–87), and the National Library (T. E. Hansen, 1859, 1885, 1888–91). But they built a great deal more besides, and so did their pupil Ernst Ziller (1837–1923), who arrived in Athens in 1861, and their rivals and emulators, the Frenchmen François-Louis-Florimond Boulanger (1807–1875) and E. Troumpe and the Greek architects Panayotis Kalkos (1800–1870), Stamatios Kleanthes (1802–1862), and Lysandros Kaftanzoglu (1812–1885). Kaftanzoglu was trained in both Paris and Rome. These men were naturally active mainly in Athens, creating such extravaganzas as the circular court of the Zappeion (F. L.-F. Boulanger began this in 1874, but it was taken over by T. E. Hansen) and

560. Benjamin Latrobe, Roman
Catholic cathedral, Baltimore,
Maryland, 1804–18

Ilion Melathron, the house of no less a personality than Heinrich Schliemann (now the Supreme Court) by Ziller, of 1890. But major neoclassical buildings were put up also in Piraeus and scattered as far afield as Patras and the remoter islands. Their crisp, rigid forms and details were copied throughout Greece, transforming even the humblest of houses into models of classical rectitude. As late as 1920 the style survived, virtually unaltered and altogether intact. Now many of the lesser buildings are being destroyed. Others have been drastically altered, as was the Dimetrion House (1842–43) on Syntagma Square, by T. E. Hanse, which became the Hotel Grande Bretagne and survived as such until 1958, when it was demolished and rebuilt, only the ironwork being incorporated into the new hotel. Certainly this extraordinary postscript to the neoclassical movement has been much underestimated, by foreigners no less than by the Greeks themselves.

THE UNITED STATES OF AMERICA

The enthusiast for full-scale Greek Revival architecture will find no country so satisfying as North America. Here in the first half of the nineteenth century flowered prolifically, if sometimes coarsely, the seeds planted by James Stuart in his Doric temple at Hagley in 1758. Thomas Jefferson (1743–1826) and Benjamin Henry Latrobe (1764–1820) were the most interesting architects in late eighteenth-century America. Though many others were anxious to emulate their example during the Greek Revival of the nineteenth century, none possessed quite the quality of Latrobe. For another classical architect of comparable imagination, America had to wait for the emergence, in the 1870s, of Charles Follen McKim (1847–1909), trained in Paris.

The architect Charles Bulfinch (1763–1844) reflects the uncertain impact on America of the classicism of Chambers and Adam. His domed and colonnaded Massachusetts State House, Boston (1795–98), is a gross and inflated version of the work of Perrault, Chambers, and Adam, but it set the pattern for much official building in the nineteenth century. In the meantime, the more subtle Jefferson was working on the ever-changing designs for his own house, Monticello, at Charlottesville, Virginia. It was conceived in 1771 on a plan taken from Robert Morris's *Select Architecture* (1755) and adapted to a facade from Palladio's *Quattro libri*. The construction of this carefully thought-out, but not, by English standards, especially remarkable, building was carried out between 1771 and 1782. Work was resumed in 1793, and by 1809 the building had been completely transformed into a much more interesting and complex, though basically one-storied, house. With its varied and original planning, its Picturesque parkland setting, and its superb views of mountain scenery, Monticello realized Jefferson's dream of re-creating the Roman villas described by Pliny, admired by Lord Burlington and the English Palladians, and recorded

in Robert Castell's *Villas of the Ancients Illustrated* (1728).

In 1785-89 Jefferson designed the Virginia State Capitol, at Richmond, with a vast and rather vapid Ionic portico supposedly inspired by the Corinthian-columned Maison Carrée at Nîmes, which he had seen and admired a year or so earlier. In 1790 the site of the new federal city of Washington was selected and plans were drawn up by the Frenchman Pierre-Charles L'Enfant (1754–1825). On Jefferson's suggestion, competitions were held in 1792 for the president's house and the Capitol. The Irishman James Hoban (c. 1762-1831) won the competition for the former with an old-fashioned design copied from James Gibb's *Book of Architecture* (1728). The competition for the Capitol was inconclusive, and the rather pedestrian pile executed between 1792 and 1828 was the outcome of an uneasy alliance between the Frenchman Stephen Hallet and three English-born architects, Dr. William Thornton (1758–1828), George Hadfield (c. 1763–1826), and Benjamin Latrobe. The side wings and commanding dome with its cast-iron frame were added in 1851–65 by Thomas U. Walter (1804–1887).

It is a relief to turn from the Capitol to the novelty and charm of Jefferson's University of Virginia, at Charlottesville. The idea of an "academical village" consisting of small, linked buildings surrounded by grass and trees had been growing in Jefferson's mind between 1804 and 1810, but it was not until 1817 that the final plans were drawn up and the foundation stone laid. The captivating arrangement, with its two groups of five Palladian pavilions linked by colonnades and facing each other across a great lawn, seems to have been inspired (ironically, given the libertarian views of Jefferson) by the most remarkable monument of French absolutism, Louis XIV's Château de Marly, which Jefferson had visited with Maria Cosway when in Paris. In fact, Jefferson was anticipated by Soane, whose unexecuted designs of 1809 for the Royal Academical Institution in Belfast, Ireland, had also been inspired by the pavilion layout of Marly. With its low, detached buildings grouped around a huge lawn, William Wilkin's Downing College, Cambridge, England (designed 1804-6; executed 1807–20), was also a precedent for the University of Virginia. Each of Jefferson's ten pavilions, containing lecture rooms and living accommodations for ten professors, was differently designed than the others. Most contained references to such ancient Roman structures as the Ionic order of the Temple of Fortuna Virilis (Pavilion II) and the Doric order of the Baths of Diocletian (Pavilion I). Pavilion IX, with its central exedra, may have been inspired by Ledoux's Hôtel de Guimard (1770) or by Soane's project for Shotesham Park, Norfolk (1785). On Benjamin Latrobe's recommendation, Jefferson placed at the head of the whole composition a great Pantheon or Rotunda (executed 1823–27) containing a suite of three oval rooms and a superb circular library.

Latrobe arrived in Virginia in 1796, having been trained in England by the original if eccentric architect Samuel Pepys Cockerell. Latrobe's first

563. William Strickland, Second
Bank of the United States (later
Custom House), Philadelphia, plan,
1818
564. Thomas U. Walter, Andalusia,
near Philadelphia, 1835–36

565. Thomas U. Walter, Girard
College, Philadelphia, main building,
1833–47
566. Henry Walter, Ohio State
Capitol, Columbus, designed 1838,
built 1848 onward

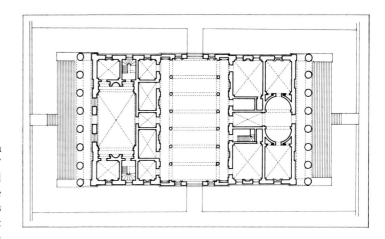

important work in America was his State Penitentiary at Richmond, Virginia
(1797–98), whose powerful arched entrance gate is in Soane's "primitivist"
style. Latrobe was soon attracted northward to Philadelphia, the national
capital from 1790 to 1800, and the largest city in America. In 1798 he
received the commission for the Bank of Pennsylvania there. Latrobe's
austere templar building, a simple rectangle with a Greek Ionic portico at
each end, culminated in a central, circular domed space articulated with a
logic and purity evidently derived from the doctrines of Laugier; the top-lit
dome recalled Soane's Stock Office of 1792 at the Bank of England. The
demolition of Latrobe's building in the 1860s was a major loss for America.
His next endeavor was the Philadelphia Waterworks (1798–1801; demolished 1827); here a rotunda rose from a rectangular base articulated with
a radical Greek Doric order, and the whole seems to have echoed Ledoux's
Rotonde de la Villette.

In 1803 Latrobe became Surveyor of the Public Buildings of the United
States, a post that called for completing Thornton's Capitol Building in
Washington, D. C. Latrobe's first House of Representatives was an oval
colonnaded space with capitals derived from the Choragic Monument of
Lysicrates in Athens. His Soane-like vestibule, with American maize-leaf
capitals, built in the east basement in 1809, was rebuilt by him after the fire
of 1814. Like Soane at the Bank of England and the Law Courts, Latrobe
responded imaginatively to the task of working in cramped existing
structures. After the fire he also rebuilt the Senate and House of
Representatives on an improved plan incorporating a small rotunda with
tobacco-leaf capitals of his own invention. Based on plans Latrobe had made
as early as 1806–7, his Supreme Court Chamber, of 1815–17, beneath the
Senate Chamber, is one of the most imaginative American classical spaces.
Its trio of arches supported on stunted Greek Doric sandstone columns and
its floating half-dome, strangely lobed, owe much to Ledoux and Soane.

Latrobe's best-known building is the Roman Catholic cathedral in
Baltimore. With its low segmental dome and emphatically segmental arches,
the interior recalls Soane's Bank of England, though the whole is unlike
any church Soane ever designed. A masterpiece of sobriety and refinement,
the building was designed in 1804–8 and executed in 1809–18; the
onion-shaped tops to the belfry towers were added in 1832—but not to
Latrobe's designs; his Ionic portico was not completed until 1863, and in
1890 the choir was tactfully lengthened.

Latrobe's pupils Robert Mills (1781–1855) and William Strickland
(1788–1854) dominated the architectural scene until the 1840s. Mills
worked in Latrobe's office from 1803 to 1808; his early works were centrally
planned churches in Philadelphia and in Richmond, Virginia. In his
octagonal Monumental Church in Richmond (1812), Mills interpreted the
Greek Revival with a characteristically aggressive but thoughtful originality
that established him as the heir of such architects as Bonomi and Gentz. In
a similar vein was his Country Records Office of 1822 at Charleston, South

Carolina, designed in an unfluted Doric style and known, because of the manner of its construction, as the "Fireproof Building." His reputation was made with the Washington Monument at Baltimore (1814–29), a giant unfluted Doric column. After its completion, Mills moved to the city of Washington. He quickly set his mark on the capital with such large public buildings as the Treasury, the Patent Office, and the Washington Monument—all designed in 1836—and the Post Office of 1839. Bacause of their giant porticos and colonnades and, in the case of the Washington Monument, huge height, they created a more powerful and effective national image than the comparable though slightly earlier buildings in England by Wilkins and Smirke.

William Strickland rose to prominence with his remarkable Second Bank of the United States (later Custom House; 1818–24) in Philadelphia, the first American public building to be based on the Parthenon. His United States Mint (1829–33), in Washington, is an unremarkable classical block, but in 1832–34 came his most imaginative contribution to the Greek Revival, the Philadelphia Merchants' Exchange. The circular Corinthian colonnade of the Exchange, crowned by a tall lantern based on the Lysicrates Monument, has an impressive drama lacking in his last major work, the Tennessee State Capitol, at Nashville (1845–49), where the Lysicratean lantern is less happily related to the building below.

At least as successful as Strickland were his pupils Thomas U. Walter and Alexander Jackson Davis (1803–1892), who formed a partnership in 1829 with Ithiel Town (1784–1844). Town's templar State Capitol for Connecticut, at Hartford (1827), was a worthy successor to Strickland's Second Bank in Philadelphia and led to commissions for similar capitol buildings. The Parthenon was also the model chosen by Davis and Town for their impressive United States Custom House, New York City (now the Sub-Treasury), of 1833–42, and then by Ammi B. Young (1800–1874) for his domed, colonnaded, granite-built Custom House in Boston, Massachusetts (1837–47). Ithiel Town's Bowers House, Northampton, Massachusetts (1825–26), with its giant Ionic portico, is characteristic of countless temple-like houses of the first half of the nineteenth century; James Coles Bruce's Berry Hill, Virginia (1835–40), in the Greek Doric style, stands even closer to the paradigm: Wilkins's Grange Park of 1809. Yet another dramatically archaeological house worthy of comparison with Grange Park is Andalusia, north of Philadelphia, designed in 1835–36 by Thomas U. Walter. His patron was the influential Nicholas Biddle, who, unusual in his generation of Americans, had investigated Greek remains at first hand, in 1806. From Biddle also came the inspiration for Walter's singularly beautiful Girard College in Philadelphia (1833–47), whose centrally placed, Corinthian peripheral temple "contains an ingeniously planned three-story complex of groin-vaulted spaces, entirely of the latest (Millsian) fireproof construction" (W. H. Pierson, *American Buildings and Their Architects,* vol. 1, 1970, p. 437). The central temple is flanked on each side by a pair of templar dormitory buildings, the whole suggesting a highly colored version of the theme Wilkins had essayed at Downing College, Cambridge. For the giant portico of his Hibernian Hall in Charleston, South Carolina (1835), Thomas U. Walter adopted the Greek Ionic of the Erechtheum, but Henry Walter's Ohio State Capitol, Columbus (designed 1838 with the assistance of A. J. Davis; built from 1848 on by William Russell West and Nathan B. Kelly), is conceived on an altogether more heroic scale. Its vast octostyle Doric portico *in antis* builds up to a cylindrical cupola in a truly monumental composition. Uniting the styles of Ledoux and Schinkel, Walter here realized the fantastic unexecuted scheme of 1834 by Thomas Rickman and Edward Hussey for the Fitzwilliam Museum, in Cambridge, England.

This fecund classical tradition, gradually failing in quality if not in quantity, dominated American architecture until the 1860s. The return from Paris to Boston in 1865 of Henry Hobson Richardson (1838–1886) opened a new phase in the history of American architecture. Though he had been trained at the École des Beaux-Arts in Paris (1859–62) and had subsequently worked under Labrouste and Hittorff, Richardson did not import French classicism to America. His early works, including the Grace Episcopal Church, Medford, Massachusetts (1867–69), and the B. H. Crowninshield House, Marlborough Street, Boston (1868–69), owe something to contemporary Gothic Revival buildings in England. But in the 1870s, Richardson developed a rock-faced Romanesque—for example, the Brattle Square (now First Baptist) Church and Trinity Church in Boston, of 1870–72 and 1873–77—which owed more to France, and particularly to J.-A.-E. Vaudremer. Perhaps Richardson's finest works were such private houses of the 1870s and 1880s as the William Watts Sherman House, Newport, Rhode Island (1874–75), and Stoughton House, Cambridge, Massachusetts (1882–83), in a tile-hung Manorial style, with spreading plans recalling the work of Richard Norman Shaw.

Thus, Richardson has no real part in the present chapter. It was Charles Follen McKim, also a student at the École des Beaux-Arts (1867–70), and an assistant of Richardson, who instituted an academic classical revival in America. With his two partners, William Rutherford Mead and Stanford White, he produced a series of superlative classical masterpieces with a Roman rather than a French flavor. Despite the brilliance of their Boston Public Library (1887) and of their extensive work in New York City—the Villard houses (1882), Columbia University (1893), the University Club (1899), the Pierpont Morgan Library (1903), and the Pennsylvania Railroad Station (1904–10)—the determinist bias of recent architectural historians has prevented the firm of McKim, Mead & White from receiving the critical attention it deserves.

ENGLAND: *Walpole to Rickman*

By 1750 the Gothic Revival already had a long history in England. One of the most striking and earliest examples of the style is the library of St. John's College, Cambridge, of 1623–24. Justifying the elaborately Gothic design of its windows, a contemporary wrote to the master of the college: "Some men of judgement liked the best the old fashion of church window, holding it most meet for such a building." This justification of Gothic on grounds of environmental propriety was to be echoed for the next hundred years. Its most striking monuments are Sir Christopher Wren's Tom Tower at Christ Church, Oxford (1681), and Nicholas Hawksmoor's additions to All Souls' College, Oxford (1715–34), and his western towers at Westminster Abbey, London (1735–45). One of the first architects to imply that Gothic might have a romance and a quality in its own right was Sir John Vanbrugh, although he never employed the Gothic arch. However, his narrow, tall battlemented house at Greenwich, begun in 1717, is undoubtedly "emotionally Gothic" (J. Summerson, *Architecture in Britain, 1530–1830,* 5th ed., 1969, p. 237). He also argued keenly for the preservation of the "Holbein" Gate at Whitehall and, as we saw in Chapter 2, for the ruins of old Woodstock Manor in the park at Blenheim. If Vanbrugh provided a new emotional stimulus, William Kent created the new language of form that became known as "Georgian Gothic." Kent's innovatory role is thus of immense stylistic significance, but it is to be noted that the following list of his principal Gothic works contains not one that is anything more than an addition to an existing medieval or Tudor building: Esher Place, Surrey (1729–33); the gateway at Hampton Court, Middlesex (1732); the Courts of Chancery and of King's Bench, Westminster Hall (1739); and the pulpit at York Minster and choir-screen at Gloucester cathedral (both 1741). Kent's lighthearted, medievalizing style was basically an inaccurately Gothic treatment of the classical orders and, as such, proved easy to imitate. Batty Langley (1696–1751) developed Kent's hints and codified their details in his book confidently entitled *Gothic Architecture Improved by Rules and Proportions* (1747), though he evidently had some firsthand knowledge of medieval work.

The fruits of all this, in the later 1740s and 1750s, are particularly associated with the name of the Warwickshire squire and amateur architect Sanderson Miller (1717–1780). In addition to erecting sham castles at Edgehill, Warwickshire (1745–47), Hagley Park, Worcestershire (1747–48), and Wimpole Hall, Cambridgeshire (1750), Miller was one of a number of architects responsible for remodeling Arbury Hall, Warwickshire, from 1750 onward for Sir Roger Newdigate. Arbury was a Tudor house with pre-Reformation monastic origins, so the choice of Gothic could be justified on associational grounds. Its dramatic and beautiful Gothicization, which extended throughout the second half of the eighteenth century, is largely the work of the architect Henry Keene (1726–1776), and, though it contains a number of references to medieval sources, the overall impression is entirely of the eighteenth century. At Lacock Abbey, Wiltshire, Sanderson Miller added a delightful Gothic gateway and great hall in 1754–55 intended to be in keeping with the existing monastic structures. But his most surprising Gothic building is one for which no claims to what we have called "environmental propriety" could possibly justify the choice of style. This is the astonishing Pomfret House built in Arlington Street, London, in 1760 for the widowed Countess of Pomfret. It was as though James Gibbs's Gothic temple at Stowe (1741) had been transferred from a rural to an urban setting.

The choice of Gothic as a style to be admired in its own right, not simply for associational reasons, had been anticipated by Horace Walpole at Strawberry Hill from 1749 to the 1790s. His selection of the Gothic style as a matter of taste is one of the three most important features of the house, the development of which has been so often told it scarcely need be repeated here. The two other points of importance are its asymmetrical growth, in which fortuitous development was emphasized, and the increasing archaeological knowledge that lies behind its stylistic details. With numerous borrowings from an astonishing variety of medieval sources, including tombs at Westminster Abbey and Canterbury, Salisbury, Ely, and Worcester cathedrals, as well as motifs taken from Old St. Paul's, Henry VII's Chapel at Westminster Abbey, and Rouen cathedral, Strawberry Hill was equally the product of collective endeavor as far as a "design team" was concerned. Between the 1750 and 1790s the learned amateurs Richard Bentley, John Chute, Thomas Pitt, and James Essex were assisted by a number of professional architects, including William Robinson, Robert Adam, James Wyatt, and the master mason at Westminster Abbey, Thomas Gayfere. Chute and Gayfere collaborated on the design of the Chapel in the Woods in 1772–74. With a facade based on Bishop Audley's chantry tomb at Salisbury cathedral, it was the most solid and convincing piece of Gothic at Strawberry Hill, for everywhere else the mood was one of rococo gaiety. Indeed, the house that Walpole had bought from the proprietress of a successful London toy shop always retained the aura of a plaything. Walpole's own attitude to it is captured both in a description of the staircase given to a friend in 1753—"[It is] so pretty and so small that I am inclined to wrap it up and send it to you in my letter"—and also in his comment, eight years later, "My buildings are paper, like my writings." Strawberry Hill, though visually so gay, was indeed a kind of paper architecture since many of its details were copied not directly from medieval buildings but from engravings of them in books in Walpole's library, notably Sir William Dugdale's *Warwickshire* (1656) and *St. Paul's* (1658) and John Dart's *Westminster* (1723) and *Canterbury* (1726). Paradoxically, the closest parallel to this Picturesque archaeology is the process by which the park at Shugborough, Staffordshire, was adorned by James Stuart during the 1760s with miniature versions of the Athenian buildings he was publishing with Revett in the *Antiquities of Athens.*

569. *James Wyatt, Fonthill Abbey, Wiltshire, plan, 1796–1807*

570. *James Wyatt, Fonthill Abbey, Wiltshire, view from the southwest, 1796–1807*

571. *James Wyatt, Fonthill Abbey, Wiltshire, view through St. Michael's Gallery and the central octagon to King Edward's Gallery, 1796–1807*

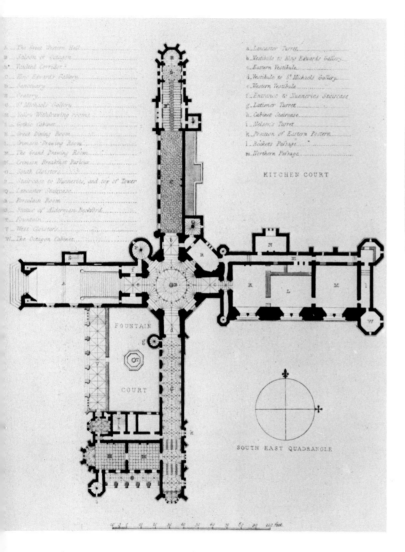

The product of a similar antiquarianism, of which Walpole highly approved, was the house of his friend Thomas Barrett, at Lee Priory, Kent (1783–90). Here James Wyatt, who had possibly been recommended by Walpole to Barrett, devised an extravaganza that was a little more archaeologically correct in some of its details than Strawberry Hill and yet, at the same time, almost more fanciful in its provision of an octagonal tower and spire. There were no medieval or monastic associations at Lee ("Priory" being a spurious addition by Barrett) so the choice of Gothic was purely aesthetic. Indeed, Wyatt prepared both classical and Gothic designs for Barrett to choose between. What particularly attracted Barrett and Walpole was Wyatt's ability to suggest growth and change in a building whose owner intended to create the impression of a small convent adapted for domestic use, presumably after the Reformation. In a letter of 1785 Walpole admired the make-believe that led one to "consider the whole as Gothic modernized in parts, not as what it is—the reverse." Its extreme irregularity of plan and outline also gave great pleasure to the eye nurtured on Picturesque principles. The domed octagonal library that forms the striking centerpiece of the whole composition may owe something to the fourteenth-century lantern over the crossing at Ely cathedral.

Ely, or possibly the plates in J. Bentham's *History and Antiquities of Ely* (1771), is also the source of the staggering central tower of Fonthill Abbey, Wiltshire, which Wyatt built for William Beckford between 1796 and 1807. But from Wyat's imagination alone came the brilliant cruciform plan with its breathtaking vista, more than ninety meters (three hundred feet) long, from the oriel at the end of St. Michael's Gallery, through the central octagon, to the oratory at the north end of King Edward's Gallery. Beckford's original idea, analogous to Barrett's for Lee Priory, was to create

a building resembling a convent, partly ruinous and partly converted to domestic use, which he could use for occasional picnics or supper parties. His obsession with the place grew until in 1805 he finally decided to live in it permanently. The grounds were landscaped and planted in such an appropriately sublime and exotic manner that house and setting eventually became the high-water mark of Picturesque Gothic.

So far, we have seen the Gothic Revival as an aspect of the Picturesque theory that developed from Vanbrugh, through Strawberry Hill and Payne Knight's Downton Castle, to Fonthill Abbey and Nash's brilliant asymmetrical Irish castles Killymoon, near Cookstown (1803), Shanbally, County Tipperary (1812), and Lough Cutra, County Galway (c. 1817)—not forgetting, of course, Nash's own country seat, East Cowes Castle, Isle of Wight (c. 1798; now demolished). We must investigate two other traditions, associated respectively with castle and with church, which owe rather less to the Picturesque. At Clearwell Castle, Gloucestershire (1727), and Inveraray Castle, Argyllshire (begun 1745), Roger Morris (1695– 1749) echoed the formal, symmetrical castles of the Middle Ages, which had already been revived in the Elizabethan and Jacobean periods at Mount Edgecumbe, Cornwall, Lulworth Castle, Dorset, and Ruperra Castle, Glamorganshire. From here it was but a step to James Wyatt's Kew Palace, Surrey (1802–11), and Ashridge Park, Hertfordshire (begun 1808); to Robert Smirke's Lowther Castle, Westmorland (1806); and to Eastnor Castle, Herefordshire (1812), and Taymouth Castle, Perthshire (1806–10), by Archibald and James Elliott (1760–1823; 1770–1810).

Church- far more than castle-building in the Gothic style seems almost to have had a momentum of its own. The numerous Gothic churches erected between the time, say, of the younger Wing's church at King's Norton,

575. *Augustus Welby Northmore*
Pugin, Alton Castle, Staffordshire,
1847–51

576. *William Butterfield, vicarage,*
Coalpit Heath, Gloucestershire, 1844

577. *Augustus Welby Northmore*
Pugin, Scarisbrick Hall, Lancashire,
1837–45

578. William Butterfield, group of cottages, Baldersby, Yorkshire, 1855–57

579. George Edmund Street, church vicarage, and school, Boyne Hill, Maidenhead, Berkshire, 1854

Leicestershire (1760–75), and of Charles Barry's St. Peter, Brighton (1823–28), do not reveal any substantial development in the understanding of medieval construction, although in his St. Luke, Chelsea (1819–25), James Savage introduced for the first time a masonry rather than a plaster vault. At the church of the Holy Trinity, Theale, Berkshire (1820–28), Edward Garbett and John Buckler (1770–1851) provided a strikingly complete and serious recreation of the lancet mode of Salisbury cathedral. Since Perpendicular was the mode usually adopted in eighteenth- and early nineteenth-century churches, Theale represents a significant attempt to enlarge historical understanding of medieval architecture. By basing the design of the tower on the demolished campanile of Salisbury cathedral, Garbett and Buckler delivered a sharp rebuke to eighteenth- century Gothicists, for the destruction carried out at Salisbury was attributed, not altogether fairly, to James Wyatt.

But the new and more serious phase of the Gothic Revival—of which the design of Holy Trinity, Theale, is a harbinger—was ushered in not so much by architects as by antiquarians and publishers in what J. M. Crook has called the "bibliographical revolution" (C. L. Eastlake, *A History of the Gothic Revival,* 1872; rev. ed., 1970, ed. J. M. Crook). Between the 1790s and the 1830s John Carter (1748–1817) and John Britton (1771–1857) produced a series of influential books on medieval architecture, which combined scholarship with topography and, like Stuart's and Revett's *Antiquities of Athens,* provided architects with an authentic new vocabulary. Carter's publications included the books *Views of Ancient Buildings in England* (1786–93), *Ancient Architecture of England* (1795 and 1807), as well as numerous articles in the *Gentleman's Magazine* attacking the ill-treatment and ignorant restoration of medieval buildings. Britton's principal works were *The Architectural Antiquities of Great Britain* (1804–14) and, more important, the superbly illustrated, fourteen-volume *Cathedral Antiquities of Great Britain* (1814–35). Thomas Rickman's *An Attempt to Discriminate the Styles of English Architecture* (1817) provided a vocabulary of identification—"Early English," "Decorated," and "Perpendicular"—that was a reassuring parallel to the familiar "Doric," "Ionic," and "Corinthian" of classical architecture, and that had the similar advantage of being easily memorized and applied. Finally, Augustus Charles Pugin's *Specimens of Gothic Architecture* (1821–23) spelled out the language of Gothic detail in technical drawings for the benefit of craftsmen and draftsmen. The scene was now set for the arrival of the hero, and, at the risk of writing determinist or progressivist history, it cannot be denied that Pugin's celebrated son, Augustus Welby Northmore Pugin, seemed destined in every way to fulfill that very role.

ENGLAND: *Pugin and His Impact*

A. W. N. Pugin (1812–1852) has probably exercised as much influence over English architecture and architectural theory as any other architect of

580. *Augustus Welby Northmore Pugin, St. Giles, Cheadle, Staffordshire, 1839–44*

581. *Augustus Welby Northmore Pugin, St. Giles, Cheadle, Staffordshire, interior 1839–44*

582. *Augustus Welby Northmore Pugin, St. Augustine, Ramsgate, Kent, choir, 1845–50*

any period. In a series of compelling books, by turns amusing, polemical, and scholarly—*Contrasts* (1836), *The True Principles of Pointed or Christian Architecture* (1841), *The Present State of Ecclesiastical Architecture in England* (1843), and *An Apology for the Revival of Christian Architecture in England* (1843)—Pugin made a case for the adoption of Gothic, not as one of a number of styles chosen on grounds of beauty or association but as *the* style, indeed, as "truth." Gothic was the truthful expression of true construction and function, of true religion (i.e., Roman Catholicism), and of the true genius of the English people. Thus, Pugin could claim that what he was defending was "not a style but a principle" (*An Apology,* p. 44). In so doing, he laid the foundations of Victorian architecture and—by implying the special merit of a building that reveals its construction—of modern architecture as well. Whatever our feeling about his conclusions, it cannot be denied that Pugin was one of the few Englishmen who have theorized coherently about architecture; however, to say that he was English is not strictly true. A. C. Pugin was a French emigré, and it is to the intellectual tradition of French theorists from Perrault to Laugier and beyond that his son belonged. Pugin's first book, *Contrasts,* upheld the Gothic cause by an entertaining attack on the Reformation as the begetter of a false religion and a false (i.e., classical) architecture; however, five years later, guessing perhaps that an English Protestant audience might require a wider variety of argument, Pugin justified his passionate adherence to Gothic by echoing the language of eighteenth-century neoclassical rationalism. The equation of architectural beauty with structural honesty was familiar in France and Italy through the writings of such men as Cordemoy, Laugier, and Lodoli, but it had made little impact in England. The rational and academic analysis of Gothic structure as a basis for a modern architecture initiated by Cordemoy was brought to a climax by Pugin's contemporary Viollet-le-Duc. Pugin's contribution to this tradition was less influential than his sociological and ethical interpretation of architecture as the true index of the state of society. This was the vision that fired the Victorian Gothicists Butterfield, Street, Pearson, and Bodley: Christian architects creating a Christian society with Christian buildings, schools, colleges, parsonages, convents, and churches. One of Pugin's principal contributions to the language of form was his insistence that the elevation of a building should be subservient to its plan. Though this principle was derived from his belief in truthfulness, it led, ironically, to a type of self-consciously asymmetrical architecture that closely resembled the products of the Picturesque that Pugin was committed to despise.

In Chapter 2 we emphasized the importance of Salvin's Scotney Castle, Kent (1835–43), in the Picturesque tradition, particularly because of its relation through a landscaped garden to the ruins of the medieval Scotney Castle. Salvin's new building (see illustration 33) was itself equally revolutionary. The asymmetrical separation of part from part on the entrance front, the apparently functional placement of windows and chimneys

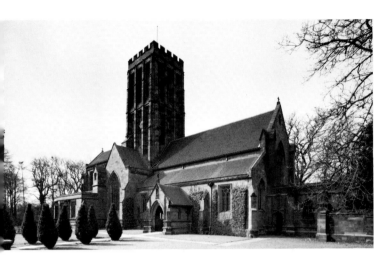

584. George Frederick Bodley, Holy Angels, Hoar Cross, Staffordshire, 1872–1900

585. George Frederick Bodley, Holy Angels, Hoar Cross, Staffordshire, interior, 1872–1900

contrasting eloquently with areas of blank wall, the vigorous diagonality of line—all this could be described as Puginesque, though, paradoxically, the twenty-three-year-old Pugin was not yet capable of work of this quality.

The kind of buildings Pugin was designing in 1835 we can see at his own house, St. Marie's Grange, Wiltshire. Here, though on a much smaller scale, is the same determined asymmetry that characterizes Scotney, and that is supposed to enable us to read the internal disposition of the building. The house was altered and enlarged, probably by Pugin himself, but its original appearance is recorded in a sketch by him of 1835 in which he is careful to show its relation to the distant view of Salisbury cathedral (and here, of course, is another parallel with Scotney). The cramped, narrow proportions of St. Marie's Grange, the aspiring verticality of its all roofs and turrets, its steeply sloping site and drawbridge are all unexpected reminders of another pioneering house built by an architect for his own occupancy more than a century earlier, Vanbrugh Castle, Greenwich.

Though Salvin's later career was prolific and in many ways distinguished, he did not quite fulfill the particular promise of Scotney. It was Pugin who developed the language of domestic Gothic in a paradoxical combination of functional and Picturesque that was used to such brilliant effect by Richard Norman Shaw. Between St. Marie's Grange and Shaw's superb Adcote, Shropshire (designed 1875), lie Pugin's Scarisbrick Hall, Lancashire (1837–45), and especially Alton Castle, Staffordshire (1847–51), with its staccato separation of part from part, each functional element with its own appropriate and distinct shape and roof. A humbler line of dwellings also sprang from Pugin's early experiment at St. Marie's Grange. Between 1840 and 1843 he developed the theme of "Picturesque utility" (S. Muthesius, *The High Victorian Movement in Architecture, 1850–1870*, 1971, pp. 4–10)

586. *Edward Buckton Lamb, Nunn Appleton Hall, Yorkshire, 1864*
587. *William Butterfield, All Saints, Margaret Street, London, interior, 1849–59*

588. *William Butterfield, All Saints, Margaret Street, London, pulpit*
589. *William Butterfield, All Saints, Margaret Street, London, plan*

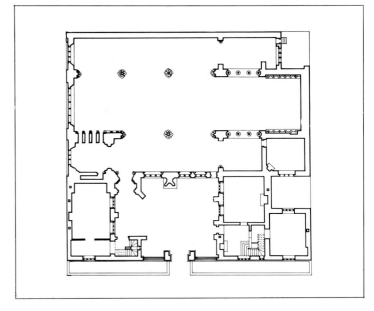

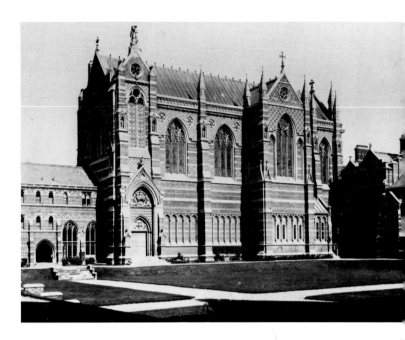

in a series of important and influential houses—Bishop's House, Birmingham (demolished), the Catholic school and teacher's house at Spetchley, Worcestershire, and his own house, The Grange, at Ramsgate, Kent. This earnest and supposedly "truthful" way of building caught on immediately with the Ecclesiological Society, which was busy popularizing in the Anglican church ideas Pugin had claimed were essentially Catholic. Butterfield's Coalpit Heath vicarage, Gloucestershire (1844), and the village of Baldersby, Yorkshire (1855–57); George Edmund Street's Colnbrook vicarage, Buckinghamshire (1853), and group of church, vicarage, and school at Boyne Hill, Maidenhead, Berkshire (1854); and William White's vicarages at Lurgashall, Sussex (1852), and Little Baddow, Essex (1857–58), are all unthinkable without the precedent of Pugin. Not least in importance is the building that stands at the end of this rather glum and cerebral development, Red House at Upton, near Bexleyheath, Kent, designed for William Morris (1834–1896) in 1859 by Philip Webb (1831–1915), which for so long, and so ironically, was hailed as a stepping-stone to the modern movement.

Pugin's church design had probably less influence on his contemporaries than his domestic design. Nonetheless, he has left us some singularly beautiful interiors, ranging from the early St. Chad's cathedral, Birmingham (1839), with its curiously attenuated proportions, to the solidly Early Victorian St. Giles, Cheadle, Staffordshire (1839–44)—elaborately stenciled in imitation of the treatment then being given to the Ste.-Chapelle in Paris—and finally to his late St. Augustine, Ramsgate, Kent (1845–50), possibly his finest church. At Ramsgate, which he paid for largely himself, Pugin was able to indulge his profound feeling for the powerful structure and profuse ornament of English early fourteenth-century Gothic. The result is a moving piece of living archaeology, which deeply influenced such followers of Pugin as Sir George Gilbert Scott, John Loughborough Pearson (1817–1897), and George Frederick Bodley (1827–1907). Pearson's opulent and sophisticated church of St. Mary at Dalton Holme, Yorkshire (1858–61), is a realization of the Puginesque dream as is the sumptuous, much later Holy Angels, Hoar Cross, Staffordshire (1872–1900), by Bodley, in whose career we can trace a Pugin revival. Bodley's All Saints, Cambridge (1861–70), came at the turning point when he rejected the exuberance of the 1850s for the calmer medievalism of Pugin.

ENGLAND: *High Victorian Architecture*
We have just spoken of exuberance as characteristic of the 1850s. It is generally accepted that between 1850 and 1870 the Gothic Revival passed rather unexpectedly through a violent period recognizably different from what preceded and succeeded it. It is by turns muscular and geometrical, naturalistic and polychromatic, often unaccommodating and even brutal. It is particularly associated with Butterfield, Lamb, Teulon, Burges, White,

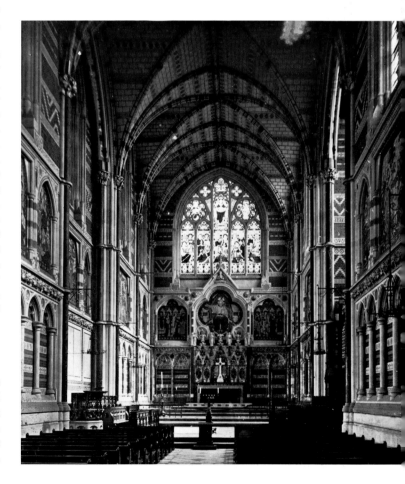

592. *George Edmund Street,*
St. James-the-Less, London, apse,
1859–61

593. *George Edmund Street,*
St. James-the-Less, London, interior,
1859–61

Brooks, and Street and Bodley in their early work. The elaborate secular buildings of Scott and Waterhouse must also be considered as High Victorian.

The oldest architect working in this new manner was Edward Bruckton Lamb (1805–1869). His bizarre and assertive Gothic style had its origins in the Picturesque, pre-Puginesque world of John Claudius London (1783–1843) and his circle. He found it early and did not develop it according to the doctrines of Pugin and Butterfield. He was consequently spurned by the Ecclesiological Society, yet the violence of his work in the 1850s and 1860s—for example, at Nunn Appleton Hall, Yorkshire (1864)—justifies his placement in the High Victorian movement. The harsh but roguish complexities of the tower of his Christ Church, West Hartlepool, County Durham (1854), reappeared with undiminished vigor at St. Martin, Vicars Road, Gospel Oak, London (1862–65). Of St. Martin's tower, Sir John Summerson brilliantly observed, "Most towers answer a question. This one asks" (*Victorian Architecture: Four Studies in Evaluation,* 1970, p. 73).

An architect with an equally individual and strident language was William Butterfield (1814–1900). With Pugin he was the most original and influential of the mid-century ecclesiastical architects. The Ecclesiologists were much more concerned than Pugin with the problems of urban church-building; they were more attracted by force and power in architectural form, and, though deeply influenced by his appeal for constructional honesty, tended to interpret this in terms of structural polychromy: Thus, the English country church of the fourteenth century, which had been Pugin's ideal, was temporarily forsaken in favor of an original amalgam that drew on the more massive forms of the thirteenth century and in which the polychromatic effects of the medieval architecture in Italy and Spain were daringly elaborated in brick. Butterfield's "model church" for the Ecclesiological Society—All Saints, Margaret Street, London (1849–59)—is a doctrinal statement of this new reformed Gothic. It is a forceful and compelling work in which it is hard not to discern a desire to shock. In his distinguished monograph *William Butterfield* (1971) Paul Thompson has tried to absolve Butterfield from the attachment to a kind of creative ugliness that has sometimes been seen in his work. Yet we should not overlook the fact that the Ecclesiological Society's own organ referred to a "deliberate preference of ugliness" in an article on the consecration of the church in 1859 (*The Ecclesiologist,* vol. 20, p. 185). In the early 1850s Butterfield dropped his structural polychromy but returned to it with passion in such churches as St. Alban, Holborn (1859–62), and in one of his most powerful and best-known masterpieces, Keble College, Oxford (1866–83).

As brilliant as Butterfield, and possibly more versatile, was George Edmund Street (1824–1881). His early vicarage and theological college at Cuddesdon, Oxfordshire (1852), and church at Boyne Hill, Maidenhead, contained the seeds of that massive and deceptively simple style that led Charles Eastlake to believe that Cuddesdon College and East Grinstead

convent "have literally no architectural character beyond what may be secured by stout masonry, a steep roof, and a few dormer windows, though he claimed at the same time that "there is a genuine *cachet* on each design which it is impossible to mistake. They are the production of an artist hand" (*History of the Gothic Revival,* p. 323).

In 1855 Street published *Brick and marble of the Middle Ages: Notes of a Tour in the North of Italy,* in which he defended the combination of motifs from different styles and countries. In the late 1850s and 1860s he went on to produce a group of vividly original churches in which he developed his firsthand knowledge of the color and constructional detail of Italian Gothic. From the year 1859 date three remarkable churches in very different parts of the country: St. John the Evangelist, Howsham, Yorkshire; St. Philip and St. James, Oxford; and St. James-the-Less, Westminster, London. The massive chunkiness of St. John the Evangelist, Howsham, with its somewhat Italianate western porch, reappears in the bigger and more sculptural church at Oxford, but it is St. James-the-Less that reveals Street at his most forceful and most brilliant. Of striped and diapered red and black brick it is an electrifying blend of Butterfield's style with early French and north Italian details, dominated by a massive Ruskinian campanile, forty-one meters (one hundred thirty-four feet) of unbuttressed brickwork. Its forceful exterior geometry is echoed internally in the insistent patterning of tile, marble, and mastic. For Charles Eastlake, the whole church was "evidence of a thirst for change which Mr. Street could satisfy without danger, but which betrayed many of his contemporaries into intemperance. Even here there is something to regret in the restless notching of edges, the dazzling distribution of stripes, the multiplicity of pattern forms, and exuberance of sculptural detail" (*History of Gothic Revival,* p. 321).

The "intemperance" Eastlake noted can surely be found in the work of William White (1825–1900) and Samuel Sanders Teulon (1812–1873). Notched, polychromatic, and willful is White's bizarre church of St. Michael at Lyndhurst, Hampshire (1858–59), which has many features in common with Street's St. James-the-Less but markedly lacks its overall balance. But even White's work pales into normality by the side of Teulon's Shadwell Park, Norfolk (1856–60), freakishly muscular, or Burges's additions to Gayhurst, Buckinghamshire (1859). Teulon's early work—for example, Tortworth Court, Gloucestershire (1849–53)—is rather in the busy manner of E. B. Lamb, but by the late 1850s he was producing work in a sculptural idiom similar to Street's but more assertive, exemplified by such buildings as St. Mark, Silvertown, Essex. But it was in country-house design that Teulon's idiosyncratic genius found its fullest expression. His Elvetham Hall, Hampshire (1859–62), for the fourth Lord Calthorpe, is a secular counterpart of Street's contemporary St. James-the-Less, as is also John Prichard's and John Pollard Seddon's Ettington Park, Warwickshire (1858–63). Perhaps the climax of this instantly recognizable and permanently unforgettable Teulon manner is Bestwood Lodge, Nottinghamshire

XLII. Giuseppe Venanzio Marvuglia
with Giuseppe Patricola, La Favorita
(or Palazzina Cinese), Palermo,
1799–1802

596. *John Loughborough Pearson,
St. Peter, Vauxhall, London,
1860–65*

597. *James Brooks, St. Columba,
Haggerston, London, 1867*

598. *William Burges, Cardiff Castle,
Glamorganshire, Smoking Room
ceiling, 1868–74*

d'antiquités monumentales, was published between 1830 and 1841; his *Abécédaire* did not appear until 1851. In 1834 he founded the Société Française d'Archéologie, organizing congresses each year in different parts of France and publishing in the *Bulletin monumental* the papers that were read. The *Bulletin* was from the start, and has remained, a stern, authoritative journal. It demonstrated that the romantic ghost could be exorcised from medieval studies.

Not that an archaeological standard of taste was at once accepted by exponents of Gothic; such men were as much inspired by the rhetoric of Michelet's circle, and in particular by that of Victor Hugo, whose rallying cry was contained in the novel *Notre-Dame de Paris,* first published in 1831. He spurred two of the most active propagandists of the first phase of the Gothic Revival, Adolphe-Napoléon Didron (1806–1867) and Charles Forbes, Comte de Montalembert (1810–1870). Didron, then a young civil servant, wrote to Hugo enraptured when he had read *Notre-Dame de Paris.* Hugo advised him to travel to Normandy. During the following months he walked, rucksack on his back, from one medieval building to another, thus initiating those archaeological studies that he was to diffuse first as editor of the *Bulletin monumental,* then after 1844 in the pages of the *Annales archéologiques.* In 1845 he published the *Manuel d'iconographie chrétienne grecque et latine.* Montalembert's fascination with Hugo had been stirred earlier, in 1830, with the production of *Hermani.* He, too, was dispatched to Normandy, which he explored by carriage, moving thence to England and then to Ireland, before returning to take up the romantic Catholic revival preached by Félicité-Robert de Lamennais and J.-B.-Henri Lacordaire. Neither of these men had much liking for Gothic architecture. Lacordaire listened long to Montalembert's expositions on Gothic only to find that even Ste.-Croix at Orléans escaped his understanding; "Je crois avoir un peu compris," he wrote to Montalembert on September 1, 1831. Yet Montalembert managed to initiate in their paper, *L'avenir,* the policy of which he was to become the most consistent and effective exponent in France: of regarding Gothic architecture as the Catholic style par excellence. The papal suppression of *L'avenir* in 1832 diminished none of his fervor; rather, it served to increase it. In Rome, where he traveled with Lamennais and Lacordaire, Montalembert met the German Nazarene painter Johann Friedrich Overbeck; in Florence he found a childhood acquaintance, Alexis François Rio (1797–1874), whom he inspired with his new-found passion. The result was *De la poésie chrétienne dans son principe, dans sa matière et dans ses formes,* the first volume of which Rio published in 1836. This won no immediate success: After five months no more than twelve copies had been sold. But in 1840 the English *Quarterly Review* devoted a long article to the book, and it later earned John Ruskin's respect, influencing much of the second part of his *Modern Painters.* The second part of Rio's book, *De l'art chrétien,* was published in 1855.

The only architect Montalembert inspired, Louis-Alexandre Piel (1808–

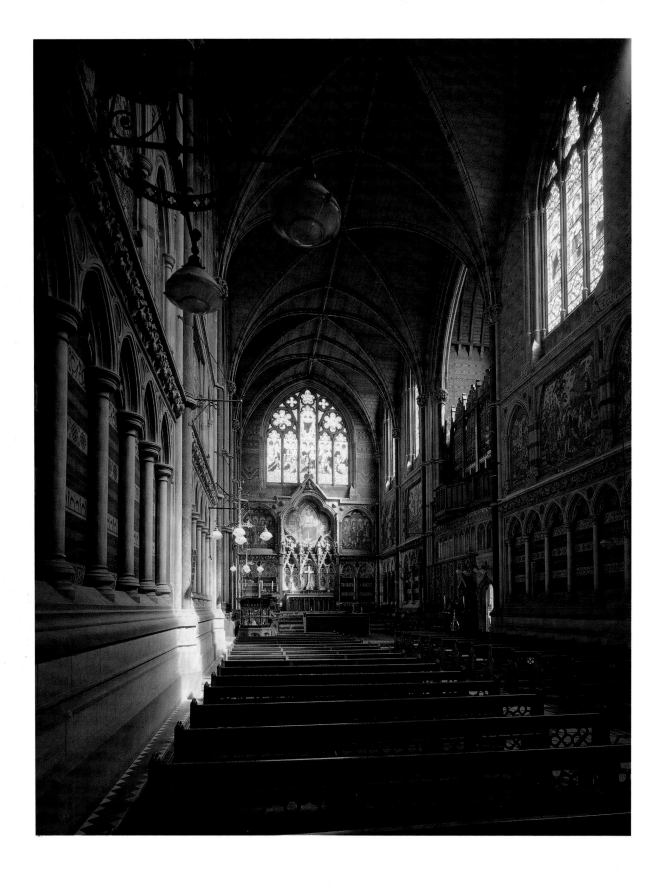

1841), is likewise little known. His active career was extremely short. He was a pupil of Francois Debret but, spurred by Montalembert, he traveled to Germany (writing a series of articles in 1836, "Voyage en Allemagne," for *L'européen*) and returned to design a village church in the Franche-Comté and then, in 1837, St.-Nicolas at Nantes (which was to be taken over by J.-B.-A. Lassus). In 1840 he left for Rome, where he was received into Lacordaire's Dominican order. In 1841, at the age of thirty-three, he died. But his influence was not ineffectual. He had written two more articles for *L'européen,* "Le temple de la Madeleine" and "Déclamation contre l'art païen," which served to set fashionable opinion against the adaptation of classical forms for church architecture.

Montalembert's own collection of articles *Du vandalisme et du catholicisme dans l'art,* issued in 1839, was shallow and unsustained by vigorous thought. He relied largely on the ideas of Hugo, Overbeck, and Pugin; but although he described St. Marie's College at Oscott and employed the methods of the *Contrasts,* he made no mention of Pugin by name. Yet Montalembert's influence was felt strongly in France, and even in England. In 1844 the Camden Society made him an honorary member, an honor he hastened to reject, publishing a pamphlet in English in which he accused the members of the society of being guilty of mortal sin. Gothic in France was to be practiced as a Catholic religious discipline, and the first phase of the revival was thus confined—almost exclusively—to the design of churches.

For all practical purposes the Gothic Revival in France began about 1840. There were several earlier experiments: a Protestant chapel with Gothic trimmings, in the Rue d'Aguesseau, Paris, dating from 1835, and another in a thirteenth-century style, begun in the same year, for the Dames de la Congrégation Notre-Dame, 84 Rue de Sèvres, Paris (now demolished), by François-Marie Lemarié (1795–1854), a pupil of Debret. But the only noteworthy project of the Gothic Revival to date from before 1840 is that for St.-Paul at Nîmes, designed in competition with thirty other architects, in 1835, by Charles-Auguste Questel. This church is one of the great representative buildings of the Romanesque Revival in France and also, by a curious freak, the first. It is the work, moreover, of an architect who does not figure as an important influence in either the Romanesque or the Gothic revivals. However, it is fair to note that Questel's restoration of St.-Martin d'Ainay at Lyons and, in particular, the magnificent copper-gilt altar front and the furnishings he designed for that church were acclaimed and thoughtfully scrutinized by a great many visitors, French and foreign, when they were exhibited at the international exhibition in 1855, alongside Viollet-le-Duc's similar altar front and furnishings for the cathedral of Clermont-Ferrand. But Questel is remembered today for a dull, classical *palais de justice* at Nîmes or the livelier, if still academic, *préfecture* and library on the Place de Verdun at Grenoble.

St.-Paul was begun only in 1838, after the drawings had been considerably revised in accordance with the dictates of the Conseil Général des Bâtiments

610. *Charles-Auguste Questel, St.-Paul, Nîmes, designed 1835, built 1838–50*

611. *Charles-Auguste Questel, St.-Paul, Nîmes, interior, designed 1835, built 1838–50*

Civils, and was not completed until November 1850. It emerged then as an adequate if slightly gutless interpretation of southern Romanesque architecture, with ribbed vaults over the nave and aisles, an apse colorfully decorated with murals by Jean-Hippolyte Flandrin, and stained-glass windows by Maréchal Guyon of Metz, but all handled with greater confidence and maturity than one might be led to expect from a pupil of Duban, even a precocious one. Much was no doubt due to the help of the archaeologist Charles Lenormant, Questel's brother by adoption.

There were far more uncertainty and awkward lapses of knowledge in other early attempts to revive the medieval styles: in St.-Clément at Nantes, for instance, built between 1841 and 1847 by François-Léon Liberge (1800–1860); or in the large church that Alexandre-Charles Grigny (1815–1867) erected between 1842 and 1846 for the sisters of the Adoration Perpétuelle du Saint Sacrement at Arras. And even more laxity and indecisiveness are in that handful of maverick commissions awarded by Louis-Philippe: the chapel dedicated to Saint Louis at Carthage, designed by Charles-Joseph Jourdain and consecrated on April 25, 1841 (now gone); the fanciful Gothic *cloche* that was placed in 1842 by Pierre-Bernard Lefranc (1795–1856) over the family chapel at Dreux, built initially by Cramail in the form of a Doric temple between 1816 and 1822; and, most astonishing of all, the mausoleum for Ferdinand d'Orléans, the Chapelle St.-Ferdinand (now the Place de la Porte des Ternes), Paris, built between July 1842 and July 1843, in something of a Romanesque manner, by none other than P.-F.-L. Fontaine, with windows to the design of Ingres and surrounds drawn by Viollet-le-Duc. Other oddities and disasters could be listed, for, the liturgical enthusiasms of the clergy having once been aroused, there was much experimentation throughout France. But only a few of the early provincial exponents of Gothic need be considered before turning our attention to the focus of the revival, which was in Paris.

In Normandy, as was appropriate, two architects of more than usual distinction emerged, H.-C.-M. Grégoire (1791–1854) and Jacques-Eugène Barthélemy (1799–1882). Grégoire, who had studied under Percier, began his career in 1837 with a small chapel in brick with trimmings of stone for the *hospice* at Yvenot (the similar chapel built there two years later for the seminary was by C.-L.-N. Robert). His major work was the fragile facade that he added to the late Gothic church of St.-Ouen at Rouen between 1845 and 1851. This was an architectural tour de force that displays neither originality nor real scholarship, yet evinces genuine powers of compositional skill. Not that Didron agreed: "Ce travail est inutile, nuisible, impossible," he wrote in the *Annales archéologiques* (p. 320) in 1845, when work was just begun; a year later he described the church as "l'édifice hybride et disgracieux [*sic*]" (p. 188). Barthélemy, who later became diocesan architect to Rouen, was better informed. In 1840 he began Notre-Dame-de-Bon-Secours at Blosseville, just outside the town. By 1847 building was complete. The fittings and colorful decorations inside were added during

the reign of Louis-Napoleon. The church, entirely of stone, was in the thirteenth-century style. The composition is careful rather than interesting, though Barthélemy showed himself singularly resourceful in adapting recondite elements and details. Altogether, it gives evidence of archaeological sensibility and stands thus as a landmark for the beginning of the Gothic Revival in France. It bears comparison, moreover, with many of Pugin's early works. In 1844 Barthélemy started on a chapel in the thirteenth-century style at the Château du Plessis, near Port Audemer; two years later he built a small church in the same manner at St.-Aubin, near Elbeuf. However, when in 1847 he was commissioned to design the church of Ventes-St.-Rémi, near Saint-Saëns, he chose a Romanesque style. All his works have pretensions to archaeological accuracy—pretensions that are not altogether unfounded.

Less well known though no less earnest than Barthélemy were the architects Hippolyte-Louis Durand (1890-1881), Victor Gay, and the brothers Charles-Victor and Gustave Guérin. Hippolyte Durand studied under Lebas and Vaudoyer at the École des Beaux-Arts. When he left the school he took to sending studies of Gothic buildings to the Salons and was soon rewarded with the commission to restore St.-Rémy at Rheims—a work that won Montalembert's praise. In 1845 Durand exhibited designs for a number of small churches in the thirteenth-century style and conceived the idea, together with Didron, of publishing a catalogue of them, "Parallèle de projets d'églises en style ogival du XIIIᵉ siècle." The project was abandoned. But in the same year Durand began his first Gothic building, a thirteenth-century chapel for M. d'Orjault at Beaumont (Allier). In the following year he designed a church in the same style for Peyrehorade (Landes)—a church, as we shall see, that was to be the subject of some controversy at the Conseil Général des Bâtiments Civils. In 1849 Durand was made diocesan architect in the Basses-Pyrénées and in the years that followed built a number of churches in that area, all of them orthodox but dull. He was an architect of no great distinction.

Victor Gay, of whom much less is known, is perhaps more important. In 1846 he designed a large church—it was thirty-eight meters (one hundred twenty-five feet) long—for St.-Sulpice-les-Feuilles, near Arnac (Haute-Vienne). The church was conceived as a frame construction—the buttresses, the piers, and the ribs of the vaults of granite, the rest of the masonry of a light, less durable stone. The significance of the arrangement was at once apparent to all French theorists of Gothic construction, foremost among them Viollet-le-Duc, who was at that time publishing a series of articles on the subject in the *Annales archéologiques.* In the same year Gay designed a similarly organized chapel at Nanterre—it was exhibited at the Salon in 1846—but this seems to have aroused little interest in the architectural world. Indeed, almost nothing is known of Gay's activities after his early outburst. He designed some notable church furnishings, made by L. Bachelet, but, like Piel, may well have ended up in Rome, for the church

614. Gustave Guérin and Charles-
Victor Guérin, St. Étienne, Tours,
interior, 1869–74

615. Gustave Guérin and Charles-
Victor Guérin, St.-Étienne, Tours,
1869–74

it was a determined attempt to give expression to Viollet-le-Duc's latest doctrines, and was acknowledged as such when it was finished, in 1864. The curé's house and the village hall, also by Boeswillwald, are in the same style, with an attempt at Picturesque grouping. But the architecture cannot be judged a success; nor was it of any great influence, though its decorative motifs were taken up later by Félix Narjoux for his schools in Paris. In the south of France, in the hills to the southeast of St.-Jean-Pied-de-Port, Boeswillwald built the small chapel of St.-Sauveur; at Biarritz, starting in 1863, and later at Beaumetz, he built other chapels, covered inside and out with geometrical designs in colored stone, brick, and tile. These were crude, self-conscious adaptations of Byzantine and other Eastern models to which the medieval architecture of the region was thought to relate. They owed something, no doubt, to A. L. Couchaud's *Choix d'églises byzantines de la Grèce,* of 1842, and even more, perhaps, to C. F. Texier's and R. P. Pullan's *Architecture byzantine,* of 1864. Boeswillwald's one ambitious domestic undertaking was the grotesque rebuilding of the Château de Montigny, near Masny (Nord), complete with octagonal towers of varying diameters and crow-stepped gables—all derived, it would seem, from an unexecuted project by Viollet-le-Duc, of May 1863, for the Château de Merinville. Boeswillwald was, through life, a close friend of Viollet-le-Duc and also of his mentor, Mérimée. In the autumn of 1854 he traveled with them to Germany; he owed the commission of the Biarritz chapel to Mérimée and in 1860 succeeded him as *Inspecteur Général des Monuments Historiques,* the first architect to be appointed to the post.

Maurice-Augustin-Gabriel Ouradou (1822–1884), a pupil of Lebas, the third of the early disciples of Viollet-le-Duc to be trained at Notre-Dame, became his son-in-law in 1857 and worked thereafter in close conjunction with him; indeed, such houses as that for Auguste Griois, at Ambrières-les-Vallées (Mayenne), designed in 1857 but begun only in 1865, and the Hôtel Duranti, 184 Boulevard Haussmann, Paris, both to be credited on completion to Ouradou, were commissioned from and first sketched by Viollet-le-Duc. One can well understand his reluctance to accept credit for these miserable works. Ouradou did little else to match even their small distinction—some minor restorations, church furnishings, and tombs. Eugène-Louis Millet (1819–1879), a pupil of Labrouste, entered the École des Beaux-Arts in 1837; three years later he was working for Viollet-le-Duc. He started in 1848 to restore the cathedrals of Châlons-sur-Marne and of Troyes, where he was to build the Chapel des Soeurs de la Providence, and in 1855 was commissioned to restore the Château de St.-Germain-en-Laye, near Maisons Lafitte, where in 1867 he began the new church in the Rue de la Muette. Three years after Lassus's death in 1857 Millet took over the work of the cathedral at Moulins and, similarly, succeeded to the restoration of the cathedral at Rheims in 1874, after Viollet-le-Duc's resignation as *Inspecteur Général des Édifices Diocésains.* Millet's special influence on the Gothic movement was exerted, however, not as an architect but as a teacher

*XLVI. George Edmund Street,
SS. Philip and James, Oxford,
1860-62*

of craftsmen, in particular, the members of the Cercle des Ouvriers maçons et Tailleurs de Pierres, for whom he built a small center in Paris, at 9 Rue des Chantiers.

To the list of architects already considered one might add the names of Jean-Charles Laisné (1819–1891), Victor-Marie-Charles Ruprich-Robert (1820–1887), Jean-Juste-Gustave Lisch (1828–1910), Joseph-Eugène-Anatole de Baudot (1834–1915), Édouard-Jules Corroyer (1835–1904), Félix Narjoux (1836–1891), and Edmond-Armand-Marie Duthoit (1837–1889). All of these men worked long and with distinction both for the Commission des Monuments Historiques and for the Service des Édifices Diocésains and upheld, if in some cases only to a limited extent, the ideals of Viollet-le-Duc. But they were certainly not consistent Gothic Revivalists. Ruprich-Robert, a pupil of Constant-Dufeux, in 1840 became Viollet-le-Duc's assistant and later his successor at the École de Dessin. He began three churches in 1855, with the plates of the *Dictionnaire raisonné de l'architecture française* in mind: the church of Athis (Orne), St.-Jean-Baptiste at Flers (Orne; 1855–68), and the Chapelle du Petit Séminaire at Sées (Orne). He built little else in this manner, but instead demonstrated his attachment to Viollet-le-Duc in theories of ornamental design, proposed first in 1866 in the *Flore ornementale: essai sur la composition de l'ornement, éléments tirés de la nature et principes de leur application,* a work of considerable importance, completed in 1876. His great literary contribution, however, was *L'architecture normande aux XIe et XIIe siècles en Normandie et en Angleterre,* published posthumously.

Juste Lisch, a pupil of both Vaudoyer and Labrouste, likewise showed early Gothic sympathies, with his design for the bishop's palace at Luçon, though he turned soon after to classical sources for inspiration. His late works, the Gare de Le Havre and a host of buildings set up for the Paris exhibition of 1878—in particular, the Gare du Champ de Mars—and others for the Paris exhibition of 1889 (one of which survives as the Gare de Javel) were all designed with exposed frameworks of iron filled in with luridly colored panels of glazed bricks and tiles. They show undivided loyalties to the doctrines set down by Viollet-le-Duc in the second volume of the *Entretiens sur l'architecture.* Édouard-Jules Corroyer and Félix Narjoux, pupils of Constant-Dufeux, allied themselves always with Viollet-le-Duc and were active and sympathetic restorers of Gothic monuments. Corroyer began with the restoration of Mont Saint-Michel, a project later taken over by another of Viollet-le-Duc's disciples, his biographer, Paul-Émile-Antoine Gout (1852–1923). Narjoux started his career in 1857 with the restoration of the cathedral of Limoges. Both were early supporters of the Gothic Revival, Narjoux most notably in a house he built in his native Chalon-sur-Saône, closely modeled on the thirteenth-century houses of Cluny. Despite this interest in Viollet-le-Duc and Gothic architecture, both Corroyer and Narjoux spent most of their active careers developing a style that was far closer to the heart of Charles Garnier than that of Viollet-le-Duc. Only the three schools that Narjoux built in Paris (after 1872, when the Paris council

voted to erect thirty-five such buildings) were to be organized and detailed in a manner responsive to the teachings of Viollet-le-Duc.

Anatole de Baudot and Edmond Duthoit alone of this group should be considered as determined and evolving exponents of the Gothic cause. Even so, their roles must be carefully defined. Duthoit was the son and the nephew of stone carvers at Amiens, trained and employed first by Viollet-le-Duc. But he spent much of his life outside France—in north Africa, where from 1872 onward he was actively engaged in restoration work, and in the Middle East, in Palestine and Syria in particular, where he traveled first in 1861, on the expeditions of the Comte de Vogüé and W. H. Waddington. There he measured and sketched a number of Early Christian and Byzantine churches, regularly sending drawings to the Salons and articles to the *Gazette des architectes et du bâtiment.* He was even tempted to try his hand at designing in the Eastern manner: He built two churches in Beirut. Yet his most adventurous work was done in France. For Viollet-le-Duc he supervised the reconstruction of the fifteenth-century Château d'Arragori, near Hendaye, on the Spanish border, designed for the explorer and astronomer Antoinine d'Abbadia. He greatly elaborated Viollet-le-Duc's designs, introducing an array of highly colored decorative motifs, partly Gothic in character but equally inspired by Eastern sources. "Mon arabe," he said, "sent le gothique, et mon gothique a un arrière goût d'arabe ou de byzantin." His Château du Roquetaillade, southeast of Bordeaux, near Langon, once again begun on the basis of Viollet-le-Duc's designs in 1864, on this occasion for M. de Mauvesin, was even more spectacular. No detail, no piece of furniture, even, fails to show something of the exotic image Duthoit had evolved. The Rose Bedroom, the Green Bedroom, and the chapel are Duthoit's alone. It is the only building in France that may be compared—if unfavorably—to William Burges's contemporary work at Cardiff Castle (see illustrations 598, 599). Duthoit, unfortunately, produced little else: churches of a modest sort at Champeaux (Deux-Sèvres; c. 1878), Bryas (Pas-de-Calais; 1880-84), and Souverain-Moulin (Pas-de-Calais; c. 1883), and of a spectacular sort at Albert (Somme; 1883-97), where he erected the highly colored, almost exotic pilgrimage church of Notre-Dame-de-Brebières.

Anatole de Baudot was perhaps a more fitting heir to Viollet-le-Duc, his defender and constant support. He came to him first when Labrouste closed his *atelier* in 1856. By 1857 he had been set to work on the restoration of the cathedral at Puy-en-Velay (Haute-Loire) and was soon after appointed diocesan architect at Clermont-Ferrand. During the years that followed he restored no fewer than twenty-five churches. His original buildings are almost as numerous, usually adventurous. However, it is difficult to assess his particular genius at this period, for his early works were designed under the watchful eye of Viollet-le-Duc, and only after his death did de Baudot learn to extend his abilities. Then he emerged as an innovator of great distinction. Not, of course, that he did not himself early inflect the works of his mentor. The house that Viollet-le-Duc built about 1863, for M.

Sauvage, a building contractor, on a site bounded by Rue Le Peletier, Rue La Fayette, and Rue Chauchat in Paris, is largely the work of de Baudot, and undoubtedly owes much of its decoration in the form of outsized grotesques and gargoyles to his supervision. "Réussie ou non," de Baudot wrote in 1865 in the *Gazette des architectes et du bâtiment,* "cette façade a le mérite de l'originalité" (p. 83). At the same time he erected a more conventional building, with scarcely a hint of Gothic in its detailing, 21 Rue de Leningrad (originally Rue de Saint Petersbourg); then another at 34 Rue Saint-Lazare, finished in 1866, more boldy—one might say clumsily— detailed. This has something of the quality of Viollet-le-Duc's apartments for M. Milon, put up between 1857 and 1860, at 15 Rue de Douai. The Gothic features in the design, as one might expect at this period, are not obtrusive. De Baudot's slightly later church at La Roche Millay (Nièvre), of 1870, was likewise derived from a design by Viollet-le-Duc; the second for the tower and west front of St.-Martin at Ussel (Corrèze), dating from 1852 (the first was done in 1843), which was supervised by Millet and later credited to him. It is just possible that Viollet-le-Duc was indeed the designer of the La Roche Millay church also, for early sketches relating to it are still among his papers.

De Baudot's first important church, St.-Lubin at Rambouillet, designed in 1865 in competition with fifty-four other architects, relates rather to Viollet-le-Duc's more venturesome theories, taken up already, as we have seen, by Boeswillwald for the church at Masny. Along the nave are columns of iron, set two feet in front of piers of stone, serving together to support the walls and stone vaults above. The arrangement, taken perhaps from the lower chapel of the Ste.-Chapelle, or, more probably, from the fourteenth-century church of Tour (Calvados), restored later by de Baudot, avoids the use of flying buttresses while retaining an air of lightness internally. Though technically sound, the design was strongly attacked. Bourgeois de Lagny ridiculed it as a naive paraphrase of Gothic in the *Moniteur des architectes,* in 1866. César Daly followed up the attack in the *Revue générale de l'architecture* thirteen years later, when the church was finally completed. De Baudot determined not to use exposed ironwork in his later designs for churches, three of which—Levallois-Perret (1869), Sèvres (1870), and St.-Bruno at Grenoble (1870)—were won in competition and were at once castigated in the established architectural press, and then not built—though St.-Justin at Levallois-Perret was eventually erected, in a modified form, between 1892 and 1911. The project for the church at Privas (Ardèche), which de Baudot exhibited at the Salon in 1876, was, however, carried out. All were thoughtful if straightforward adaptations of simple thirteenth-century structures. They were related to Viollet-le-Duc's designs for the church at Aillant-sur-Tholon and, in particular, to St.-Denys-de-l'Estrée. What distinguishes all these churches, whether by Viollet-le-Duc or by his followers, is that they were modeled on the parish churches of France, not the cathedrals that Lassus and his contemporaries had sought to emulate,

632. Joseph-Auguste-Émile Vaudremer, St.-Pierre-de-Montrouge, Paris, 1864–72

if only in miniature. The limited extent of the aspirations of both Viollet-le-Duc and de Baudot at this period is to be measured by the two lackluster volumes of their manual of instruction, *Églises de bourgs et villages,* published in 1867. Only long after Viollet-le-Duc's death did de Baudot demonstrate the truly startling quality of his imagination, beginning in 1882 with the building of the Lycée Lakanal at Sceaux, in which some of Boeswillwald's innovations at Masny were to be exploited and developed, but especially after 1890, when he initiated his astonishing experiments in reinforced brickwork and concrete, including the Lycée Victor Hugo, 27 Rue de Sévigné (1894–96), and the church of St.-Jean-de-Montmartre (1894, 1897–1904), both in Paris. This development culminated in 1914 in his famous design for a giant exhibition hall, in all things a presage to the works of Pier Luigi Nervi. In de Baudot the intellectual promise of the Gothic Revival might be held to have been fulfilled.

There is a great deal more in the history of the Gothic Revival in France outside the orbit of Viollet-le-Duc urgently requiring investigation: the two early churches that Ferdinand Leroy is reported to have built at Châteauroux (Indre), by 1844, for example; or the ten that Paul Pechinet, an architect active at Langres, is said to have built in the Haute-Marne by 1846; or that extraordinary series on the outskirts of Paris, all by Claude Naissant (1801–1879), of a spare and taut geometry derived from Romanesque models. The critic of *The Ecclesiologist* had begun to remark upon some of the latter as early as 1855: St.-Lambert, Rue Bausset, Vaugirard (1848–56); Notre-Dame-de-la-Gare, Place Jeanne d'Arc, Ivry (now Gobelins; 1855–64); St.-Charles-Borromée at Joinville-le-Pont (1856–66); St.-Pierre, Place de l'Église, Charenton-le-Pont (1857–59): Ste.-Geneviève, Rosny-sous-Bois (1857–66); and Notre-Dame-de-la-Médaille-Miraculeuse, 80 Avenue Pierre Larousse, Malakoff (1861). Also of interest is the imposing church of Notre-Dame-de-la-Croix, Rue Julien Lacroix, at Ménilmontant in Paris, by Louis-Jean-Antoine Héret (1821–1899), another of Lebas's pupils, built between 1863 and 1880, all in stone apart from the ribs of the vaults of the nave, which are of iron lattice construction. Even more demanding of comment is St.-Pierre-de-Montrouge, on the Place Victor Basch, Paris, built between 1864 and 1872 by Joseph-Auguste-Émile Vaudremer (1829–1914), the most outstanding of Blouer's and Gilbert's pupils. This church, though once again based on Romanesque models, was even more consciously indebted to a restoration study of Qal'at Saman, in Syria, that Duthoit had showed at the Salon and had then published in the *Gazette des architectes et du bâtiment* in 1864, the year before the Comte de Vogüé's two great volumes *La Syrie centrale* started to appear. Vaudremer was attempting to produce a building of solid dignity—a quality noticeably lacking in the works of Viollet-le-Duc and his followers—that was clearly ecclesiastical in character, but in no way attested to the Gothic Revival. And he succeeded. St.-Pierre is perhaps the only church of the period of any architectural quality. He was less adept in his subsequent experiments—Notre-Dame-

d'Auteuil, Place d'Auteuil, Paris, of 1876–80, which hints at a knowledge
of Abadie's work; the gable-fronted Protestant Temple de Belleville, 97 Rue
Julien Lacroix, Paris, put up between 1877 and 1880; the Greek Orthodox
church in the Rue Georges Bizet, Paris, of 1890–95—though his last,
St.-Antoine-des-Quinze-Vingts, 66 Avenue Ledru-Rollin, Paris, of 1901-3,
reveals unusual and surprising powers of asymmetrical composition. Other
classically trained architects sought similar evasive expedients along the lines
suggested by the engineers François-Léonce Reynaud, in his *Traité d'architecture,* of 1850–58, and F. de Dartein in his *Étude sur l'architecture lombarde,*
issued between 1865 and 1882. Lombard Gothic, it seemed, had the merit
of being Italian, not French. Louis-Joseph Duc adopted it for the chapel of
the Lycée Michelet, Paris, as did P.-R.-L. Ginain, to much less pleasing result
at Notre-Dame-des-Champs, in the Boulevard du Montparnasse, Paris, of
1867–76. Such compromises, however, had little convincing effect. They
made no impact on subsequent architecture.

Whether or not one notes and pursues the instances listed above, the
pattern of the development of the Gothic Revival in France must already
be clear. Support came in the first instance from the Commission des
Monuments Historiques and later and more forcefully, after 1850, from the
Service des Édifices Diocésains. Nearly all the architects we have considered
had restored at least one Gothic building before they undertook to build
anything new. They were thus amateur archaeologists and at once
acknowledged an archaeological standard of taste. The focus for all their
discussion, their source of information and ideas, was thus the *Annales
archéologiques,* started by Didron in 1844. The tone of this review was from
the first stridently militant. Didron delighted to provoke friends and
enemies alike. The Gothic Revival was deliberately encouraged by scores
of articles on medieval music, stained glass, and, above all, architecture. Félix
de Verneilh established the national status of Gothic in a series of articles
in 1845; Lassus preached the merits of the thirteenth-century style in the
same year; while Viollet-le-Duc, as we have seen, beginning in 1844 and
continuing until 1847, outlined in full those theories on Gothic that he was
to elaborate later in life. These were the years of the highest hopes and
excitement. Building in the Gothic style started just before 1840, though
the first admired achievement, Barthélemy's Notre-Dame-de-Bon-Secours,
was not completed until 1847. The Gothic movement during the 1840s was
being firmly consolidated. In 1852 Didron estimated that two hundred
churches of a mock-medieval kind had been built or were under construction
in France. The chapter house of Notre-Dame in Paris was then complete,
resplendent with murals and rich new furnishings, but the mature works
of Lassus and Viollet-le-Duc were yet to come. At just this period, however,
the sap and savor that had sustained the whole movement failed. Lassus
remained a convinced revivalist, but Viollet-le-Duc, though he continued
to design in a Gothic style, was no longer wholehearted in his support. He
had given notice of this crisis of faith as early as 1844, concluding one of

his articles in the *Annales archéologiques* with the words, "Ces secondes poussées n'ont jamais le vigueur, la sève des premières; elles sont souvent pâles et étiolées. Mais enfin ce sont encore les rejetons d'une bonne souche, et il faut bien se garder de les dédaigner" (p. 179). Already he was looking for an alternative form of architecture, Gothic in its principles but not in its appearance. He was determined to forge a new style. Although he remained friendly with Didron after 1848, he ceased to provide propaganda in the *Annales archéologiques*. Instead, he wrote after 1852 for the *Revue générale de l'architecture* and then for the *Encyclopédie d'architecture*, the review founded in 1851 by Adolphe Lance (1813–1874) and Victor Calliat (1801–1881). Viollet-le-Duc was not alone in his misgivings; many of the most active and serious-minded adherents of the Gothic movement sought a solution to the dilemmas of nineteenth-century architecture outside the restrictions of a revivalist doctrine. They built churches in the Gothic style—or in an interpretation of it—but little else. They were not sure of their cause. Apart from the limited creative ability of the architects involved, this lack of strong conviction must be held largely accountable for the rapid decline into eclecticism of the Gothic Revival in France. Very little of value in the way of building was to emerge.

The cause, the catalyst of this crisis of faith, was, paradoxically, the erection of Ste.-Clotilde, in Paris, the most conspicuous of the early monuments to the Gothic Revival, and one for which Didron and all his host fought tenaciously. The history of this battle is little known. It begins, surprisingly, in 1834, when Prosper Mérimée, as *Inspecteur Général des Monuments Historiques,* suggested, wisely enough, that all plans for restoration work to be undertaken by the Commission des Monuments Historiques be submitted to the Conseil Général des Bâtiments Civils. This procedure was followed happily for five years and more, for Jean Vatout, president of the Commission, was at the same time president of the Conseil. But at the end of 1839 control of the Conseil was transferred from the Ministère de l'Intérieur to the Ministère des Travaux Publics. Vatout was obliged to resign his position on the Commission, which was thus deprived of its president and of the intimate cooperation of the staff of the Conseil. The Commission, now presided over by Ludovic Vitet, decided to assert its independence; in this it was successful, but at the expense of the Conseil's trust. Thereafter the two bodies were in all things opposed. And their antipathy became more marked with the quickening interest in Gothic, for, though the members of the Commission were by no means Gothic enthusiasts to a man, almost all the members of the Conseil opposed the Revival. They were, for the most part, members of the Académie.

The changes in administration had an irritating consequence for the Commission: the virtual loss of control over several important historic monuments, among them the church of St.-Denis, which François Debret had been restoring for a number of years. In 1839 he began work on the west front. More than an inch of stone was cut from the face of the building;

niches and altogether unwarranted detail were also added to the north
tower, which had been struck two years before by lightning. The
Commission complined repeatedly. It demanded Debret's removal. Then,
in 1844, the north tower was found to be collapsing under its own weight.
All Gothic men were aghast. Didron attacked Debret and the Conseil
viciously in the *Annales archéologiques.* The members of the Conseil lost no
time in retaliating. Early in 1845 they arbitrarily refused to allow
construction of three churches in the Gothic style strongly championed by
Didron: St.-André, a diminutive version of St.-Nicaise, at Rheims; St.-Aubin
at Toulouse, designed in competition the year before by Gaston Virebent;
and St.-Étienne at Tours, by Gustave Guérin. The plans of St.-Étienne had
already been passed and work was stopped only at the last moment by
telegram. Didron was furious. He launched a new offensive. St.-André and
St.-Aubin were not built, and St.-Étienne was begun only in 1869; but
Didron's campaign resulted in the acceptance of the plans of the more
conspicuous, and thus even more controversial, church of Ste.-Clotilde. Th
earliest plans for this, in the classical style, were by Jean-Nicolas Huyot
(1780–1840). Two years before he died he was succeeded as architect by
his friend Franz Christian Gau (1790–1854), a native of Cologne who had
crossed the Rhine in 1809 to study under Lebas and Debret. The *Préfet de
la Seine,* Claude-Philibert-Barthelot Rambuteau, a friend of Mérimée,
demanded a church in the Gothic style. After some delay Gau produced
a project in a fourteenth-century style. This was rejected by the Conseil in
1840 on the grounds that too many iron cramps and tie-rods were proposed
in the construction. In the years that followed Gau modified his design no
fewer than three times. On each occasion it was rejected. By 1845
Rambuteau had lost patience. He demanded acceptance of the desaign. The
Conseil made no move. Then, early in 1846, the north tower of St.-Denis,
collapsing slowly for two years, had to be hastily demolished. Debret was
dismissed, but he was made a member of the Conseil. Rambuteau responded
at once. Under the threat of a full-scale enquiry into the conduct of the work
at St.-Denis, he forced the Conseil to approve the plans of Ste.-Clotilde. They
were passed by one vote. Didron was triumphant. He disliked Gau and he
disliked Gau's design, but he was overjoyed that a victory had been won
for the Gothic cause in the teeth of the Conseil's—and thus the Académie's—
opposition. The Académie was no yet prepared to concede the victory. A.-N.
Caristie, a member of both the Conseil and the Commission, submitted a
specially prepared questionnaire to the Académie. "Est-il convenable à nôtre
époque," he asked, "de construire une église dans le style dit gothique?"
This memoir and the discussion that followed were summarized by
Désiré-Raoul Rochette and published at once as an academic encyclical. A
copy was sent to the Ministère de l'Intérieur. Didron, Lassus, and
Viollet-le-Duc all responded with vigor, and no fewer than six other
pamphlets were written to support them. Viollet-le-Duc was appointed
architect for the restoration of St.-Denis. In the same year, the Conseil

attempted to prevent the election of Hippolyte Durand's church at Peyrehorade, but was thwarted. By 1847 eighteen of the twenty plans for churches passed by the Conseil were in some medieval style or other.

Work was at once begun on Ste.-Clotilde. Responsibility, however, was placed in the hands of Théodore Ballu rather than of Gau, who had become deaf and unduly querulous. Ballu kept to Gau's designs as far as possible, being forced to reduce the height of the towers for reasons of economy. He retained the two spires, modifying their design. By December 1857 the church was complete. Didron disliked it with a rare intensity, as indeed did all committed revivalists. They thought it too florid in detail and were not proud of their victory.

The dispute forced many admirers of Gothic architecture to consider seriously the merits of a Gothic Revival; they had been unnerved by the feebleness of their own arguments, Viollet-le-Duc no less than anyone else, and there is ample evidence to suggest that they soon found the style insupportable. Churches like Gau's were not worth fighting for. The movement declined. It would not be unfair to say that it failed. The French had for only a very few years felt impelled to imitate Gothic.

637. Joseph-Auguste-Émile Vaudremer, Lycée Buffon, Paris, courtyard, 1885–90, 1895–99

Historians of modern architecture have looked to the nineteenth century, if at all, for prophets of the modern movement. Such theorists who have held rational, apparently utilitarian ideals—Horatio Greenough, A. W. N. Pugin, Edward Lacy Garbett, and Viollet-le-Duc—have been singled out and upheld as extraordinary visionaries who owed nothing or almost nothing either to their predecessors or to the societies in which they lived. Yet they evolved their ideas in relation to both, and if we hope ever to understand their intentions and meanings we must assess them in relation to the complex contexts from which they emerged. To abstract and isolate their ideas is to falsify them and to give them new meanings. This might, indeed, be stimulating. But to view history as triumphant progress toward the present is to view it through a distorting glass.

The nineteenth-century radicals were not what they have seemed. Those moments in their careers when they have appeared to err or to falter have for the most part been ignored or set aside as embarrassments. Take Sir Joseph Paxton (1801–1865), the duke of Devonshire's head gardener at Chatsworth, who had already designed for the estate the Great Conservatory in 1836 and the *Victoria regia* greenhouse in 1850, before he put up the Crystal Palace, in London, in 1850–51. This marvel of prefabrication, of iron and glass—and also, it must be stressed, a great deal of timber construction—has a forceful clarity of expression that has rarely failed to satisfy. But it was not always thought of as "Architecture," which is how we have been taught to consider it. Paxton himself regarded the structure only as a specific solution to a particular dilemma. Iron and glass were not generally applicable to Victorian architectural needs, nor were the methods of building he had developed. When he launched into, among many other careers, that of architect after the Great Exhibition, he started to build Mentmore House in Buckinghamshire, a solid Elizabethan pastiche, for the Baron de Rothschild. He built much more of this sort. For the Rothschilds in France, with whom he had business dealings, he started a whole sequence of houses, beginning in 1853 with Ferrières, outside Paris, and ending, as we have seen, with the Château de Pregny, outside Geneva, where he was to be joined by Viollet-le-Duc. These great ungainly châteaux are all in a rich and florid style. They were clearly conceived as appropriate solutions to the problems Paxton considered as set; they were as fitted to their purposes as the Crystal Palace. And the lessons we have derived from this particular building—if lessons are wanted from history—we might as readily have read into the stones of Pregny.

Owen Jones (1809–1874), an architect of as clear and commonsensical a cast of mind as Paxton, was appointed Superintendent of the Works at the Crystal Palace with the injunction to give it something of the effect of Architecture. He applied, as we might think proper, no ornamentation; instead, he invented a system of colored decoration designed to give body and depth to the framework of iron and timber. He painted the interior with stripes of red, yellow and blue, all separated by white, an arrangement

based on Michel Eugène Chevreul's *De la loi du contraste simultané des couleurs,* of 1839—a law that Hittorff had tried to interpret so very differently at St.-Vincent-de-Paul—and also based on the color experiments of George Field. The theory was all science and calculation, but the effect was as of a fairy palace. "Looking up the nave with its endless rows of pillars," wrote the correspondent of the *Illustrated London News* on May 1, 1851, "the scene vanished from extreme brightness to the hazy indistinctness which Turner alone can paint." The outside was all blue and white. In 1856 Jones published his *Grammar of Ornament,* in which he made clear his belief that the generative forces of the nineteenth century—like religious or moral belief in the past—were science, industry, and commerce, and that it was the business of designers to express these. The artistry that was to give style to this utilitarian form—outlined in his thirty-seven propositions—consisted in proportion systems, geometrical arrangements of pattern and color, scientifically applied. At the end of his book were suggested decorative appliqués evolved from plant forms, a fashion that may have begun in England with Pugin's *Floriated Ornament,* of 1849. It was certainly taken up and marvelously expanded there by such men as James Kennaway Colling, John Lindley, Ralph Nicholson Wornum, Christopher Dresser, Frederick Edward Hulme, and Lewis Foreman Day. In France, as we have seen, Viollet-le-Duc and Ruprich-Robert pursued this path to somewhat different ends. The magical aura that Owen Jones had conjured up with his science at the Crystal Palace he successfully captured once again in his halls of arts and commerce—St. James's Hall, off Regent Street, London, of 1855 to 1858, the Crystal Palace Bazaar, between Great Portland and Oxford streets, London, of 1858, and Osler's shop, Oxford Street, of 1858 to 1860—all long since gone. Each had a roof of iron and glass and plaster painted in primary colors. They caused a sensation. But when it came to providing homes for the solid citizens who paid to hear music or shopped in these emporiums Owen Jones chose to design in a heavy Italianate style, as he did, for example, No. 8 Kensington Palace Gardens, London. He considered it appropriate to the station and needs of his clients.

When one turns to the career of that febrile French seer Hector Horeau (1801–1872), who in 1849, even before Paxton, submitted an iron and glass structure in the Crystal Palace competition, one finds the same candid acceptance of common propriety in the field of domestic and other architecture. A pupil of Eugène-Charles-Frédéric Nepveu (1777–1862) and then of François Debret, he failed to win the Grand Prix in 1826 but, like Owen Jones, traveled for three years throughout Europe and later, in 1837, to North Africa, before settling down to his chosen, constantly frustrating career. He published a spectacular and highly colored *Panorama de l'Égypte et de la Nubie* in 1841. But first he made a name for himself as a builder of iron and glass structures: In 1846 he designed a *jardin d'hiver* at Lyons (built in the following year) and the Château des Fleurs (a bandstand, in effect) for the corner of the Rue Vernet and the Rue Galilée, off the

639. Owen Jones, Osler's shop,
45 Oxford Street, London, 1858–60

640. Augustus Welby Northmore
Pugin, Medieval Court, Crystal
Palace, London, 1851

641. Sir Joseph Paxton, Crystal
Palace, 1851, being reerected at
Sydenham, 1854

Champs-Elysées, in Paris, much praised in 1847 in the *Revue générale de l'architecture* (pp. 254, 410). He published a number of ambitious schemes for improving the drainage of the city, for *abattoirs,* markets, and exhibition buildings. His design for the Halles Centrales, the central market of Paris, a great iron and glass structure similar in appearance to Philibert de l'Orme's design for the Salles des Fêtes Royales, the forerunner of C.-L.-F. Dutert's Galerie des Machines, was first presented in 1844 and developed in the following years. When Victor Baltard and F.-E. Callet were appointed to build that market and began with a ponderous pavilion of stone, Horeau initiated a campaign that brought Baron Haussmann, in 1853, to order its demolition—thus leading to the erection of the iron and glass structures that Baltard and Callet eventually designed. Horeau was furious. He moved in 1855 to England, where he suggested a whole new range of street improvements and exhibited them all, four years later, in the Hanover Square Rooms, London. By then he had built a house in Surrey (untraced) and another at Primrose Hill, London (probably The Poplars, at 18 or 20 Avenue Road; demolished in 1934), illustrated in the review established by Viollet-le-Duc's son, the *Gazette des architectes et du bâtiment,* in 1868. The plan is imaginative, if symmetrical, with splayed wings, but the elevation is decorated with conventional Italian-inspired motifs. In the first volume of the elder Viollet-le-Duc's *Habitations modernes,* of 1875, another of Horeau's houses is illustrated, a farmstead at Ostend, in Belgium, with clumsy brick decoration around the door and window openings, and boldly projecting timber bargeboards and balconies with frets and rude arabesques. A Swiss chalet, it seems, has strayed. Later in life Horeau moved to Madrid, where in 1868 he designed an iron and glass market for the Plaza Cebada. A few years after—while serving a prison sentence in Paris for overenthusiastic support of the Commune—he sketched proposals for a new *hôtel de ville,* once again an ordinary enough, unpretentious sort of building, but with a great glass-roofed court in which all business was to be conducted. Horeau was a hard thinker and a man of immense enterprise and no little adventure, but he, too, accepted, without qualm it seems, that for certain types of building, the conventional hybrid modes were the best.

In America James Bogardus (1800–1874), a manufacturer of machinery, was making four- and five-story fronts for buildings, all of iron and glass, from the late 1840s onward, but he chose to cast them in classically modeled molds, and with his increasing success made them ever more rich and intricate in decoration. The Renaissance style that he applied was to him an essential and fitting part of the whole conception. And, though he had an arrogant disregard of all conventional opinion and ranked the products of engineering extremely high, even James Fergusson (1808–1886), that bombastic philistine, one-time indigo merchant, and archaeologist, the architectural historian who was probably more widely read than any other during the nineteenth century, thought that such buildings as the Crystal Palace were lacking in a sense of solidity and mass, and could not, as he

expressed it, "be elevated to the class of the Fine Arts." Fergusson, it is to be remarked, was general manager, from 1856 to 1858, of the Crystal Palace Company, at Sydenham, where Paxton and Jones had set up an even grander variant of the Hyde Park structure. His most entertaining and certainly most provocative book was *History of the Modern Styles of Architecture,* of 1862 (published together with his *Illustrated Handbook of Architecture,* of 1855, as part of the even more compendious *History of Architecture in All Countries, from the Earliest Times to the Present Day,* issued between 1865 and 1867). At the end of his *History of the Modern Styles of Architecture,* having rejected Greek and Gothic as moribund, and having ranted and raved at the shams of modern architecture, Fergusson yet felt compelled to recommend to his contemporaries that they take up a Renaissance style. "There is yet one other style within whose limits progress still seems possible," he wrote despairingly. "The Renaissance Italian is by no means worked out." Fergusson sought an architecture that was altogether sensibly designed and built, strong and durable, reflecting both in its forms and in its decoration—which he considered of the highest importance—the aspirations and the communal sense of the society that produced it: a banal aim, one might judge, but one that, together with so many other contemporaries, he thought best fulfilled in the Renaissance manner.

No less bathos attaches to those agonized theories offered in that now little-known but, in the nineteenth century, much-read *Rudimentary Treatise on the Principles of Design in Architecture,* first printed in 1850. The author was Edward Lacy Garbett, who was to appeal so much to Horatio Greenough and later American theorists. He staunchly upheld the importance of structural principles, recognizing two systems of structural purity, the Greek and the Gothic, but rejected them at length in favor of a third, as yet unresolved—that of the Italian Renaissance.

Other nineteenth-century prophets—those who most strongly affected nineteenth- and even twentieth-century sensibilities—came to somewhat different conclusions, though they inclined to agree with Fergusson as to the merits of the Crystal Palace. A. W. N. Pugin, that brilliant proselytizer of Gothic, described the building in casual asides in his letters as "the crystal humbug" and "a glass monster." This was not because he disapproved of iron construction or other modern devices and inventions, for he wrote in 1843 in *An Apology for the Revival of Christian Architecture in England,* "Any modern invention which conduces to comfort, cleanliness or durability should be adopted by the consistent architect." Moreover, he made clear in other of his works his approval of modern plumbing systems, gaslights, all manner of mechanical devices, and even the railways, provided that they were designed directly and simply with reference to their use. He liked best what he called "the substantial manner." He loathed the evident lack of mass of the Crystal Palace, and even more the evident indifference to Gothic that it reflected. The Medieval Court he set up in Paxton's building was, in its rich intensity, in sharp contrast to that pared-down structure. The

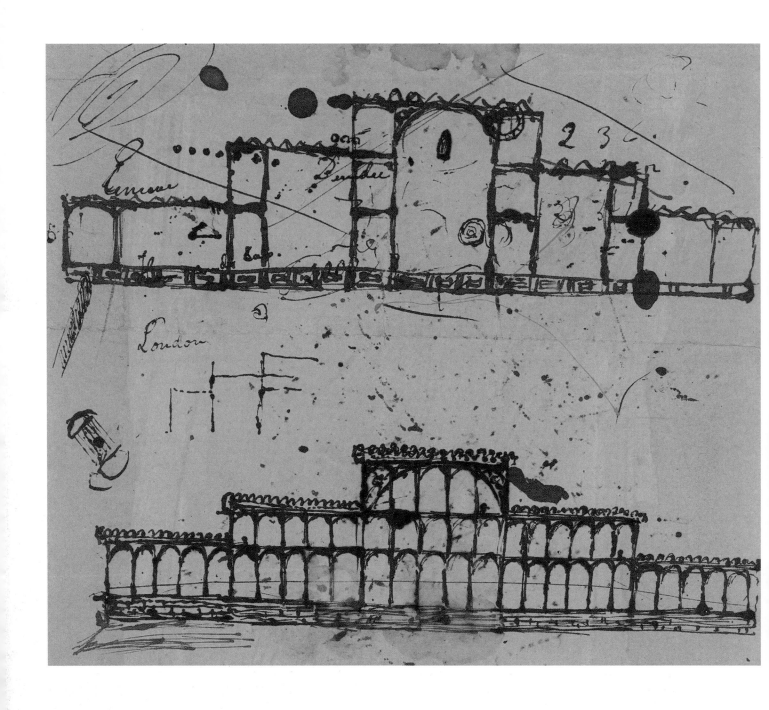

644, 645. *Louis-Auguste Boileau,*
project for a chapel at Saint-Denis,
exterior and interior, 1854

principles that Pugin laid down in 1841 on the first page of *The True*
Principles of Pointed or Christian Architecture have nothing overtly to do with
Gothic. "The two great rules for design are these: 1st, that there should
be no features about a building which are not necessary for convenience,
construction, or propriety; 2nd, that all ornament should consist of
enrichment of the essential construction of the building." However, it is
evident throughout this book, and made quite plain in the second edition,
that the only acceptable style is Gothic. Pugin countenanced no other. He
fought throughout his short and active life for its revival, for it represented
to him the last historical stage at which architecture had been a complete
expression of communities imbued with a true spiritual faith. Pugin had been
converted to Roman Catholicism in 1835. The Reformation, and all that
was associated with it, was thus to him a second fall from grace. In his early
years he adopted the late Gothic style, but as his belief grew that the
Reformation was not the root cause of the fall, merely part of a more general
decay in faith, he retreated to the styles of the early fourteenth and late
thirteenth centuries; these became for him the only true architecture for the
Revival.

Pugin's principles and much of his attitude toward Gothic—even his
identification of it as the true Catholic style—may be traced back,
surprisingly, to so academic a source as Jacques-François Blondel's *Cours*
d'architecture, to which Pugin was no doubt introduced by his father, an
architectural illustrator from France. But Pugin's perfervid moralism is new
to architectural theory. It was most forcefully expounded right from the start,
in the most devastating of all his books, *Contrasts; or, A Parallel Between the*
Noble Edifices of the Fourteenth and Fifteenth Centuries, and Similar Buildings of
the Present Day, issued in 1836. The text is short, but the sixteen contrasted
plates make his meaning clear: All the towns and buildings of the nineteenth
century are degraded and mean; those of the Middle Ages are rewarding
and full, burgeoning with ancient feelings and sentiments. " 'Tis they alone
that can restore pointed architecture to its former glorious state: without
it all that is done will be a tame and heartless copy, true as far as the
mechanism of the style goes, but utterly wanting in that sentiment and
feeling that distinguishes ancient design" (2d ed., 1841, p. 43).

The moral note struck by Pugin was to be the real contribution of England
to nineteenth-century architectural thought. John Ruskin (1819–1900) was
the most eloquent spokesman of the ethical—though not the Catholic—
attitude. His social convictions, however, were to be forcefully and
dogmatically expressed only later in life. Yet already in his very first
writings, "The Poetry of Architecture," published in 1837 and 1838, under
the pseudonym Kata Phusin ("According to Nature"), in *Loudon's Architec-*
tural Magazine, was his whole future understanding made evident. His editor
Johan Claudius Loudon, it is worth remarking, was a man of a different
stamp. All his activity was in sharp contrast to Ruskin's—his obsessive
writing apart. Loudon was a caricature of the dour, industrious Scot; he got

up at seven each morning, breakfasted, and then worked without a break until eight in the evening, writing in the course of his life over four million words, mostly on estate management and horticulture but on much else besides. He was forever producing practical proposals for such things as drainage systems and heating devices. He sought out the woman he was to marry because she had written what must rank as one of the first works of science-fiction, *The Mummy: A Tale of the Twenty-Second Century* (1827). He was building greenhouses years before Paxton and established the techniques of construction that Paxton was later to use at Chatsworth and the Crystal Palace. He was a very early protagonist of iron and glass architecture. But in his myriad publications he also offered all manner of architectural styles (he employed Charles Barry and those rogues E. B. Lamb and S. S. Teulon indiscriminately to make his designs), for, though he had explicit and very commonsensical ideas about architecture, he cared not a jot what it should look like provided that it be usefully organized and soundly built. He cared for everything that Ruskin did not; yet he did care for Ruskin and was generous in his praise of his writings. Ruskin's "The Poetry of Architecture" dealt with qualities of landscape and the manner in which a chalet, a cottage, or a farmhouse might relate to it, in the tradition of Picturesque theory already widely applied in England. However, Ruskin's particular view of the way in which such inevitable, unassuming, and "natural" architecture is a reflection not only of the skills but of the whole way of life of the people who made it was new—though it may well have derived from Jean-Jacques Rousseau's enraptured description of the life and form of a mountain village near Neuchâtel contained in his polemic of 1758 addressed to d'Alembert "*. . . Sur le projet d'établir un théâtre de comédie en [Genève].*" Goodness in architecture, for both men, arises from goodness in man. Later, in those two works most memorably concerned with architecture, *The Seven Lamps of Architecture,* of 1849, and *The Stones of Venice,* issued in three volumes in 1851 and 1853, Ruskin was to enlarge on this theme. In *The Queen of the Air,* of 1869, he was to turn it into an aphorism: "A foolish person builds foolishly, and a wise one sensibly; a virtuous one, beautifully; and a vicious one, basely."

The seven lamps—Sacrifice, Truth, Power, Beauty, Life, Memory, Obedience—have not much to do with architecture, certainly not in any conventional fashion. Ruskin was not greatly interested in the way a building might work, in its organization, or in its structure (though he was vehement in his denunciation of what he recognized as structural deceit). There are no more than one or two plans illustrated in his published works, and no sections; nor, if we are to judge by his drawings and descriptions, was he much taken with mass or volume in architecture. His skill as a draftsman and his passion in writing are directed to details: to doorheads and windows, to capitals and moldings. He focused always on discrete fragments. Architecture itself, he thought, resided in surface adornment, in moldings and sculpture. "Thus," he wrote in "The Lamp of Sacrifice," "I suppose

648. William Slater, project for a
church in the Gothic style with cast-
iron columns, 1856

no one would call the laws architectural which determine the height of a
breastwork or the position of a bastion. But if to the stone facing of that
bastion be added an unnecessary feature, as a cable moulding, *that is*
Architecture." But what excited him above all else was surface pattern, the
texture of things, whether in architecture or nature. His delight in drawing
or describing such patterns was sensual, almost erotic. He saw in the surface,
whether worked by man or weathered by time, the imprint of all nature,
to be caressed by the hand and the eye. No matter if the surface was rough
and ungainly, scarred and broken, provided it be a truthful expression. He
abominated all restoration in architecture, battling furiously against it
through life, and in 1874 refusing the Gold Medal of the Royal Institute
of British Architects became the company included men who were defacing
the ancient buildings he loved. The surface of structures had for him a
sanctity that must not be disturbed (shades here of Chateaubriand). There
was more to it than visual delight. The surface revealed the nature of the
man who had worked it, giving expression to all his joys, passions, and
beliefs; it thus also expressed the nature of the society of which that man
was a part. For good architecture to arise, those responsible must have good
lives and be happy.

Ruskin's ideal society was set somewhere in the Middle Ages, a notion
he had derived first from Thomas Carlyle and later from Pugin. However,
good Evangelical that he was and fearing lest he be tainted by Pugin's
Catholicism, he sharply denied any such influence. He thus rejected all
Renaissance architecture as a sham and upheld Gothic as an image of the
good and the true. But just as there is not as much as one might expect of
architecture in the *The Seven Lamps,* so there is not much in it on Gothic—nor
is there even in *The Stones of Venice.* Ruskin's crusade was not a national one.
He disliked the damp and the gloom of the north and did not look long
at the Gothic monuments of England, or even at those of France (though
in time he learned to admire some of the latter). He preferred the south.
Italian Gothic became for him the symbol of all he loved in architecture—
Giotto's tower at Florence and, even more, the Doges' Palace, at Venice.
Hastily written and added almost haphazardly to the second volume of *The
Stones of Venice,* his chapter "The Nature of Gothic" served nonetheless as
a catechism for the serious-minded architects of England. William Morris,
of whom nothing need here be said, solemnly printed a separate edition
at the Kelmscott Press in 1892. He described it then as "one of the very
few necessary and inevitable utterances of the century." It was the spur to
his career, and to that of Philip Webb, William Lethaby, and a great many
others. "The Nature of Gothic" is, as might be expected, unspecific. Ruskin
approaches his subject through broad categories: savageness, imperfection,
changefulness, redundance, and rigidity. Yet one emerges from it inspired
with a new reverence and feeling for the idea of Gothic. Absolutely, it was
the most potent of all Ruskin's writings on architecture.

In time he turned his attention away from architecture: He thought rather

649, 650. Louis-Auguste Boileau, St.-Paul, Montluçon (Allier), interior, 1864–69

on the nature of society and on what it might be. He became one of the most radical thinkers of his age. He aimed to make England a good, egalitarian society—with equal wages for all (he himself had been left 197,000 pounds on his father's death). Architects, he saw, were impotent; only when the nature of society changed would good architecture arise. In 1864 he was invited to lecture at the Mechanics Institute at Bradford, where a competition was being held for the design of a new exchange. He was expected to advise on the style, which no one doubted he would designate as Gothic. Instead, he told the assembled burghers and businessmen that *he* didn't care a damn what style they got, because *they* didn't. All that concerned them was the making of money. And he thundered on and on about the immorality of their lives and the consequent ugliness of their city. "The only absolutely and unapproachably heroic elements in the soldier's work," he told his audience, "seems to be—that he is paid little for it—and regularly: while you traffickers, and exchangers, and others occupied in presumably benevolent business, like to be paid much for it—and by chance. I never can make out how it is that a *knight*-errant does not expect to be paid for his trouble, but a *pedlar*-errant always does;—that people are willing to take hard knocks for nothing, but never to sell ribands cheap; that they are ready to go on fervent crusades, to recover the tomb of a buried God, but never on any travels to fulfil the orders of a living one;—that they will go anywhere barefoot to preach their faith, but must be well bribed to practise it, and are perfectly ready to give the Gospel gratis, but never the loaves and fishes.

"If you chose to take the matter up on any such soldierly principle; to do your commerce, and your feeding of nations, for fixed salaries; and to be as particular about giving people the best food, and the best cloth, as soldiers are about giving them the best gunpowder, I could carve something for you on your exchange worth looking at. But I can only at present suggest decorating its frieze with pendent purses" (*The Works of Ruskin,* ed. E. T. Cook and A. Wedderburne, vol. 18, p. 450).

The one building with which Ruskin was said to have been closely involved, the University Museum at Oxford, by Sir Thomas Deane and Benjamin Woodward, was not a successful expression of his ideals. He was less involved, though, than is usually thought. He was out of England for much of the building period and was writing hard for most of the rest of the time. The final design was made in 1854, and construction began in the following year, with workmen brought over from Ireland led by the rumbustious James O'Shea. He was to demonstrate in his work all Ruskin's cherished obsessions, thought his insolent disregard for the dignitaries of Oxford led to his deportation in 1860, before the work of carving was complete. Woodward died in the following year, and funds were lacking, so little more was done. The bulk of the work was, however, by then largely executed, with a fantastical covered court all in iron and glass, Gothic in style. Ruskin cannot have much approved of the use of iron, but he was

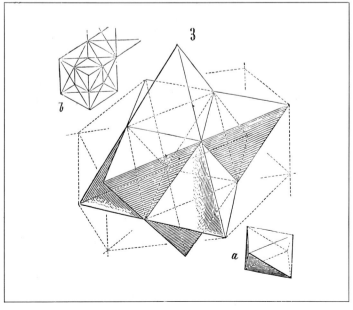

never strongly critical about it. His concern for the joy of a man in his work and for the way he might make his mark on the finished surface had led him, inevitably, to reject the large-scale use of iron in architecture as well as all methods of prefabrication. The workman, he said, was thus degraded. Critics might see the effects of a painting by Turner (a painter he revered) in the nave of the Crystal Palace, but 1851, Ruskin retorted, was the very year in which Turner had died. In fact, Turner was keenly interested in the Crystal Palace. But for Ruskin there was nothing in it either of Turner or of Architecture. "The quantity of thought it expresses is, I suppose," he wrote in 1855 in a note to the second edition of *The Seven Lamps*—a note, incidentally, directed against Garbett—"a single and very admirable thought of Sir Joseph Paxton's, probably not a bit brighter than thousands of thoughts which pass through his active and intelligent brain every hour—that it might be possible to build a greenhouse larger than ever greenhouse was built before. This thought, and some very ordinary algebra, are as much as all that glass can represent of human intellect" (*Works*, vol. 9, p. 456). When he viewed the influence of his own works and writings in 1874 in the preface to the third edition of *The Stones of Venice*, "which has mottled our manufactory chimneys with black and red brick, dignified our banks and drapers' shops with Venetian tracery, and pinched our parish churches into dark and slippery arrangements for the advertisement of cheap coloured glass and pantiles," he felt bound to reject them, too, as pernicious.

On the Continent ethics and social morality were not permitted to dominate architectural theory: No one of any great influence took up architecture as a religious crusade, no one veered from architecture to political theory. Nonetheless, many—indeed, all the key figures—held strong, sometimes violent, political views. Gottfried Semper, the German spokesman, was forced to flee to Belgium and then to France when the antimonarchical revolution in which he was involved had failed. In France, Horeau, as we have seen, was imprisoned for his part in the Commune. Earlier, Gilbert, Blouet, Labrouste, and Duc had been passionately stirred by the ideas of Saint-Simon and Comte, while César Daly, editor of that most influential and sumptuous of journals, the *Revue générale de l'architecture,* was a Fourierist, and even designed a *phalanstère,* which he illustrated in outline in his *Revue.* But there was little else of this sort in it.

Viollet-le-Duc himself had fought on the barricades when young and, after the Franco-Prussian war, when the mood of the country was at a very low ebb, he thought to take up an active political stance. He started to write regularly for *Le centre gauche, Le peuple,* and *Le bien public.* In 1873 he stood in the first municipal elections and was chosen as Republican candidate for Montmartre, a position he was to hold for no more than a year, for he decided then that the Republican government was without morality. He denounced it in *Le centre gauche* and resigned his seat and all government appointments, including that of *Inspecteur Général des Édifices Diocésains.* He was reelected to the city council, although under a different political banner,

653. Eugène-Emmanuel Viollet-le-
Duc, section of a Gothic church, from
his Dictionnaire raisonné de
l'architecture française 1859

and sat on it until his death in 1879. These were honest and courageous steps to take, but there is no need to exaggerate their importance. Viollet-le-Duc had for too long been a compliant courtier under the Second Empire; he had done nothing then to use his influence to improve the world.

The focus of all Viollet-le-Duc's interest in architecture was on construction. He was determined to show that the proper expression of structural principles would produce proper architecture. No one who has read Henry Adam's *Mont-Saint-Michel and Chartres,* packed with quotations from Viollet-le-Duc, can be in any doubt that he was also a man of sensitivity and feeling, acutely responsive to the poetry of Gothic architecture, and that he may be interpreted also in this light; but in his battle against the established architectural conventions, and in particular those established by the École des Beaux-Arts, he was forced to steel his arguments with the most ruthless logic and to interpret Gothic architecture—indeed, all good architecture, in which he included Greek and also Byzantine—as the readily explicable results of determined ends. The principles he adduced in his analysis were to be applied in the fashioning of an architecture for the nineteenth century and even after. He emerges thus as a harsh materialist, crude and overbearing. Yet even those structural principles he had so early explained in the pages of the *Annales archéologiques* were to be but tentatively applied to the exigencies of nineteenth-century architecture. From the first he accepted that new materials, especially iron, must serve as an essential part of nineteenth-century renewal. He was even prepared to use iron for restoration work: He ordered iron window frames for Ste.-Madeleine at Vézelay in 1845, just as Lassus had done for St.-Germain-l'Auxerrois. However, in a report to the Commission des Monuments Historiques of 1850 on the ridiculous cast-iron spire that J.-A. Alavoine had set on top of Rouen cathedral in 1824, Viollet-le-Duc firmly rejected—in much the same manner as had Pugin—the notion that iron might be used to reproduce forms or ornaments that had evolved under different circumstances. There was to be no cast-iron Gothic. He was vehement in his denunciation of all such experiments. On January 11, 1854, Louis-Auguste Boileau (1812-1896), the son of a joiner and himself the maker and carver of the organ loft at St.-Germain-l'Auxerrois, the architect also of a simple mock-Gothic church at Mattaincourt (Vosges) that included cast-iron pews, published a proposal in *La presse* for a church with columns of cast iron to be erected in the Chaussée-d'Antin. On February 18 this was again published, in *L'illustration,* with an enthusiastic commentary by Albert Lenoir. Within a short time a pupil of Percier and Fontaine, Louis-Adrien Lusson (1790–1864), had taken up the idea and proposed it to the archbishop of Paris for a site on the corner of the Rue Monthyon (now Rue Ste.-Cécile) and the Rue du Conservatoire. Work began in the month of March. Boileau, as might be expected, protested most strongly. He replaced Lusson as architect and by December 21, 1855, his new church of St.-Eugène had been consecrated. Externally it is an ordinary enough red-brick box, stuccoed here

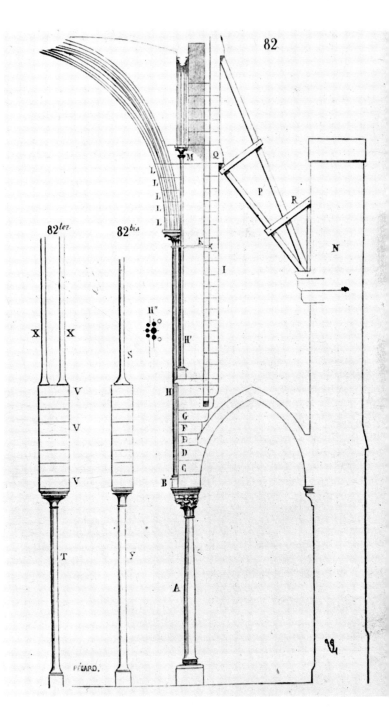

and there and broken by pointed windows, with three gables on the entrance
facade. Internally it is a curious Gothic paraphrase similar to that designed
(possibly in the same year) in England for the Ecclesiological Society, by
William Slater, Richard Cromwell Carpenter's pupil and successor, but
published in *Instrumenta ecclesiastica* only in 1856. All the columns and ribs
and even the traceries of Boileau's church are of iron. The vaults are covered
with sheets of metal. The building caused much excitement and comment.
César Daly condemned it early, in February 1855, long before its
completion, in the *Revue générale de l'architecture,* as a conception of the utmost
naivety. Two years later he was to reject it as too much the railway shed:
"Dans lesquelles toutefois la colonne en fonte réussit très bien, parce que
là l'effet d'art résulte uniquement de l'aménagement, non pas le plus
monumental, dans le sens propre du mot, mais le plus commode, d'un grand
espace qu'on doit disposer, autant que possible, de façon à en utiliser toutes
les parties et à y laisser largement pénétrer le jour; dans une église, au
contraire, la colonne, il nous semble, est tout à la fois faite pour soutenir
et pour meubler" (p. 100). But Michel Chevalier published a highly
appreciative account of Boileau's paraphrase in the *Journal des débats* on June
1, 1855, and at once proposed that the system be adopted for the cathedrals
of Moulins and Marseilles and also for the new churches at Montpellier and
Lille. Chevalier's tribute drew forth a rude reply from Viollet-le-Duc. In
the *Encyclopédie d'architecture,* in the same month, he wrote, "Un système dont
toute la solidité réside dans l'extrême précision des assemblages se
rapproche plus de l'art du mécanicien que de l'art de l'architecture. . . . M.
Boileau, le directeur de la construction de Saint-Eugène, quelque ingénieux
qu'il soit, n'était pas architecte, c'était un fort habile menuisier, et quoi qu'on
fasse, la première éducation pratique ne se remplace pas." It was, he added,
a puerile pastiche in bad taste. Boileau replied in the following month with
more restraint than might be expected. He was doing no more, he said, than
Viollet-le-Duc himself had suggested in his writings. Approving of the
principles of Gothic construction, he had tried to interpret them in the way
in which thirteenth-century masons themselves might have done had they
had present-day resources. Viollet-le-Duc's distaste, he suggested, was
aroused because the forms and arrangements of Gothic had not been
slavishly copied. Viollet-le-Duc was enraged. He responded in the same
issue of the *Encyclopédie d'architecture,* raising a host of technical issues and
also that question pertinent to the whole problem: "Pourquoi des arcs,
quand on peut avoir des poutres de fonte ou de tôle d'une énorme portée?
Pourquoi ne pas se servir de ces matières comme les ingénieurs anglais et
français sont arrivés à le faire, c'est-à-dire en simplifiant de jour en jour les
formes, en rompant franchement avec les vieilles traditions imposées par
la routine?" But there is small cause to think that Viollet-le-Duc would have
liked St.-Eugène any better had it resembled more closely a railway shed.
Along with César Daly and most of his fellow critics in France, he had not
admired the Crystal Palace. Henri Sirodot had dismissed it in the *Revue*

655. Jules Saulnier, Menier chocolate factory, Noisiel-sur-Marne, 1869, 1871–72

656. Eugène Train, Collège Chaptal, Paris, 1863–75, a celebrated example of mixed brick, terra-cotta, colored ceramic, and exposed iron construction that started a fashion even before its completion

générale de l'architecture in 1851 as no more than a giant greenhouse, without pretensions to architecture (p. 154).

Boileau was unabashed. Already in a small brochure issued in September 1854 he had published his first, and even more startling, project for a church of iron as *La nouvelle forme architecturale.* He showed tenuous columns of iron supporting a system of segmental arches and ribs of iron, carrying in turn an array of ribbed vaults, built up one against another to form a pyramidal composition. The curved vaults are exhibited both inside and out. The columns of iron, boldly expressed inside, are sheathed on the outside perimeter with stone. But the window areas between remain unusually large. The traceries with which they are filled are yet more unusual. They are made up of intersecting arcs to form a pattern of lines that relates to the segmental arches of the vaults. Two towers of a similar idiosyncratic composition stand at the west end of the church. Altogether, the design is freakish, inspired not only by Gothic examples but also, there is little doubt, by Moorish architecture (extracts from Owen Jones's lavish book on the Alhambra were published in the *Revue générale de l'architecture* in 1844, and one plate in particular seems to have provided the prototype for Boileau). He was later to produce many and far more ambitious variations on this design, to illustrate them, and to issue them together with the most persuasive of literary propaganda: In 1881 he published *Les principes et exemples d'architecture ferronnière,* five years later the *Histoire critique de l'invention en architecture,* and in 1889 *Les préludes de l'architecture du XXᵉ siècle et l'exposition du centenaire,* a work of prophetic intention. But, apart from the great Magasins du Bon Marché, a department store begun, together with his son Louis-Charles, in 1869, his executed works showed little advance on St.-Eugène, if indeed they attained its standard of consistency. He added an iron-ribbed dome to his early reinforced-concrete church of Le Vésinet (Yvelines) in 1863, in the same year began St.-Paul, Place J. Dormoy, at Montluçon (Allier), and then in 1869 started work on St.-Étienne at Juilly (Seine-et-Marne)—where Lamennais and his disciples had installed themselves in 1830—a church not unlike St.-Eugène. In 1868 he built Notre-Dame-de-France in Leicester Place, London, a curious, iron-framed structure (demolished in 1957) set within the circular shell of Robert Barker's old panorama.

Viollet-le-Duc ignored this activity. His disciple J.-E.-A. de Baudot, however, attacked Boileau's designs for the church at Le Vésinet in 1863 in the *Gazette des architectes et du bâtiment* and three years later castigated the project Boileau had submitted in the Rambouillet competition (won, it may be remembered, by de Baudot himself, with a design incorporating columns of iron). "Le parti général adopté par l'architecte," he wrote, "n'est pas un système, mais simplement l'application de métal à des formes qui ne résultent pas des propriétés des matériaux employés" (p. 97). De Baudot sought thus firmly to disassociate his design from Boileau's. Later he was to find that Boileau was, after all, a liberating stimulus; when he came to design a church at Montmartre he took up a great deal from him. But the dispute with

Boileau forced Viollet-le-Duc at once to consider more seriously the role of iron in architecture. In the article on construction in the fourth volume of the *Dictionnaire raisonné de l'architecture française,* issued in 1860, he showed very simply how iron, and timber, too, might be substituted for the structural members of a Gothic church, suggesting in this way how iron might be used in the nineteenth century. He himself used it thus unenterprisingly (as Butterfield and other such Gothic enthusiasts had done earlier in England) for the trusses of the sacristy of the cathedral at Rheims, designed in July 1862, but not built until 1870, and also for the more adeptly designed trusses for the roofs of the Château de Pierrefonds (1862). The Maison du Personnel at Notre-Dame in Paris, also with simple trusses of iron, was built in 1866. The use of iron was a particularly sensitive issue for Viollet-le-Duc at this period (hence de Baudot's shamefaced attack on Boileau's Rambouillet design) because Alfred Darcel, reviewing architecture at the Salon of 1864 in the *Gazette des beaux-arts* and, more important, César Daly in the editorial and in an assessment of a confessional designed twenty years earlier by Lassus for St.-Germain-l'Auxerrois included in the *Revue générale* in 1866, and also Bourgeois de Lagny in his review of the Salon of the same year in the newly founded *Moniteur des architectes,* had all vigorously attacked those tendencies that they associated then with Viollet-le-Duc. The Rambouillet church designs were a particular pretext for scorn. "L'école rationaliste," wrote Daly (thus categorizing Viollet-le-Duc and his disciples), "qui tend en ce moment à transformer l'*art architectural* en *architecture industrielle,* proclam[e] ainsi devant tous son scepticisme en matière d'art, son respect exclusif pour la science et l'utile" (p. 5). Bourgeois de Lagny, like Darcel earlier, even associated Viollet-le-Duc and his disciples with Boileau—an association they dreaded. Everyone regarded Boileau as a crank. But Bourgeois de Lagny was perhaps even more damaging when he linked them with the Realists, then being so widely discussed. "Le réalisme architectural (ou la construction avec l'absence d'art)," he concluded, "n'a qu'un rôle très-secondaire à remplir dans le développement de l'art monumental" (p. 81). Viollet-le-Duc had long been a friend of Champfleury and, in the *Journal des débats,* on August 7, 1863, had reviewed his collected essays, *Réalisme,* with what best tact he could. However, when he commented on other products of the Realist school, the novels of Flaubert, in letters to Mérimée, he was unequivocal in his contempt. Mérimée shared his opinions: "J'ai lu le roman de Flaubert," he wrote on December 29, 1869, of *L'éducation sentimentale.* "Hélas! C'est un mathématicien qui se trompe," a remark that both Daly and Bourgeois de Lagny would willingly have applied at that time to Viollet-le-Duc.

Viollet-le-Duc's answer to this onslaught was the astounding designs contained in the twelfth *Entretien,* dating from 1866 or just after. There, in illustrations for a *hôtel de ville* supported by V-poles and for other large halls combining struts and frameworks of iron supporting masonry vaults— but especially in his hall for three thousand people—he showed how an

architecture for the future might be forged. Modest in his estimation of his creative abilities, he no doubt saw that his designs were ungainly and lacking in style, but they were yet an attempt of a determined and desperate sort to achieve style. The polyhedral hall is indeed a naive illustration of style as defined in that very same year, 1866, not in the *Entretiens,* as one might expect, but in the eighth volume of the *Dictionnaire raisonné de l'architecture française. "Le style,"* Viollet-le-Duc wrote (no longer part, if it ever had been for him, of period styles), *"est la manifestation d'un idéal établi sur un principe"* (p. 475). To him, this great guiding principle was, ultimately, that of the world, of the universe itself. The secret of all its structure, of all its stability, was the equilateral triangle, upon which all the structure of all matter, all fine form, was based. The earth's crust had style. There is a lot more to his argument, and more subtlety than is here indicated, but even this short exposition is enough to demonstrate how he had moved from Gothic Revivalism to the most inclusive of guiding principles and how he hoped that they might be interpreted. No one would say that he succeeded, but the breadth of his outlook was without equal.

Not many of his contemporaries were better equipped than Viollet-le-Duc to take up his challenge or to provide an example of his intentions. Those that did make the attempt were not trained by him. A pupil of Horeau, Jules-Désiré Bourdais (1835–1915), about 1868 built a small chapel at Négreplisse (Tarn-et-Garonne) with a roof supported by four conspicuous timber struts, composed in a manner reminiscent of the illustrations offered in the *Entretiens.* Jules Saulnier completed a series of great brick structures for the Menier chemical factory at Saint-Denis in 1865; then, four years after, began the design of that celebrated iron-framed building across the Marne at Noisiel, for the Menier chocolate works. Building did not start for another two years but was sufficiently advanced for Viollet-le-Duc to draw it to the attention of his readers in the eighteenth *Entretien,* written in 1871 or early in 1872. It was illustrated in full in the *Encyclopédie d'architecture* in 1874 and in the years that followed, together with Saulnier's subsidiary buildings and remarkable workers' housing. The splendid building over the river gleaming with richly colored and patterned glazed bricks is thought to be the first complete iron-framed structure ever erected. This may indeed be the case. But the diagonal metal framework that is so boldy exposed on the facade commemorates a timber-framed structure erected on the same site between 1840 and 1855 by Saulnier's master, Bonneau, which in turn was based on a surviving medieval construction. Viollet-le-Duc may, nonetheless, have acted as a stimulus to Saulnier. Less doubtful is his influence on the architect of the library of the École de Droit, Rue Cujas, Paris, built between May 1876 and June 1878 by Louis-Ernest Lheureux (1827–1898), a pupil of Henri Labrouste. Lheureux had worked with Labrouste on the Collège Ste.-Barbe, just across the street, where he also built the Salle de Dessin. All these buildings—the facade of the College apart—are now gone, as is the second hall that Lheureux added to the first, beginning in 1880.

659. Louis-Ernest Lheureux,
Bibliothèque de l'École de Droit,
Paris, second reading room, 1880,
1893–98

In both, arrangements of cast-iron brackets and ceiling beams, with infilling panels of brickwork, were striking interpretations of Viollet-le-Duc's ideas but they were even more notable as examples of the reserve and monumental splendor that one associates with the name of Labrouste. The stone facade of the first hall, admirably articulated with three tall arches and a panel of lettering, was among the finest examples of French nineteenth-century architecture. Lheureux did little else of this quality, though his designs for the Entrepôt, the wine warehouses, at Bercy, Paris, approved in 1877 by Viollet-le-Duc himself—in his role as committee member for the city council—were not unworthy successors; iron-framed buildings, with infilling panels of glazed brickwork. The first phase of building was complete by 1886, but this has now disappeared. There is not much else dating from this period to bear witness to the theories of Viollet-le-Duc.

"Nous faisons de l'architecture de sentiment," Viollet-le-Duc wrote angrily in 1871 in the seventeenth *Entretien,* "comme nous avons fait de la politique de sentiment, la guerre de sentiment. . . . Il faudrait songer à faire intervenir en tout ceci la froide raison, le bon sens pratique, l'étude des nécessités du temps, des perfectionnements fournis par l'industrie, des moyens économiques, des questions d'hygiène et de salubrité" (p. 296). This was the note he struck again in the conclusion to the *Entretiens,* an emphasis upon practical wisdom and analytical investigation, which he believed was best expressed in the work of engineers: in particular, that engineer of the École des Ponts et Chaussées Auguste Choisy (1841–1919).

Choisy, in his studies of the art of construction in history, even more perhaps in his devasting *Histoire de l'architecture,* of 1903, fittingly resolved all these issues, over which Viollet-le-Duc had pondered and puzzled, in a most ruthless conclusion. Choisy's brilliant illustrations reduced the complexities of all architecture to a few simple lines. Choisy provides the natural ending to the period we have studied, for he condensed not only Viollet-le-Duc's but all architectural theory into the simplest of aphorisms and diagrams. His very last work was an edition of Vitruvius, published in 1909, the final occasion on which that old Roman was edited for architects—and how very different it was from Perrault's, though one can see the connection. But there is yet one more architect who demands consideration before our conclusion is reached. That man is Gottfried Semper, a pupil of Gärtner, an architect of a distinctly lackluster kind.

Semper, like Viollet-le-Duc, was ultimately concerned with the problem of style. His preoccupation with this question antedated even Viollet-le-Duc's. His first attempt to explain it was in *Die vier Elemente der Baukunst,* published in Brunswick late in 1851, but based on lectures he had prepared in London, where he was established from 1851 to 1855. While in London, he was in close contact with Owen Jones and Henry Cole, for whom he acted as an investigator of Meyer's enameling process at Sèvres and Minton's tileworks at Trent. Semper was also responsible for the arrangement of some of the exhibits at the Crystal Palace. He could not, however, approve of

660. Auguste Choisy, isometric view of J.-G. Soufflot's Ste.-Geneviève, Paris from Choisy's Histoire de l'architecture, *1903*

661. Gottfried Semper, Wreath, *plate from his* Der Stil, *vol. 1, 1860*

this building since he believed that iron, when thus logically used, was unable to produce monumental form. One of his pupils, whom we know only by his initials, L. H., writing in 1900 in *La construction moderne,* summed up his beliefs: "Il y a deux catégories de constructions: 1ᵉ celles dont chaque élément est en lui-même stable (comme le temple de Paestum). C'est ce qui caractérise la construction monumentale; 2ᵉ celles dont les éléments ne doivent leur stabilité qu'à leur assemblage; c'est ce qui caractérise la construction des meubles, des chaises, par example. Entre ces deux extrêmes il y a toute une série de degrés qui donnent des structures plus ou moins monumentales suivant qu'elles se rapprochent de l'un des systèmes ou de l'autre. La cathédrale gothique serait donc moins monumental que le temple de Paestum, et le Palais de cristal ne serait pas du tout monumental" (p. 525). But it was there, at the Crystal Palace, overwhelmed by the sheer number and variety of artifacts, that he determined to evolve some system whereby the meaning of all such creative endeavor might be grasped and explained. He had earlier marveled in Paris at the ordering devices adopted at the Jardin des Plantes by that great biologist Georges Cuvier, who had first put forward a classificatory system based not on the resemblance of creatures and their parts but rather on the functioning of their organs and other vital processes. The key to the theory that Semper was to propose for the works of man was a small exhibit at the Crystal Palace, a model of a Carib hut, from the village of Arima, near Port of Spain, Trinidad. This was the work of Manuel Sorzano and was filled with utensils and other objects, mostly of Spanish or modern West Indian origin. It was not a primitive hut, but it made manifest the four processes that Semper was to uphold as the prime generators of everything made by man. He made no differentiation between the arts and the crafts. His developed theory is contained in *Der Stil,* published in Munich in two volumes, in 1860 and 1863. The third volume, which was to treat of architecture, was never completed. But this scarcely matters. The tenor of the theory is clear. Semper conceived four essential processes of making: weaving, molding, building in timber, and building in stone, sometimes reduced to heaping (to which he reluctantly appended metalworking). Each of these involved particular materials: textiles, ceramics, wood, and stone. Each in turn resulted in a particular element of architecture: the enclosing wall and all decorative pattern; the base and the hearth; the system of support; and the masonry wall, which might eventually serve to replace any of the former. Everything in art and architecture and all the crafts he held to be reducible to these processes and the materials associated with them. The highest form of expression was architecture, as it contains them all. But it was not, as must already be evident, the first of the arts to emerge; indeed, it derived from the four crafts, and thus suggests that Semper upheld a theory of the practical and useful origin of all art and architecture. His "materialist" stance has often been derided. But this is to misinterpret him willfully, for he believed that the crafts were originally developed for symbolical purposes. Long before man

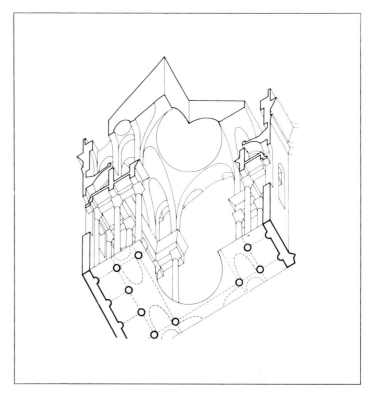

made a house, before he molded a hearth or a pot, he had started to weave and to plait, to make a wreath. The wreath is offered at the beginning of *Der Stil* as the first of the fully fashioned, expressive products of man.

According to Semper's theory, most patterns spring from the art (or the craft, if we prefer to call it that) of weaving. Patterns thus precede the development of structural form, so that ornament may be seen as more basic than structure. The developed theory also includes the way in which religious, social, and political institutions condition the processes of making to give fit and poetic expression to forms. But Semper himself was never to succeed in giving adequate shape to his ideas—not even to the extent that Viollet-le-Duc did. He built hugely—in Dresden, where he put up two successive opera houses (begun in 1837 and 1871); in Zurich, where he became professor in 1855 at the Eidgenössische Technische Hochschule and began to build the new school in 1859; and in Vienna, where he started construction on the Kunst und Naturhistorisches Museums and Hofburgthe-

ter in 1872. There was a lot more besides, but his architecture is all undistinguished. In the prolegomena to *Der Stil* he was able to hold up no more challenging a style for future development than that of the cinquecento, it "not being complete in itself." "Die Gefahr für die Erhaltung jener Baukunst der Wiedergeburt die, zugleich mit der Malerei und der Bildnerei des Cinquecento, und in gleichem Grade, unübertroffen dasteht, ohne, wie das Gothische, in sich fertig zu sein, keine Seite zu weiterer Entwicklung zu bieten, liegt in der Thatsache, dass sie nur durch wahrhaft künstlerische Hand ausführbar ist, aber durch Pfuscherei, die heutzutage verlangt wird, sofort in trivialste Formengemeinheit ausartet" (vol. 1, p. xvii). Semper despised Gothic, in particular after 1844 when he was overtaken by Sir George Gilbert Scott in the Nikolaikirche competition at Hamburg. The ideas of the three great European theorists—Ruskin, Viollet-le-Duc, and Semper—were not readily absorbed. They were not to be taken up outside their own countries until late in the century. Semper's stay in England from 1851 to 1855 no doubt ensured an early interest in his work, in particular in the orbit of the South Kensington Schools of Design, but none of his works was translated. His ideas on the design of urns or vases were adopted in 1862 by Christopher Dresser (1834–1904) for *The Art of Decorative Design,* and later, without acknowledgment, for *Principles of Decorative Design* (1873). Yet as late as 1884, when Lawrence Harvey read "Semper's Theory of Evolution in Architectural Ornament" to the Royal Institute of British Architects, he began with the words, "Perhaps many of my British colleagues have never heard of Semper" (*Transactions,* 1885, vol. 1, p. 29).

One might think that Semper's earlier sojourns in France, in 1826 and 1827, in 1829 and 1830, and from 1849 to 1851, also ensured a heightened interest in his works when they appeared, but there is no hint of any. Viollet-le-Duc owned a copy of *Der Stil,* but was not equipped to read it. His analysis of urns or water vessels in the sixth *Entretien,* which might be taken as a rebuke to or even as a parody of Semper's, was written in 1859, before the publication of Semper's book. Semper, however, had read the four *Entretiens* issued in 1858, for he was quick to reject Viollet-le-Duc's notions on the design of Doric columns; he mocked him in *Der Stil* as a materialist.

Ruskin, so widely read in England, was but slowly acknowledged in France. Mérimée intended to write an article on him as early as 1856, a few years after Mérimée's return from England with Viollet-le-Duc, but nothing came of it. Viollet-le-Duc made no mention of Ruskin. The first article to appear in France on Ruskin, signed "J. C," in the *Revue britannique* of 1856, was hostile. The first important studies were J.-A. Milsand's two articles in the *Revue des deux mondes* of July 1860 and August 1861, issued together as a book in 1864. But it was not for his architectural criticism that Ruskin was admired. Robert de La Sizeranne's celebrated *Ruskin et la religion de la beauté* produced the same reaction in France in 1897 that had been provoked exactly twenty years before in England, when Walter Pater's blasphemous

essay "The School of Giorgione" was published in the *Fortnightly Review*. "Art, then," Pater wrote (and he thought this of architecure too), "is ... always striving to be independent of the mere intelligence, to become a matter of pure perception, to get rid of its responsibilities to its subject or material" (p. 530). Ruskin's message was seen in France in this light; the moral and intellectual elements in art that he so staunchly upheld were largely overlooked—though it is fair to note that Charles Lucas, writing his obituary in *La construction moderne*, in January 1900, described Ruskin as a moralist. Marcel Proust became his greatest admirer; to him Ruskin and Pater represented all that Viollet-le-Duc was not. By 1904 Proust had published his translation of *The Bible of Amiens*. Four years earlier *The Seven Lamps of Architecture* had appeared in French. By then Ruskin had died, like Pugin, mad.

Ruskin himself, surprisingly, looked upon the works of Viollet-le-Duc with a measured respect. He saw to it that the great *Dictionnaire raisonné de l'architecture française* was purchased for his students at Oxford, though he mentioned it only with passing scorn in his lectures of 1873; but he returned to the subject eleven years later as Slade Professor: "And here I must advise you that in all points of history relating to the period between 800 and 1200, you will find M. Viollet-le-Duc, incidentally throughout his *Dictionary of Architecture*, the best-informed, most intelligent, and most thoughtful of guides. His knowledge of architecure, carried down into the most minutely practical details—(which are often the most significant,) and embracing, over the entire surface of France, the buildings even of the most secluded villages; his artistic enthusiasm, balanced by the acutest sagacity, and his patriotism, by the frankest candour, render his analysis of history during that active and constructive period the most valuable known to me, and certainly, in its field, exhaustive. Of the latter nationality his account is imperfect, owing to his professional interest in the mere *science* of architecture, and comparative insensibility to the power of sculpture" (*Works*, vol. 33, p. 465).

This passage, long, eloquent, and rambling, it typical of the late Ruskin, but its general tone is unexpected in its sympathy. For, though fully conscious of what he regarded as Viollet-le-Duc's failings in sensibility, and horrified by them, Ruskin was yet willing to recognize the achievement represented by the *Dictionnaire raisonné de l'architecture française:* "Were you not glad when that book came out?" Sir Sidney Cockerell asked him in 1888. "No, I was very jealous," he replied, "I ought to have written it myself." Certainly he read it again and again, and recommended it often. He was fascinated by it, and also by Viollet-le-Duc. On October 18, 1882, he recorded this poignant note in his diary: "Disturbed sleep, dreaming I had introduced myself to M. Viol[let]-le-Duc and that he wouldn't have anything to say to me."

But perhaps more revealing of Ruskin's relation to Viollet-le-Duc is his response to another of his books, *Le massif du Mont Blanc*, of 1876. Almost exact contemporaries, strongly opposed in sentiment and outlook, Ruskin and Viollet-le-Duc yet shared interests to an uncanny degree. Both were passionate geologists, both traveled on all possible occasions to view the Swiss Alps. After the disappointments of 1863, when he was hounded out of the École des Beaux-Arts by the students he had thought to indoctrinate, Viollet-le-Duc first sought solitude, strength, and reassurance in the healing springs of alpine scenery. Thereafter he went back each year, for eight weeks in the summer. In 1872 he built himself a chalet at Chamonix, two years later a house at Lausanne, La Vedette (demolished in 1976), where he died and was buried. Viollet-le-Duc was not a climber, but his relentless urge to activity drove him up the mountains. He started to survey Mont Blanc, often climbing steadily for eight hours to reach a vantage point, only to find the mountains obscured by clouds. Undeterred, he would return the next day to take his readings. He was tireless in his task. By 1876 he was able to issue both a most detailed map of Mont Blanc and a study of that mountain. Cutting the leaves of that book in this same year, as he set out on his journey to Switzerland, Ruskin contemplated, he wrote, "the splendid dash of its first sentence into space—'La croûte terrestre, refroidie au moment du plissement qui a formé le massif du Mont Blanc,'—with

———. *Parere su l'architettura.* Rome, 1765.

———. *Diverse maniere d'adornare i cammini.* Rome, 1769.

———. *Différentes vues de quelques restes de trois grands édifices qui subsistent encore dans le milieu de l'ancienne ville de Pesto.* Rome, 1778.

PUGIN, A. W. N. *Contrasts; or, A Parallel Between the Noble Edifices of the Fourteenth and Fifteenth Centuries, and Similar Buildings of the Present Day.* London, 1836.

———. *The True Principles of Pointed or Christian Architecture.* London, 1841.

———. *An Apology for the Revival of Christian Architecture in England.* London, 1843.

QUATREMÈRE DE QUINCY, A.-C. *Le Jupiter Olympien; ou, l'art de la sculpture antique considérée sous un nouveau point de vue.* Paris, 1815.

RONDELET, J. *Traité théorique et pratique de l'art de bâtir.* Paris, 1802–3.

RUSKIN, J. *The Seven Lamps of Architecture.* New York, 1849.

SCHINKEL, K. F. *Sammlung architektonischer Entwürfe.* 28 portfolios. Berlin, 1819–40.

———. *Werke der höheren Baukunst für die Ausführung erfunden.* 2 vols. 1842–48.

SCOTT, G. G. *Personal and Professional Recollections.* London, 1879.

SEMPER, G. *Der Stil in den technischen und tektonischen Kunsten.* Frankfurt-am-Main, 1860–63.

SOANE, J. *Plans, Elevations, and Sections of Buildings Erected in the Counties of Norfolk, Suffolk, Yorkshire, etcetera.* London, 1788.

———. *Sketches in Architecture.* London, 1798.

———. *Designs for Public and Private Buildings.* London, 1828.

———. *Description of the House and Museum on the North Side of Lincoln's Inn Fields, the Residence of John Soane.* London, 1835–36.

SPON, J. *Voyage d'Italie, de Dalmatie, de Grèce, et du Levant, fait aux années 1675 et 1676.* Lyons, 1676.

STUART, J., and REVETT, N. *The Antiquities of Athens.* 4 vols. London, 1762–1816.

TALLIS, J. *Tallis's History and Description of the Crystal Palace.* London and New York, 1852.

VIOLLET-LE-DUC, E.-E. *Dictionnaire raisonné de l'architecture française du XIe au XVIe siècle.* 10 vols. Paris, 1854–68.

———. *Entretiens sur l'architecture.* Paris, 1863–72.

FRANCE

BABEAU, A. A. *La ville sous l'Ancien Régime.* Paris, 1880.

BALLOT, M. J. *Le décor intérieur au XVIIIe siècle à Paris et dans la région parisienne.* Paris, 1930.

BELEVITCH-STANKEVITCH, H. *Le goût chinois en France au temps de Louis XIV.* 1910. Reprint. Geneva, 1970.

BENOIT, F. *L'art français sous la Révolution et l'Empire: les doctrines, les idées, les genres.* Paris, 1897.

BLOMFIELD, R. *A History of French Architecture from 1661 to 1774.* 2 vols. London, 1921.

BRAUNSCHWIG, M. *L'Abbé Dubos, renovateur de la critique au XVIIIe siècle.* Toulouse, 1904.

BRUNEL, G., ed. *Piranèse et les français, 1740–1790.* Rome, 1978.

CASSIRER, K. *Die ästhetischen Hauptbegriffe der französischen Architektur-Theoretiker von 1650–1780.* Berlin, [1909?].

CHANGNEAU, C. et al. *Jardins en France, 1760–1820.* Exhibition catalogue. Paris, 1977.

CHARVET, E.-L.-G. *Lyon artistique: architectes, notices biographiques et bibliographiques avec une petite note des édifices et la liste chronologique des noms.* Lyons, 1899.

CHOPPIN DE JANVRY, O. "Le Desert de Retz." *Bulletin de la Société de l'Histoire de l'Art Français,* Année 1970, pp. 125–48.

CLOZIER, R. *La Gare du Nord.* Paris, 1940.

CONTET, F. et al. *Les vieux hôtels de Paris.* 2 vols. Paris, 1908–37.

CORDIER, H. *Le Chine en France au XVIIIe siècle.* Paris, 1910.

COUSSILLAN, A. A. [HILLAIRET, J.]. *Dictionnaire historique des rues de Paris.* 2 vols. Paris, 1968.

DARTEIN, F. DE. *Études sur les ponts en pierre remarquables par leur décoration: Antérieurs au XIXe siècle.* 4 vols. Paris, 1907–12.

DELABORDE, H. *L'Académie des Beaux-Arts depuis la fondation de l'Institut de France.* Paris, 1891.

DESHAIRS, L. *Bordeaux, architecture et decoration au dix-huitième siècle.* Paris, 1907.

———. *Aix-en-Provence, architecture et décoration aux dix-septième et dix-huitième siècles.* Paris, 1909.

———. *Dijon, architecture et décoration au dix-septième et dix-huitième siècles.* Paris, 1909.

DREXLER, A., ed. *The Architecture of the École des Beaux-Arts.* New York, 1978.

ERIKSEN, S. *Early Neo-Classicism in France.* London, 1974.

D'ESPOUY, H., ed. *Les Grands Prix de Rome d'architecture: 1850–1900, 1900–1905.* 2 vols. Paris, n.d.

———. *Monuments antiques, relevés et restaurés par les architectes pensionnaires de l'Académie de France à Rome.* 2 vols. Paris, n.d.

GALLET, M. *Paris Domestic Architecture of the 18th Century.* London, 1972.

GANAY, E. DE. "Les jardins à l'anglaise en France." 1923. Ms. in 2 vols., Bibliothèque des Arts Décoratifs, Paris.

GIEDION, S. *Bauen in Frankreich, Eisen, Eisenbeton.* Leipzig, 1928.

GRUBER, A. C. *Les grandes fêtes et leurs décors à l'époque de Louis XVI.* Geneva, 1972.

HAUTECOEUR, L. *Histoire de l'architecture classique en France.* Vols. 3–4. Paris, 1950–57.

———. *Paris de 1715 à nos jours.* Paris, 1972.

———. "Les places en France au XVIIIe siècle." *Gazette des beaux-arts* 85 (1975): 89–116.

HÉLIOT, P. "La fin de l'architecture gothique dans le nord de la France aux XVIIe et XVIIIe siècles." *Bulletin de la Comm. Royale des Monuments et des Sites* 8 (1957).

HERMANN, W. *Laugier and 18th-Century French Theory.* London, 1962.

HUNT, H. J. *Le socialisme et le romantisme en France.* Oxford, 1935.

JARRY, P. *La guirlande de Paris; ou, maisons de plaisance des environs, au XVIIe et au XVIIIe siècle.* Paris, 1928–31.

KALNEIN, W. G., and LEVEY, M. *Art and Architecture of the Eighteenth Century in France.* Baltimore and Harmondsworth, 1972.

KIMBALL, S. F. *The Creation of the Rococo.* 1943. Reprint. New York, 1964.

LEITH, J. A. *The Idea of Art as Propaganda in France, 1750–1799.* Toronto, 1965.

LELIÈVRE, P. *L'urbanisme et l'architecture à Nantes au XVIIIe siècle.* Nantes, 1942.

LÉON, P. *La vie des monuments français: destruction, restauration.* Paris, 1951.

LEONARD, C. M. *Lyon Transformed: Public Works of the Second Empire, 1853–1864.* Berkeley and Los Angeles, 1961.

LOCQUIN, J. *La peinture d'histoire en France de 1747 à 1785.* Paris, 1912.

LUCAS, C. L. A. *Étude sur les habitations à bon marché en France et à l'étranger.* Paris, 1899.

MAGNE, L. *L'architecture française du siècle.* Paris, 1889.

MALLION, J. *Victor Hugo et l'art architectural.* Paris, 1962.

MARION, M. *Dictionnaire des institutions de la France aux XVIIe et XVIIIe siècles.* Rev. ed. Paris, 1968.

MAROT, P. *La Place Royale de Nancy.* Nancy, 1966.

MIDDLETON, R. D. "The Abbé de Cordemoy and the Graeco-Gothic Ideal: A Prelude to Romantic Classicism." *Journal of the Warburg and Courtauld Institutes* 25 (1962): 278–320; 26 (1963): 90–123.

MORNET, D. *Le sentiment de la nature en France de J.-J. Rousseau à Bernardin de Saint-Pierre.* Paris, 1907.

———. *Le romantisme en France au XVIIIe siècle.* Paris, 1912.

MORTIER, R. *La Poetique des ruines.* Geneva, 1974.

MOULIN, M. *L'architecture civile et militaire au XVIIIe siècle en Aunis et Saintonge.* La Rochelle, 1972.

MULLER, E., and CACHEUX, E. *Habitations ouvrières et agricoles.* Paris, 1855–56.

NIÈRES, C. *La reconstruction d'une ville au XVIIIe siècle: Rennes 1720–1760.* Paris, 1972.

NOLHAC, P. DE. *Hubert Robert.* Paris, 1910.

———. *Histoire du château de Versailles: Versailles au XVIIIe siècle.* Paris, 1918.

PARISET, F. G. *Histoire de Bordeaux, 1714–1814.* Vol. 5. Bordeaux, 1968.

PINKNEY, D. H. *Napoleon III and the Rebuilding of Paris.* Princeton, N.J., 1958.

SAISSELIN, R. G. *Taste in Eighteenth-Century France.* New York, 1965.

SCHNEIDER, R. *L'esthétique classique chez Quatremère de Quincy (1805–1825).* Paris, 1910.

———. *Quatremère de Quincy et son intervention dans les arts (1788–1830)*. Paris, 1910.

STAROBINSKI, J. *The Invention of Liberty, 1700–1789*. Geneva, 1964.

———. *1789: les emblèmes de la raison*. Paris, 1973.

STEINHAUSER, M. *Der Architektur der Pariser Oper*. Munich, 1969.

SUTCLIFFE, A. *The Autumn of Central Paris: The Defeat of Town Planning, 1850–1970*. London, 1970.

THIBERT, M. *Le rôle social de l'art d'après les Saint-Simoniens*. Paris, 1926.

TOURNIER, R. *Les églises comtoises: leur architecture des origines au XVIIIᵉ siècle*. Paris, 1954.

———. *Maisons et hôtels privés du XVIIIᵉ siècle à Besançon*. Paris, 1970.

VAUDOYER, A.-L.-T., and BALTARD, L. P., eds. *Grands Prix d'architecture, 1801–1831*. 3 vols. Paris, 1818–34.

VERLET, P. "Le mobilier de Louis XVI et de Marie-Antoinette à Compiegne." 1937. Ms., Louvre, Paris.

———. *French Furniture and Interior Decoration of the Eighteenth Century*. London, 1967.

GERMANY AND AUSTRIA

BEENKEN, H. *Schöpferische bauideen der deutschen romantik*. Mainz, 1952.

DU COLOMBIER, P. *L'architecture française en Allemagne au XVIIIᵉ siècle*. 2 vols. Paris, 1956.

GROTE, L., ed. *Die deutsche Stadt im 19. Jahrhundert*. Munich, 1974.

MANN, A. *Die Neuromanik: eine rheinische Komponente im Historismus des 19. Jahrhunderts*. Cologne, 1966.

MUTHESIUS, S. *Das englische Vorbild*. Munich, 1974.

PLAGEMANN, V. *Das deutsche Kunstmuseum, 1790–1870*. Munich, 1967.

ROBSON-SCOTT, W. D. *The Literary Background of the Gothic Revival in Germany*. Oxford, 1965.

VOGT, G. *Frankfurter Bürgerhäuser des Neunzehnten Jahrhundert*. Frankfurt, [1970?].

WAGNER-RIEGER, R. *Wiens Architektur im 19. Jahrhundert*. Vienna, 1970.

WAGNER-RIEGER, R., ed. *Die Wiener Ringstrasse: Bild einer Epoche*. Cologne, Graz, and Vienna, 1969–. (9 vols. to date.)

GREAT BRITAIN

ALLEN, B. S. *Tides in English Taste (1619–1800)*. 2 vols. 1937. Reprint. New York, 1969.

AMES, W. *Prince Albert and Victorian Taste*. London and New York, 1968.

ANSON, P. F. *Fashions in Church Furnishings, 1840–1940*. Rev. ed. London, 1965.

ARMYTAGE, W. H. G. *Heavens Below: Utopian Experiments in England, 1560–1960*. London, 1961.

BOASE, T. S. R. *English Art, 1800–1870*. Oxford, 1959.

BURKE, J. *English Art, 1714–1800*. Oxford, 1976.

CHADWICK, G. F. *The Park and the Town: Public Landscape in the 19th and 20th Centuries*. London and New York, 1966.

CLARK, K. *The Gothic Revival*. London, 1928. Reprint. New York, 1974.

CLARKE, B. F. L. *Church Builders of the 19th Century*. 1938. Reprint. Newton Abbot, Devon, 1969.

———. *Parish Churches of London*. London, 1966.

CLIFTON-TAYLOR, A. *The Pattern of English Building*. Rev. ed. London, 1972.

COLVIN, H. M. *A Biographical Dictionary of British Architects, 1600–1840*. London, 1978.

CRAIG, M. J. *Dublin, 1660–1860*. Rev. ed. London, 1969.

CROOK, J. M. *The Greek Revival: Neo-Classical Attitudes in British Architecture, 1760–1870*. Feltham, 1968.

———. *The British Museum*. London and New York, 1972.

CROOK, J. M., and PORT, M. H. *The History of the King's Works*. Vol. 6 (1782–1851). London, 1973.

DYOS, H. J. *Victorian Suburb: A Study of the Growth of Camberwell*. Leicester, 1966.

DYOS, H. J., and WOLFF, M., eds. *The Victorian City: Images and Reality*. 2 vols. London, 1973.

FAWCETT, J., ed. *Seven Victorian Architects*. London, 1976.

FERRIDAY, P., ed. *Victorian Architecture*. London, 1963.

FOWLER, J., and CORNFORTH, J. *English Decoration in the 18th Century*. London, 1974.

GARRIGAN, K. O. *Ruskin on Architecture: His Thought and Influence*. Madison, Wis., 1973.

GIROUARD, M. *The Victorian Country House*. Oxford, 1971.

———. *Sweetness and Light: The Queen Anne Movement, 1860–1900*. Oxford, 1977.

GOMME, A., and WALKER, D. *Architecture of Glasgow*. London, 1968.

GOODHART-RENDEL, H. S. *English Architecture Since the Regency*. London, 1953.

HITCHCOCK, H.-R. *Early Victorian Architecture in Britain*. 2 vols. 1954. Reprint. New Haven, Conn., 1972.

HOBHOUSE, H. *Lost London*. Boston and London, 1971.

HOPKINS, H. J. *A Span of Bridges*. New York and Newton Abbot, 1970.

HUNT, J. D., and WILLIS, P., eds. *The Genius of the Place: The English Landscape Garden, 1620–1820*. London, 1975.

HUSSEY, C. *The Picturesque*. 1927. Reprint. New York, 1967.

———. *English Country Houses: Late Georgian, 1800–1840*. London, 1958.

———. *English Country Houses: Mid-Georgian, 1760–1800*. Rev. ed. London, 1963.

JERVIS, S. *High Victorian Design*. Ottawa, 1974.

KELLET, J. R. *The Impact of Railways on Victorian Cities*. London, 1969.

London, County Council. *Survey of London*. London, 1896–. (39 vols. to date.)

MACAULAY, J. *The Gothic Revival, 1745–1845*. Glasgow and London, 1975.

MACLEOD, R. *Style and Society: Architectural Ideology in Britain, 1835–1914*. London, 1971.

MORRIS, W. *Collected Works of William Morris*. Edited by M. Morris. 24 vols. London, 1910–15.

MUTHESIUS, H. *Die neuere kirchliche Baukunst in England*. Berlin, 1901.

MUTHESIUS, S. "The 'Iron Problem' in the 1850's." *Architectural History* 13 (1970): 58–63.

———. *The High Victorian Movement in Architecture, 1850–1870*. London, 1971.

OLSEN, D. J. *Town Planning in London: The Eighteenth and Nineteenth Centuries*. New Haven, Conn., 1964.

———. *The Growth of Victorian London*. London, 1976.

PEVSNER, N. *The Buildings of England*. 46 vols. Harmondsworth, 1951–74.

———. *Some Architectural Writers of the 19th Century*. Oxford, 1972.

PORT, M. H. *Six Hundred New Churches: A Study of the Church Building Commission, 1818–1856*. London, 1961.

PORT, M. H., ed. *The Houses of Parliament*. New Haven, Conn., 1976.

RICHARDSON, A. E. *Monumental Classic Architecture in Great Britain and Ireland During the Eighteenth and Nineteenth Centuries*. London, 1914.

Royal Institute of British Architects (RIBA). *Catalogue of the Drawings of the Royal Institute of British Architects*. London, 1969–. (17 vols. to date.)

RUSKIN, J. *The Works of John Ruskin*. Edited by E. T. Cook and A. Wedderburn. 39 vols. London, 1903–12.

SAXL, F., and WITTKOWER, R. *British Art and the Mediterranean*. London, 1948.

SHERBURNE, J. C. *John Ruskin; or, The Ambiguities of Abundance*. Cambridge, Mass., 1972.

STEEGMANN, J. *Consort of Taste, 1830–1870*. London, 1950.

SUMMERSON, J. *Heavenly Mansions, and Other Essays on Architecture*. 1949. Reprint. New York, 1963.

———. *Architecture in Britain, 1530–1830*. 5th ed. London, 1969.

———. *Georgian London*. Rev. ed. London, 1970.

———. *Victorian Architecture: Four Studies in Evaluation*. New York, 1970.

———. *The London Building World of the 1860s*. London, 1973.

———. *The Architecture of Victorian London*. Charlottesville, 1976.

WATKIN, D. J. *Morality and Architecture: The Development of a Theme in Architectural History and Theory from the Gothic Revival to the Modern Movement*. Oxford, 1977.

WHIFFEN, M. *Stuart and Georgian Churches: The Architecture of the Church of England Outside London, 1603–1837*. London and New York, 1948.

WHITE, J. F. *The Cambridge Movement: The Ecclesiologists and the Gothic Revival*. Cambridge, 1962.

WOODBRIDGE, K. *Landscape and Antiquity: Aspects of English Culture at Stourhead, 1718 to 1838*. London, 1970.

YOUNGSON, A. J. *The Making of Classical Edinburgh, 1750–1840*. Edinburgh, 1966.

GREECE

RUSSACK, H. H. *Deutsches Bauen in Athen*. Berlin, 1942.

SINOS, S. "Die Gründung der neuen Stadt Athen." *Architectura* 1 (1974): 41–52.

TRAVLOS, J. *Architecture néoclassique en Grèce*. Athens, 1967.

ITALY

ANGELINI, L. *L'avvento dell'arte neoclassica in Bergamo*. Bergamo, 1966.

BASSI, E. *Architettura del sei e settecento a Venezia*. Naples, 1962.

BORSI, F. *La capitale a Firenze e l'opera de G. Poggi*. Rome, 1970.

BRUSATIN, M. *Illuminismo e architettura del '700 Veneto*. Castelfranco Veneto, 1969.

HASKELL, F. *Patrons and Painters: A Study in the Relations Between Italian Art and Society in the Age of the Baroque*. 1963. Reprint. New York, 1971.

LAVAGNINO, E. *L'arte moderna dai neoclassici ai contemporanei*. 2 vols. Turin, 1956.

MEZZANOTTE, G. *Architettura neoclassica in Lombardia*. Naples, 1966.

POMMER, R. *Eighteenth-Century Architecture in Piedmont:*

The Open Structures of Juvarra, Alfieri and Vittone. London and New York, 1967.

PROZZILLO, I. *Francesco Milizia, teorico e storico dell' architettura*. Naples, 1971.

VENDITTI, A. *Architettura neoclassica a Napoli*. Naples, 1961.

WITTKOWER, R. *Art and Architecture in Italy, 1600 to 1750*. 3d ed. Baltimore and Harmondsworth, 1973.

ZUCCA, L. T. *Architettura neoclassica a Trieste*. Trieste, 1974.

PORTUGAL

FRANCA, J. A. *Lisboa Pombalina, e o iluminismo*. Lisbon, 1965. (First published as *Une ville des lumières: la Lisbonne de Pombal*. Paris, 1965.)

RUSSIA

BATER, J. H. *St. Petersburg: Industrialization and Change*. London, 1976.

EGOROV, I. A. *The Architectural Planning of St. Petersburg*. Athens, Ohio, 1969.

HAMILTON, G. H. *The Art and Architecture of Russia*. Baltimore and Harmondsworth, 1954.

HAUTECOEUR, L. *L'architecture classique a Saint-Pétersbourg à la fin du XVIIIᵉ siècle*. Paris, 1912.

ILYIN, M. *Moscow Monuments of Architecture: Eighteenth–the First Third of the Nineteenth Century*. 2 vols. Moscow, 1975.

KIRICHENKO, E. *Moscow Architectural Monuments of the 1830s–1910s*. Moscow, 1977.

SPAIN

CAREDA, J. *Memorias para la historia de la Real Academia de San Fernando y de las Bellas Artes en España*. 2 vols. Madrid, 1867.

GAYA NUÑO, J. A. *Arte del siglo XIX*. Ars Hispaniae, vol. 19. Madrid, 1966.

NAVASCUES PALACIO, P. *Arquitectura y arquitectos Madrileños del siglo XIX*. Madrid, 1973.

PARIS, P. "L'art en Espagne et en Portugal de la fin du XVIIIᵉ siècle à nos jours." In *Histoire de l'art*, by A. Michel, vol. 8. Paris, 1926.

SWITZERLAND

CARL, B. *Die Architektur der Schweiz: Klassizismus 1770–1860*. Zurich, 1963.

CORBOZ, A. *Invention de Carouge, 1772–92*. Lausanne, [1968].

GERMANN, G. *Der protestantische Kirchenbau in der Schweiz*. Zurich, 1963.

UNITED STATES OF AMERICA

HAMLIN, T. *Greek Revival Architecture in America*. New York, 1944.

PIERSON, W. H. *American Buildings and Their Architects*. Vol. 1 (*The Colonial and Neo-Classical Styles*). New York, 1970.

STANTON, P. B. *The Gothic Revival and American Church Architecture*. Baltimore, 1968.

175, 176, 324, 330

Revue britannique, 386

Revue des deux mondes, 386

Revue générale de l'architecture et des travaux publiques, 238, 245, 352, 363, 366, 378, 380-382

Reynaud, François-Léonce, 31, 365

Rheims
cathedral, 367, 382
St.-Rémy, 350

Richardson, A. E., 233

Richardson, Henry Hobson, 322

Richmond (Virginia)
Monumental Church, 321
State Penitentiary, 321
Virginia State Capitol, 320

Rickman, Thomas, 322, 324-330

Rigaud, John Francis, 87

Rimini: Tempio Malatestiano, 233

Rio, Alexis François, 346

Robert, C.-L.-N., 348

Robert, Hubert, 35, 72, 134, 184, 186, *Plates 297, 298*

Robertson, William, 182-183

Robinson, William, 324

Rochechouart, *abattoir,* 211

Rochette, Désirée-Raoul, 97, 99, 367

Rodi, Faustino, 306

Romano, Giulio, 122, 196

Rome
Basilica of Maxentius, 172
Baths, 142, 166, 211, 259, 320
Campidoglio, 157
Cloaca Maxima, 75
Colosseum, 184, 229, 301
Festa della Chinea, 35, 69, 72, 105, 151, *Plates 76, 77*
Fontana di Trevi, 293
Mausoleum of Augustus, 184
Mausoleum of Hadrian, 184
Palazzo Vidoni-Caffarelli, 147
Pantheon, 151, 160, 184
Piazza del Popolo, 301
Piazza S. Ignazio, 293
Pyramid of Cestius, 184
S. Costanza, 151

S. Paolo fuori le Mura, 217
S. Maria del Priorato, 300
S. Trinità dei Monti, 117, *Plate 152*
St. Peter's, 14, 110, 122, 300
Spanish Steps, 293
Temple of Aesculapius, *Plate 523*
Temple of Castor and Pollux, 195
Temple of Fortuna Virilis, 81, 320
Temple of Minerva Medica, 199
Temple of Vesta, 170, 253
Temple of Virtue, 39
Theater of Marcellus, *Plate 88*
Tomb of Caecilia Metella, 151, 170, 184
Villa Albani, 300
Villa Madama, 87, 157
Villa Mattei, 39
Villa Torlonia, 301

Romé de l'Isle, Jean-Baptiste-Louis, 184

Rondelet, Jean-Baptiste, 28, 30, 31, 32, 211, 257, *Plate 23*

Root, John Wellborn, 389

Roquetaillade, Château de, 362, *Plate 628*

Rose, Joseph, Jr., 87, 160, 166

Roskilde, cathedral, 290, *Plate 497*

Rosny-sous-Bois: Ste.-Geneviève, 364

Rossi, Giuseppe Ignazio, 104

Rossi, Karl Ivanovich, 285, *Plates 490, 491, XXXIX*

Rothschild, Baron de, 34, 368

Rouen
cathedral, 348, 379
St.-Ouen, 348, *Plate 613*

Rousham (Oxfordshire), 36, 39, 83, *Plates 36-38*

Rousseau, Jacques, 140

Rousseau, Jean, 119

Rousseau, Jean-Jacques, 76, 374

Rousseau, Pierre, 116, 160, 174, 285, *Plates 149, 150*

Rousset, Pierre-Noël, 140

Royal Academy, London, 160, 164

Royal Residences (Pyne), 175

Rudimentary Treatise on the Principles of Design in Architecture (Garbett), 372

Ruines de Paestum (Delagardette), 229

Ruines des plus beaux monuments de la Grèce, Les (Le Roy), 29, 68, 70, 93, *Plates 24, 75*

Ruins of Athens and Other Valuable Antiquities in Greece (Sayer), 68

Ruins of Balbec, The (Dawkins and Wood), 44, 68, 87

Ruins of Paestum, The (Major), 88

Ruins of Palmyra, The (Dawkins and Wood), 68, 87

Ruins of the Palace of the Emperor Diocletian at Spalato (Adam), 154

Rundbogenstil, 290

Ruperra Casle (Glamorganshire), 328

Ruprich-Robert, Victor-Marie-Charles, 361, 369

Ruskin, John, 7, 58, 237, 258, 271, 314, 346, 373-378, 386, 387, 388, 389, *Plate 643*

Ruskin et la religion de la beauté (La Sizeranne), 386

Russia, classical architecture in, 283-287

Rysbrack, John, 44

Saggio sopra l'architettura (Algarotti), 22

Saggio sopra l'architettura gotica (Frisi), 312

St. Alban's Court (Kent), 65

St.-André-de-Cubzac (Gironde): Château de Bouilh, 119, *Plate 176*

Saint-Aubin, Gabriel de, 113, *Plate 144*

St.-Aubin (near Elbeuf), church, 350

St.-Chamas (near Marseilles): Flavian bridge, 231

St.-Cloud, palace, 213

Saint-Denis
chapel, 344, 366, 367, *Plates 640-645*
Menier chemical factory, 383
St.-Denys-de-l'Estrée, 358, 363, *Plate XLVII*

Saint-Florentin, Comte de, 121

St.-Germain-en-Laye, 360, St.-Louis, 122, *Plate 197*

St.-Jean-Pied-de-Port: chapel of St.-Sauveur, 360

St.-Laurent-de-Chamousset (Rhône): Château de Chamousset, 357

St.-Maur, Benedictine congregation of, 14, 16

Saint-Non, Richard de (Abbé), 68

St. Paul's (Dugdale), 324

St. Petersburg, *See* Leningrad

Saint-Simon, Claude-Henri, Comte de, 30, 221, 234, 378

Saint-Simonists, 221, 231, 233, 238

Salisbury (Wiltshire), cathedral, 324, 330, 333

Salvin, Anthony, 36, 65, 332, 333, 340, *Plates 33, 574*

Saly, Jacques, 72

Sandford Priory (Berkshire), 170

Sangallo, Antonio da, 268

Sangallo family, 122

Sansovino, Jacopo, 233

Sansovino, Pietro, 269

Santi, Lorenzo, 300, *Plate 519*

Saonara (near Padua): Villa dei Conti Cittadella Vigodarzere, 300

Sarti, Antonio, 301

Saulnier, Jules, 383, *Plate 655*

Savage, James, 330

Sayer, Robert, 68

Scalfarotto, Giovanni Antonio, 296

Scandinavia, classical architecture in, 287-293

Scarisbrick Hall (Lancashire), 333, *Plate 577*

Scarsdale, Lord, 86

PHOTOGRAPH CREDITS
The numbers listed refer to the plates

Aerofilms, London: 43

Angel, H., Farnham: IV

Andrews, W., Grosse Pointe, Michigan: 563

Archives Municipales, Bordeaux: 176, 177

Archives Photographiques, Paris: 166, 179, 225, 350, 352

Austin, J., London: 119, 130, 149, 150, 214, 215, 363, 392, 397, 401, 412

Balestrini, B., Milan: 1, 9, 10, 11, 13, 15, 19, 20, 21, 27, 104, 113, 114, 116, 120, 127, 128, 129, 132, 133, 134, 135, 136, 155, 156, 157, 158, 161, 167, 169, 178, 180, 182, 183, 184, 185, 189, 198, 202, 206, 208, 211, 219, 236, 237, 295, 299, 300, 301, 303, 308, 312, 346, 347, 348, 349, 351, 356, 359, 360, 361, 362, 364, 365, 368, 370, 371, 372, 374, 375, 378, 379, 380, 381, 382, 383, 384, 390, 391, 393, 394, 395, 399, 400, 402, 403, 404, 408, 409, 410, 411, 413, 414, 415, 416, 418, 419, 425, 426, 428, 429, 430, 432, 433, 434, 478, 502, 503, 504, 505, 506, 509, 510, 511, 512, 516, 517, 518, 519, 520, 521, 522, 523, 524, 526, 527, 528, 530, 531, 532, 533, 534, 535, 538, 543, 544, 545, 546, 547, 549, 550, 551, 552, 610, 611, 612, 613, 614, 615, 616, 617, 619, 620, 621, 622, 623, 624, 625, 629, 630, 631, 632, 633, 634, 635, 636, 637, 646, 649, 650, 654, 655, 656, XXII

Bibliothèque Nationale, Paris: 137, 138, 143, 159, 202, 207, 282, 283, 284, 285, 286, 287, 288, 289, 290, 344, 398, XXXII

Bildarchiv Preussischer Kulturbesitz, Berlin: XXXV

Bulloz, Paris: 151, 304, 405, XI

Cirani, N./Ricciarini, L., Milan: XXXI, XXXIX, XLIII, XLVI, XLVII

Combier, J., Macon: 317

Country Life, London: 33, 34, 35, 41, 42, 48, 50, 51, 54, 55, 56, 68, 93, 96, 97, 98, 101, 103, 105, 106, 111, 153, 238, 239, 240, 241, 244, 247, 251, 252, 253, 254, 255, 256, 257, 258, 260, 262, 264, 265, 268, 269, 271, 272, 274, 275, 280, 281, 328, 437, 454, 455, 458, 459, 460, 463, 464, 465, 573, 575, 577, 587, 588, 595, 598, 599, V

Courtauld Institute of Art, London: 64, 67, 95, 246, 248, 249, 270, 333, 466, 592, 593, 600, 601

Dalton, C., Daventry: 99, 100

Danver, A.G., Bordeaux: X

De Grivel, J., Besançon: 190, 191, 192, 193, 194

Deutsche Fotothek Dresden, Dresden: 59, 60, 61

Fitzwilliam Museum, Cambridge: 152

Fotocielo, Rome: 540

Gibson, J.M., Guildford, Surrey: 69

Giraudon, Paris: 4, 78, 174, 187, 201, 216, 217, 221, 223, 298, 314, 385, 386, 387, 396

Godfrey New Photographics Ltd., Sidcup: XIV, XLV

Greater London Council, Photographic Unit Department of Architecture and Civil Design, London: 435, 451, 467, 469

Irish National Trust Archive, Dublin: 572

Kersting, A.F., London: 263, 462, 604, VI, XV, XVI, XVII, XVIII, XIX, XX, XXI, XLIV

Kupferstich Kabinett und Sammlungen der Zeichnungen, Berlin: XXXVI

Landesbildstelle, Berlin: 109, 110, 470

Lauros-Giraudon, Paris: II, XII, XIII, XXV, XXVI, XXVII, XXVIII, XXX

Leeds Art Galleries, Leeds: 267

Library of Congress, Washington, D.C.: 557, 558, 559, 560, 561, 562, 564, 565, 566, 567

Liot, R., St.-Germain-en-Laye: 197

Mayer, N./Ricciarini, L., Milan: VIII

Mensy, Besançon: 80

Münchner Stadtmuseum, Munich: 477

Musée de Strasbourg, Strasbourg: 186

Musei Vaticani, Archivio Fotografico, Rome: 513, 514, 515

National Monuments Record, London: 336

National Museet, Copenhagen: 497, 498, 499, 500

National Trust, London: 39, 45, 65, 66, 574

Newbert, S.W., London: 342

Novosti Press, Rome: 482, 483, 484, 485, 486, 487, 488, 489, 490, 491, 492, 494, 495, 496

Pagliarani, A., Verona: 507

Perret, F., La Chaux-de-Fonds: 195, 196

Photo Pierrain-Carnavalet, Paris: 79, 125, 131, 165, 204, 205

Pineider, G.B., Florence: 525

Pitkin Pictorials Ltd., London: XLVIII

Studio Pizzi, Milan: XXIX

Reilly and Constantine Commercial, Birmingham: 639

Ricciarini, L., Milan: XL, XLII

H. Roger-Viollet, Paris: 406, 407

Royal Commission on Ancient Monuments (Scotland), Edinburgh: 108, 259, 261, 447, 448

Royal Commission on Historical Monuments (England), London: 329, 335, 336, 338, 438, 439, 440, 441, 443, 444, 446, 459, 461, 576, 578, 580, 581, 582, 583, 584, 585, 590, 591, 594, 596, 597, 607, VII. All rights reserved.

Royal Library, Copenhagen: 498

Scott, T., Edinburgh: 44

Semper-Archiv der ETH, Zurich: 662, 663, 664

Service Photographique des Archives Nationales, Paris: 323

Simion, F./Ricciarini, L., Milan: I, IX, XLI

Smith, E., London: 445

Sir John Soane's Museum, London: 242, 243, 330, 331, 339, 340, 343, XXIII, XXIV

Staatliche Antikesammlungen, Munich: XXXVII, XXXVIII

Staatliche Schlösser und Gärten, Berlin: XXXIV

Stoedtner, F., Düsseldorf: 472

Tate Gallery, London: 115

Thorvaldsen Museum, Copenhagen: 501

Topical Press, London: 341. All rights reserved.

University Library, Warsaw: 154

Verroust, J., Neuilly: 2

Verwaltung der Staatlichen Schlösser, Gärten, und Seen, Munich: 479

Victoria and Albert Museum, London: 30, III, XLIX

Wallace Collection, London: 144. All rights reserved.

Work in Progress/Ricciarini, L., Milan: XXXIII